The Ethics of Fur

The Ethics of Fur

Religious, Cultural, and Legal Perspectives

Edited by

Andrew Linzey and Clair Linzey

LEXINGTON BOOKS
Lanham • Boulder • New York • London

Published by Lexington Books
An imprint of The Rowman & Littlefield Publishing Group, Inc.
4501 Forbes Boulevard, Suite 200, Lanham, Maryland 20706
www.rowman.com

86-90 Paul Street, London EC2A 4NE

British Library Cataloguing in Publication Information Available

Library of Congress Cataloging-in-Publication Data

Names: Linzey, Andrew, editor. | Linzey, Clair, editor.
Title: The ethics of fur : religious, cultural, and legal perspectives / edited by Andrew Linzey, Clair Linzey.
Description: Lanham : Lexington Books, 2023. | Includes bibliographical references and index.
Identifiers: LCCN 2023010656 (print) | LCCN 2023010657 (ebook) | ISBN 9781666937947 (cloth) | ISBN 9781666937954 (ebook)
Subjects: LCSH: Fur trade--Law and legislation. | Fur trade--Moral and ethical aspects. | Selling--Fur garments. | Fur garments--Labelling--Law and legislation. | Animal welfare--Law and legislation | Animal rights.
Classification: LCC K3947.F87 E84 2023 (print) | LCC K3947.F87 (ebook) | DDC 343.08/7397--dc23/eng/20230421
LC record available at https://lccn.loc.gov/2023010656
LC ebook record available at https://lccn.loc.gov/2023010657

This book is dedicated to
Susan and Dan Boggio,
courageous pioneers of animal protection

Contents

Introduction

Increasing Ethical Sensitivity around Fur

Andrew Linzey and Clair Linzey

I.

There is a joke that circulates among animal people that goes like this: an animal rights activist decides to go to a church service. She sits in one of the pews and, to her horror, sees that the woman in front of her is wearing a fur coat. She tries to control herself, but eventually her outrage takes over. She taps the shoulder of the person in front of her and says, "What poor, innocent, defenseless creature had to die for you to wear that fur coat?" The woman turns around and replies, with tears running down her face, "My auntie."

The joke works in many ways. First, there is the ironic encounter between the two people: a probably burned-out animal activist goes to church presumably for spiritual solace only to meet her ideological enemy, wearing the dead skin of (in her view) a creature murdered for the sake of vanity. Second, there is the issue of when or how to protest and what good it will do if one does. The activist struggles to control her emotions, but the attempt is a failure. She must speak out even though the fur wearer is a fellow congregant, and the context may be inappropriate. She carefully crafts her question to best express her moral outrage—not a condemnation, but a simple question. The unexpected response takes her aback. The incongruity produces humor.

The third, and perhaps most striking, issue lies in the question of guilt and innocence. Animal people normally assume that others have considered the morality of fur and, if they decide to wear it, have an appropriate justification. Not so in this case. The decision to wear fur is decided by another factor—namely, the person's love for her relative who has died. The contrast, then, is between the moral innocence of the dead animal and the apparent innocence of wearing the fur.

It is this latter point that should give us pause. Not everyone who wears fur (or in this case, inherits such a garment) has thought about the origin of the fur in question—how the creature was raised or how the creature was killed. This is not a far-fetched scenario. One of us can recall questioning his mother's wearing of a beaver's coat and being told that the creatures[1] in question had all died from natural causes.

That fur-wearing involves unnatural death and frequent suffering has taken a long time to fully register in our consciousness. Of course, there were pioneers, such as seventeenth-century Thomas Tryon, who came to this realization and even recognized the connection between the exploitation of animals and that of other humans.[2] But it has been, until comparatively recently, a slow business. Even the renowned antivivisectionist leader Frances Power Cobbe was depicted wearing fur apparel.[3] Despite her admirable work in defense of animals used in laboratories, she obviously overlooked fur as a moral issue. Perhaps she simply thought, like many others, that fur was "harvested" from cadavers. As indicated in *Veritatis Splendor*, there is a thing called invincible ignorance, "an ignorance of which the subject is not aware and which he is unable to overcome by himself."[4] For many years, this ignorance of how fur was obtained prevailed.

II.

But various factors in the nineteenth and twentieth centuries made an uneducated conscience less and less possible. We select just three.

The first was the increasing realization of the realities of trapping and what it entails. The most common trap used is the steel-jaw leghold trap. When the steel jaws shut on the victim's leg, flesh and muscle are torn, and bones may be splintered and broken. Animals remain caught in traps for hours, days, even weeks, until the trapper comes to kill them. They suffer pain, fear, thirst, exhaustion, and hunger—and they are, of course, subject to injury or death by predators. When the trapper comes, it is not usual to kill the animal with bullets because that would damage the fur. Instead, trappers kill the animals by beating them around the head with an axe handle or stick or by suffocating them, through standing on their necks. The use of the steel-jaw trap is banned in one hundred countries, including the UK, according to the Library of Congress.[5]

The two other common methods used are the conibear trap and the snare. The conibear is designed to kill the animal entering the trap by breaking his or her neck or back, but this can happen only when the animal caught is of the right size and enters the trap at the necessary angle. All too often, the animal is left alive, his or her body crushed between strong wire jaws, for hours, even days. Snares are still commonly used to trap furred animals. At its most basic, the snare is a piece of wire looped into a noose that is placed on a known animal trail or on a branch, to catch the first creature who runs through it. Death in snares can occur in several ways. An animal may die of strangulation if caught around the neck or may have his or her throat slowly cut if the wire gradually makes its way into the neck. Many animals are caught around the body. Obviously, the degree of suffering involved depends greatly on the type of snare set and the size of the animal caught.

All the main methods used to trap animals for their fur have one thing in common—they are nonselective and indiscriminate. Many domesticated and free-living animals, including sheep, cats, dogs, deer, swans, and even golden eagles, are trapped in these devices every year. The fur trappers have a word for these creatures. They call them "trash." It is possible that for every furred animal trapped, a "trash" animal is also trapped and discarded.[6]

As these realities became clear, the animal protection movement was galvanized in protest. Organizations were created specifically to campaign against fur. These included, inter alia, the Humanitarian League, Fur Bearers International, Fur Free Alliance, and Respect for Animals. The campaign was on.

The second factor that increased awareness of the issues surrounding fur was the growth in the international trade in fur. The Hudson's Bay Company, the pioneer of the international fur trade, was incorporated by an English royal charter in 1670.[7] Its centuries of work were first lauded as a successful imperial innovation, with the company trading with indigenous Canadians to ship fur back to England and later to the rest of the world. But in reality the company thrived on the back of colonial exploitation. As John Richards details, the relationship between the company and the indigenous people was an inherently unequal one: "when they [indigenous people] became commercial hunters they entered an inherently unstable and unsustainable realm . . . commercial hunters caught up in the all-consuming market."[8] Hence, in the commercialization of the indigenous communities arguably previously sustenance-based fur trapping by the colonial settlers, there was a double exploitation and two victims: the animals and the Canadian natives themselves. It was only as colonization was deemed morally unacceptable that the full facts of this double exploitation became apparent.[9]

In this way, fur increasingly became an indisputable fashion accessory. However desirable wearing fur might have been, it was difficult to justify animal suffering for an inessential garment. As far as we know, no one ever died from lack of fur. The international trade also compromised the often-made argument that trapping animals was essential for survival and sustainable to boot. Trade, by its very nature, is not subsistence. Even today, less than 1 percent of fur trapping is for indigenous purposes.[10] Regarding the judgment that anti-fur is anti-indigenous, we know that the Canadian government deliberately used First Nation peoples in a cynical public relations move to provide an alternative emotional focus to thwart the anti-fur movement, especially seal hunting. A 1985 discussion paper from the Canadian government suggests using "contradictory emotional themes of interest to the same target publics, e.g., preservation of traditional indigenous cultures."[11]

Moreover, far from being sustainable, trapping virtually wiped out the beaver population. Before the European settlement in North America, beavers were thought to number somewhere between sixty and four hundred million. Their populations were decimated, and only now are they beginning to recover, with estimates of six to twelve million.[12]

A third factor was the emergence of industrial fur farming. The realization descended that most fur came from industrial fur-farming units that deprived these animals of their natural behaviors and induced suffering, mental and physical, over an even longer time than trapping, which is where we are today.

As one of us has written elsewhere,[13] "animals are kept in rows of barren wire cages in open-sided sheds. A typical mink cage measures seventy centimeters long by forty wide and forty-five high, and a cage for two arctic foxes would typically measure 110 centimeters square." Compared to the one- to three-kilometer territories that mink normally cover on a daily basis when free-roaming, this is quite a reduction of space. The reduction is even greater for foxes: red foxes cover on average ten kilometers daily, and an arctic fox migrates around one hundred kilometers in one season. In addition, mink are normally semiaquatic animals who live solitary lives—having no access to water and being kept in close conditions on fur farms represents a large change to their natural environment. Foxes are social animals who form complex social bonds and live together in large dens that they dig. Fur farm conditions give them no opportunities to socialize or dig, frustrating their natural behavior. It is a similar story with chinchillas, who are kept in cages that are on average fifty centimeters high by fifty centimeters wide by fifty centimeters deep. Free-living chinchillas cover a great deal of ground at speed and have been known to jump up to two meters. They are nocturnal social animals who live in large groups, enjoy dust-bathing, and retreat to crevices to nest. In the life afforded to chinchillas on fur farms, their social needs are not met, they rarely have access to nesting areas or dust-bathing, and their nocturnal lifestyle is compromised by being inspected in the daytime.

The conditions of factory fur farms mean it is impossible for animals farmed for their fur to express their normal species-specific behavior. The inability to live their normal expressive life leads to behavior known as "stereotypies" and harms that include psychological stress–induced fur-chewing, self-injury, and biting. Moreover, the slaughtering of animals factory-farmed for fur is not without considerable suffering. "Since the aim of producers is not to damage the actual fur, slaughter practices have to aim for a kill by unusual means, which include electrocution (using electrodes clamped in the mouth and inserted in the rectum), gassing, cervical dislocation, and sometimes (homemade) poisoning. All these methods are controversial."[14]

This last development has cemented the link between fur and suffering and has turned people and politicians against fur.

Consider the following comparatively recent developments.[15] In 2004, six of the nine federal states in Austria banned fur farming. The remaining three began to enforce such strict animal welfare regulations that fur farming is now no longer economically feasible. In 2018, the Flemish government of Belgium adopted a decree to end fur farming, following bans in Wallonia in 2015, and Brussels in 2017. The remaining seventeen Belgian mink farms are to be closed by 2023. In 2009, Bosnia and Herzegovina passed an anti–fur farming law that would prohibit raising animals for fur. After a phaseout period, the ban was due to go into effect in January 2018. However, the phaseout period was extended. In October 2019, the state veterinary authority announced that sixty chinchilla farms had already ceased operations, and the remaining fur farms would be closed by 2028.

Croatia's Ministry of Agriculture decided in 2006 to ban fur farms. After a phaseout period of ten years, the ban went into effect in January 2017. In 2017, the Czech Republic passed an animal protection law that ended fur farming in January 2019. Hungary introduced an immediate ban on the breeding of mink, foxes, polecats, and coypu for fur in November 2020, following concerns about animal welfare and coronavirus outbreaks on mink fur farms across Europe. The ban was introduced as a precautionary measure to prevent fur farmers from moving their operations there.

In 2006, Japan passed the Invasive Alien Species Act, which restricted the breeding of the non-native species American mink, raccoon, and coypu. The act in effect outlawed fur farming, and ten years later, the last fur farm shut down. Luxembourg's animal welfare law was passed in June 2018 and prohibited fur farming from October 2018. Luxembourg currently had no operating fur farms, but the legislation prevents any from opening. The Netherlands passed a ban on farming mink for their fur in 2015; a phaseout began, with the production of mink fur set to end entirely by 2024. This deadline was brought forward to March 2021 following the serious COVID outbreak discovered on Dutch fur farms in spring 2020. Fur farming is now banned in the Netherlands. In 1995, the Netherlands became the first in the world to ban farming foxes for their fur, after which it banned farming chinchillas for fur in 1997.

There have been similar bans in Norway, Slovakia, Slovenia, Serbia, and the United Kingdom, as well as stricter legislation that makes fur farming economically unfeasible in countries such as Germany, Italy, Sweden, and Switzerland. In addition, some cities and countries also have moved toward banning the sale and importation of fur, including California (2019), Los Angeles (2018), New Zealand (2013), San Francisco (2018), and São Paulo (2015).

That so many countries and states have moved against fur and fur factory farming is remarkable. Within a span of only twenty to thirty years, fur production has turned from being a contentious activity to being illegal in around twenty countries. Fur has probably become the most legislated-against activity regarding animals in the last fifty years. Also important is the number of fashion houses that have given up selling and producing fur. These include Gucci, Michael Kors, Armani, Calvin Klein,[16] and most recently, Canada Goose.[17] The tide seems to be turning.

But it is important to recognize that these are not ad hoc developments. They naturally flow from the determinations in 2001 of the Scientific Committee on Animal Health and Animal Welfare of the European Union, which concluded on welfare grounds that "mink and foxes generally suffer from being kept in cages because it limits their natural [behavior] as wild animals."[18]

However, the number of animals used in farming is still huge. Fur is a multimillion-dollar business. It is estimated that over one hundred million animals are killed on fur farms worldwide annually. It is hard to give precise figures as to the number of animals killed in fur farming worldwide since Russia and China, two of the largest producers of fur, do not provide statistics. In addition, fur farming takes place across parts of Europe, Canada, and the United States.[19]

It is worth returning to the notion of innocence with which we began. You will recall how the outraged animal activist referred to how the poor creature was defenseless and innocent. It goes without saying (but it needs to be said) that the animals killed for their fur *are* morally innocent and invariably defenseless too. No one we know of has died through beaver, mink, or arctic fox attacks. All these animals want to do is live their lives in the way nature has made possible.

They are not moral agents (even if sometimes they appear to show signs of moral sense) and therefore are not morally culpable in the sense that they have free will to make decisions and are therefore responsible for their actions. People sometimes decry the violence in nature, but animals eat others for survival, not for sport, profit, or fashion. It is the very innocence and relative defenselessness of these animals that should rightly engender human moral solicitude. As one of us has argued elsewhere, "inflicting pain on those who can never deserve nor merit it increases our responsibility; it raises the bar of moral responsibility even higher."[20] As C. S. Lewis observed, "so far as we know beasts are incapable of sin or virtue; therefore they can neither deserve pain nor be improved by it."[21]

III.

This book is divided into three parts. The first is "Historical and Religious Perspectives," the second is "Ethical and Cultural Perspectives," and the third is "Political and Legal Perspectives." A brief overview may be helpful.

Adam Bridgen ("From the Pleistocene to COVID-19: A Brief History of Fur") opens part 1 with a fascinating overview of the use of fur throughout the ages, highlighting the various shifts of moral perspective and cultural change. Bridgen also provides a further chapter on Thomas Tryon, the standout figure in the anti-fur movement ("'Thou Shalt Not Use the Skins of Any Living Creature': The Original Anti-Fur Activist, Thomas Tryon [1634–1703]"). Inter alia, Tryon's objections to violence against animals, especially his emphasis on fur as sinful vanity, anticipated the later protests against fur in the nineteenth and twentieth centuries. In the following chapter, Linda M. Johnson ("The New England Fur Trade: The Ethics of Puritan Dress in a Portrait of Lieutenant Governor William Stoughton") takes us into the Puritan world and its tensions about excessive adornment as illustrated by the portrait of Lieutenant Governor William Stoughton. Robyn Hederman ("The Nineteenth-Century Boycott against Feathered Hats") takes a sideways look at the anti-plumage campaign in the late nineteenth century and illustrates the importance of women's activism and the success of their boycott. There is much here that is instructive for contemporary anti-fur campaigners. Sidney Blankenship in his essay ("Corpse 'Contamination' as a Religious Approach to Fur") analyzes the biblical notion of purity found in Leviticus 11 and the New Testament and how this relates to the Native American approach to nature, which was essentially violated by the transatlantic fur trade. Kurt Remele ("Of Ermines, Cats, and 'the Best-Dressed Pontiff Ever': The Ethics of Fur-Trimmed Clerical Garb") brings us up-to-date with a critique of the late fur-dressed Pope Benedict, who apparently demonstrated little regard for the pains of fur animals.

Part 2, "Ethical and Cultural Perspectives," begins with a chapter by Frances M. C. Robinson ("A Case of Wrongful Use: An Ethical Analysis of the Use of Animal Fur") that addresses the fundamental question of whether fur is morally justifiable and, after careful analyses of the concepts of person, autonomy, and human objectification of animals, concludes that the case against is enough to label the practice as wrongful use. Taking their cue from Wittgenstein, K. York ("If a Fox Could Talk: Wittgenstein and the Calculated Silencing of Animals in Industrial Fur Production") argues that fur farming is an extreme case of how we silence animals by refusing to acknowledge the pain of animals or their desire for freedom. Rebecca Rose Stanton in her chapter ("'All Fur Coat and No Knickers!' The Speciesism of Fur in Disney Media") shows how Disney films dichotomize animal products, the result of speciesism in which one species is arbitrary favored over another. In "Bringing Nonhuman Animals into Anthropologies of Fur," Jen Clements indicates how traditional anthropologies have been dominated by a materialist paradigm, which has all but left animals out of the picture. Ambrose Tinarwo ("Video Killed the Animal for Fur: An Analysis of the Influence of Pop Music Culture on Perceptions about Fur") concludes this section by showing how popular music and popular culture reinforce fur fashion and thus influence contemporary debate.

The third section, "Political and Legal Perspectives," opens with Simon Brooman's chapter ("Politics, Law, and Grasping the Evidence in Fur Farming: A Tale of Three Continents"), which examines international fur farming through the regulatory and sociopolitical situation in three continental areas—Europe, North America, and Asia/Oceania—and explores the possibilities for change. Letícia Albuquerque and Gabriela Franziska Schoch Santos Carvalho look specifically at the situation in Brazil ("Legislation against Animals Reared for Fur in Brazil") and document the legislative attempts at regulation or prohibition. Heather Pickett offers a scientific perspective on the adverse welfare experienced by mink and foxes farmed for fur production ("Animal Welfare Standards in European Fur Production and the 'WelFur' Assessment Program"). She particularly critiques the WelFur program proposed by fur traders as misleading since "best current practice" still represents what most people would consider to be an unacceptable level of welfare. Kimberly Moore addresses the promotion of fur to children ("The Ethics of Marketing Fur to Children") and makes policy recommendations to safeguard children from misleading information. Justin Marceau, Jess Beaulieu, Kate Sanford, and Chloe Gleichman examine the use of the argument for free speech ("Fur and Free Speech"); they maintain that the argument works both ways and suggest that there should be more scholarly discourse on the tensions that arise in the context of free speech and animals, especially in relation to fur farming. Next, Kimberly Moore ("The Myth That 'Fur Is Green' and the Real Impact of the Fur Industry on the Environment") details the impact that the fur trade has on lakes, rivers, and other local waterways, on soil and air quality, and ultimately on climate change.

IV.

This is the first multidisciplinary book that addresses the ethics of fur. It tilts against fur. Whatever might have been true of the past, the production of fur is now morally problematic in terms of both necessity and suffering. There is no necessity in killing animals for nonessential purposes, such as adornment, fashion, or vanity. The argument for utility simply doesn't hold up. Alternative clothing is now readily available, enduring, and less costly. Worse still, since we know that the animals exploited are sentient, causing them suffering or making animals liable to suffering is arguably intrinsically wrong.

The purpose of this volume is to open up and advance further the ethical, political, and specifically legislative endeavors now moving at a pace and to encourage the anti-fur movement. That said, there is much to learn from this book about the history, culture, and political arguments for and against fur that should interest scholars and students, as well as those engaged on either side of the debate. It is not common for academics to engage with pressing and contentious moral issues, and we pay tribute to our eighteen contributors for leading the way. Academic "neutrality" can sometimes be an excuse for moral cowardice—not so with our contributors.

As we invariably say in the introduction to our books, we as editors have had to pay special attention to the question of ethical language. So much of our historic language denigrates animals as "beasts," "brutes," "sub-humans," or "dumb brutes" or deploys negative metaphors about animals, such as "snake in the grass," "cunning as a fox," "greedy as a pig," and "stupid cow." With these terms we libel animals—and not only animals, of course. Therefore, we have found it essential to pioneer ethical or at least more objective terminology. We have used "he" or "she" instead of "it" for individual animals. We have used "free-living," "free-roaming," or simply "free" instead of "wild" because wildness has negative connotations. We also have used the term "companion animal" rather than "pet." Needless to say, exceptions to ethical language have been made in the quotation of texts, particularly historical writings.

This book is a project of the Oxford Centre for Animal Ethics, and many of the contributors are fellows of the Centre. The aim of the Centre is to pioneer ethical perspectives on animals through academic research, teaching, and publication, and the Centre has a worldwide fellowship of more than one hundred academic fellows. All royalties from the sale of this book will go the Centre to further its work.

Our special thanks go to our copyeditor Stephanie Ernst for her outstanding and patient work on the text.

NOTES

1. It takes nine beaver skins to make a fur coat. See Jorina Fontelera, "Animals Used to Make Fur Coats," *Our Everyday Life*, September 28, 2017, https://oureverydaylife.com/animals-used-to-make-fur-coats-12209351.html.

2. See Adam Bridgen's essay, "'Thou Shalt Not Use the Skins of Any Living Creature': The Original Anti-Fur Activist, Thomas Tryon (1634–1703)," in this volume.

3. See the book cover of Lori Williamson, *Power and Protest: Frances Power Cobbe and Victorian Society* (London: Rivers Oram Press, 2001).

4. John Paul II, *Veritatis Splendor* (encyclical letter, 1993), 6.2, www.vatican.va/content/john-paul-ii/en/encyclicals/documents/hf_jp-ii_enc_06081993_veritatis-splendor.html.

5. Tom Knudson, "More Than 100 Countries Ban This Cruel Trap: The US Isn't One of Them," *Reveal News*, September 14, 2016, https://revealnews.org/blog/more-than-100-countries-ban-this-cruel-trap-the-us-isnt-one-of-them/.

6. The last three paragraphs are adapted from "The Fur Trade Today" in Andrew Linzey, ed., *Cruelty and Christian Conscience: Bishops Say No to Fur* (Nottingham: Lynx, 1992), 22–32.

7. Although the Hudson Bay Company still exists today, it is primarily a retail store and says that "HBC is no longer involved in the fur trade." See "HBC and the Fur Trade," *HBC Heritage*, www.hbcheritage.ca/classroom/virtual-museum/the-business-of-fur/hbc-and-the-fur-trade.

8. John F. Richards, *The Unending Frontier: An Environmental History of the Early Modern World* (Oakland: University of California Press, 2003), 507–8.

9. For details on how colonialization exploited indigenous Canadians, see Facing History and Ourselves, "Stolen Lives: The Indigenous Peoples of Canada and the Indian Residential Schools," *Facing History and Ourselves*, www.facinghistory.org/stolen-lives-indigenous-peoples-canada-and-indian-residential-schools/historical-background/dispossession-destruction-and-reserves. See especially the sections "Colonization," "Colonial Power Struggle," and "Dispossession, Destruction, and the Reserves." See also a discussion in this volume: Adam Bridgen, "From the Pleistocene to COVID-19: A Brief History of Fur."

10. Linzey, "The Fur Trade Today," 32.

11. Department of External Affairs, Canada, *Defence of the Fur Trade*, a discussion paper, May 1985, 9. We are grateful to Dr. David Lavigne for this reference.

12. See the website of Beavers Northwest at https://beaversnw.org/about-beavers.

13. Quotations in the following two paragraphs come from Andrew Linzey, *Why Animal Suffering Matters: Philosophy, Theology and Ethics* (Oxford: Oxford University Press, 2009), 98.

14. Linzey, *Why Animal Suffering Matters*, 98.

15. The following information is adapted from Fur Free Alliance, "Fur Bans," https://www.furfreealliance.com/fur-bans/.

16. See Sophie Hirsh, "12 Luxury Fashion Brands That Have Gone Fur-Free," *Green Matters*, updated April 1, 2021, www.greenmatters.com/p/fur-free-luxury-fashion.

17. "Canada Goose Fashion Brand to Go Fur-Free by the End of 2022," *Sky News*, June 25, 2021, https://news.sky.com/story/canada-goose-fashion-brand-to-go-fur-free-by-the-end-of-2022-12341143.

18. Scientific Committee on Animal Health and Animal Welfare, "New Report Recommends Improved Conditions in Fur Farms" (press release), December 19, 2001.

19. For more information on the statistics on fur farming, see Andrew Linzey and Clair Linzey, *An Ethical Critique of Fur Factory Farming* (Basingstoke: Palgrave Macmillan, 2022).

20. For further discussion, see chapter 1 of Linzey, *Why Animal Suffering Matters*, 35.

21. C. S. Lewis, *The Problem of Pain* (London: Geoffrey Bles, 1940), 117.

REFERENCES

Beavers Northwest. "About Beavers." *Beavers Northwest*. Accessed February 17, 2023. https://beaversnw.org/about-beavers.

Department of External Affairs, Canada. *Defence of the Fur Trade*. A Discussion Paper. May 1985.

Facing History and Ourselves. "Stolen Lives: The Indigenous Peoples of Canada and the Indian Residential Schools." *Facing History and Ourselves*. Accessed February 17, 2023. www.facinghistory.org/stolen-lives-indigenous-peoples-canada-and-indian-residential-schools/historical-background/dispossession-destruction-and-reserves.

Fontelera, Jorina. "Animals Used to Make Fur Coats." *Our Everyday Life*. September 28, 2017. Accessed February 17, 2023. https://oureverydaylife.com/animals-used-to-make-fur-coats-12209351.html.

Fur Free Alliance. "Fur Bans." Accessed June 25, 2021. https://www.furfreealliance.com/fur-bans/.

HBC Heritage. "HBC and the Fur Trade." *HBC Heritage*. Accessed February 17, 2023. www.hbcheritage.ca/classroom/virtual-museum/the-business-of-fur/hbc-and-the-fur-trade.

Hirsh, Sophie. "12 Luxury Fashion Brands That Have Gone Fur-Free." *Green Matters*. Updated April 1, 2021. Accessed June 25, 2021. www.greenmatters.com/p/fur-free-luxury-fashion.

John Paul II. *Veritatis Splendor*. Encyclical Letter, 1993. www.vatican.va/content/john-paul-ii/en/encyclicals/documents/hf_jp-ii_enc_06081993_veritatis-splendor.html.

Knudson, Tom. "More Than 100 Countries Ban This Cruel Trap: The US Isn't One of Them." *Reveal News*. September 14, 2016. https://revealnews.org/blog/more-than-100-countries-ban-this-cruel-trap-the-us-isnt-one-of-them/.

Lewis, C. S. *The Problem of Pain*. London: Geoffrey Bles, 1940.

Linzey, Andrew. Ed. *Cruelty and Christian Conscience: Bishops Say No to Fur*. Nottingham: Lynx, 1992.

Linzey, Andrew. *Why Animal Suffering Matters: Philosophy, Theology and Ethics*. Oxford: Oxford University Press, 2009.

Linzey, Andrew and Clair Linzey. *An Ethical Critique of Fur Factory Farming*. Basingstoke: Palgrave Macmillan, 2022.

Richards, John F. *The Unending Frontier: An Environmental History of the Early Modern World*. Oakland: University of California Press, 2003.

Scientific Committee on Animal Health and Animal Welfare. "New Report Recommends Improved Conditions in Fur Farms." Press Release. December 19, 2001.

Sky News. "Canada Goose Fashion Brand to Go Fur-Free by the End of 2022." *Sky News*. June 25, 2021. https://news.sky.com/story/canada-goose-fashion-brand-to-go-fur-free-by-the-end-of-2022-12341143.

Williamson, Lori. *Power and Protest: Frances Power Cobbe and Victorian Society*. London: Rivers Oram Press, 2001.

PART ONE

Historical and Religious Perspectives

Chapter 1

From the Pleistocene to COVID-19

A Brief History of Fur

Adam Bridgen

THE CONTESTED ORIGINS OF FUR-WEARING

Whether our early ancestors wore the fur of other animals is in and of itself a contentious question. Recently, archaeologists have argued that clothing was a critical human invention that emerged during the last Ice Age, as a response to humans' "biological nakedness"—that is, their unusual lack of the fur covering that most other mammals have.[1] There are various ideas as to when and why our ancestors lost their fur, the most popular theory being environmental.[2] Although the genus *Homo* evolved (some two million years ago) in Africa when global temperatures were 2–3°C higher than today (perhaps leading them to lose their fur), they subsequently lived through a period—the Pleistocene—dominated by ice ages.[3] The most recent of these glacial cycles began 120,000 years ago, and at the period's coldest point, air temperatures were on average 3–5°C lower.[4] On this basis, Ian Gilligan argues that wearing the fur of other animals became a "thermal . . . necessity," at least for those living in areas beyond the tropics.[5] However, as Gilligan admits, the material evidence for fur-wearing is sparse: only indirect suggestions exist, such as scraping and cutting tools, awls, and needles.[6] The actual extent of fur-wearing, therefore, and whether it was in fact "necessary" for human survival are entirely a matter of interpretation. It must be kept in mind, as other scholars argue, that the modern idea of "man the hunter" is a myth, based on archaeological findings in Africa in the 1920s.[7] The myth persists because it says something about humanity's understanding of itself.[8]

Fur and Power in the Ancient World

What we know for sure is that by the period in which written history emerged, the wearing of fur was increasingly evident. While it can be argued that the "revolution" of woven textiles offered clothing choices far better suited to the milder, more humid conditions of the Holocene, fur-wearing nevertheless appeared in this period—primarily as a signifier of wealth and power.[9] In the ancient Mediterranean world, for example, larger animals such as foxes and bears were valued for their fur, as were weasels and beavers.[10] In pagan societies, individuals might wear fur in ritual contexts to take on the attributes of a given animal spirit or god.[11] Fur also had a prominent place in the iconography of this period, with the panther skin of Dionysus indicating his decadent "eastern" origins and the lion pelt of Heracles reflecting his superhuman strength and courage (it was a prize he took after slaying the Nemean lion). The wearing of fur or skins as a means of conspicuous display was also adopted by powerful rulers, such as Alexander the Great, who was at one point portrayed wearing the skin of an elephant with a ram's horn protruding through it. This is thought to have "symbolised his victory over the eastern realms whence the [elephant] came, with an underlying connotation of military prowess."[12] The use of fur as a status symbol can be seen throughout the ancient world, such as in pre-imperial China. One text from the *Shijing*, or *Book of Poetry*, from circa 600 BCE, describes how rural communities would "catch those foxes and racoon-dogs/and make fur garments for a young gentleman"—a passage that points to the ways in which fur production was already being marketized and driven not just by need, but by elite demands for fine clothing.[13]

Global Transits in Antiquity

Admittedly, as the much newer technology of woven textiles was adopted throughout the ancient world, animal fur might have begun to attract some more negative associations.[14] In the case of the ancient Greeks, a rethinking of fur might have occurred due to emerging social and geographical hierarchies. Alastair Harden suggests that in the early classical period, there was a growing urban disdain for animal skins and those who produced and wore them, while textiles were becoming associated with sophistication and civilization.[15] Some ancient philosophers also began to stress moral concern for animals and less violent means of clothing. In the third century AD, Porphyry wrote in his *On Abstinence from Animal Flesh*:

> The comparison of plants with animals is obviously forced. It is the nature of animals to have perceptions, to feel distress, to be afraid, to be hurt, and

therefore to be injured. Plants have no perceptions, so nothing is alien or bad to them, nothing is harm or injustice: for perception is the origin of all appropriation and alienation. . . . We see that many people live only by perception, having no intellect or *logos*, and many surpass the most terrifying beasts in savagery and anger and aggression. . . . How can it not be irrational to think that there is justice between us and these, but none between us and the ox that ploughs, the dog that lives with us, the creatures that feed us with their milk and clothe us with fleece? How can it not be wholly contrary to reason?[16]

The existence of woven materials that did not directly involve slaughter (whether plant-based, such as flax, or from shearing domesticated animals, such as wool) might have facilitated this embryonic reimagining of human relations with animals. However, this association of fur with backwardness—if not also violence—was relatively unusual. Across the world, free-living animals continued to be hunted for their skins and, increasingly, traded as the demand for fur grew in the wealthy centers of powerful empires. Indeed, from late antiquity if not earlier, the trade in fur began to span continents, with Viking traders bringing Scandinavian furs to market in the Byzantine and Abbasid empires and with the Xiong-nu and Han empires in China serving as a similar center for the fur trade in Asia. As Jonathan Schlesinger points out, "the product was high value, low weight, easy to carry, and durable and so remarkably well suited for long-distance trade in preindustrial economies."[17] Similarly, in the Aztec empire, while animal skins had long been worn by nomadic hunters, they were increasingly goods of trade and gift exchange, with rulers bestowing rabbit-skin capes on warriors and merchants who distinguished themselves in service.[18] Rabbit fur was also woven into cotton cloth as a form of decoration.[19]

Fur as Status Symbol: Sumptuary Laws in the Middle Ages and Renaissance

Evidently, fur was not outmoded by woven garments, nor did fur's association with untamed nature prevent it from becoming a valuable and sought-after commodity. Throughout medieval Europe, fur was esteemed not only for the yet-unparalleled degree of warmth it offered but also, increasingly, for its distinctiveness and exclusivity—a factor that was only enhanced by global trade. The most expensive furs (such as those from Baltic squirrels, ermines, and sable, as well as bears, otters, and lynx) were imported and worn by those of the highest social rank, while poorer sorts might wear the pelts of domesticated or other animals (such as hares, rabbits, lambs, and wolves).[20] By the thirteenth and fourteenth centuries, Europe's growing mercantile classes displayed their wealth by adopting the clothing of the aristocracy—including, importantly, wearing furs.[21] In 1513, a Venetian envoy remarked, "In England it is always windy, and however warm the weather the natives invariably wear furs."[22] So significant was fur-wearing to the display of the nobility that sumptuary laws across Europe were passed "to restrict the wearing of certain furs, fabrics, and styles to members of particular social and economic classes, ranks, or 'states.'"[23] In a similar vein, religious authorities would often warn against the moral dangers of extravagant clothing. In his searing rebuke of popular culture, *The Anatomie of Abuses* (1583), the Puritan Philip Stubbes argued that "this sinne of excesse in Apparell, remayneth as an Example of Evyll before our eyes, and as a provocative of sinne, as Experience daily showeth . . . for doth not the apparel styrre uppe the heart to pride?"[24] Julia Emberley argues that Stubbes sought "not so much to curb extravagance as to preserve certain commodities for the wealthy, ensuring that symbolic displays of wealth were reserved to the property-owning classes."[25] While concerns like these continued, the desire to restrict fine clothing to elites became impractical: by the late sixteenth century, the meaning of "fashion" had grown to encompass its more modern meaning as "the mode of dress . . . adopted in society for the time being."[26] Moreover, with the emergence of a more commercial ethos in England, by the mid-seventeenth century, the new mantra was that "luxury and fashion are acceptable because they stimulate consumption, which in turn generates trade and employment."[27]

Early Modern Consumer Culture and European Expansion

Throughout the sixteenth and seventeenth centuries, the birth of consumer culture in Europe drove to new heights the demand for, and global trade in, fur.[28] One particularly important development in the use of fur was the felt hat, or "beaver," which—as Timothy Brook argues—holds a central place in the history of commercialization and globalization.[29] Beaver fur was prized for its barbed hairs, which made it an invaluable material for making waterproof, sleek, and strong yet flexible felt hats. Such hats had been known in England since the fourteenth century, albeit as a Dutch product. The Ellesmere Manuscript describes Chaucer's merchant "Hye on horse . . . Upon his head a Flaundryssh bever hat."[30] It was not until the start of the sixteenth century that the technology of felt-making became known in England.[31] Paralleling the expiry of sumptuary laws in 1604, the fashion for hats spread throughout English society, from high to low, in a dizzying variety of styles.[32] As a consequence of the rising demand for this very specific kind of fur, by the sixteenth century beavers had been hunted to near extinction in Europe, and they were fast disappearing elsewhere.[33] However, the incursion of Russian, French, and English adventurers into northernmost America, originally in hopes of discovering the fabled "Northwest Passage," opened up this vast, forested region to the global fur trade.[34] Subsequently, London became the center of the fur trade and European hat production. The Hudson's Bay Company, established in 1670, oversaw England's interests in the region; its beaver-studded crest and underlying motto, *pro pelle cutem* ("the skin for the fur"), reflected the reality that "beaver skins were wanted not to wear but for hats."[35] Beaver fur remained a critical material for hat-making, constituting until 1775 more than half of the value of English fur imports and almost 30 percent of English exports of fur.[36] As one historian writes, "the early history of the fur trade is essentially a history of the trade in beaver fur."[37]

The North American Fur Trade and Its Impacts

Due to this extraordinary European demand for felt hats, argues John F. Richards, "the North American beaver became the most valuable furbearer of the New World and prey to one of the longest sustained hunts for a single species in world history."[38] The scale of the killing was immense: from a previously flourishing population of some sixty to one hundred million, over the course of the seventeenth and eighteenth centuries, beavers were practically wiped out in North America.[39] It always had been the case, of course, that the fur trade caused immense suffering to those animals who were hunted and killed through a variety of methods, whether with shot or arrow or through snares, traps, or poison. As killing for fur increased to meet growing demand, however, harm extended to more than just hunted animals; habitats and the various other animals who relied upon them also suffered harm. The dark side of the fur trade became more apparent as it reached ever further into the waterways of the Great Lakes region and what is now Canada. The North American fur trade was distinctive in that it relied upon asymmetrical trading agreements between European colonists and Native Americans. Through the trade of European manufactures and consumable products (such as sugar, tobacco, and rum) for furs, colonists struck trading agreements with tribes that led to a cascade of environmental problems. While technologies such as the musket enabled indigenous populations "to gain a livelihood more easily—to obtain their supply of food, as in the case of moose, more quickly, and to hunt the beaver more effectively," as Harold Innis writes, these "radical innovations brought about such a rapid shift in the prevailing Indian [*sic*] culture as to lead to the wholesale destruction of the peoples."[40] The gun not only instigated a veritable arms race between neighboring tribes but also allowed beavers to be hunted in ever-increasing numbers—both of which increased the demand for European goods. However, as beaver populations were destroyed, so were the unique water habitats they created by damming.[41] This, in turn, reduced the number of fish, waterfowl, and deer—previously a source of food for indigenous peoples. "The end result," Richards writes, "was a dependency that grew more pervasive and demeaning over time," and by the end of the seventeenth century, many Native American tribes had been driven to selling furs to European traders merely to gain enough food to survive through the long boreal winter.[42] The appetite for fur in fashion led to devastation elsewhere. Moreover, fur meant death to animal and hunter alike. It was, as some workers in the fashion industry perceived, a "stinking trade," and "the price of Blood, for the most part procured by great hazard, trouble, and labour."[43]

The Invention of Fur Farming in the Modern Period

By the end of the nineteenth century, across the world, populations of fur-bearing animals of almost all kinds were nearing collapse due to over-hunting and habitat destruction. While beaver populations were able to bounce back, that was not the case for other keystone species, such as wolves, wolverines, and martens, and these practically disappeared across North America.[44] Similar extinctions (and consequent fur shortages) occurred in China, in Russia and Siberia, and on both sides of the Pacific, in California, Mexico, and Japan.[45] Although the farthest-flung areas experienced their fur boom much later, their economies suffered similar collapses when animals later were hunted to the point of collapse, such as Alaska in the 1920s.[46]

Gradually, the apparent solution to the recurrent issue of extinction and the unreliability of fur became to take fur production into the organized and controlling structure of the farm. Of course, fur farming had its earliest beginnings among those who were observant enough to notice the variation of animals and to seek to produce the most valuable types through artificial selection, as was the case in eleventh-century China, where cats were said to have been bred for patterned furs.[47] However, it was the logic of colonization that led to the modern fur farm. Adventurous eighteenth-century merchant Andrean Tolstykh, for example, established isolated populations of "blue" arctic foxes in the Aleutian Islands (the string of islands in the Bering Sea).[48] These small islands were in effect the first fur farms and gave rise to further attempts to artificially control fur production to maximize profitability. Subsequently, it was in Alaska at the turn of the twentieth century that fur farming was further intensified, with the now familiar factory-like systems of enclosures, feeding stations, breeding pens, and mechanized means of slaughter and processing.[49] Once again, the violence of the fur trade was not limited to furbearers: in Alaska, eagles and other predators were considered nuisance ("pest") animals and eradicated due to the risk they posed to the fox pups farmers were breeding, while Alaska natives were pushed off their land.[50] In addition, fur farming had other dangerous side effects, such as diseases that spread through previously free-roaming animals when they were penned closely together and that veterinary science struggled to prevent.[51]

THE END OF FUR? ETHICAL RESISTANCE, SYNTHETIC ALTERNATIVES, AND GLOBAL HEALTH

Fur remained in high demand in the twentieth century, met by new fur farms as well as the further spread of the fur trade to remote regions such as Amazonia.[52] Although during World War II, the consumption of fur—like other nonessential goods—temporarily bottomed out, it boomed in the 1950s as a fashion accessory, famously sported by Hollywood film stars. However, fur was beginning to face existential threats in the form of growing ethical resistance as well as new synthetic materials. Animal advocates had long expressed concerns about fur; American anticruelty campaigners such as Caroline Earle White (1833–1916) took a stance against it in the second half of the nineteenth century, and from the 1920s to the 1950s, the American Society for the Prevention of Cruelty to Animals offered a cash prize to anyone who could invent a "humane" furbearer trap.[53] One critical development was the mass production of synthetic clothing during the World Wars.[54] While one long-standing defense of fur was its apparent necessity, as Sarah Isto writes, "with the availability of warm synthetics in the last half of the twentieth century, opponents of wearing fur felt that killing fur animals for cold-weather clothing was neither necessary nor acceptable."[55]

Subsequently, in the 1970s, the organized anti-fur movement sparked a public outcry against fur.[56] Leading this charge was the British-based anti-fur organization Lynx, which utilized striking advertising campaigns.[57] After the demise of Lynx, Respect for Animals took up the cause against fur and won multiple victories against fur farming, especially in Europe.[58] Subsequently, fur farming was banned first in the UK in 2000 and then in Austria in 2005, and numerous other European countries followed suit. Countries beyond Europe also passed legislation against mink farming and imports, such as Japan, India, and New Zealand. In 2019, California became the first US state to ban all fur sales—the strictest of regulatory measures.[59] Of course, the fur industry responded to these changes by shifting production to other countries and with attempts to disguise or minimize fur's violence to animals, such as through "welfare washing."[60]

While legislation has thus far been only partial and piecemeal, perhaps one of the biggest catalysts for more sweeping change is the SARS-CoV-2 pandemic. Not only is this zoonotic disease thought to have been spread to humans through the fur trade in Asia, but it also subsequently led to outbreaks of variants on fur farms in Europe and America.[61] In 2021 the UK government began a consultation on finally ending fur imports.[62] Meanwhile, France and Ireland committed to their first farming bans, while other countries brought forward their plans to phase out fur farming.[63] While the global history of fur shows the devastating impact it has had upon animals, environments, and humans, it shows also the remarkable endurance of this industry. If the history of fur, in turn, highlights how far anti-fur campaigners have come in changing attitudes, it also reminds us of the global scale of the challenge of abolishing the fur trade altogether.

NOTES

1. Ian Gilligan, *Climate, Clothing, and Agriculture in Prehistory: Linking Evidence, Causes, and Effects* (Cambridge: Cambridge University Press, 2019), 23.
2. Gilligan, *Climate, Clothing, and Agriculture*, 28–55.
3. Gilligan, *Climate, Clothing, and Agriculture*, 24.
4. Gilligan, *Climate, Clothing, and Agriculture*, 7.
5. Gilligan, *Climate, Clothing, and Agriculture*, 28, 57.
6. Gilligan, *Climate, Clothing, and Agriculture*, 25–26.
7. See especially Matt Cartmill, *A View to Death in the Morning: Hunting and Nature through History* (Cambridge, MA: Harvard University Press, 1993).
8. Cartmill explains that his work, *A View to Death*, "is about the connections that various people have tried to draw between hunting and being human . . . The book's concluding chapters express my doubts about the meaning and reality of the distinctions we draw between artifice and nature and between people and animals" (xi–xiii).
9. Gilligan, *Climate, Clothing, and Agriculture*, 124.
10. Michael MacKinnon, "Fauna of the Ancient Mediterranean World," in *The Oxford Handbook of Animals in Classical Thought and Life*, ed. Gordon Lindsay Campbell (Oxford: Oxford University Press, 2014), 156–79, 163–65, 168.
11. Graham Harvey, *Contemporary Paganism: Religions of the Earth from Druids and Witches to Heathens and Ecofeminists*, 2nd ed. (New York: NYU Press, 2011), 166.
12. Angela McDonald, "Animals in Egypt," in *The Oxford Handbook of Animals in Classical Thought and Life*, ed. Gordon Lindsay Campbell (Oxford: Oxford University Press, 2014), 441–60, 453.
13. Robert Weisser, *Student Study Guide to the Ancient Chinese World* (Oxford: Oxford University Press, 2005), 22.
14. E. J. W. Barber, *Prehistoric Textiles: The Development of Cloth in the Neolithic and Bronze Ages with Special Reference to the Aegean* (Princeton, NJ: Princeton University Press, 1991).
15. Alastair Harden, "'Wild Men' and Animal Skins in Archaic Greek Imagery," in *Interactions between Animals and Humans in Graeco-Roman Antiquity*, ed. Edmund Thomas and Thorsten Fögen (Berlin, Germany: De Gruyter, 2017), 369–88.

16. Porphyry, *On Abstinence from Killing Animals*, trans. Gillian Clark (Ithaca, NY: Cornell University Press, 2000), 91, 3.19.

17. Jonathan Schlesinger, *A World Trimmed with Fur: Wild Things, Pristine Places, and the Natural Fringes of Qing Rule* (Stanford, CA: Stanford University Press, 2017), 132.

18. Francis F. Berdan, *Aztec Archaeology and Ethnohistory* (Cambridge: Cambridge University Press, 2014), 37, 86, 130–32, 169.

19. Berdan, *Aztec Archaeology*, 112.

20. Friedrich Heer, *The Medieval World: Europe 1100–1300*, trans. Janet Sondheimer (London: Weidenfeld & Nicolson, 1962), 92; Elspeth M. Veale, *English Fur Trade in the Later Middle Ages* (Oxford: Oxford University Press, 1966), 4–5.

21. Heer, *Medieval World*, 92–93; Veale, *English Fur Trade*, 9.

22. Quoted in Veale, *English Fur Trade*, 3.

23. Marjorie Garber, *Vested Interests: Cross-Dressing and Cultural Anxiety* (New York: HarperPerennial, 1992), 25; Susan Vincent, *Dressing the Elite: Clothes in Early Modern England* (Oxford: Berg, 2003), 119, 126–27.

24. Phillipe Stubbes, *The Anatomie of Abuses* (London, 1583; repr. Amsterdam, 1972), sigs. B7v, C6r.

25. Julia V. Emberley, *The Cultural Politics of Fur* (Montreal: McGill-Queen's University Press, 1997), 43–44, 59.

26. *OED Online*, "fashion, n." (Oxford University Press, 2021), accessed June 25, 2021.

27. Christopher J. Berry, *The Idea of Luxury: A Conceptual and Historical Investigation* (Cambridge: Cambridge University Press, 1994), 104.

28. For an excellent overview of the scholarly periodization of the birth of consumer society, see the introduction to *The Oxford Handbook of the History of Consumption*, ed. Frank Trentmann (Oxford: Oxford University Press, 2012), 1–19, esp. 4–5. The classic work relocating consumer revolution to the early modern period is Joan Thirsk's *Economic Policy and Projects: The Development of a Consumer Society in Early Modern England* (Oxford: Clarendon Press, 1978).

29. Timothy Brook, *Vermeer's Hat: The Seventeenth Century and the Dawn of the Global World* (London: Profile, 2008), 29–53.

30. Geoffrey Chaucer, "Canterbury Tales: General Prologue," in *The Complete Works of Geoffrey Chaucer*, ed. F. N. Robinson, 2nd ed. (Oxford, 1957), p. 19, line 272.

31. Judy Vero, *A Concern in Trade: Hatting and the Bracebridges of Atherstone, 1612–1872* (Warwick, UK: Warwickshire Books, 1995), 14.

32. Emberley, *Cultural Politics of Fur*, 68. For the felt hat's popularization, see John H. Smith, *The Great Human Exploit: Historic Industries of the North-West* (Chichester, UK: Phillimore, 1973), 41; Eric Kerridge, *Textile Manufactures in Early Modern England* (Manchester: Manchester University Press, 1985), 138.

33. Veale, *English Fur Trade*, 175; J. F. Crean, "Hats and the Fur Trade," *Canadian Journal of Economics and Political Science* 28 (1962): 373–86, 376.

34. John R. Bockstoce, *Furs and Frontiers in the Far North: The Contest among Native and Foreign Nations for the Bering Strait Fur Trade* (New Haven, CT: Yale University Press, 2009).

35. *Hudson's Bay Company: A Brief History* (London: Hudson's Bay Company, 1934), 1.

36. Murray G. Lawson, *Fur: A Study in English Mercantilism 1700–1775* (Toronto: University of Toronto Press, 1943), 3.

37. Harold A. Innis, *The Fur Trade in Canada: An Introduction to Canadian Economic History* (Toronto: University of Toronto Press, 1999), 391.

38. John F. Richards, *The Unending Frontier: An Environmental History of the Early Modern World* (Berkeley: University of California Press, 2003), 467.

39. Richards, *Unending Frontier*, 470.

40. Innis, *Fur Trade in Canada*, 392.

41. For a history of beavers themselves, see Ben Goldfarb, *Eager: The Surprising, Secret Life of Beavers and Why They Matter* (London: Chelsea Green, 2018).

42. Richards, *Unending Frontier*, 475, 502–9. See also Daniel K. Richter, *Facing East from Indian Country: A Native History of Early America* (Cambridge, MA: Harvard University Press, 2001), 49–51, 54.

43. Quoted in Marcus Rediker, *The Fearless Benjamin Lay: The Quaker Dwarf Who Became the First Revolutionary Abolitionist* (Boston: Beacon Press, 2017), 21–22; Thomas Tryon [Philotheos Physiologus, pseud.], *The Way to Health, Long Life, and Happiness* (London: Andrew Sowle, 1683), 470–71. See my chapter on Tryon in this collection for further details.

44. Richards, *Unending Frontier*, 509–15.

45. Schlesinger, *A World Trimmed with Fur*, 129–66.

46. Sarah Crawford Isto, *The Fur Farms of Alaska: Two Centuries of History and a Forgotten Stampede* (Fairbanks: University of Alaska Press, 2012).

47. Timothy H. Barrett and Mark Strange, "Walking by Itself: The Singular History of the Chinese Cat," in *Animals through Chinese History: Earliest Times to 1911*, ed. Roel Sterckx, Martina Siebert, and Dagmar Schäfer (Cambridge: Cambridge University Press, 2018), 84–98, 97.

48. Isto, *Fur Farms of Alaska*, 10–14.

49. Isto, *Fur Farms of Alaska*, 23–42, esp. 32.

50. Isto, *Fur Farms of Alaska*, 55–57, 96–97, 161–62.

51. Isto, *Fur Farms of Alaska*, 94, 108, 154.

52. André P. Antunes et al., "Empty Forest or Empty Rivers? A Century of Commercial Hunting in Amazonia," *Science Advances* 2, no. 10 (October 12, 2016): e1600936.

53. Diane Beers, *For the Prevention of Cruelty: The History and Legacy of Animal Rights in America* (Athens: Ohio University Press, 2006), 83–84; Isto, *Fur Farms of Alaska*, 174.

54. Isto, *Fur Farms of Alaska*, 141–55; Arthur J. Ray, *The Canadian Fur Trade in the Industrial Age* (Toronto: University of Toronto Press, 1990), 96–112.

55. Isto, *Fur Farms of Alaska*, 174–75.

56. An excellent account of the debates is in Emberley, *Cultural Politics of Fur.*

57. Janice Li, "Dumb Animals: Lynx's Campaign against the Fur Industry," *Victoria and Albert Museum Blog*, January 7, 2019, accessed June 25, 2021, www.vam.ac.uk/blog/projects/dumb-animals-lynxs-campaign-against-the-fur-industry.

58. Respect for Animals, "About," accessed June 25, 2021, respectforanimals.org/about/.

59. For an excellent up-to-date overview of current and prospective legislation, see Fur Free Alliance, "Fur Farming Bans," accessed June 25, 2021, www.furfreealliance.com/fur-bans/.

60. I borrow the term from Kristian Bjørkdahl and Karen Lykke Syse, "Welfare Washing: Disseminating Disinformation in Meat Marketing," *Society & Animals* (2021): 1–19. For an account of welfare washing specifically in relation to fur, see Lise Skov, "The Return of the Fur Coat: A Commodity Chain Perspective," *Current Sociology* 53, no. 1 (2005): 10–32.

61. Dina Fine Maron, "What the Mink COVID-19 Outbreaks Taught Us about Pandemics," *National Geographic*, February 24, 2021, accessed June 25, 2021, www.nationalgeographic.com/animals/article/what-the-mink-coronavirus-pandemic-has-taught-us.

62. Kalyeena Makortoff, "People in Great Britain Being Asked for Views on Fur Trade Ban," *Guardian*, May 31, 2021, accessed June 25, 2021, www.theguardian.com/business/2021/may/31/uk-government-to-ask-citizens-if-it-should-ban-fur-trade.

63. Fur Free Alliance, "Fur Farming Bans."

REFERENCES

Antunes, André P., et al. "Empty Forest or Empty Rivers? A Century of Commercial Hunting in Amazonia." *Science Advances* 2, no. 10 (October 12, 2016): e1600936.

Barber, E. J. W. *Prehistoric Textiles: The Development of Cloth in the Neolithic and Bronze Ages with Special Reference to the Aegean*. Princeton, NJ: Princeton University Press, 1991.

Barrett, Timothy H., and Mark Strange. "Walking by Itself: The Singular History of the Chinese Cat." In *Animals through Chinese History: Earliest Times to 1911*, edited by Roel Sterckx, Martina Siebert, and Dagmar Schäfer, 84–98. Cambridge: Cambridge University Press, 2018.

Beers, Diane. *For the Prevention of Cruelty: The History and Legacy of Animal Rights in America*. Athens: Ohio University Press, 2006.

Berdan, Francis F. *Aztec Archaeology and Ethnohistory*. Cambridge: Cambridge University Press, 2014.

Berry, Christopher J. *The Idea of Luxury: A Conceptual and Historical Investigation*. Cambridge: Cambridge University Press, 1994.

Bjørkdahl, Kristian, and Karen Lykke Syse. "Welfare Washing: Disseminating Disinformation in Meat Marketing." *Society & Animals* (2021): 1–19.

Bockstoce, John R. *Furs and Frontiers in the Far North: The Contest among Native and Foreign Nations for the Bering Strait Fur Trade*. New Haven, CT: Yale University Press, 2009.

Brook, Timothy. *Vermeer's Hat: The Seventeenth Century and the Dawn of the Global World*. London: Profile, 2008.
Cartmill, Matt. *A View to Death in the Morning: Hunting and Nature through History*. Cambridge, MA: Harvard University Press, 1993.
Chaucer, Geoffrey. "Canterbury Tales: General Prologue," in *The Complete Works of Geoffrey Chaucer*, edited by F. N. Robinson, 2nd ed. London: Oxford University Press, 1957.
Crean, J. F. "Hats and the Fur Trade." *Canadian Journal of Economics and Political Science* 28 (1962): 373–86.
Emberley, Julia V. *The Cultural Politics of Fur*. Montreal: McGill-Queen's University Press, 1997.
Fur Free Alliance. "Fur Farming Bans." Accessed June 25, 2021. www.furfreealliance.com/fur-bans/.
Garber, Marjorie. *Vested Interests: Cross-Dressing and Cultural Anxiety*. New York: HarperPerennial, 1992.
Gilligan, Ian. *Climate, Clothing, and Agriculture in Prehistory: Linking Evidence, Causes, and Effects*. Cambridge: Cambridge University Press, 2019.
Goldfarb, Ben. *Eager: The Surprising, Secret Life of Beavers and Why They Matter*. London: Chelsea Green, 2018.
Harden, Alastair. "'Wild Men' and Animal Skins in Archaic Greek Imagery." In *Interactions between Animals and Humans in Graeco-Roman Antiquity*, edited by Edmund Thomas and Thorsten Fögen, 369–88. Berlin, Germany: De Gruyter, 2017.
Harvey, Graham. *Contemporary Paganism: Religions of the Earth from Druids and Witches to Heathens and Ecofeminists*. 2nd ed. New York: NYU Press, 2011.
Heer, Friedrich. *The Medieval World: Europe 1100–1300*. Translated by Janet Sondheimer. London: Weidenfeld & Nicolson, 1962.
Hudson's Bay Company: A Brief History. London: Hudson's Bay Company, 1934.
Innis, Harold A. *The Fur Trade in Canada: An Introduction to Canadian Economic History*. Toronto: University of Toronto Press, 1999.
Isto, Sarah Crawford. *The Fur Farms of Alaska: Two Centuries of History and a Forgotten Stampede*. Fairbanks: University of Alaska Press, 2012.
Kerridge, Eric. *Textile Manufactures in Early Modern England*. Manchester: Manchester University Press, 1985.
Lawson, Murray G. *Fur: A Study in English Mercantilism 1700–1775*. Toronto: University of Toronto Press, 1943.
Li, Janice. "Dumb Animals: Lynx's Campaign against the Fur Industry." *Victoria and Albert Museum Blog*, January 7, 2019. Accessed June 25, 2021. www.vam.ac.uk/blog/projects/dumb-animals-lynxs-campaign-against-the-fur-industry.
MacKinnon, Michael. "Fauna of the Ancient Mediterranean World." In *The Oxford Handbook of Animals in Classical Thought and Life*, edited by Gordon Lindsay Campbell, 156–79. Oxford: Oxford University Press, 2014.
Makortoff, Kalyeena. "People in Great Britain Being Asked for Views on Fur Trade Ban." *Guardian*, May 31, 2021. Accessed June 25, 2021. www.theguardian.com/business/2021/may/31/uk-government-to-ask-citizens-if-it-should-ban-fur-trade.

Maron, Dina Fine. "What the Mink COVID-19 Outbreaks Taught Us about Pandemics." *National Geographic*, February 24, 2021. Accessed June 25, 2021. www.nationalgeographic.com/animals/article/what-the-mink-coronavirus-pandemic-has-taught-us.

McDonald, Angela. "Animals in Egypt." In *The Oxford Handbook of Animals in Classical Thought and Life*, edited by Gordon Lindsay Campbell, 441–60. Oxford: Oxford University Press, 2014.

OED Online. "fashion, n." Oxford University Press, 2021. Accessed June 25, 2021.

Porphyry. *On Abstinence from Killing Animals*. Translated by Gillian Clark. Ithaca, NY: Cornell University Press, 2000.

Ray, Arthur J. *The Canadian Fur Trade in the Industrial Age*. Toronto: University of Toronto Press, 1990.

Rediker, Marcus. *The Fearless Benjamin Lay: The Quaker Dwarf Who Became the First Revolutionary Abolitionist*. Boston: Beacon Press, 2017.

Respect for Animals. "About." Accessed June 25, 2021. respectforanimals.org/about/.

Richards, John F. *The Unending Frontier: An Environmental History of the Early Modern World*. Berkeley: University of California Press, 2003.

Richter, Daniel K. *Facing East from Indian Country: A Native History of Early America*. Cambridge, MA: Harvard University Press, 2001.

Schlesinger, Jonathan. *A World Trimmed with Fur: Wild Things, Pristine Places, and the Natural Fringes of Qing Rule*. Stanford, CA: Stanford University Press, 2017.

Skov, Lise. "The Return of the Fur Coat: A Commodity Chain Perspective." *Current Sociology* 53, no. 1 (2005): 10–32.

Smith, John H. *The Great Human Exploit: Historic Industries of the North-West*. Chichester, UK: Phillimore, 1973.

Stubbes, Phillipe. *The Anatomie of Abuses*. London, 1583. Reprint, Amsterdam, 1972.

Thirsk, Joan. *Economic Policy and Projects: The Development of a Consumer Society in Early Modern England*. Oxford: Clarendon Press, 1978.

Tryon, Thomas [Philotheos Physiologus, pseud.]. *The Way to Health, Long Life, and Happiness*. London: Andrew Sowle, 1683.

Trentmann, Frank. *The Oxford Handbook of the History of Consumption*. Oxford: Oxford University Press, 2012.

Veale, Elspeth M.. *English Fur Trade in the Later Middle Ages*. Oxford: Oxford University Press, 1966.

Vero, Judy. *A Concern in Trade: Hatting and the Bracebridges of Atherstone, 1612–1872*. Warwick, UK: Warwickshire Books, 1995.

Vincent, Susan. *Dressing the Elite: Clothes in Early Modern England*. Oxford: Berg, 2003.

Weisser, Robert. *Student Study Guide to the Ancient Chinese World*. Oxford: Oxford University Press, 2005.

Chapter 2

"Thou Shalt Not Use the Skins of Any Living Creature"

The Original Anti-Fur Activist, Thomas Tryon (1634–1703)

Adam Bridgen

I. A HYPOCRITICAL THINKER?

The London hat-maker, religious dissenter, and popular self-help writer Thomas Tryon (1634–1703) is considered one of the most important voices in the development of vegetarianism in the Western world. From 1682 to the early 1700s, Tryon wrote on a vast array of subjects—from brewing, husbandry, and account keeping to education, trade, and dream interpretation—but was above all concerned with a brand of Christian dietary pacifism "recommending . . . Temperance, Cleanness, and Innocency of Living; and admonishing Mankind against Violence, Oppression, and Cruelty, either to their own Kind, or any inferior Creatures."[1] His best-known work, the 583-page *Way to Health, Long Life, and Happiness* (1683), argued on several fronts, but discussed in particular the sanctity of all living creatures and the admonitions against violence and flesh-eating in the Bible, as well as the corresponding evils of carnivorism for human health and society.[2] Tryon presented his temperate, pacifist regimen not only as a present good, therefore, but also as a means of redeeming humankind from its proud and tyrannous fallen state. The *Way to Health* was reprinted at least five times before 1700 and is said to have prompted the playwright Aphra Behn (c. 1640–1689) to give up meat as well as leather, and it had a similar, if not more formative, influence on the US Founding Father Benjamin Franklin (1706–1790) and the Quaker abolitionist Benjamin Lay (1682–1759).[3] Recognized now as the backbone of a veritable vegetarian revival during the eighteenth century, Tryon's writing continued to exert an influence long after his death, inspiring the Romantic-period vegetarians Percy Shelley and Joseph Ritson, as well as vegetarian campaigners throughout the nineteenth century.[4] Tryon was also an early antislavery writer, producing a tract in 1684 in which he dramatizes principled African resistance to slavery and connects European demand for exotic goods such as sugar with the "extravagant viciousness" of plantation life.[5]

Tryon was clearly concerned about the violence involved in producing many sought-after commodities. His criticism of other animal-made products, especially skins and fur in clothing, has been overshadowed, however, by the fact of his work as a hatter. Born into poverty in rural Gloucestershire, Tryon began working in the clothing industry at the tender age of six, when his parents taught him to spin and card wool. Tryon was highly driven: in his adolescence he became a shepherd and scrupulously saved his earnings to buy reading materials, even trading a sheep for writing lessons at one point. When he was eighteen, he sold his small flock, left for London, and there bound himself as an apprentice to an Anabaptist hat-maker. Crucially, in the fifth year of his apprenticeship, Tryon had a series of divine revelations, which—he later recalled—steered him toward an "abstemious self-denying Life" that precluded "eating any kind of Flesh or Fish."[6] During the 1660s, Tryon relocated to Barbados to ply his trade, before opening his own shop back in London.[7] While hat-making was Tryon's route to prosperity and hence, eventually, to publication, it was nevertheless a gift to his early critics. In response to the *Way to Health*, the Quaker censor John Field published *The Absurdity & Falseness of Thomas Trion's Doctrine Manifested* (1685). Angered at Tryon's attempts to bring, as he put it, "a judgment over all them living that desire to eat flesh," Field launched a point-by-point attack on Tryon's theories and suggested his hypocrisy given his occupation, asking "whether he doth not Trade, Merchandize, or deal in the Skins of Beasts, and get Gain and Money by the same."[8] In this particular case, evidence would appear to bear out Field's accusation: beaver fur, shorn from the pelt, was an essential component of the fashionable felt hats of this period, so much so that the hats were colloquially termed "beavers" (or "Castors," from the Latin). In addition to drawing fire at the time, the uncomfortable fact of Tryon's occupation also has meant that his anti-fur arguments have been overlooked in modern scholarship. Seeking to explain away the apparent contradiction, Alan Rudrum ingeniously suggests (although with little evidence) that Tryon may have used "imitation fur," while Geoffrey Plank comprehends the problem under the more general claim that Tryon's "guide to human conduct in this less-than-perfect world was riddled with compromises and apparent contradictions."[9] Such criticism might lead us to think that Tryon's experience as a hatter was of little significance to his vegetarian thinking or an embarrassment he tried to forget.

This essay offers a more nuanced account of Tryon's hat-making career, exploring the influence that this experience had upon his writing and, above all, his arguments against fur. As I argue, while Tryon's occupation undoubtedly made him an accessory to the fur trade, it also made him an insightful critic of fur's far-reaching destructiveness. Throughout his writing, Tryon argues that his culture's unthinking use of animal skins for clothing (and for fashionable garments in particular) was a depraved custom that, much like meat-eating, contravened the pacifist tenets of Christianity, and doing violence to animals also further depraved humankind. While Tryon may have echoed some of the anti-luxury arguments of other religious sectarians, such as the Puritans, he looked beyond their anthropocentric concerns by stressing not only the evils of fur for those who wore it, but also the very real, physical harm it caused animals as well as those involved in its procurement—a case he made particularly astutely in his account of the cataclysmic effects of the North American fur trade, in *The Country-Man's Companion* (1684). As well as commanding his followers "not [to] use the skins of any living creature for shoes, gloves, saddles or any other thing whatsoever," Tryon also proposed a range of nonviolent textile alternatives.[10] By finally bringing to light Tryon's arguments against fur, his alternative recommendations, and also his onward influence, I hope to show that Tryon was—in spite of his trade—one of the earliest and most remarkable anti-fur activists.

II. "MAKING BEAVERS TO SUCCESS": TRYON THE HATTER

Undoubtedly, Tryon's occupation as a hat-maker would have meant that he worked with beaver fur. To appreciate the nature of this contact, however, we need to understand the precise process of hat-making in the period. Following is John F. Richards's helpful description:

> Skilled master hatters bought cleaned and graded beaver wool sheared from the skin. Journeymen boiled lesser quality wool with water and urine to enhance its felting qualities; the best quality needed no preparation. Next, the workers passed a large taut bow, similar to a violin bow, over the pile of wool. When vibrated, the bow's magnetic force aligned the hairs all in the same direction. Using heat and pressure, the hatter shaped the wool into batts of felt. Two large and two joining batts were pressed together to form a hat. After shaping or

blocking, the hat underwent a finishing process that involved dyeing, stiffening, waterproofing, reblocking, ironing, trimming, and final shaping.[11]

Before the introduction of (poisonous) mercury salts in the 1730s, beaver fur was essential to the making of felt hats. Given the "barbed" nature of its hairs, beaver wool felted with ease, and while lower-grade wools would make a substandard felt, the mere addition of beaver resulted in a hat that was light, smooth, waterproof, and durable, keeping its shape for many years. One of the reasons for the success of the "beaver" was the range of shapes it could take—such as the wide-brimmed "cavalier" or the tall, flat-topped "sugar-loaf."[12] Satirizing these shifts in fashion, Thomas Dekker joked that "the blocke for [the Englishman's] heade alters faster than the felt maker can fitte him, and thereupon we are called in scorne *Blockheads*."[13] Due to the demand for these hats in Europe, by the end of the sixteenth century, beavers had been hunted to near extinction throughout Eurasia.[14] Penetrating into North America, English and French colonists soon found a new, untapped source of beaver pelts (which they could gain, with relative ease, through trade with native peoples). Consequently, Richards notes, "the North American beaver became the most valuable furbearer of the New World and prey to one of the longest sustained hunts for a single species in world history."[15]

The violent and exploitative origins of these foreign wools may not have been immediately apparent to workers, however, or especially apprentices. As Richards's earlier summary indicates, novices like Tryon would have first learned easier, more menial tasks, such as trimming, while the art of distinguishing between different types and grades of wool would be mastered later (and even then, these wools were bought wholesale, already shorn from the pelts). That said, Tryon could not have remained unaware for long, and the more proficient he grew as a hatter, the more he would have had to consider the nature of the materials he worked with. Having completed his apprenticeship, in 1663 Tryon traveled to Barbados, where he remained for almost five years "making Beavers to Success," as he characterfully put it.[16] Such a venture was fraught with risks, but Tryon's calculation paid off. Nuala Zehedieh calculates, "The number of hats exported from London to the plantations increased almost sixfold from about 7,400 in 1663 to 41,500 in 1686," with nearly half of these going to the West Indies.[17] By taking his skills to Barbados on the crest of this wave, Tryon was ideally positioned to benefit. As a result, when Tryon returned to London in the late 1660s, he had stored up enough capital to open his own shop—where, he writes, "I stuck as close to my working Trade, as ever before."[18]

This account of Tryon's rise from an obscure shepherd boy to a successful London business owner brings into better focus the predicament he faced—particularly in light of the ascetic, pacifist transformation he had undergone in the fifth year of his apprenticeship. While Tryon's *Memoirs* (1705) indicate that he was a stalwart believer in the virtues of "Industry," he was also convinced of the importance of living an "Innocent Life" based on simplicity and peacefulness, rather than (all-too-often violent) material greed.[19] The "Voice of Wisdom" inspired Tryon not only to forgo "Meat and Fish" but also to wear only "mean and thin" clothing (given a concern for "what Garments are most useful and most beneficial to Nature").[20] The contradiction that his trade of "making Beavers" thus would have posed is clear, and it is hard to imagine that Tryon was unaware of this—even if the economic benefits persuaded him against abandoning the trade. In 1684, condemning the hunting practices of Quaker settlers in the New World, Tryon wrote:

> They say, and do not. They pray God would incline their hearts not to commit any violence, and yet the profession, the very trade of killing, is one of the most honourable callings amongst them in their esteem. They with their lips desire the Lord would forgive them their oppressions and violences, and in their hearts resolve upon, and by their practices continue, the same outrages.[21]

Calling out this hypocrisy might seem doubly hypocritical, but it suggests that Tryon was already wrestling with such issues himself and hence that John Field's scathing criticism of him the following year "could not have . . . completely surprised" him, as Plank suggests.[22] It was only later that Tryon was able to give up hat-making, and later still that he disowned it explicitly: although hatters were "Second *Beautifyers*" who had little to do with killing animals, he reasoned, theirs was nevertheless a "Trade or Employment concern'd about the Dead *Bodies* of the Creatures"; in an ideal world, he wrote, there would be no "Dressers of the Skins of the inferior Creatures, Shoemakers, . . . Hat-makers, nor no bloody Butchers."[23] This concatenation was no accident of Tryon's: in his sage opinion, "Man both feeds and cloaths himself by Violence and Oppression."[24]

Viewing the matter in this light, we might venture a closer connection between Tryon's work with fur and his subsequent vegetarian philosophy. Indeed, some of the most prominent vegetarians of this period had a background working with fur. The former English Civil War soldier, Leveller, and vegan Roger Crab (1621–1680) had also been "a Felt-maker" and "a Haberdasher of hats,"[25] while one of Tryon's later followers, Benjamin Lay, was apprenticed as a glover (a "stinking trade," as Lay termed it).[26] It is impossible to tell whether Tryon's work "making Beavers" may have, consciously or otherwise, prompted his vegetarian transformation in the 1650s. What *is* patently clear, however—and as I will go on to explore—is that his experience in this industry made him a particularly perceptive critic of the atrocious consequences of fur-wearing for animals as well as humans more generally.

III. DRESSING DOWN: TRYON'S VEGETARIAN CRITIQUE OF FASHION CONSUMPTION

Tryon's work in the fashion industry, in combination with his radical spiritualism and pacifist theological beliefs, helps to explain why his arguments against the violence of fur were so extensive and so unprecedented for his time. Luxury clothing like fur was, of course, a central topic among moralists in the early modern period, usually in terms of its sinful vanity. In *The Anatomy of Abuses* (1583), the Puritan pamphleteer Philip Stubbes argued that "this sinne of excesse of Apparell remayneth as an Example of Euyll before our eyes, and as a prouocative to sinne, as Experience daily sheweth," asking, "For doth not the apparel styrre vppe the heart to pride?"[27] Although Stubbes rejected fashionable fur-wearing (as well as beaver hats), his motivation was purely anthropocentric: in fact, while he disliked ostentation, he supported the wearing of (more simple) animal skins as a means of "mark[ing] on the human self-abasement [as] the closest that fallen man can come to holiness," to quote Erica Fudge.[28] Although William Prynne (1600–1669), by contrast, argued that animal skins might in fact bestialize wearers, until the end of the seventeenth century, it nevertheless remained the case that moralists were concerned only with the negative consequences of fur-wearing for humans, while any consideration of animals was secondary (see, for example, Linda Johnson's essay in this collection).[29] Tryon offers a more biocentric rejection of fur-wearing, in which the inherent bloodiness of fur as a commodity was front and center. Tryon wrote extensively on the subject, and so for the purposes of this essay, I separate his objections to fur into three core areas, focusing in turn upon his ideas about fur's violent effect on wearers, on producers, and above all, on animals.

The most characteristic way in which Tryon criticized fur was on the basis of its detrimental health effects. Central to Tryon's philosophy is his theory that the violent energies contained in slaughtered animals could be communicated to the human body—a spiritualist understanding that, as critics suggest, was likely inspired by the mystical theories of the Lutheran theologian Jakob Boehme (1575–1624).[30] As Tryon argued in his first work, *Healths Grand Preservative* (1682), by eating meat, humans defiled their bodies with "all kind of Beastial Passions, as Anger, Revenge, Covetuousness, Love and Hate, which dispositions and Passions of the Flesh, but especially the Blood, doth retain after such Animals are Killed."[31] Because by a "sympathetical operation" eating meat awakened a "wrathful savage Nature" in people, it also threatened humankind's bodily, psychological, and social harmony.[32] Food was centrally important to Tryon; however, it was far from the only form of consumption with which he was concerned. Indeed, based on his spiritualist theories, he argued that fur-wearing led to the "Uniting of the Bestial Nature with the humane," particularly because "the revengeful Spirits" contained in the blood of a murdered animal "often spread . . . through the whole Body [of the wearer]."[33] For this reason, in contrast to early modern ideas of fur as a protective barrier against pollutants and disease, Tryon claimed that "Intemperately Superfluous" luxuries like fur in fact overheated the body and sped the onset of disease, as well as disturbing the wearer psychologically, given the violent energies they contained.[34] He continued, "Whether it be *Meats, Drinks, Employments,* or *Communications,* that very thing, be it what it will, shall powerfully impose the true property of its Spirit on the Man, by way of *Simile.*"[35]

While Tryon's concerns about the trans-naturing power of fur are in some ways comparable to those of earlier religious thinkers such as Prynne, his critique is distinguished by its focus on the brutal violence of which fur was inevitably a product. Looking beyond the more personal, bodily effects of fur-wearing, in his early writing Tryon also demonstrated how fur was intimately connected with more societal and economic forms of violence, particularly given its role as a fashionable marker of status. Indeed, in one of Tryon's most famous vignettes on carnivorous culture, flesh-eating and fur-wearing are depicted as working hand in glove, involving the exploitation of both men and animals. He writes:

> It was a shame in former Ages for a Man to be seen to buy Flesh, or to have carried it openly in the Streets of Cities, but now the best Citizens count it the contrary, and make nothing to go openly to the Flesh-Markets in their Plush Coats, and load a Porter two or three times a Week, with the Spoils of their Slaughtered Fellow-Creatures.[36]

Tryon selects this scene of the "Sabbath" to stress the extent of the inversion of any self-consciousness or humility surrounding humankind's reliance upon animals for food and clothing and of the transformation of animal products into a matter of vanity and show in a highly class-conscious society.

While principally focused on the exploitation of animals, this passage goes on to consider the ancillary labors demanded of servants in order to satisfy the daily "Feasting" of "the best Citizens"—the butchering, portering, and "dressing" of meat. It also, importantly, draws attention to another form of "dressing"—namely, the "Plush Coats," "Finest Cloaths," and "newest Fashions" the elite wore. As Tryon well knew, the taste for fine clothing engaged a different range of productive processes that were no less destructive for workers or animals. In distinction from meat-eating, however, the exponential increase in luxury consumption in the seventeenth century produced a new, more global, and more dangerous context for work. Tryon warned in the *Way to Health*:

> None of the little perishing Goods of this World are to be obtained without trouble and difficulty; do not *Youths* serve seven years, enduring hard Labour and many other Inconveniencies for a Trade, whereby to get an outward Livelihood? Do not *Men* Travel by *Sea* and *Land* through a thousand Miseries, even to the hazarding of their Lives and Liberties for Meat, Drink and a little Rayment?[37]

As had been the fate of Tryon himself, the necessity of gaining an "outward Livelihood" compelled many poor young Englishmen to enter laborious seven-year apprenticeships and even to risk their lives plying their trade overseas. The superficial, materialist "Goods" they produced purely to meet their own basic needs—and the dangers they undoubtedly faced in traveling the world to do so—made manifest the increasing *human* cost of luxury. Although Tryon was more fortunate than most, his work "making Beavers to Success" did not leave him with any grand illusions. "All those needless Dainties," he wrote, were "the price of Blood, for the most part procured by great hazard, trouble, and labour."[38]

Based on his insights as a worker in the fashion industry, Tryon offered a radically different view of the ethical consequences of fur-wearing for human society. Specifically, and in distinction to other moralists at the time, Tryon connected these destructive consequences to the original violence by which fur was procured and thus placed a concern for animals at the forefront of his critique. This connection is most powerfully demonstrated in Tryon's 1684 pamphlet *The Country-Man's Companion*, which was directed at Quaker colonists in North America. As Geoffrey Plank argues, Tryon was responding to a letter that the Quaker leader William Penn had published the year prior, in which he had "detailed the progress of Pennsylvania, and in a list of the many advantages the colonists enjoyed . . . mentioned good hunting and the tasty variety of local mammals and birds."[39] Rejecting Penn's mercantilist advertisement of the various animals available for food and/or profit, Tryon argued that widespread hunting of animals was corrupting the Quakers' dream of leading peaceful, innocent lives in the New World. In the final chapter of this work ("The Complaints of the *Birds* and Fowls of Heaven to their Creator, for the Oppressions and Violences most Nations on the Earth do offer unto them, particularly the People called *Christians,* lately settled in several Provinces in *America*"), Tryon adopted the perspective of a fowl in order to persuade Quaker settlers not only of the "unparallell'd Barbarity" of killing innocent animals as "an Occupation and a Trade," but also of its catastrophic wider effects.[40] Describing the shift away from Native Americans' hunter-gatherer society to a commercialized one (under European influence), the bird states:

> Whereas before the *Christians* Arrival they only were able to kill some few of us, and that too, as it were, for Necessity, for Food, and Skins to cover them in the Winter; but [now] they will sell the choicest of their *Skins & Furs* to procure a little *Rum* or *Brandy,* or a *Gun, Powder, Shot,* and the like, which only tend to their own Destruction, as well as ours; for as with the one they take away our *sweet Lives,* so with the other they ruin their own *Healths,* contract various Diseases never before heard of amongst them; and besides, put themselves to a World of needless Slavery and Toil to procure . . . these Mischiefs.[41]

Although this "complaint" chapter sought to further persuade Quaker settlers against the ownership of weapons and hunting of animals (these arguments also appear in the prior chapter), it also focused on the North American fur trade as a phenomenon of far grander scale and consequence. As Tryon perceived, well before modern historians began to account for it, Native Americans' exchange of furs for various European foods and manufactures would speed their doom—obliterating the balance of their former ways of life and the ecosystems they relied upon and bringing tribes into ever greater conflict, while colonists exploited such disturbance to gain further footholds within the tribes' territories.[42]

Although this passage exposed the debauching effects of luxury consumption on indigenous peoples, it firmly lay the blame at the door of Christians and, more broadly, the European commodification of animals. Instead of exemplifying models of Christian virtue, English colonists had merely exported violence into the New World, it would seem, in service of the Old. In asking, "Wherefore dost thou thus degrade thy self to become a *Setter*, a *Trappan*, a *Snare*, a *Plague* and a *Torment* to all the rest of the Innocent Inhabitants of the four Worlds, wherein yet thou plaguest thy self more than any of them?" the bird draws a causal connection between colonialism and carnivorism, indicating that it was humans' intemperate desires that were the principal root of such evils on both sides of the Atlantic.[43] Nowhere is this more manifest than in Tryon's antislavery pamphlet from the same year. In the final dialogue between an enslaved African speaker and his enslaver, Tryon has the African reject his enslaver's view that Africans' relative nudity was a sign of their inferiority, making them "the very next Door to *Beasts*." The enslaved African replies:

> As for our poor Coverings, or going Naked, as long as Man remained in the innocent State, he wanted no Garments; and you are forced to *Rob* several sorts of Creatures to cover your *Shame*. . . . But how depraved and dishonourable does it look, for that *noble Creature* [Man], not only to be glad to borrow

> of his inferior Creatures to hide his Shame, but also to grow *Proud* of those Ornaments?[44]

Turning the accusation of beastliness back upon the accuser, the enslaved man's allusion to the fashionable wearing of animal skins among Christians worked to undermine the very basis of the superiority that their "civilized" clothing technologies were meant to signify.[45] In this exchange, Tryon draws upon the Christian view of luxury dress as, in Susan Vincent's words, "a two-fold immorality," being "not only evidence of pride—the chief of all vices—but . . . pride in our morally flawed state."[46] Developing this idea further, Tryon stresses the more immediate and underlying evil of fashionable fur-wearing: its biological cost. This expanding European custom was particularly "depraved and dishonourable" because animals were killed and stripped of their skins for reasons far from necessity, merely for the sake of social one-upmanship. As the wise African made clear, in addition to leading men to "study to out-try and exceed each other," such extravagance "is attended with another sore Evil, for that it *cannot be maintained* but chiefly by *great Oppression* of Men and Beasts" elsewhere.[47]

IV. CONCLUSION: THE FIRST ANTI-FUR ACTIVIST

I think we can see, therefore, that fur was in fact a central consideration in Tryon's vegetarian philosophy, rather than an oversight. The works he produced in 1684, at the very least, suggest the extent to which Tryon was already thinking about these problems, even as he was soon after attacked by John Field for his apparent hypocrisy. It is important to note that Tryon not only argued against the wearing of fur and commanded his followers "not [to] use the skins of any living creature for shoes, gloves, saddles or any other thing whatsoever," but also advocated practical, nonviolent clothing alternatives.[48] This included simple "White Linnen and Woollen" garments instead of animal skins, "Wooden Shooes instead of Leather," wood fires instead of "Candles made of the Fat of the Beasts," and also—not surprisingly, perhaps—"Straw-Hats . . . instead of Beavors and Castors."[49] In fact, by the end of his life, Tryon was articulating a holistic, ethical, and forward-looking clothing aesthetic, maintaining that "the *Original Beauties* of the *Human Nature*" will only ever "appear internally and externally in their own comely Native Dress"—that is, when humankind forgoes violent and artful extravagance of every kind and adheres to the beatific notion "to *do unto others as we would that others should do unto us*; and . . . unto the whole sensible Creation as much as in us lies, in all our Conversation and Corporeal Actions of Life."[50] It is this, and not fur or other cruel fashions,

Tryon argues, that constitutes "the compleating of all our Furniture, and the most beautiful Dress . . . Human Nature can be Cloathed with: No other Array is so Glorious."[51]

While Tryon was thus the first thinker to consider fur from an animal rights position, he was also the first moralist to consider the ethics of clothing as a *global* commodity and to critique its effects upon *producers* as much as consumers. This focus on the extensive chain of production not only was timely but also made his recommendations (which empowered the consumer to make ethical decisions) highly germane, and this may explain the far-reaching influence of Tryon's writing against fur. Tryon's contemporaries, such as Aphra Behn and Benjamin Lay, are known to have adopted his ethical clothing policies, and his influence persisted well into the eighteenth century.[52] In the 1760s one of his readers, James Williamson, tersely wrote that "Men are Justly punished for Animal murders[.] [F]or example[,] the late War in America arose about fishing and the fur Trade of Deer & Beaver skins[,] in place of which men sold one another scalps."[53] Although he took a far more sarcastic tone than the ever-serious Tryon adopted, Williamson nevertheless developed on Tryon's critique of the complex links between animal and human exploitation. Therefore, while Tryon's employment in the fashion industry was a site of discomfort, it spurred his vegetarian philosophy far beyond the abstract treatments of previous theologians, prompting him to comment on the human consumption of animals as a problem of truly global proportions and as a result to invent new, practical ways of responding to it. Just as some of the most destructive forces were unleashed upon the modern world, Tryon rose against this trend, and his expansive oeuvre remains as timely as ever.

NOTES

1. Thomas Tryon, *Some Memoirs of the Life of Mr. Tho. Tryon* (London: T. Sowle, 1705), 54–55. Covering the first forty-eight years of his life, Tryon's unfinished biography was published after his death by his friends and followers. The biography occupies pages 1–56, including eighteen additional pages, numbered 1–18, inserted between pages 34 and 35, detailing Tryon's philosophy. When referencing these pages on his philosophy, I will give the page number (1–18) followed by "(second pagination)."

2. For overviews of Tryon's arguments and his theological and philosophical influences, see Rod Preece, *Sins of the Flesh: A History of Ethical Vegetarian Thought* (Vancouver: University of British Columbia Press, 2008), 172–73; Tristram Stuart, *The Bloodless Revolution: Radical Vegetarians and the Discovery of India* (London: HarperPress, 2006), 60–77; Alan Rudrum, "Ethical Vegetarianism in Seventeenth Century Britain: Its Roots in Sixteenth Century Theological Debate," *The Seventeenth*

Century 18, no. 1 (2003): 80–82; Anita Guerrini, "A Diet for a Sensitive Soul: Vegetarianism in Eighteenth-Century Britain," *Eighteenth-Century Life* 23, no. 2 (1999): 34–36.

3. See Geoffrey Plank, "Thomas Tryon, Sheep and the Politics of Eden," *Cultural and Social History* 14 (2017): 3; Dana Medoro, "Benjamin Franklin's Autobiography as an Eighteenth-Century Omnivore's Dilemma," *English Studies in Canada* 36, no. 4 (2010): 95; Marcus Rediker, *The Fearless Benjamin Lay: The Quaker Dwarf Who Became the First Revolutionary Abolitionist* (Boston: Beacon Press, 2017), 110–11, 126.

4. Timothy Morton, "The Plantation of Wrath," in *Radicalism in British Literary Culture, 1650–1830*, ed. Timothy Morton and Nigel Smith (Cambridge: Cambridge University Press, 2002), 65–66, 81. For example, Tryon was quoted by the American whole-food advocate Sylvester Graham in *Lectures on the Science of Human Life* (London: Horsell, Aldine Chambers, 1849), 234, and by the influential anthologist of vegetarian thought Howard Williams in *The Ethics of Diet: A Catena of Authorities Deprecatory of the Practice of Flesh-Eating* (1883; Urbana: University of Illinois Press, 2003), 309–14.

5. Kim F. Hall, "'Extravagant Viciousness': Slavery and Gluttony in the Works of Thomas Tryon," in *Writing Race across the Atlantic World*, ed. P. Beidler and G. Taylor (Basingstoke: Palgrave Macmillan, 2005), 93–111. For a discussion of the connections between Tryon's antislavery and animal rights arguments, see Adam Bridgen, "Thomas Tryon (1634–1703): A Theology of Animal Enslavement," in *Animal Theologians*, ed. Andrew Linzey and Clair Linzey (New York: Oxford University Press, 2023).

6. Tryon, *Memoirs*, 26–27.

7. For further details about Tryon's life, see Virginia Smith, "Thomas Tryon (1634–1703)," *Oxford Dictionary of National Biography*, September 2004, accessed June 30, 2020, doi.org/10.1093/ref:odnb/27783.

8. John Field, *The Absurdity & Falseness of Thomas Trion's Doctrine Manifested* (London: Tho. Hawkins, 1685), [4], 14.

9. Rudrum, "Ethical Vegetarianism," 82; Plank, "Politics of Eden," 8.

10. Tryon, *Memoirs*, 85–86.

11. John F. Richards, *The Unending Frontier: An Environmental History of the Early Modern World* (Berkeley: University of California Press, 2003), 468.

12. Fiona Clark, *Hats* (London: Batsford, 1982), 9–10, 15.

13. Thomas Dekker, "Seven Deadly Sinnes of London" (1606), in *Non-Dramatic Works*, ed. Alexander Grosart (New York: Russell & Russell, 1963), 2:60.

14. J. F. Crean, "Hats and the Fur Trade," *Canadian Journal of Economics and Political Science* 28, no. 3 (1962): 376.

15. Richards, *Unending Frontier*, 467.

16. Tryon, *Memoirs*, 41.

17. Nuala Zehedieh, "London and the Colonial Consumer in the Late Seventeenth Century," *Economy History Review*, 2nd ser., 47, no. 2 (1994): 256.

18. Tryon, *Memoirs*, 25.

19. Tryon, *Memoirs*, 5, 35.

20. Tryon, *Memoirs*, 26–27, 2 (second pagination).

21. Thomas Tryon [Philotheos Physiologus, pseud.], *The Country-Man's Companion, or a New Method of Ordering Horses & Sheep* (London: Andrew Sowle, 1684), 159.

22. Plank, "Politics of Eden," 8.

23. Thomas Tryon, *The Knowledge of a Man's Self . . . Or, the Third Part of the Way to Long Life, Health and Happiness* (London: Tho. Bennet, 1704), 336, 368.

24. Thomas Tryon, *The Knowledge of a Man's Self . . . Or, the Second Part of the Way to Long Life, Health and Happiness* (London: Tho. Bennet, 1703), 405.

25. Ariel Hessayon, "Roger Crab (c. 1616–1680), Hermit," *Oxford Dictionary of National Biography*, September 2004, accessed June 30, 2020, doi.org/10.1093/ref:odnb/6548.

26. Rediker, *Benjamin Lay*, 21–22.

27. Philip Stubbes, *Anatomy of the Abuses in England in Shakspere's Youth, A.D. 1583*, ed. Frederick J. Furnivall, 2 vols. (London: N. Trübner, 1877), 1:30, 39. See also page 50 for Stubbes's note on beaver hats.

28. Erica Fudge, "Renaissance Animal Things," in *Gorgeous Beasts: Animal Bodies in Historical Perspective*, ed. Joan B. Landes, Paula Young Lee, and Paul Youngquist (University Park: Pennsylvania State University Press, 2012), 48.

29. Fudge, "Animal Things," 49.

30. For more on Boehme's influence, see Morton, "Plantation of Wrath," 66–68.

31. Thomas Tryon, *Healths Grand Preservative* (London, 1682), 14–15.

32. Thomas Tryon [Philotheos Physiologus, pseud.], *The Way to Health, Long Life, and Happiness* (London: Andrew Sowle, 1683), 98, 348.

33. Thomas Tryon, *A Treatise of Cleanness in Meats and Drinks* (London, 1682), 19, 16.

34. Tryon, *Healths Grand Preservative*, 7. Susan J. Vincent, *Dressing the Elite: Clothes in Early Modern England* (Oxford: Berg, 2003), 49–50.

35. Tryon, *Way to Health*, 347.

36. Tryon, *Healths Grand Preservative*, 22.

37. Tryon, *Way to Health*, 63.

38. Tryon, *Way to Health*, 470–71.

39. Plank, "Politics of Eden," 11.

40. Tryon, *Country-Man's Companion*, 144, 151.

41. Tryon, *Country-Man's Companion*, 152–53. Tryon misdiagnoses the actual cause of disease here, since the new illnesses affecting Native Americans at the time were not caused by what they ate so much as by contact with infectious colonists.

42. See, for example, Richards, *Unending Frontier*, 472–75, 502–15; Daniel K. Richter, *Facing East from Indian Country: A Native History of Early America* (Cambridge, MA: Harvard University Press, 2001), 49–51, 54.

43. Tryon, *Country-Man's Companion*, 153

44. Thomas Tryon [Philotheos Physiologus, pseud.], *Friendly Advice to the Gentlemen Planters of the East and West Indies* (London: Andrew Sowle, 1684), 166, 192, 194.

45. Gordon Sayre, *Les Sauvages Américains: Representations of Native Americans in French and English Colonial Literature* (Chapel Hill: University of North Carolina Press, 1997), 152–53.

46. Vincent, *Dressing the Elite*, 123.

47. Tryon, *Friendly Advice*, 166

48. Tryon, *Memoirs*, 85–86.

49. Thomas Tryon, *Wisdom's Dictates, or, Aphorisms & Rules, Physical, Moral, and Divine* (London: Tho. Salisbury, 1691), 84.

50. Tryon, *Knowledge . . . Second Part*, 321, 44–45.

51. Tryon, *Knowledge . . . Second Part*, 45.

52. Plank, "Politics of Eden," 3; Rediker, *Benjamin Lay*, 115, 123. For a further discussion of Tryon's influence in Britain during the eighteenth century, see Adam Bridgen, "Humphrey Primatt (1735–1777): Animal Protection and Its Revolutionary Contexts," in *Animal Theologians*, ed. Andrew Linzey and Clair Linzey (New York: Oxford University Press, 2023).

53. Quoted in David Allen, "Greeks, Indians, and the Scottish Presbyterian: Dissident Arguments for Vegetarianism in Enlightenment Scotland," *1650–1850: Ideas, Aesthetics, and Inquiries in the Early Modern Era* 6 (2001): 293. See also Stuart, *Bloodless Revolution*, 249.

REFERENCES

Allen, David. "Greeks, Indians, and the Scottish Presbyterian: Dissident Arguments for Vegetarianism in Enlightenment Scotland." *1650–1850: Ideas, Aesthetics, and Inquiries in the Early Modern Era* 6 (2001): 265–97.

Bridgen, Adam. "Humphry Primatt (1735–1777): Animal Protection and Its Revolutionary Contexts." In *Animal Theologians*, edited by Andrew Linzey and Clair Linzey. New York: Oxford University Press, 2023.

———. "Thomas Tryon (1634–1703): A Theology of Animal Enslavement." In *Animal Theologians*, edited by Andrew Linzey and Clair Linzey. New York: Oxford University Press, 2023.

Clark, Fiona. *Hats*. London: Batsford, 1982.

Crean, J. F. "Hats and the Fur Trade." *Canadian Journal of Economics and Political Science* 28, no. 3 (1962): 373–86.

Dekker, Thomas. "Seven Deadly Sinnes of London." In *Non-Dramatic Works*, edited by Alexander Grosart, vol. 2. New York: Russell & Russell, 1963.

Field, John. *The Absurdity & Falseness of Thomas Trion's Doctrine Manifested.* London: Tho. Hawkins, 1685.

Fudge, Erica. "Renaissance Animal Things." In *Gorgeous Beasts: Animal Bodies in Historical Perspective*, edited by Joan B. Landes, Paula Young Lee, and Paul Youngquist, 41–56. University Park: Pennsylvania State University Press, 2012.

Graham, Sylvester. *Lectures on the Science of Human Life*. London: Horsell, Aldine Chambers, 1849.

Guerrini, Anita. "A Diet for a Sensitive Soul: Vegetarianism in Eighteenth-Century Britain." *Eighteenth-Century Life* 23, no. 2 (1999): 34–36.
Hall, Kim F. "'Extravagant Viciousness': Slavery and Gluttony in the Works of Thomas Tryon." In *Writing Race across the Atlantic World*, edited by P. Beidler and G. Taylor, 93–111. Basingstoke, UK: Palgrave Macmillan, 2005.
Hessayon, Ariel. "Roger Crab (c. 1616–1680), Hermit." *Oxford Dictionary of National Biography*. Oxford University Press, September 2004. Accessed January 15, 2020. doi.org/10.1093/ref:odnb/6548.
Medoro, Dana. "Benjamin Franklin's Autobiography as an Eighteenth-Century Omnivore's Dilemma." *English Studies in Canada* 36, no. 4 (2010): 91–107.
Morton, Timothy. "The Plantation in Wrath." In *Radicalism in British Literary Culture, 1650–1830*, edited by Timothy Morton and Nigel Smith, 64–85. Cambridge: Cambridge University Press, 2002.
Plank, Geoffrey. "Thomas Tryon, Sheep and the Politics of Eden." *Cultural and Social History* 14 (2017): 1–17.
Preece, Rod. *Sins of the Flesh: A History of Ethical Vegetarian Thought*. Vancouver: University of British Columbia Press, 2008.
Rediker, Marcus. *The Fearless Benjamin Lay: The Quaker Dwarf Who Became the First Revolutionary Abolitionist*. Boston: Beacon Press, 2017.
Richards, John F. *The Unending Frontier: An Environmental History of the Early Modern World*. Berkeley: University of California Press, 2003.
Richter, Daniel K. *Facing East from Indian Country: A Native History of Early America*. Cambridge, MA: Harvard University Press, 2001.
Rudrum, Alan. "Ethical Vegetarianism in Seventeenth Century Britain: Its Roots in Sixteenth Century Theological Debate." *The Seventeenth Century* 18, no. 1 (2003): 80–82.
Sayre, Gordon. *Les Sauvages Américains: Representations of Native Americans in French and English Colonial Literature*. Chapel Hill: University of North Carolina Press, 1997.
Smith, Nigel. "Of Enthusiasm and Enlightenment: Food, Filth, and Slavery." In *The Country and the City Revisited*, edited by Donna Landry, Gerald McLean, and Joseph P. Ward, 106–18. Cambridge: Cambridge University Press, 1999.
Smith, Virginia. "Thomas Tryon (1634–1703)." *Oxford Dictionary of National Biography*. Oxford University Press, September 2004. Accessed January 15, 2020. doi.org/10.1093/ref:odnb/27783.
Stuart, Tristram. *The Bloodless Revolution: Radical Vegetarians and the Discovery of India*. London: HarperPress, 2006.
Stubbes, Philip. *Anatomy of the Abuses in England in Shakspere's Youth, A.D. 1583*. Edited by Frederick J. Furnivall. 2 vols. London: N. Trübner, 1877.
Tryon, Thomas [Philotheos Physiologus, pseud.]. *The Country-Man's Companion, or a New Method of Ordering Horses & Sheep*. London: Andrew Sowle, 1684.
———[Philotheos Physiologus, pseud.]. *Friendly Advice to the Gentlemen Planters of the East and West Indies*. London: Andrew Sowle, 1684.
———. *Healths Grand Preservative*. London, 1682.

———. *The Knowledge of a Man's Self . . . Or, the Second Part of the Way to Long Life, Health and Happiness*. London: Tho. Bennet, 1703.

———. *The Knowledge of a Man's Self . . . Or, the Third Part of the Way to Long Life, Health and Happiness.* London: Tho. Bennet, 1704.

———. *Some Memoirs of the Life of Mr. Tho. Tryon*. London: T. Sowle, 1705.

———. *A Treatise of Cleanness in Meats and Drinks*. London, 1682.

———[Philotheos Physiologus, pseud.]. *The Way to Health, Long Life, and Happiness*. London: Andrew Sowle, 1683.

———. *Wisdom's Dictates, or, Aphorisms & Rules, Physical, Moral, and Divine*. London: Tho. Salisbury, 1691.

Vincent, Susan J. *Dressing the Elite: Clothes in Early Modern England*. Oxford: Berg, 2003.

Williams, Howard. *The Ethics of Diet: A Catena of Authorities Deprecatory of the Practice of Flesh-Eating*. 1883. Urbana: University of Illinois Press, 2003.

Zehedieh, Nuala. "London and the Colonial Consumer in the Late Seventeenth Century." *Economy History Review*, 2nd ser., 47, no. 2 (1994): 239–61.

Chapter 3

The New England Fur Trade

The Ethics of Puritan Dress in a Portrait of Lieutenant Governor William Stoughton

Linda M. Johnson

In 1683, an anonymous writer known as the Compassionate Conformist pertinently addressed the court, nobility, and gentry of the city of London in a treatise, which stated that Englishmen were committing the sin of pride in the wearing of strange apparel beyond the bounds of "Prudence, Moderation, and Hability." Largely referring to the use of animal products in clothing, the writer stated:

> We rob and spoil all Creatures almost of the world to cover our back and to adorn our bodies withal; from some we take their wool, from many their skins, from diverse their Furrs, from sundry their very Excrements, as the silk which is nothing else but the very Excrement of the worm; not content with this, we come to Fishes and do beg from them their Pearles to hang about us, . . . And having borrowed all this of other Creatures, we jett up and down, provoking men to look upon us, as if . . . all that beauty came from us.[1]

While late-seventeenth-century English exhortations such as those made in this anonymous tract were used as a means to shame the indulgent for their neglect of true religion, the Compassionate Conformist here delivers a rather curious empathetic appeal toward animals. He suggests that domesticated and free-roaming animals were being exploited for mere prideful arrogance that exceeded any scriptural sanction permitting their bodies to be used for necessary clothing. Moreover, he brings into play the plundering of the earth's resources in stating that the "wearing of diverse Furrs" was only to meet the demands of the proud peacocks in fashion.

Since the earliest times, humans have used fur and leather to clothe and protect their bodies from climate and harm.[2] While animal skin was sanctioned in Genesis 3:21, it was not necessarily deemed acceptable as decorative material for the popular fashion trends that had become central to the way of life in modern England and her colonies.[3] In an earlier treatise written in 1583, titled *The Anatomie of Abuses*, Englishman Philip Stubbes expressed astonishment at the lengths taken to procure exotic materials for fashion purposes. In a critique of the North American fur trade, Stubbes attests to the vanity of wearing fur:

> And as the fashions bee rare and strange, so is the stuff whereof there hattes be made divers also: for some are of silke, some of Velvet, some of Taffatie, some of Garcenet, some of Wooll, & whiche is more curious some of a certaine kind of fine haire: These they call Bever hates . . . fetched from beyond the Seas, from whence a greate sorte of other vanities doe come besides.[4]

This curious kind of "haire" Stubbes refers to, from across the seas, was the main catalyst that set the stage for the hunting of free-roaming animals in North America. With the colonization of New France and New England between the seventeenth and eighteenth centuries, western European furriers, hatters, and leather manufacturers were assured an almost unlimited supply of pelts. In the early 1600s, the growing demand for luxury and fashion furs by the nobility and the new mercantile classes led to the opening of new trade routes and the establishment of fur-trade monopolies. Contrary to the myth of religious zealots setting sail for the New World, historian Francis Moloney states that it was the fur traders who selected locations in the colonies, arranged for purchase of lands from the Indians, and took the lead in all practical affairs of the new towns.[5] Moloney affirms that it was a well-managed fur trade, largely involving the hunting of beavers, that saved Plymouth colony from extinction and gave the settlers a chance to repay heavy debts to the London merchants for the advances that funded their passage.[6]

To explore the issue of fashion consumption and the slaughtering of fur-bearing animals in North America, I will examine the portrait of Massachusetts Bay lieutenant governor William Stoughton in the context of Puritan doctrine, as a window into the anthropocentric response toward fur-bearing animals in colonial New England.[7]

A close reading of his portrait in light of the economic issues surrounding the New England fur trade provides new evidence, albeit indirect, within the methodology of art historical analysis.[8] The emblematic conventions of his portrait can be read as the embodiment of his involvement in the polemics of

Figure 3.1. Unidentified Artist, William Stoughton (1631–1707), Harvard University Portrait Collection, Gift of John Cooper to Harvard College, 1810, Photo © President and Fellows of Harvard College, H37.

Massachusetts Bay's survival. A strong case can be deduced that Stoughton's legalistic propensity was to advocate for the short-term material gain of the fur trade rather than the long-term notion of eternal life inherent to a Calvinist eschatological faith. Art historian Jules D. Prown affirms that paintings are artistic signs that illuminate beliefs embodied within the objects themselves. He states, "Human objects reflect consciously and unconsciously the beliefs of the individuals who commissioned, purchased, or used them."[9]

While many of Stoughton's political failures to maintain the doctrines of Puritan orthodoxy have been mined by scholars, such as his inept handling of the Massachusetts Charter, the Salem witchcraft trials, and his inability to prolong and secure the New England Way, Stoughton's legalistic tendency gave way to a materialistic rather than a spiritual worldview that was at odds with notions of Puritan frugality and Christian stewardship.[10] Calvinist tenets that recognized unnecessary cruelty to animals as morally wrong were part of a wider conversation between natural philosophers during the early modern period. Keith Thomas states, "By the end of the seventeenth century the most common view held by intellectuals was that beasts had a kind of reason, but an inferior one."[11] New Englanders such as Stoughton were not removed from the philosophical arguments on animal stewardship and were part of a frequent transatlantic discourse with their nonconformist brothers across the pond on matters of scriptural exegesis, politics, and economics, as well as culture.[12] In fact, Stoughton's background connects him with Latitudinarian thinkers such as those in the Hartlib circle and the new sciences of Robert Boyle, as well as a long line of nonconformists whose eschatology was millennialist in nature, placing animals beside humankind in God's evolutionary plan.[13]

To be sure, the early modern world was anthropocentric. However, John Foster states that despite John Calvin's emphasis on the primacy of humanity in the Noahic covenant, he argued for a real covenantal benefit being extended to the creatures of the earth.[14] In Calvin's *Commentaries on Genesis*, Foster states, Calvin relates a duty to "brute animals," stating, "[God] declares that he will be propitious also to brute animals, so that the effect of the covenant towards them, might be the preservation of their lives."[15] Moreover, Calvin suggests that this "duty" has eternal conditions and repercussions in which humankind will be accountable and therefore judged for lack of adherence to this injunction:

> Scripture declares that [earthly blessings] have all been given us by the kindness of God, and appointed for our use under the condition of being regarded as trusts, of which we must one day give account. We must, therefore, administer them as if we constantly heard the words sounding in our ears, Give an account of your stewardship.[16]

Yet despite all the materialist and scientific interpretations by religious leaders and philosophers revering nonhuman life, somehow the exclusion of fur-bearing animals from consideration (other than those used for fox or hare coursing) constituted a signifying absence in Puritan discourse. Their lives, if discussed at all, were referenced only in relation to the brutalizing effects hunting had on men's character, and their worth was considered only in terms of quick monetary return in a precarious market of European competition. When the beaver, otter, marten, and mink (to name only a very few) were discussed, it was only in terms of their products. Unlike animals used for food and transport, who received at least a cursory nod of concern in exchange for their labor and meat, the fur-bearing animals remained casually discarded in religious language and stewardship as the goods of human greed and concupiscence.[17]

In this essay, I claim that Stoughton's portrait is a visual declaration of this indifference and represents his indecisive moral compass regarding the massive slaughtering of fur-bearing animals and that this may be one way of examining the fall of New England Puritanism, as it became a culture that abandoned its religious covenant to achieve economic gain, colonial power, and land control.

THE PORTRAIT OF LIEUTENANT GOVERNOR WILLIAM STOUGHTON, C. 1701

A cursory look at Stoughton's dress depicts many embellishments on his cloak, known as a tabard, an old-fashioned garment typically lined with fur that became associated with antiquity and various forms of male learned professions.[18] The viewer cannot discern his occupation, but his sartorial choices in portraiture boast of success. Stoughton was close to seventy years of age at this portrait sitting, and his choice of costume as an elder aligns with seventeenth-century allegories depicting the tabard's association with old age and winter.[19] Tabards carried connotations of prestige, so much so that in 1531, Charles V established a sumptuary law particular to the tabard, prohibiting all but the members of high nobility from wearing tabards that were embellished with gold cloth or fur.[20] In the early Tudor period, fur had been the chief symbol of wealth, and as such it remained strictly governed by sumptuary legislation.[21] In Western Europe, furs such as ermine, mink, sable, and arctic fox were reserved for royalty, nobility, high-ranking clergy, and the bourgeoisie. Most if not all tabards were lined with high-quality furs that were imported from Scandinavia and Russia.[22]

An unknown artist completed Stoughton's image, and its style is provincial in nature. Most colonial artists were not academically trained, and

Stoughton's portrait is considered "liney" in the Elizabethan tradition.[23] Yet having traveled to England on a few occasions for political reasons, Stoughton was surely aware of cosmopolitan painterly renderings that boasted modeling, light, and shadow. His stylistic choice demonstrates his choice of an unsophisticated persona. As Wendy Katz states, strong shadows were a departure from a gentlemanly style, which left the image of the sitter suspect, promoting a "cunning style of illusionism."[24] Thus, as Abbott Lowell Cummings states, New England portraiture is not necessarily primitive or indicative of a limited ability by the artist but represents a stylistic option of truthfulness preferred by a significant number of clients.[25]

Stoughton wears the tabard casually over his shoulders, enveloping what is most likely a three-piece suit consisting of a jacket, a waistcoat, and matching breeches.[26] The volume and weightiness of the fabric consume the canvas and conceal Stoughton's corporeal form. The tabard's dark green color reflects popular ideas of fashion at the time; Henry Peacham's *Compleat Gentleman* stressed that dark clothing reflected modesty and demonstrated a sober and trustworthy character.[27] The dark brown color painted underneath Stoughton's tabard most likely connotes a lining of fur from a beech marten, marten (a tree weasel), polecat (a weasel with dark brown fur), or American beaver. Although these fur-bearing animals were native to Massachusetts Bay, the origins of Stoughton's tabard remain uncertain.[28]

Two rather large, elaborate gold-embroidered buttons are fastened through the matching gilded buttonholes clasping Stoughton's coat. At least three more are hidden underneath his long neck cloth known as a cravat, worn over the neckband of his shirt. As Doriece Colle states, a long decorative neck cloth displayed fine linen and expensive lace. Stoughton's cravat falls to mid-abdomen, denoting the expense of additional fabric.[29] The brown and gold epaulet-shaped collar of his verdant robe is rendered with tight curled loops of golden-brown paint, vibrantly depicting the luster and silkiness of expensive fur. Gold tie cords hang in a serpentine arrangement along Stoughton's slightly distended neck. His long, under-curled white wavy hair covers his ears and falls to his shoulders. A snug fur cap accentuates a high forehead.[30] According to Marie De Winkel, dress is always a personal statement, invaluable for discerning the messages the sitter is attempting to portray.[31] Stoughton's constructed persona is associated with notions of gravitas and dignity, as well as studiousness, and depicts a fitting "uniform" for the magisterial profession. Colonial itinerant artists, much like their Northern Renaissance predecessors, made deliberate use of clothing to emphasize the character or social status of the sitters and to heighten the drama in portraiture. Stoughton's dress, while somber and academic, boasts a lavish volume of luxury fabrics, such as brocade, linen, silk, and fur, woven with raised patterns and sewn with gold or silver threads, which was somewhat atypical in Puritan New England, where modesty and simplicity demonstrated one's saintly status.[32]

In London, Puritan Divines perceived that popular fashion trends were the cause of immorality and pride.[33] Moreover, the English civil authorities defined what constituted proud apparel and established elaborate sumptuary legislation.[34] Garments that displayed a prideful heart were those made of expensive fabrics such as velvet or silk and embellished with excessive ornamentation. Conversely, modest clothing expressed a humble heart.[35] New England was no stranger to excesses in apparel. Massachusetts Bay authorities established sumptuary laws in 1634, within four years after arrival in New England.[36] Yet the breach of sumptuary laws indicates the extent to which Massachusetts Bay failed to make sartorial morality its concern, more than likely due to a shifting mixture of dogma and economics. Moreover, with luxurious goods, there was a tension that produced an embarrassment of riches in Puritan sensibility, at odds with the notion that wealth was perceived as a blessing from God.

Increase Mather, a close friend of Stoughton, was particularly concerned with pride in clothing and adhered to the sumptuary laws in prohibited the lower classes from dressing like their betters. Yet he agreed that elaborate dress should express one's professional role, stating, "Those in high office should dress according to their station."[37] To be sure, Stoughton led the colonial settlement toward the Promised Land of Massachusetts Bay dressed in material finery. It is telling, however, that before entering the political realm, Stoughton had begun a career in the ministry.[38] Dissatisfied with this role, he would continue to refuse to serve the church in his own town every year between 1662 and 1670. It appears that despite his father's generous yet presumptive bequest to him of "halfe" of his library "for his incourag [encouragement] to apply himself to studies, especially to the Holy Scriptures; unto which they are most helpful," he time after time declined requests to lead in various church positions at Dorchester.[39] He recognized his lack of passion after twelve years of preaching in various English dissenting congregations, stating, "I had some objections within myself against the motion."[40] In 1671, John Hull affirmed Stoughton's refusal, stating that his passion was focused elsewhere: "Mr. William Stoughton, an able preacher and very pious, but not yet persuadable to take any office charge in any church, was chosen into the magistracy, and accepted the same."[41] Having had the title of "Moses of New England" bestowed upon him by Increase Mather's son, Cotton, Stoughton instead became a powerful figure, serving in various governmental roles in Massachusetts Bay, such as commissioner and deputy of courts, selectman of Dorchester, chief magistrate in the Salem witch trials, and acting governor from 1692 until his death in 1701.[42] Nevertheless, Stoughton's blatant portrayal of wealth in an embellished fur-lined tabard cloak and cap may be viewed as a deviation from Puritan humility, where outward "signs" were understood to be reflective of inward grace.[43] According to Cummings, Puritans were less concerned with the character of the face than with the emblematic conventions of objects and the costume a person chose.[44] Pride expressed in clothing was seen as the worst offense in Puritan society. Puritan apologists like Philip Stubbes stated that pride in dress is the greatest sin of all, "more than pride of the harte or pride of the mouthe."[45]

According to religious historian Martha Finch, Puritans like Stoughton espoused the theology of the body: the correspondence between soul and body and the notion that the presence of grace could be verified by the "outward evidences" of one's appearance and behavior.[46] Therefore, Puritan belief cohered nicely with common ideas about self-fashioning. This conviction, of course, included not only dress but also manners, gender, level of education, economic status, social rank, and occupation. Therefore, visible saints strove to embody plain honesty, and nonconformists of all stripes shunned elaborately ornamented dress and excessive hairstyles and feared disguises. Stoughton's image may be a duplicity of sorts, as if Massachusetts Bay had been founded on grace alone rather than the fur trade itself. A more pervasive hypocrisy underlay the patents, stocks, and profits established from the sale of beaver pelts for clothing by the Massachusetts courts, because the same governing body that promoted the fur trade prohibited the wearing of beaver hats in the colonies in sumptuary laws written in 1641.[47]

THE FUR TRADE

From 1621 to the end of the century, legislative leaders such as Stoughton as well as Puritan and Separatist ministers were involved in the business of the fur trade, since Massachusetts Bay was surrounded by merchants, traders, Indians, fur-trading posts, and trucking houses, which extended from Plymouth to the Connecticut River Valley and upward toward Maine and the Merrimack River.[48] The fashion in Europe of wearing beaver hats caused a larger demand for beavers' fur, and European traders sure of a ready market were quick to urge Indians to trade beaver skins for blankets, cloth, ribbon, kettles, axes, knives, guns, and liquor.[49] Beaver furs were becoming scarce and expensive because the free-ranging beavers in Britain had been hunted to extinction, and the sources in Northern Europe had become exhausted. Massachusetts Bay governors such as John Winthrop and William Stoughton selected special traders and supported companies of merchant adventurers to extend the fur trade beyond the bounds of Massachusetts and into territory claimed by the Dutch and the French.[50] By the time Charles II gave a charter to the Hudson's Bay Company, most of the beaver furs were coming from the colonists in New England, and the supply was not enough to meet the demand.[51]

Early in Plymouth colony's existence, Separatists like William Bradford and Roger Williams participated in the fur trade as a luxury export from New England not only to pay off their investors, but also to buy necessary goods from Europe and acquire modest fortunes.[52] Beaver fur was easy to transport and small in bulk, and its high value could bear the heavy overhead cost of long voyages, always finding a ready market. From 1631 to 1636, twelve thousand pounds of beaver skins and one thousand pounds of otter skins were sent to England. Governor Bradford estimated that "the sale of beaver for these years was 10,000 Pounds . . . A great sume of money.[53]"

Yet as early as 1627, Bradford complained about the consequences of overhunting, suggesting that the killing of animals beyond the debt to England was abusive. While Bradford was involved in the fur trade, he criticized its exploitative intentions for reasons not that dissimilar from the reasons Philip Stubbes expressed in his passionate discourse on abuse of animals.[54] Stating that fishermen had begun to leave fishing for the sake of quicker profits from the fur trade, Bradford described these men as "greedy and [full of] covetousness."[55] Moreover, the overhunting of other fur-bearing animals, such as martens, otters, mink, and black foxes, meant that huntsmen were often not paid by investors. The difficulty in conducting business long-distance is summed up in a lament from Bradford: "It is a shame to us to have 1800 lbs. of beaver lying by us and more owing than the bills come to."[56]

Moloney affirms that most investors treated the colonists like loan sharks: the more beaver fur and other commodities the colonists sent to England, the more the debt grew. Many of the settlers left the trade, but only after the initial debt was paid off in 1648, and many had to sell houses and large parcels of land to make up the balance.[57] While Rhode Island founder Roger Williams left the trade in 1641, having called it a "murderous affair," he lamented the monetary losses. He recognized that the trade yielded "the most profitable employment in these parts of America, and by which many persons of mean degree advanced to considerable estates."[58] While his protests toward the beaver trade were largely regarding the sale of artillery to Indians for beaver pelts, he protested against the slaughtering of the animals to the elders of Massachusetts Bay, stating, "For myself . . . I have refused the gain of thousands by such a murderous trade."[59] Williams's discouragement regarding human greed and waste is telling. He described the American wilderness "as a clear resemblance of the world, where greedy and furious men persecute and devour the harmless and the innocent as wild beasts devour the hinds and roes."[60]

It appears that below the economic gain of the fur trade, there were many traces of guilt, unease, and defensiveness about the slaughter of fur-bearing animals and the immoral practice of trading. Many Puritan leaders, obligated by a certain moral courage, did sustain a significant loss of income by prohibiting the trade, if only based on the ethics of exchanging fur for guns and liquor. Stoughton's predecessor, John Winthrop, wrote that "the law prohibiting of the trade with the Indians in guns and powder recently passed by the Commissioner of the united colonies had drawn the greater part of the beaver trade to the Dutch and the French by whom the Indians were constantly furnished with those things. So as our means of returns for English commodities were grown very short."[61]

Yet controversies ensued as the "profitable employment" of killing beavers described by Williams was scripturally sanctioned by New England Divine Cotton Mather, who in his unpublished work *Biblia Americana*, explained that Genesis 1:28 allowed humankind the controlling and "free use" of "unruly" animals. The sanctioning of control of free roaming animals such as the fur-bearing beaver, through scriptural exegesis, might have been one factor that promoted the indifferent slaughter of such animals. However, Mather did qualify his statement, noting that in "subduing" the undomesticated animal, moderation and necessity were integral. He stated, "The Almighty gave man the Privilidge of cultivating and improving the Earth into a pleasant habitation for themselves by Subduing the more Wild, and unruly Kinds of Animals, and (afterwards) granting them free use of Such of them as were proper for their Food and Nourishment."[62]

While Mather's anthropocentric view was largely accepted, the definition of the term "proper" was argued by many theologians and discounted by traders. Modern theological opinion defined Mather's notion of proper use by clarifying that humankind was fully entitled to domesticate animals and to kill them for food and clothing, but humans were not to tyrannize or cause unnecessary suffering or kill for decorative embellishment. Philip Stubbes went even further than Mather in his flagship of all moral diatribes, *The Anatomie of Abuses*, where he contended that despite the danger of free-living animals, their purpose was to glorify God. Stubbes declared:

> For although they be bloody beast to mankind and seek his destruction, yet we are not to abuse them for his sake who made them and whose creatures they are. For notwithstanding that they be evil to us and thirst after our blood, yet are they good creatures in their own nature and kind and made to set forth the glory and magnificence of the great God . . . and therefore for his sake not to be abused.[63]

Stubbes is referring specifically to undomesticated animals since the "bloody beast[s]" who "seek [our] destruction" and "thirst after our blood" are typically predatory carnivores. Puritan stewardship denoted that domesticated animals should be allowed food, rest, and painless deaths and that free-living animals could be killed only for food or defense.

In 1641, a Massachusetts law was written to protect animals. However, it did not apply to those who lived free in nature. It echoed John Calvin's call for gentle handling of "brute animals," prohibiting "tyranny or cruelty toward any brute creatures which are usually kept for the use of man."[64] The word "kept" implies the protection of only domesticated animals as property, rather than free-living animals who were, in Mather's words, "unruly" and in need of "subduing." Nevertheless, this law suggests changing attitudes toward stewardship and sentience.

Yet by 1657 the volume of trade in the area north of Massachusetts Bay was greater than two thousand pounds of beaver skins annually. During Stoughton's tenure, the Massachusetts Bay General Court continued to be heavily involved in the fur trade, choosing appointed commissioners in the New England Confederation to expand locations and hunt more beavers north of the colony's patent. This was strictly regulated, not for the sake of the beaver population but admittedly under the provision of the common good. In the *Laws and Liberties of Massachusetts* written in 1646, penalties were given if any trading outside of governmental practice occurred. One of the laws, regarding the trading of the hides and skins of beavers, moose, and otters, stated:

> Whereas some persons more seeking their own private advantage then the good of the publick doe transport raw hydes & pelts, it is ordered and by this Court enacted, That Henceforth no person shall deliver aboard any ship or other vessel, directly or indirectly any raw hyde, skin, pelt, or leather unwrought with intent to have the same transported out of this Jurisdiction upon pain to forfeit the same or the value thereof. . . . [65]

The fur trade was now a highly competitive commercial enterprise for the state authorities of Massachusetts Bay, ironically paying for the building of churches and the salaries of ministers and governors. The stronger the government of the colony, the tighter was its control over the fur trade. Stoughton surely was surrounded by Puritan invectives against extravagances in dress as well as against the business of the fur trade, even though the trade had changed considerably by the close of the century.

In 1670, while the fur trade was in full progress under the various leadership positions Stoughton enjoyed, he was bemoaning New England's vanities and greed for worldly things in his only published sermon, titled *New England's True Interest Not to Lie*. In it, he harked back to the founding of the colony, lamenting what he saw as a decline in Massachusetts society. He wrote:

> God sifted a whole nation that he might send choice grain over into this wilderness. Thy God did expect better things from thee and thy children; not worldliness and insatiable desire after perishing things; such as "whoredoms," "drunkenness," "oaths," "oppressions," "slanderings," "rudeness," "not an itching after new things and ways," "not a growing weary of government and a drawing loose in the yoke of God; not these things, but better things, O New England, hath thy God expected from thee.[66]

Stoughton's admonition refers to the lack of virtue and character in his congregation, as embodied in lewd behavior and an insatiable desire of "itching after new things," yet his portrait is redolent of self-aggrandizement and material goods.[67] His dress reflects the worldly things he coveted from the very "wildness" he wished to subdue. Stoughton's own insatiable desires may be seen as a personal failure projected onto his congregants. The behavior of the community in Puritan doctrine was deemed a reflection of its leadership.[68]

THE PORTRAIT

Through the rectangular aperture to the left of Stoughton's portrait, the viewer sees a landscape of cone-shaped hills framing a prominent red-brick building, whose foundation falls upon the horizontal line extending across the center of the composition. Stoughton's thin, bony right hand peeks out in a solicitous gesture from under the sleeve of white lace painted close to his body. This rigid arm draws the viewer's eye upward to Stoughton Hall, where a small heraldic-shaped crest inscribed in stone is an allusion to royal ancestry.[69] Nuanced tiers of black, gray, and gold foreshadow an ominous horizon, which glows dramatically above both features. Cotton Mather praised Stoughton's generosity in building Stoughton Hall, one of the buildings at Harvard College named for him. Mather stated, "[Stoughton] who was the first benefactor of this institution, has bound all true sons of Harvard to himself in bonds of everlasting gratitude."[70] Yet Harvard librarian and biographer John Sibley reported in the 1800s that Stoughton Hall's construction was shoddy at best. According to Sibley, the bricks had come from the long-unused Indian College, where the early printing presses had produced Increase Mather's books, and the building did not stand the test of time: "Being originally an unsubstantial piece of masonry, it grew weak by age and having been injured, it is said, by the earthquake of 1755, after undergoing many repairs it was finally taken down in 1780."[71] According to another account,

> Master builder Willis appears to have scampd on his work; for as early as 1714 the Corporation had to repair the roof, and in 1721, the Overseerers represented

> the desperate and Dangers Condition of Stoughton House. A survey showed the building to be "so exceedingly bow'd and broken" that the Overseers recommended it be taken down and rebuilt. Nothing was done, however; and the walls became so bulgy and wobbly that everyone expected the earthquake of Lisbon in 1755 to shake it down into a heap of bricks.[72]

A stationary object, perhaps a wide curtain, pillar, or tree in varying degrees of darkness, sharply bisects Stoughton's image contiguously to the picture plane, pushing his body forward, as if to topple it out of the painting. A cap fuses his head posteriorly to the erect vertical feature, loosely securing Stoughton within the portrait. This instability creates displacement of Stoughton's inner thought and relates to the tension between greed, blessing, and wealth.[73] His verticality in the portrait and the asymmetry of the building creates an up/down, erratic, or haphazard interchange alluding to an anxious depiction. The awkward divisional structure of the portrait gives rise to pulling and pushing movements of the competing vertical and horizontal lines of light and darkness, which meet on the surface of the painting, creating a disturbance in viewing rather than a culminating focal point for the audience's eyes to rest upon.[74] Despite Stoughton's upturned welcoming right palm, viewers are unable to enter the space.

The weighted fabric of his dress conceals a torso that may be a bony frame, judging by his pallor and skull-shaped head. The flat affect of his facial countenance and cast-iron gaze mimics the eeriness represented in the darkened clouds hovering above the man-made structure of Stoughton Hall. A spectral effect of doom indicates his image may be a posthumous portrayal, demonstrated by the long strip of cloth knotted under his chin—the proxy for his cravat, which resembles a cranial bandage wrap. When imaginatively raised and tied along the top of his head, it could support his jaw, keeping it shut in death. A pale complexion is the foundation from which an elongated jawline and pursed lips are encircled by a dark shadowing. His brows are heavy and well-defined semicircles that look somber above the dark bulbous eyes. A camouflaged (or missing) arm, along with the poorly defined bodily form, lies beneath the luxurious, fur-lined bulging fabric of the tabard, an emblem for the winter of Stoughton's life. Rather than a royal robe embellishing him for perpetuity, the tabard robe has expansive edges that can be drawn together, evoking a shroud-like mantle, enveloping Stoughton as well as the beaver's body within it. The serpentine movement of the golden cords weaves about his neck as a personification of evil. A physiognomic reading of his drawn and resolute face and the conventions of a formidable horizon suggest a supernatural knowledge of his own mortality and despondency toward eternal life. Mystically, an apocalyptic glow layered in a faraway horizon sets in the sky of Stoughton's portrait, appearing as a clairvoyant signifier, ominous in the truth of the demise of his personal ambition and subsequent downfall. Stoughton's phantom visage and decaying building portray him as being returned to dust. His hand points to the earth, where the resurrection of his body and soul remains suspect, perhaps meeting the same mortal fate as his building. Literally and metaphorically, the building's future belies the commemoration due him as he nears the end of his life. The illusory ancestral line forged into the heraldic crest in the center of the building cannot usher his memory into the future.

CONCLUSION

Stoughton's devotion to his Puritan community is enshrouded in the material finery of a fur-laden tabard that speaks loudly in the visual language of his portrait to his worldly allegiances. It is revealing, among other digressions and failures in Puritan doctrinal orthodoxy during his tenure as lieutenant governor, that his anthropocentric beliefs were not in keeping with John Calvin's statement on stewardship toward nonhuman life. As noted by scholars, the wealth of Massachusetts Bay hinged on the fur trade, a trade based on the demise of Native American relationships, European competition, massive slaughter and oppression of animals, and debts in luxury commodities owed to king and colony. Stoughton's constructed persona and emblematic conventions embody this mix of dualistic tension in his extravagant dress, at odds with Puritan self-effacement and humility. Stoughton's portrait is telling of his personal ideology, which vacillated to and fro, similar to the extinction of beaver populations and the trade itself, which moved farther west and out of the control of Massachusetts Bay. While the solid brick appearance of Stoughton Hall, the fur-collared tabard robe, and the lace cravat represent Stoughton's superficial benevolence and his accomplishments in education, wealth, and power, the thematic elements convey Stoughton's ethereal nature of pride, ambition, and indifference toward fur-bearing animals in a "murderous trade" that finally crumbled like the bricks in the shaky structure of Stoughton Hall.

NOTES

1. The Compassionate Conformist [pseud.], *England's Vanity or The Voice of God against the Monstrous Sin of Pride, in Dress and Apparel* [. . .] (London: Printed for John Dunton, at the Black Raven in the Poultry, 1683). EEBO.

2. Aileen Ribeiro, *The Art of Dress* (New Haven, CT: Yale University Press, 1995), 3.

3. Authorized King James Version. All biblical citations in this chapter refer to this version.

4. Phillip Stubbes, *Anatomy of the Abuses in England in Shakspere's Youth, A.D. 1583*, edited by Frederick J. Furnivall (London: Trübner, 1877), 50.

5. Francis X. Moloney, *The Fur Trade in New England 1620–1676* (Hamden, CT: Archon Books, 1967), 14.

6. Moloney, *Fur Trade*, 13–15.

7. John Langdon Sibley, *Biographical Sketches of Graduates of Harvard University in Cambridge, Massachusetts* (Cambridge, MA, 1873), 1:194–208.

8. Anne D'Alleva, *Look Again: Art History and Critical Theory* (Upper Saddle River, NJ: Prentice Hall, 2005), 88–120, 133–34. D'Alleva references major psychoanalysts such as Sigmund Freud, Jacques Lacan, Ernest Gombrich, and Carl Jung who documented the connections between art and the unconscious mind.

9. Jules David Prown, *Art as Evidence: Writings on Art and Material Culture* (New Haven, CT: Yale University Press, 2000), 69–91. Prown's methodology is a three-step format of interpretation—description, deduction, and speculation; the last utilizes critical theories such as psychoanalysis to examine portraits as a process of interpretative hypothesis.

10. Sibley, *Biographical Sketches*, 194–208.

11. Keith Thomas, *Man and the Natural World: Changing Attitudes in England 1500–1800* (London: Penguin Books, 1983), 125, 154.

12. Francis Bremer, "Increase Mather's Friends; The Trans-Atlantic Congregational Network of the Seventeenth Century," *Proceedings of the American Antiquarian Society* 94 (1984): 59–96. The Mathers were good friends with William Stoughton and corresponded frequently with those in England regarding the new sciences and the exposition of biblical narrative. As members of the Royal Society in England, they were founding members of the New England Philosophical Society. Their relationship with chemist Robert Boyle exposed them to new modes of scientific inquiry, the Hartlib circle, and sentience of animals, which surely did not escape Stoughton's observation. Stoughton himself funded the philosophical departments at Harvard as well as Cotton Mather's large compendium *Magnalia Christi Americana*, in which Cotton lauded the colony's modernity.

13. Thomas, *Man and the Natural World*, 170. Thomas states that the evolution of the "man of feeling" can be traced back to Anglican divines of the Latitudinarian tradition, who from the early years of the Restoration preached and wrote on the ethics of benevolence, "good nature," and tender sentimental feeling toward all of creation, hinging on the positive interpretation of Romans 8.

14. Jason Foster, "The Ecology of John Calvin," *Reformed Perspectives Magazine* 7, no. 51 (2005), 5.

15. Ibid., 15, fn. 43.

16. John Calvin, *Institutes of the Christian Religion*, trans. from the original Latin and collated with author's last edition in French by John Allen (Philadelphia: P. H. Nicklin, 1816), 3.10.5.

17. Thomas, *Man and the Natural World*, 23.

18. Marieke De Winkel, *Fashion and Fancy: Dress and Meaning in Rembrandt's Paintings* (Amsterdam: Amsterdam University Press, 2006), 27–50.

19. De Winkel, *Fashion and Fancy*, 29, 48.

20. De Winkel, *Fashion and Fancy*, 28.

21. Martha Finch, *Dissenting Bodies: Corporealities in Early New England* (New York: Columbia University Press, 2010), 5, 113–15.

22. De Winkel, *Fashion and Fancy*, 27–29.

23. Rosemary Troy Krill and Pauline K. Eversmann, *Early American Decorative Arts 1620–1860: A Handbook for Interpreters* (New York: Rowman and Littlefield, 2001), 219–30.

24. Wendy Katz, "Portraits and the Production of the Civil Self in Seventeenth Century Boston," *Winterthur Portfolio* 39 (2004): 124–60. Colonial Americans were painting in the "Tudor-like" tradition of limners, which was consistently criticized by Europeans as being too liney, flat, and old-fashioned, devoid of Renaissance principles. Colonial New Englanders were aware of stylistic choices and were conscious of, although not necessarily ready for, the new painterly "naturalism," using shadow to create displacement of inner thought.

25. Abbott Lowell Cummings, "Seventeenth-Century Boston Portraiture: Profile of the Establishment," in *Painting and Portrait Making*, ed. Peter Benes (Boston: Dublin Seminar for New England Folk Life Annual Proceedings, 1994), 17–21.

26. Aileen Ribeiro, *Dress and Morality* (New York: Holmes & Meier, 1986), 87.

27. Henry Peacham, *Compleat Gentleman, 1634* (Oxford: Clarendon Press, 1906), 227–28; Janet Mayo, *A History of Ecclesiastical Dress* (London: B. T. Batsford, 1987), 77–88.

28. Susan Sleeper- Smith, *Rethinking the Fur Trade* (Lincoln: University of Nebraska Press, 2009).

29. Doriece Colle, *Collars, Stocks, and Cravats: A History and Costume Dating Guide to Civilian Men's Neckpieces 1655–1900* (Emmaus, PA: Rodale Press, 1972), 77–119.

30. De Winkel, *Fashion and Fancy*, 30.

31. De Winkel, *Fashion and Fancy*, 11.

32. Linda Johnson, "Spiritual Autobiography in Puritan Portraiture" (PhD diss., Michigan State University, 2011). Johnson catalogues 184 images (either portraits or prints) and 217 images by the amount of repetition of emblems, objects, and costume and the manner of posture, gesture, and settings of the subjects, disclosing the transmission of style in a quantitative analysis.

33. Jane Ashelford, *The Art of Dress; Clothes and Society, 1500–1914* (London: National Trust Enterprises, 1996), 27–50.

34. Paul Raffield, "Reformation, Regulation and the Image: Sumptuary Legislation and the Subject of Law." *Law and Critique* 13 (2002): 127–50.

35. Finch, *Dissenting Bodies*, 110.

36. Ribeiro, *Dress and Morality*, 15.

37. Increase Mather, "Burnings Bewailed" (Boston, 1711), in *Departing Glory: Eight Jeremiads*, ed. Lee Schweninger (New York: Scholar's Facsimiles & Reprints, 1986), 23.

38. Sibley, *Biographical Sketches*, 196.

39. Sibley, *Biographical Sketches*, 194–99.

40. Sibley, *Biographical Sketches*, 196.

41. Quoted in Sibley, *Biographical Sketches*, 196.

42. Cotton Mather, *Magnalia Christi Americana; or, The Ecclesiastical History of New-England: From its First Planning the Year 1620, unto the Year of Our Lord 1698, in Seven Books* (New York: Russell & Russell, 1852), 2:11.

43. Finch, *Dissenting Bodies*, 110.

44. Cummings, "Seventeenth-Century Boston Portraiture," 17.

45. Stubbes, *Anatomy of the Abuses*, 30.

46. Finch, *Dissenting Bodies*, 5, 12.

47. Max Farrand, ed., *The Laws and Liberties of Massachusetts, Cambridge, Printed According to the Order of the General Court* (1647; repr., Cambridge, MA: Harvard University Press, 1929), 16.

48. Moloney, *Fur Trade*, 27.

49. Sleeper-Smith, *Rethinking the Fur Trade*, xx–xxv.

50. Moloney, *Fur Trade*, 46–47.

51. Sleeper-Smith, *Rethinking the Fur Trade*, xxvii. In 1600–1640, the Dutch, English, Swedes, and French struggled to control access to North American peltry.

52. Moloney, *Fur Trade*, 16, 43.

53. Quoted in Moloney, *Fur Trade*, 27.

54. Aubrey Townsend, ed., *The Writings of John Bradford* (Cambridge, MA: Parker Society, 1848–53), 1.351–64. There is a strong probability that Separatist William Bradford (1590–1657) was a relative of the celebrated preacher and martyr John Bradford, who explicitly challenged the scholastic doctrine that animals were made for human sustenance.

55. Quoted in Moloney, *Fur Trade*, 103.

56. William Bradford, *Of Plymouth Plantation, 1620–1647*, ed. Samuel Eliot Morison (New York: Alfred A. Knopf, 2001), 268, 286–89.

57. Moloney, *Fur Trade*, xxv.

58. Quoted in Moloney, *Fur Trade*, 43.

59. Quoted in Moloney, *Fur Trade*, 43.

60. Roger Williams, *A Key into the Language of America*, ed. James Hammond Trumbull (Providence, RI: Narragansett Club, 1866), 1.130, 190–9.

61. Quoted in Moloney, *Fur Trade*, 114.

62. Cotton Mather, *Biblia Americana: America's First Bible Commentary—A Synoptic Commentary on the Old and New Testaments*, ed. Reiner Smolinski (Grand Rapids, MI: Baker Academic, 2010), 1:306.

63. Stubbes, *Anatomy of the Abuses*, 177–8.

64. Farrand, *Laws and Liberties*, 16.

65. Farrand, *Laws and Liberties*, 24.

66. William Stoughton, "New England's True Interest Not to Lie" (Cambridge, 1670), *Proceedings of the American Antiquarian Society* 156 (1961): 1–40. For background on the urgency of election sermons, see Harry S. Stout, *The New England Soul: Preaching and Religious Culture in Colonial New England* (New York: Oxford, 1986). Stoughton feared total loss of jurisdiction and appears to have been resolved to placate the king rather than God. He stated, "Wee are hugging our privileges and franchises to death and prefer the dissolution of our Body politique, rather than to suffer Amputation in any of its limbs." Stoughton's indecision and ill attempt at equanimity resulted in the loss of favor among his people.

67. Sibley, *Biographical Sketches*, 203–6. Stoughton's probate inventory, while extensive in property holdings, does not list clothing items and instead combines all household textiles as "stuff." Stoughton left an estate considered large for the time. His monetary legacy is a telling feature definitive of the changes in Puritan orthodoxy. He bequeathed to the church in Dorchester and to Harvard College money and silver objects such as communion plates and cups, as well as stipends for Harvard tutors and students who met graduate and residential requirements.

68. Increase Mather, *Reasons for the Confirmation of the Charters, Belonging to the Several Corporations in New England* (London, 1690–91), ProQuest.

69. Samuel Eliot Morison, *Harvard College in the Seventeenth Century* (Cambridge, MA: Harvard University Press, 1936), 520. The inscription is difficult to read in the portrait, but Morison states that it reads, "Deo Opt. Max.Bonisq.Literis S. Gulielmus Stoughton Armiger provinciae Massachuset.Nov-Anglorum Vice-Gubernator Collegii Harvardini Olim Alumnus Semper Patronus Fecit Anno Domini 1699." The crest is not the first use of inventive heraldry in Puritan pseudo-aristocracy.

70. Cotton Mather, *Magnalia Christi Americana*, 11.

71. Sibley, *Biographical Sketches*, 204.

72. Morison, *Harvard College*, 520–21.

73. Jules David Prown and Kenneth Haltman, eds., *American Artifacts: Essays in Material Culture* (East Lansing: Michigan State University Press, 2000), 1–10. Art formal analysis draws from Claude Levi-Strauss's research on binary oppositions that may suggest some of the most persistent object metaphors expressive of tensions in particular beliefs.

74. Prown and Haltman, *American Artifacts*. Through a visual language of material expression, formal analysis is explored with attention to the opposition of thematic polarities, as well as conventional and iconographical methodology. The objects the patron (or the artist) has chosen in these portraits are evident of both unconscious and conscious patterns of deep cultural and religious beliefs related to life/death, male/female, security/danger, and power/lack of control, which are expressed artistically in techniques including but not limited to light/dark, soft/hard, and transparent/opaque.

REFERENCES

Ashelford, Jane. *The Art of Dress; Clothes and Society, 1500–1914*. London: National Trust Enterprises, 1996.

Bradford, William. *Of Plymouth Plantation, 1620–1647*. Edited by Samuel Eliot Morison. New York: Alfred A. Knopf, 2001.

Bremer, Francis. "Increase Mather's Friends: The Trans-Atlantic Congregational Network of the Seventeenth Century." *Proceedings of the American Antiquarian Society* 94 (1984): 59–96.

Calvin, John. *Institutes of the Christian Religion.* Translated from the original Latin, and collated with author's last edition in French, by John Allen. Philadelphia: P. H. Nicklin, 1816.

Colle, Doriece. *Collars, Stocks, and Cravats: A History and Costume Dating Guide to Civilian Men's Neckpieces 1655–1900.* Emmaus, PA: Rodale Press, 1972.

The Compassionate Conformist [pseud.]. *England's Vanity or The Voice of God against the Monstrous Sin of Pride, in Dress and Apparel* [. . .]. London: Printed for John Dunton, at the Black Raven in the Poultry, 1683. EEBO.

Cummings, Abbott Lowell. "Seventeenth-Century Boston Portraiture: Profile of the Establishment." In *Painting and Portrait Making*, edited by Peter Benes, 17–21. Boston: Dublin Seminar for New England Folk Life Annual Proceedings, 1994.

D'Alleva, Anne. *Look Again: Art History and Critical Theory.* Upper Saddle River, NJ: Prentice Hall, 2005.

De Winkel, Marieke. *Fashion and Fancy: Dress and Meaning in Rembrandt's Paintings.* Amsterdam: Amsterdam University Press, 2006.

Farrand, Max, ed. *The Laws and Liberties of Massachusetts, Cambridge, Printed According to the Order of the General Court*. 1647. Reprint, Cambridge, MA: Harvard University Press, 1929.

Finch, Martha. *Dissenting Bodies: Corporealities in Early New England.* New York: Columbia University Press, 2010.

Foster, Jason. "The Ecology of John Calvin." *Reformed Perspectives Magazine* 7, no. 51 (2005): 1–21.

Johnson, Linda. "Spiritual Autobiography in Puritan Portraiture." PhD diss., Michigan State University, 2011.

Katz, Wendy. "Portraits and the Production of the Civil Self in Seventeenth Century Boston." *Winterthur Portfolio* 39 (2004): 124–60.

Krill, Rosemary Troy, and Pauline K. Eversmann. *Early American Decorative Arts 1620–1860: A Handbook for Interpreters.* New York: Rowman and Littlefield, 2001.

Mather, Cotton. *Biblia Americana: America's First Bible Commentary—A Synoptic Commentary on the Old and New Testaments*. Vol. 1. Edited by Reiner Smolinski. Grand Rapids, MI: Baker Academic, 2010.

———. *Magnalia Christi Americana; or, The Ecclesiastical History of New-England: From its First Planning the Year 1620, unto the Year of Our Lord 1698, in Seven Books*. Vol. 2. New York: Russell & Russell, 1852.

Mather, Increase. "Burnings Bewailed." Boston, 1711. In *Departing Glory: Eight Jeremiads*, edited by Lee Schweninger. New York: Scholar's Facsimiles & Reprints, 1986.

———. *Reasons for the Confirmation of the Charters Belonging to the Several Corporations in New-England.* London, 1690. ProQuest.

Mayo, Janet. *A History of Ecclesiastical Dress.* London: B. T. Batsford, 1987.

Moloney, Francis X. *The Fur Trade in New England 1620–1676*. Hamden, CT: Archon Books, 1967.

Morison, Samuel Eliot. *Harvard College in the Seventeenth Century.* Cambridge, MA: Harvard University Press, 1936.

Peacham, Henry. *Compleat Gentleman, 1634.* Oxford: Clarendon Press, 1906.

Prown, Jules David. *Art as Evidence: Writings on Art and Material Culture*. New Haven, CT: Yale University Press, 2000.

Prown, Jules David, and Kenneth Haltman, eds. *American Artifacts: Essays in Material Culture.* East Lansing: Michigan State University Press, 2000.

Raffield, Paul. "Reformation, Regulation and the Image: Sumptuary Legislation and the Subject of Law." *Law and Critique* 13 (2002): 127–50.

Ribeiro, Aileen. *The Art of Dress*. New Haven, CT: Yale University Press, 1995.

———. *Dress and Morality.* New York: Holmes & Meier, 1986.

Sibley, John Langdon. *Biographical Sketches of Graduates of Harvard University in Cambridge, Massachusetts.* Cambridge, MA, 1873.

Sleeper-Smith, Susan. *Rethinking the Fur Trade.* Lincoln: University of Nebraska Press, 2009.

Stoughton, William. "New England's True Interest Not to Lie." Cambridge, 1670. *Proceedings of the American Antiquarian Society* 156 (1961): 1–40.

Stout, Harry S. *The New England Soul: Preaching and Religious Culture in Colonial New England.* New York: Oxford, 1986.

Stubbes, Phillip. *Anatomy of the Abuses in England in Shakspere's Youth, A.D. 1583*. Edited by Frederick J. Furnivall. London: N. Trübner, 1877.

Thomas, Keith. *Man and the Natural World: Changing Attitudes in England 1500–1800.* London: Penguin Books, 1983.

Townsend, Aubrey, ed. *The Writings of John Bradford*. Cambridge, MA: Parker Society, 1848–53.

Williams, Roger. *A Key into the Language of America*. Edited by James Hammond Trumbull. Providence, RI: Narragansett Club, 1866.

Winthrop, John. "A Modell of Christian Charity." In *The Puritans*, edited by Perry Miller and Thomas Johnson, 195–199. New York: Harper & Row, 1963.

Chapter 4

The Nineteenth-Century Boycott against Feathered Hats

Robyn Hederman

In the 1898 editorial "Murderous Millinery," the *New York Times* reported that plume hunters were slaughtering free-living birds for the "mere gratification of tender-hearted women." This article referred to the nineteenth-century fashion craze in which women donned hats with stuffed birds perched upon their wide brims. Women paraded their bird hats along the streets of New York City. In 1886, the ornithologist Frank Chapman visited Fourteenth Street in Manhattan to observe "the number and kinds of birds that were then actually being worn."[1] Chapman recognized forty distinct species of birds on the hats of the women shoppers, including warblers, blue jays, meadowlarks, ruffled grouse, and a mourning dove.[2] The *New York Times* concluded that these "feathered-headed women" invite "public stigma by exhibiting themselves as they do in the relics of murdered innocence."[3]

The bird-plumage controversy revealed social conflicts involving gender, class, and women's role in the public sphere. Women played a prominent role in the debate. As consumers of the bird hats, women were vilified for the extermination of countless species of birds. However, women also launched a boycott of the plumes and stigmatized the wearing of feathered hats. In *Flight Maps*, the historian Jennifer Price claims that wearing a dead bird became a "threat to moral womanhood."[4]

The plumage issue acquired a greater significance than game hunting or water pollution when nineteenth-century Americans embraced "conservation as a moral issue."[5] Animal advocates, conservationists, preservationists, scientists, and members of women's clubs united to save endangered birds.[6] Robin W. Doughty, in *Feather Fashions and Bird Preservation*, describes the anti-plumage campaign as a part of the nineteenth-century back to nature movement. Alarmed by animal cruelty and the exploitation of natural resources, Americans called for new attitudes "towards the environment and its animal denizens."[7] The anti-plumage campaign ignited the conservation movement and resulted in the enactment of the first federal animal protection law in 1900.[8]

As early as 1886, the American Ornithologists' Union (AOU) estimated that "five million North American birds of about fifty species were killed annually for 'fashion.'"[9] The ornithologist W. E. D. Scott described the conditions of the Florida bird rookeries. He surveyed the Gulf Coast with Mr. Batty, a plume hunter. Scott learned that the colony "had finally been abandoned by the hundreds of birds which once frequented this point."[10] Scott watched as Mr. Batty and his workers massacred Wilson's plovers, least terns, boat-tailed blackbirds, gray kingbirds, and other small species for the millinery industry.[11] In his report, Scott concluded that the industry was a "great and growing evil" where merchants in New York and other locations were buying the "skins and plumes of Florida birds" each month.[12]

Market hunters, manufacturers, and importers abetted the millinery industry. But society reserved its condemnation for women consumers wearing bird feathers or whole birds nestled atop their heads. Magazines and newspapers claimed a "true woman" would not betray her maternal instincts by murdering bird mothers and their children. Price argues that prescribed nineteenth-century gender roles helped to exempt male hunters, businessmen, and manufacturers from blame. Mabel Osgood Wright, president of the Connecticut Audubon Society, opined "why should we expect the milliner with a living at stake to be more moral than the woman?"[13] According to Price, the responsibility for conservation shifted away from men and focused on "women's sphere of morals and civilized behavior."[14] Most conservation activists agreed that "higher-class women of superior morals" should not let "lower-class men kill mother egrets."[15]

In an 1886 article, the ornithologist Joel A. Allen analyzed the "wholesale" slaughter of native birds. "The most heartless and least defensible," Allen concluded, was "the sacrifice of birds to fashion."[16] He believed the practices of "the dead bird wearing gender" resulted in a significant annual sacrifice of bird life.[17] In *Our Vanishing Wild Life*, William Hornaday, director of the New York Zoological Society, called for a reform of the defective wildlife protection laws that were supposed to protect free-living communities of animals. He claimed that free-ranging birds were being exterminated to "furnish millinery ornaments for women's wear."[18] Hornaday concluded, "We are weary of witnessing the greed, selfishness and cruelty of 'civilized' man toward the wild creatures of the earth. We are sick of tales of slaughter and pictures of carnage."[19]

HARRIET HEMENWAY AND THE AUDUBON SOCIETY

In January 1896, Mrs. Harriet Hemenway, a prominent Boston woman, read graphic accounts of the slaying of free-living birds by market hunters. She learned that the herons produced their coveted white feathers only during their breeding season, when the male and the female egrets stayed at the nest to protect their offspring. They were easy targets for the plume hunters. The adult birds were shot, and their skin "stripped from their backs."[20]The parents were massacred, while the young starved.[21]

Hemenway was no stranger to social activism. Her father, Amos Lawrence, had been active in the antislavery movement and had been the treasurer of Harvard College. Her husband, Augustus Hemenway, also came from a civic-minded family. Harriet Hemenway once invited Booker T. Washington to be a guest in her home when he was turned away by the Boston hotels.[22] After learning about the murdered herons, Mrs. Hemenway founded the Massachusetts Audubon Society. She and her cousin, Minna B. Hall, contacted Boston society ladies who wore aigrettes on their hats or in their hair, asking them if they would be willing to give up their bird hats and join the new society.[23]

Hemenway took the name of her new organization from the New York bird protection group formed in 1886 by the "sportsman" George Grinnell.[24] Grinnell argued that a live bird "is beautiful, but ten thousand dead birds with glass or waxon eyes, withering beaks and shrunken skins, perched above the noses of ten thousand women are anything but a sense of joy."[25] Grinnell's Audubon Society sought to prevent the murder of birds for millinery.[26] Grinnell published the *Audubon Magazine*, believing that once women learned of the murder of free-living birds, they would stop wearing their bird hats. When women continued to wear their plumes and hats adorned with dead birds, Grinnell became disillusioned. He dissolved the society shortly after the release of final issue of the *Audubon Magazine* in December 1888.[27]

According to historian Kathy S. Mason, Hemenway's organization succeeded where Grinnell's had failed because, unlike Grinnell, Hemenway had funding and a governing board to arrange events. Hemenway created a professional society by recruiting prominent women, ornithologists, writers, and other educators to join.[28] The Massachusetts Audubon Society's mission was "to discourage the buying and wearing, for ornamental purposes, of feathers of wild birds, and to otherwise further the protection of native birds."[29] The ornithologist William Brewster was named the president of the new group. Due to the success of the society, the Massachusetts legislature passed a bill in 1897 outlawing the trade in feathers of free-living birds.[30]

The writer Sarah Orne Jewett became the vice president of the Massachusetts Audubon Society. Jewett's "A White Heron" represents an early plea for the conservation of birds.[31] In this short story, an ornithologist invades the woods, seeking to shoot a "little white heron." He meets a child named Sylvia who is familiar with the birds in the woods and their nesting locations. The hunter seeks Sylvia's help in finding the white heron. He tells her, "I would give ten dollars to anybody who could show it to me." Sylvia discovers the heron's nest: "She knows his secret now, the wild, light, slender bird that floats and wavers, and goes back like an arrow presently to his home in the green world beneath."[32] However, Sylvia refuses to expose the heron to the young ornithologist. Remembering how "the white heron came flying through the golden air and how they watched the sea and the morning together," Sylvia "cannot tell the heron's secret and give its life away."[33]

Another contemporary writer, Celia Leighton Thaxter, vehemently opposed women wearing bird hats. "I look at the ghastly horror of women's headgear with absolute suffering," she wrote to a friend in 1886. She continued: "No woman worthy of the name would wish to be instrumental in destroying the dear beautiful creatures; and for such idle folly!"[34] In another letter, Thaxter wrote, "There are more birds than usual this year," and "the women haven't assassinated them all for the funeral pyres they carry on their heads."[35] But the next day, Thaxter described seeing "women with carcasses of the birds [she] loved[d] borne in simple vanity above their faces."[36]

Audubon groups formed in several states, and women were predominant in these organizations.[37] In 1898, the author Mabel Osgood Wright formed the Audubon Society of Connecticut. Wright also edited the Audubon section of *Bird-Lore*, a journal established in 1899 by Frank Chapman for "the study and protection of birds."[38] Wright sought popular women writers to contribute to the magazine.[39]

The National Association of Audubon Societies for the Protection of Wild Birds and Animals was formed in 1905. William Dutcher described the objective of the new organization in *Bird-Lore*: "The object of this organization is to be a barrier between wild birds and animals and a very large unthinking class, and a smaller but more harmful class of selfish people."[40]

AMERICAN CLUBWOMEN AND BIRD CONSERVATION

Feathered fashion was not new. In the eighteenth century, Queen Marie Antoinette of France wore ostrich and peacock feathers in her piled hair and ignited a fashion trend among the aristocracy.[41] In the nineteenth century, this demand for feathers swept Europe and the United States. After the American Civil War, feathers and birds dominated middle-class ladies' fashion.[42] In his book *Birds and Men*, Robert Henry Welker describes these "showy" and "flamboyant" hats, "often combining a stuffed bird or two," as another example of the "vulgarity and the naïve enthusiasm" of the Gilded Age.[43]

The women's magazines *Godey's Ladies Book*, *Harper's Bazar*, *Ladies Home Journal*, and *Vogue* exhibited ladies' hats decorated with stuffed birds and plumage. According to Jennifer Price in *Flight Maps*, the "natural look" became a symbol of femininity in the nineteenth century. Milliners stacked women's hats with birds, flowers, leaves, and even mice and reptiles.[44] *Harper's Bazar* was primarily designed for upper-class women.[45] The magazine informed its readers as early as 1868 that feather and fur hats were being imported from Europe. By the end of the nineteenth century, bird hats had become a symbol of class, beauty, and upper-class femininity.[46] In an 1899 article, "Paris Millinery for Autumn and Winter," *Harper's Bazar* described hats trimmed "with white pigeons—the entire bird put on, the claws and beak a bright color, and the head of the bird thrust through a collar of rhinestones."[47]

Harper's Bazar and *Ladies Home Journal* also published articles focusing on bird protection issues and women's role in the plumage debate. An 1875 *Harper's Bazar* article, "The Slaughter of the Innocents," lamented the failure of Americans to recognize the inherent value of free-living communities of animals. Because of women's vanity, the millinery industry "took birds from their native haunts and perched their lifeless bodies upon the heads of our mothers and sisters and daughters." The author concluded that "the widespread belief that birds and animals were created only for the use and amusement of man is a doctrine unworthy of Christendom."[48]

Many Audubon Society ladies were also members of women's clubs, which were devoted to curing diverse social ills.[49] In *The Clubwoman as Feminist*, Karen J. Blair analyzes the emergence of the women's club movement in the 1860s. The women's club movement emerged from the moral-reform societies of the early nineteenth century—for example, temperance and anti-vice organizations.[50] The club movement flourished after the close of the US Civil War. Initially, women organized literary clubs to promote education and self-improvement. But by the 1870s, the clubs had expanded to include many areas of social reform. Women employed their womanly virtues of "piety, purity, submissiveness, and domesticity"[51] to change society. According to Barbara Welter's "The Cult of True Womanhood," women learned that "if woman was so little less than the angels, she should surely take a more active part in running the world."[52]

According to Blair, this ideology of the "lady," the belief that "every woman was a moral and domestic creature," was the backbone of the women's club movement.[53] Women, the "moral guardian[s] of the home," were virtually banished from the public sphere.[54] Nevertheless, women expanded this ideal of domesticity to "supervise the moral standards of [their] community."[55] These "domestic feminists" applied "their moral qualities to the world at large through self-improvement and reform."[56]

Toward the end of the nineteenth century, clubwomen tackled environmental and bird protection issues, as well as "problems of poverty, labor, crime, disease, and infant mortality."[57] After the near extinction of the buffalo in the 1880s, a national conservation movement emerged. Women played an active role in the early conservation movement. They lobbied against deforestation and water pollution while they worked to protect natural lands and endangered species.[58] In "Women of the Progressive Conservation Movement," Carolyn Merchant depicts the growth of the women's conservation movement, claiming that "women transformed the crusade from an elite male enterprise into a widely based movement."[59] Women joined sportsman-hunters, scientists, and protectionists to protect free-living creatures.[60] Although these clubwomen were environmental activists, they also accepted their traditional nineteenth-century gender roles as "caretakers of the nation's homes, husband, and offspring."[61]

In 1905, due to an increase in sales of the white "aigrette," the Audubon Society requested help from the National Federation of Women's Clubs. The society asked women "to take a strong stand against the usage of wild bird plumage, and especially against the use of the Aigrette . . . "[62] At the Federation's 1910 convention, the chair of the Forestry Committee asked, "Can we logically work for conservation and expect to be listened to, while we still continue to encourage the destruction of the song birds by following the hideous fashion of wearing songbirds and egrets upon our hats?"[63]

ANIMAL ADVOCACY GROUPS

Animal advocates cooperated with conservationists and clubwomen to protest feathered hats. Both Henry Bergh, the founder of the American Society for the Prevention of Cruelty to Animals, and George T. Angell of the Massachusetts SPCA became honorary vice presidents of the (National) Audubon Society. Animal advocates also believed that bird hats were a women's issue. Angell's magazine, *Our Dumb Animals*, spoke against wearing bird plumage as early as 1869. Bergh expressed disgust with this "painful and discouraging" fashion and rebuked women who wore murdered birds: "Harmless and beautiful creations of the Omnipotent are mutilated and slaughtered by the million, in the mere spirit of coquettish vanity, which binds alike the matron and the maiden to the hideous crime in which they are accomplices."[64]

Caroline Earle White and Mary F. Lovell, founders of the American Anti-Vivisection Society, also embraced protection of free-living animals.

In the *Journal of Zoophily*, White asked her readers to boycott fur and feathered hats.[65] She urged her readers to protest countries participating in the hunts.[66] Emphasizing the values of the "true woman," White asked women, in their roles of "reformers, caretakers, and consumers," to reject feathered hats.[67] Likewise, as the national director of the Department of Mercy for the Women's Christian Temperance Movement, Mary F. Lovell urged women to stop wearing furs and feathers.[68] At a meeting of the Women's National Council, Lovell announced she would not wear sealskin. When she was asked what "dress ornaments" could be obtained from animals and birds without cruelty, she replied "that she knew of no ornaments of this class except cock feathers and even they are obtained with some cruelty."[69]

In her book *For the Prevention of Cruelty*, Diane Beers claims that the animal advocates connected the "act of consumption" with "willful cruelty."[70] White specifically targeted women as mothers and managers of the household. White believed that a "women's boycott of cruel industries" would create "more humane and moral families in the future."[71] Beers points out that although White's fur boycott did not develop, the later success of the gendered feathered hat boycott demonstrates that "White was on the right track."[72] According to Beers, when women took charge of the boycott campaign, "hat sales plummeted."[73]

PROTECTION LEGISLATION

Animal advocates, national women's clubs, conservationists, scientists, and bird watchers coalesced against the feather industry. In *Animals and Their Legal Rights*, Greta Nilsson concludes that by the turn of the century, there might have been fewer than three hundred egrets left alive.[74] Yet by 1900, in response to the public furor against plume wearing, eight states had passed bird protection legislation. The strength of these protections varied. Some statutes covered only native birds, whereas some states did not prohibit any sale of plumage.[75] In 1886, New York State enacted the New York Bird Law, landmark legislation that prohibited the killing, wounding, trapping, or catching of songbirds or any other free-living birds. The law further banned the destruction of nests and eggs.[76] Many state laws already restricted the killing of native birds; however, these laws did not prevent the transport of illegally killed birds to other states.

In 1900 Congress responded to the public's appeal for protection of free-living animals and passed the Lacey Act, a federal law prohibiting the interstate transport and sale of wildlife protected by state statutes.[77] In Congressman John Fletcher Lacey's opening remarks in support of his bill, he claimed, "There is a compensation in the distribution of plants, birds, and animals by the God of Nature." Lacey warned that "man's attempt to change and interfere often leads to serious results," and "we have given an awful exhibition of slaughter and destruction, which may serve as a warning to all mankind."[78]

The legislation expanded the power of the United States Department of Agriculture (USDA) to protect and reestablish free-ranging bird populations. The statute sought to restore "game birds and other wild birds" where they have become "scarce or extinct." It further regulated "the introduction of American or foreign birds or animals" and protected "any wild animals or birds" shielded by state laws.[79] Congress utilized the Commerce Clause to restrict the markets in free-living animals and "to supplement the State laws for the protection of game and wildbirds."[80]

The Lacey Act did not apply to birds killed in states without protective laws. Its passage, however, marked a turning point in the conservation movement. The bird and "wildlife" protection organizations continued to push for more state and federal laws. In 1903, President Theodore Roosevelt established the first refuge for free-living animals at Pelican Island in Florida.[81] The Audubon Society and the AOU also hired wardens to protect the diminished bird colonies on the eastern coast. In July 1905, Guy Bradley, a warden of the National Audubon Society, was murdered by plume hunters in Florida. This tragedy galvanized bird preservationists to push for greater legal protections. Women's clubs urged ladies to relinquish their bird hats. President Theodore Roosevelt supported the Audubon Society's effort to "stop the sale and use of the so-called 'Aigrettes'—the plumes of white herons," claiming, "If anything, Mrs. Roosevelt feels more strongly than I do in the matter."[82]

Other federal protections were enacted over the first two decades of the twentieth century. The 1913 Underwood Tariff impeded the importation of free-living bird feathers into the United States. Incensed ladies were stripped of their bird hats upon their arrival from Europe and other parts of the world.[83] For example, upon her arrival from Bermuda, a Mrs. Gilchrest was relieved of her five hats by customs officials. She was told by the agents that she could keep her hats by removing the bird plumage. Mrs. Gilchrest was surprised, not having realized that Bermuda was not part of the United States.[84]

The 1913 Migratory Bird Law placed the protection of the birds within the control of the federal government. The USDA could issue regulations limiting the hunting and marketing of migratory species.[85] In 1918, President Wilson signed the landmark Migratory Bird Treaty between the United States and Great Britain on behalf of Canada. The treaty prohibited the killing of non-game migratory birds. President Wilson supported the bird protection movement to the dismay of the milliners. In 1913, the millinery trade excoriated Wilson when he and his wife attended a performance of the bird protection play *Sanctuary—A Bird Masque*, where Wilson's daughter Eleanor played Ornia, a bird spirit.[86]

CONCLUSION

In her essay "The Plumage Bill," Virginia Woolf responds to a comment by Harold J. Massingham, of the Parliamentary Plumage Group, blaming women for the failure of the 1920 Plumage Bill in Great Britain. Massingham had written, "What does one expect? They have to be shot in parenthood for child-bearing women to flaunt the symbols of it, and, as Mr. Hudson says, one bird shot for its plumage means ten other deadly wounds and the starvation of the young. But what do women care? Look at Regent Street this morning!"[87]

With the release of Woolf's essay, bird protectionists criticized her as being anti-bird. Instead, in her essay Woolf protests the plumage activists who condemned women as the sole perpetrators of the violence against egrets. In "The Plumage Bill," Woolf exposes a network abetting the murder of birds for hats. Lady So-and-So "of the stupid face and beautiful figure" views the shop windows with something "of the greedy petulance of a pug-dog's face at tea time."[88] The egret plumes are "the very symbols of pride and distinction."[89] Seeking a "lemon-colored egret," Lady So-and So enters the shop, and her "silver bag disgorges I know not how many notes."[90]

Woolf next describes the "blazing South American landscape" where decoys are tied to stakes, and "the young birds rot where they sit."[91] She asks, "But these hands—are they the hands of men or of women?"[92] According to Reginald Abbott, Woolf proposed that "while Lady So-and-So is not to be absolved of all guilt," she should not receive the primary blame for this trade.[93] Woolf concludes that "we may fairly suppose then that the birds are killed by men, starved by men, and tortured by men—not vicariously, but with their own hands."[94]

Studying the anti-plumage campaign reveals the social conflicts women faced in the late nineteenth and early twentieth centuries. Abbott points out that "The Plumage Bill" merges an "anti-plumage argument with 'an outburst of sex antagonism.'"[95]

In the 1898 *Report of the A.O.U. Committee on Protection of North American Birds*, William Dutcher condemned the majority of women who continued to use "wild birds' feathers for millinery ornaments."[96] He concluded that this was "largely due" to "an unwillingness to assume an individual responsibility."[97] "In other words, unless the wearer has a particular bird killed for her particular use, she will not assume any responsibility."[98]

Yet despite this criticism, women played a significant role in the anti-plumage campaign. Along with animal activists, scientists, and sportsman-hunters, women organized a feather boycott resulting in the collapse of hat sales. According to Diane Beers, by the second decade of the twentieth century, this campaign had transformed "something once considered a stunning fashion statement into a repulsive symbol of cruel selfishness."[99]

Although Caroline White implored her readers to boycott fur, it was the wearing of feathered hats that ignited the nineteenth-century conservation movement. Why did the feathered hats invoke such outrage? Jennifer Price suggests that the notion of the woman "as the keeper of morality" made this issue "resonate at a higher moral volume than any other."[100] Bird hats became inextricably tied to cherished values of the "true woman." Wearing dead birds could no longer be reconciled with a woman's most important role, motherhood. In 1897, the *New York Times* published an editorial lamenting that it was painful to see "pretty girls" with "dead birds of every description on their hats." The author asked, "How can Sunday-school teachers, who are supposed to teach children to be kind to God's creatures, sit with hats ornamented in this way and expect the children to listen to their teachings?"[101]

NOTES

1. Frank Chapman, *Autobiography of a Bird Lover* (New York: D. Appleton-Century, 1933), 38–39; Frank Graham Jr., *The Audubon Ark: The History of the National Audubon Society* (New York: Alfred A. Knopf, 1990), 38.

2. Chapman, *Autobiography of a Bird Lover,* 38–39; see, Graham, *The Audubon Ark*, 24–25.

3. "Murderous Millinery," *New York Times*, July 31, 1898.

4. Jennifer Price, *Flight Maps: Adventures with Nature in Modern America* (New York: Basic Books, 1999), 76.

5. Price, *Flight Maps*, 72.

6. Diane L. Beers, *For the Prevention of Cruelty: The History and Legacy of Animal Rights Activism in the United States* (Athens: Swallow Press/Ohio University Press, 2006), 84–86; Price, *Flight Maps*, 72–73.

7. Robin W. Doughty, *Feather Fashions and Bird Preservation: A Study in Nature Protection* (Berkeley: University of California Press, 1975), 50.

8. "An Act to Enlarge the Powers of the Department of Agriculture, Prohibit the Transportation by Interstate Commerce of Game Killed in Violation of Local Law, and for Other Purposes," *United States Statutes at Large* 31 (1900): 187–89.

9. Graham, *The Audubon Ark*, 25.

10. W. E. D. Scott, "The Present Condition of Some of the Bird Rookeries of the Gulf Coast of Florida," *The AUK* 4, no. 4 (October 1887): 280.

11. Scott, "Present Condition," 276–77.

12. Scott, "Present Condition," 283.
13. Quoted in Price, *Flight Maps*, 94.
14. Price, *Flight Maps*, 92.
15. Price, *Flight Maps*, 97.
16. J. A. Allen, "The Present Wholesale Destruction of Bird-Life in the United States," *Science* 7, no. 160 (February 26, 1886): 191–92.
17. Allen, "Present Wholesale Destruction," 194.
18. William T. Hornaday, *Our Vanishing Wildlife: Its Extermination and Preservation* (New York: Charles Scribner's Sons, 1913), 114.
19. Hornaday, *Our Vanishing Wildlife*, x.
20. Graham, *The Audubon Ark*, 14.
21. Graham, *The Audubon Ark*, 14–15.
22. Mary Joy Breton, *Women Pioneers for the Environment* (Boston: Northeastern University Press, 1998), 257; Kathy S. Mason, "Harriet Hemenway and the Audubon Society, 1896–1905," *The Historian* 65, no. 1 (Fall 2002): 9.
23. Breton, *Women Pioneers*, 255–56.
24. Mason, "Harriet Hemenway," 4.
25. George Bird Grinnell, "A Shameful Fashion," *Forest and Stream* 25 (January 7, 1886): 465.
26. Mason, "Harriet Hemenway," 5.
27. Mason, "Harriet Hemenway," 6.
28. Mason, "Harriet Hemenway," 6.
29. William Dutcher, "Report of the A.O.U. Committee on the Protection of North American Birds [for 1896]," quoted in Mark V. Barrow Jr., *A Passion for Birds: American Ornithology after Audubon* (Princeton, NJ: Princeton University Press, 1998), 127.
30. Mason, "Harriet Hemenway," 11.
31. Sarah Orne Jewett, "A White Heron" in *Birdwatching with American Women: A Selection of Nature Writings, ed. Deborah Strom* (New York: W. W. Norton, 1986), 112–14.
32. Jewett, "A White Heron," 126.
33. Jewett, "A White Heron," 127.
34. Celia Thaxter, "To Feroline W. Fox.. Hotel Clifford, Cortes Street, Boston, April 1, 1886" in *Letters of Celia Thaxter*, ed. Annie Fields and Rose Lamb (Boston: Houghton, Mifflin, 1898), 146.
35. Celia Thaxter, "To Bradford Torrey. Appledore, Isle of Shoals, off Portsmouth, May 1, 1890" in *Letters of Celia Thaxter*, ed. Annie Fields and Rose Lamb (Boston: Houghton Mifflin, 1898), 175
36. Celia Thaxter, "To Bradford Torrey," 176.
37. Graham, *The Audubon Ark*, 23; Price, *Flight Maps*, 62.
38. Robert Henry Welker, *Birds and Men: American Birds in Science, Art, Literature, and Conservation, 1800–1900* (New York: Atheneum, 1966), 206.
39. Carolyn Merchant, "Women of the Progressive Conservation Movement: 1900–1916," *Environmental Review* 8 (Spring 1984): 70. These writers included Olive Thorne Miller, Florence A. Merriam (Bailey), and Neltje Blanchan.

40. Graham, *The Audubon Ark*, 47.
41. Doughty, *Feather Fashions*, 1.
42. Doughty, *Feather Fashions*, 14; Graham, *The Audubon Ark*, 24.
43. Welker, *Birds and Men*, 196–97.
44. Price, *Flight Maps*, 76.
45. John Tebbel and Mary Ellen Zuckerman, *The Magazine in America: 1741–1990* (New York: Oxford University Press, 1991), 103. The current "a" in *Bazaar* was not added until 1929.
46. Price, *Flight Maps*, 77.
47. *Harper's Bazar*, "Paris Millinery for Autumn and Winter," October 7, 1899, 839, quoted in Amy D. Scarborough, "Fashion Media's Role in the Debate on Millinery and Bird Protection in the United States in the Late Nineteenth and Early Twentieth Centuries" (PhD diss., Oregon State University, 2009), 79.
48. Quoted in Amelia Birdsall, "A Woman's Nature: Attitudes and Identities of the Bird Hat Debate at the Turn of the 20th Century" (thesis, Haverford College, 2002), 6–9.
49. Price, *Flight Maps*, 65–66.
50. Karen J. Blair, *The Clubwoman as Feminist: True Womanhood Redefined, 1868–1914* (New York: Holmes and Meier, 1980), 8.
51. Barbara Welter, "The Cult of True Womanhood: 1820–1860," in *Dimity Convictions: The American Woman in the Nineteenth Century* (Athens: Ohio University Press, 1976), 21.
52. Barbara Welter, "The Cult of True Womanhood: 1820–1860," 41.
53. Blair, *The Clubwoman as Feminist*, 1.
54. Blair, *The Clubwoman as Feminist*, 2–3.
55. Blair, *The Clubwoman as Feminist*, 7.
56. Blair, *The Clubwoman as Feminist*, 8.
57. Price, *Flight Maps*, 70.
58. Merchant, "Women of the Progressive Conservation Movement," 57.
59. Merchant, "Women of the Progressive Conservation Movement," 57.
60. Vera Norwood, *Made from This Earth* (Chapel Hill: University of North Carolina Press, 1993), 212.
61. Merchant, "Women and Conservation," 73.
62. Carolyn Merchant, "Women and Conservation," in *Major Problems in American Environmental History*, ed. Carolyn Merchant (Boston: Houghton Mifflin, 2005), 346.
63. Quoted in Merchant, "Women and Conservation," 346.
64. Quoted in Zulma Steele, *Angel in Top Hat* (New York: Harper and Brothers, 1942), 277.
65. White started the journal in 1892 as a joint publication of the Society for the Prevention of Cruelty to Animals and the American Anti-Vivisection Society. See Sydney H. Coleman, *Humane Society Leaders in America: With a Sketch of the Early History* (Albany, NY: American Humane Society, 1924), 184.
66. Beers, *For the Prevention of Cruelty*, 83.
67. Beers, *For the Prevention of Cruelty*, 85.

68. Lovell was a member of the Pennsylvania WCTU and convinced the national WCTU to establish a Department of Mercy in 1891. The Department of Mercy was devoted to the prevention of cruelty to animals and was associated with the growing antivivisection movement.

69. "Women Discuss Cruelty: The National Council Considers the Birds and Seals," *New York Times*, February 24, 1895. The National Council of Women was a coalition of major women's reform movements of the time. The idea for the coalition began in 1888 when the National Women's Suffrage Association (NWSA) invited a number of women's reform groups to the fortieth-anniversary commemoration of Seneca Falls.

70. Beers, *For the Prevention of Cruelty*, 84.

71. Beers, *For the Prevention of Cruelty*, 84.

72. Beers, *For the Prevention of Cruelty*, 84.

73. Beers, *For the Prevention of Cruelty*, 85.

74. Greta Nilsson, "Birds," in *Animals and Their Legal Rights: A Survey of American Laws from 1641 to 1990*, 4th ed. (Washington, DC: Animal Welfare Institute, 1990), 207.

75. Doughty, *Feather Fashions*, 109.

76. Nilsson, "Birds," 203. The law mandated that persons found guilty shall be punished by a jail sentence of "not less than five or more than thirty days, or to a fine of not less than ten or more than fifty dollars, or both, at the discretion of the court." In *Geer v. Connecticut*, 161 US 519 (1896), the Supreme Court held that a state could forbid the export of its "wildlife" and uphold the complementary power of the state to prevent the sale of articles received in interstate commerce.

77. Nilsson, "Birds," 207. There were fines of $500 for carrying and transporting "knowingly" and $200 for "knowingly receiving such articles" (H.R. 6634). "The object of this Act is to aid in the restoration of such birds in those parts of the United States adapted thereto where the same have become scarce or extinct, and also to regulate the introduction of American or foreign birds or animals in localities where they have not heretofore existed." "An Act to Enlarge the Powers of the Department of Agriculture," *United States Statutes at Large* 31 (1900): 187–89.

78. Quoted in Theodore Whaley Cart, "The Struggle for Wildlife Protection in the United States, 1870–1900: Attitudes and Events Leading to the Lacey Act" (PhD diss., University of North Carolina at Chapel Hill, 1971), 146, citing *Congressional Record*, 56th Cong., 1st sess., April 1900, pp. 4871, 4872.

79. Cart, "The Struggle for Wildlife Protection," 147, citing the Lacey Act, sections, 1, 2, and 3.

80. Cart, "The Struggle for Wildlife Protection," 150, citing H.R. 474, 56th Cong., 1st sess., 1899–1900, vols. 2 and 3.

81. Beers, *For the Prevention of Cruelty*, 85; Welker, *Birds and Men*, 210.

82. Quoted in Graham, *The Audubon Ark*, 58.

83. Merchant, "Women of the Progressive Conservation Movement," 73.

84. "Hold Up Five Hats," *New York Times*, January 9, 1914.

85. Doughty, *Feather Fashions*, 126n53.

86. Doughty, *Feather Fashions*, 131.

87. Quoted in Reginald Abbott, "Birds Don't Sing in Greek: Virginia Woolf and 'The Plumage Bill,'" in *Animals and Women: Feminist Theoretical Explorations*, ed. Carol J. Adams and Josephine Donovan (Durham: Duke University Press, 1995), 264.

88.Virginia Woolf, "The Plumage Bill," in *The Essays of Virginia Woolf*, vol. 3, *1919–1924*, ed. Andrew McNeillie (San Diego: Harcourt Brace Jovanovich, 1988), 242.

89. Woolf, "The Plumage Bill," 242.

90. Woolf, "The Plumage Bill," 242.

91. Woolf, "The Plumage Bill," 243.

92. Woolf, "The Plumage Bill," 242.

93. Abbott, "Birds Don't Sing," 274.

94. Woolf, "The Plumage Bill," 243.

95. Abbott, "Birds Don't Sing," 278.

96. William Dutcher, "Report of the A.O.U. Committee on the Protection of North American Birds," *The AUK* 15, no.1 (1898): 81.

97. Dutcher, "Report of the A.O.U. Committee," 81.

98. Dutcher, "Report of the A.O.U. Committee," 82.

99. Beers, *For the Prevention of Cruelty*, 86.

100. Price, *Flight Maps*, 72.

101. "A Plea for the Birds," *New York Times*, letter to the editor, November 16, 1897.

REFERENCES

Abbott, Reginald. "Birds Don't Sing in Greek: Virginia Woolf and 'The Plumage Bill.'" In *Animals and Women: Feminist Theoretical Explorations*, edited by Carol J. Adams and Josephine Donovan, 263–89. Durham: Duke University Press, 1995.

Allen, J. A. "The Present Wholesale Destruction of Bird-Life in the United States." *Science* 7, no. 160 (February 26, 1886): 191–95.

Barrow, Mark V., Jr. *A Passion for Birds: American Ornithology after Audubon*. Princeton, NJ: Princeton University Press, 1998.

Beers, Diane L. *For the Prevention of Cruelty: The History and Legacy of Animal Rights Activism in the United States*. Athens: Swallow Press/Ohio University Press, 2006.

Birdsall, Amelia. "A Woman's Nature: Attitudes and Identities of the Bird Hat Debate at the Turn of the 20th Century." Thesis, Haverford College, 2002.

Blair, Karen, J. *The Clubwoman as Feminist: True Womanhood Redefined, 1868–1914*. New York: Holmes and Meier, 1980.

Breton, Mary Joy. *Women Pioneers for the Environment*. Boston: Northeastern University Press, 1998.

Cart, Theodore Whaley. "The Struggle for Wildlife Protection in the United States, 1870–1900: Attitudes and Events Leading to the Lacey Act." PhD diss., University of North Carolina at Chapel Hill, 1971.

Chapman, Frank. *Autobiography of a Bird Lover.* New York: D. Appleton-Century, 1933.

Coleman, Sydney H. *Humane Society Leaders in America: With a Sketch of the Early History.* Albany, NY: American Humane Society, 1924.

Doughty, Robin W. *Feather Fashions and Bird Preservation: A Study in Nature Protection*. Berkeley: University of California Press, 1975.

Dutcher, William. "Report of the A.O.U. Committee on Protection of North American Birds." *The AUK* 15, no. 1 (1898): 81–114.

Graham, Frank, Jr. *The Audubon Ark: A History of the National Audubon Society*. New York: Alfred A. Knopf, 1990.

Grinnell, George Bird. "A Shameful Fashion." *Forest and Stream* 25 (January 7, 1886): 465.

Hornaday, William T. *Our Vanishing Wildlife: Its Extermination and Preservation*. New York: Charles Scribner's Sons, 1913.

Jewett, Sarah Orne. "A White Heron." In *Birdwatching with American Women: A Selection of Nature Writings*, edited by Deborah Strom, 112–122. New York: W. W. Norton, 1986.

Mason, Kathy S. "Harriet Hemenway and the Audubon Society, 1896–1905." *The Historian* 65, no. 1 (Fall 2002): 1–14.

Merchant, Carolyn. "Women and Conservation." In *Major Problems in American Environmental History*, edited by Caroline Merchant, 342–51. Boston: Houghton Mifflin, 2005.

———. "Women of the Progressive Conservation Movement: 1900–1916." *Environmental Review* 8 (Spring 1984): 57–85.

New York Times. "Hold Up Five Hats." January 9, 1914.

———. "Murderous Millinery." July 31, 1898.

———. "Women Discuss Cruelty: The National Council Considers the Birds and Seals." February 24, 1895.

———. "A Plea for the Birds." Letter to Editor. November 16, 1897.

Nilsson, Greta. "Birds." In *Animals and Their Legal Rights: A Survey of American Laws from 1641 to 1990*. 4th ed. Washington DC: Animal Welfare Institute, 1990.

Norwood, Vera. *Made from This Earth*. Chapel Hill: University of North Carolina Press, 1993.

Price, Jennifer. *Flight Maps: Adventures with Nature in Modern America*. New York: Basic Books, 1999.

Scarborough, Amy D. "Fashion Media's Role in the Debate on Millinery and Bird Protection in the United States in the Late Nineteenth and Early Twentieth Centuries." PhD diss., Oregon State University, 2009.

Scott, W. E. D. "The Present Condition of Some Bird Rookeries of the Gulf Coast of Florida." *The AUK* 4, no. 4 (October 1887): 276–77.

Steele, Zulma. *Angel in Top Hat.* New York: Harper and Brothers, 1942.

Strom, Deborah, ed. *Birdwatching with American Women: A Selection of Nature Writings.* New York: W. W. Norton, 1986.

Tebbel, John, and Mary Ellen Zuckerman. *The Magazine in America: 1741–1990.* New York: Oxford University Press, 1991.

Thaxter, Celia. "To Feroline W. Fox. Hotel Clifford, Cortes Street, Boston." In *Letters of Celia Thaxter*, edited by Annie Fields and Rose Lamb, 145–146. Boston: Houghton, Mifflin, 1898.

———. "To Bradford Torrey. Appledore, Isle of Shoals, off Portsmouth, May 1, 1890." In *Letters of Celia Thaxter*, edited by Annie Fields and Rose Lamb, 175–177. Boston: Houghton, Mifflin, 1898.

Welker, Robert Henry. *Birds and Men: American Birds in Science, Art, Literature, and Conservation, 1800–1900*. New York: Atheneum, 1966.

Welter, Barbara. "The Cult of True Womanhood: 1820–1860." In *Dimity Convictions: The American Woman in the Nineteenth Century.* Athens: Ohio University Press, 1976.

Woolf, Virginia. "The Plumage Bill." *The Essays of Virginia Woolf.* Vol. 3, *1919–1924*, edited by Andrew McNeillie. San Diego: Harcourt Brace Jovanovich, 1988.

Chapter 5

Corpse "Contamination" as a Religious Approach to Fur

Sidney Blankenship

The word "fur" does not appear in the King James Bible, suggesting the paucity of native fur-bearing animals and the lack of presumed necessity because of climate and geography. A concept that does occur in the Old Testament (and in rabbinic literature), however, is corpse "contamination," primarily in relation to cultic access in the temple. This idea of contamination applies to contact with a human corpse, but it also involves contact with any dead creature within the full range of taxonomy in one measure or another, as seen in conjunction with the dietary laws of Leviticus 11 (especially verses 27–28, which cover contact with the corpse of "an animal that walks on the flat of its feet"). This concept reflects relationships between humans and the life and death of animals throughout the Bible. Such contact is not only a matter of ritual and cultic purity for the priests that informs the written tradition in which it appears. It also is an aspect of the Creator's holiness. This relationship involves more than what we think of as physical hygiene.

This research will filter out several relevant textual appearances of the concept with its theological implications. It will also note the historic disconnect between wearing animal fur as a consumer-driven luxury and indigenous and subsistence usage of fur, with its communicative function in clan-based tribal systems. Clearly, the ethical focus rests on the hunting, trapping, killing, and/or massive confinement for exploitative commerce of living creatures who have been removed from their natural habitat. There is enormous ecological disruption when respect for live animals (individually or collectively) is abandoned, and therein lies a deepening spiritual estrangement. Even some biblical examples seem unconscionable, such as Samson tying three hundred foxes' tails together and using them to set the fields of the Philistines on fire.

It is not easy to deal with biblical history in its raw unfiltered form (or its perception—the New English Bible, NEB, has "jackals" in Judges 15:4), and it is necessary to delve into the most enduring aspects of one's tradition to find ethical principles that exercise the divine intention of the Spirit for the souls of both humankind and animals.

FUR TRADE AS A MEDIUM OF EXCHANGE IN THE NORTHERN HEMISPHERE

Western expansion into the northern regions of the unexplored Western Hemisphere in the sixteenth to the eighteenth centuries by Europeans, and later by Russians from the Pacific, left an indelible mark on the natural history of native species exploited for skins, hides, and fur. It also polarized tribes who were at the colonists' mercy or who took sides in the escalating demands of one nation or another as they vied for commercial dominance. An ethical understanding from the currency of religious thought that relied on the recently translated King James Version (KJV) Bible of that era lacked the essential popular focus on a theology of nature as divine creation. Neither was there sufficient knowledge in science or geography to weigh the activity's impact. No doubt, there were some who looked upon these developments with concern, but a theological awareness from the scriptures of the Reformation did not prevail against this trade.

The wearing of fur (or animal skins) has long been a historic phenomenon for humans seeking to survive in colder climates. European trade in furs with the New World was primarily a northern commercial enterprise, whereas in more southerly latitudes—Virginia, for example—transatlantic trade involved tobacco or agricultural products. With the Spanish explorers from Mexico to South America, the quest was for gold. In claims for God and country, European Christianity sought dominance with various means of conversion to a religion in which there was no common cultural understanding of the natural world. Furs became a kind of default among native tribes in North America lacking any other valuable resource to exchange. There was no prevailing ethical reckoning for the depletion of animals that was taking place. In the words of Bob Dylan, "How many deaths will it take till he knows?"[1] How many exploited animals and species suffer because religious traditions do not voice appropriate concerns?

Subsequent European colonization displaced indigenous peoples and species from their native environments, leaving fragmented natural ecosystems supplanted by the introduction of foreign domesticated animals and human "economic" development. A map of "native trade routes" in North America before European contact (ca. 1430) is given by Ian Barnes in his *Historical*

Atlas of Native Americans.[2] Native animals (and plants) at that time could only be known in natural distribution from this kind of contact, which sometimes determined tribal migratory movements. The area depicted by Barnes is surprising in its extent, but the impact on regional fauna was minimal. Local attire, in terms of availability for survival, was practical, and furs were part of that. Deerskins and bison hides dominated in the great expanse of the prairies, but many diverse habitats and species were represented, with unique animals, reverential customs, and ecological awareness. In the subsistence way of life, there was no commercial supply of goods to access.

The fur trade of the French through the St. Lawrence Seaway and into the Great Lakes was of great consequence to Native American tribes. Francis I, King of France, sent Jacques Cartier in search of a Northwest Passage to China in 1534.[3] Thereafter, a fleet of 150 vessels under Henry IV was established to import fish to France from the Newfoundland Banks. This contact was the beginning (by 1578) of fur as a business. Besides foxes and other furbearers, by 1580 beaver pelts were an "important trade item."[4] Samuel de Champlain further explored and mapped the area into the Great Lakes in the early 1600s. By 1609 Henry Hudson had secured the British presence in the region. The competition for trade in furs culminated in warring alliances of the Iroquois siding with the English and the Hurons aligning with the French. The Dutch founded a trading post on the Hudson River in 1624. Eventually, the exhausted supply of furs (and disease-induced deaths) caused an upheaval in relations between tribes, traders, and European interests. These conflicts persisted throughout the seventeenth century, but in 1701 at Montreal, the Iroquois, exhausted by the French and their Native allies to the West, declared their neutrality in any future imperial wars between the French and English.[5]

The fur trade continued in the eighteenth century with westward exploration and the former thirteen English colonies' newly elected government of independence in 1776. By 1800 the Pacific Northwest was a "lucrative region for fur trading with local Native American tribes."[6] The Lewis and Clark expedition (1804–1806) opened an overland trail for trade in furs and pelts, but Captain James Cook already had arrived by a Pacific voyage in 1778 off Vancouver Island and had established a trade in sea otter furs with local tribes there. These were sold for high prices in China, a market also exploited by Russian traders. This proved to be catastrophic for that species and caused the same kind of tribal conflicts (and death from disease) that had resulted in the Northeast. The English fur trade, beginning with Hudson's Bay Company under Charles II in 1670 and continuing with its successors and competitors, is given credit for Native Americans "entering the capitalist system" in other items "to compensate for the eventual decline in the fur trade."[7]

Unfortunately, this history (real as it is) offers no ethical basis for cultural resolution in terms of indigenous spiritual beliefs and no positive religious insight into a Christian theology of the natural world. It is that continuing legacy that is our concern.

THE IDENTITY OF FUR-BEARING ANIMALS

The historic application of taxonomic nomenclature, both from cultural experience and from scriptural reference in translation, is important in view of modern usage. The word "fur" is commonly accepted more from commercial appropriation than anything else. It originally had a Germanic etymology as a "sheath" or outer covering of an animal.[8] This broadens the definition of potential contamination, as the modern focus is on the softness and desirable quality of a mammal's outer coat. Only mammals produce "fur" in that sense. Reptiles, birds, and fish all have "skin" or some outer covering, from the hardened scales of the crocodile to the feathers of birds. For some species it is more difficult to remove. The Jewish rabbis who compiled the Mishnah (ca. 200 BC–AD 200) wrestled with this issue as a matter of taxonomy and scriptural reference, as we shall observe later. Their designations of animals who were "clean" (*Ṯa-H-O-R*) or "unclean" (*Ṯa-Me-A*) were based on Leviticus 11 and Deuteronomy 14 in the Mosaic law.[9] Both edibility and corpse contamination are broadly addressed in the Mishnah, and the attention to different categories of animals is unique in its concept of the Lord's "holiness."

Two distinct taxonomic categories of mammals contain many of the most prized fur-bearing animals: the family Mustelidae and the order Rodentia.[10] The former includes mink, weasels, ferrets, badgers, and otters as well as the highly exploited ermine and sable of the sub-Arctic regions. These are all carnivores. Rodentia includes squirrels, beavers, and the chinchilla, who are herbivores. The members of the Canidae family (dogs and their relatives) long have been used for fur, especially foxes (e.g., the red fox and the arctic fox), but even coyotes and wolves. Then there are bears and the exotic skins of the members of Felidae (cats) and Viverridae (civets) with the allure of their coats. In the sea there are fur-bearing seals. These all find their own (seemingly unusual) place in the summary categories of Leviticus 11, but there is no category of "fur-bearing animals," and the most common use of skins in the Bible is that of sheep and goats, though wool was a shepherd's garment, and "sack-cloth" was made from goats' hair. The Old Testament Hebrew terminology employs the word for "skin" or "skins" (*`-O-R* and *`-O-R-O-Th*)[11] to embrace the broader definition across taxonomic boundaries. Lagomorphs (rabbits, hares, and pikas) also have soft fur, as does the hyrax, but their skins would all be corpse contaminants in Leviticus 11 and Deuteronomy 14.

Camelids also have thick coats, as do many species of Bovidae (sheep, goats, yak, musk ox, bison, etc.). Other hoofed mammals such as deer, horses, donkeys, and swine have been taken for their hides, though equines and swine are prohibited in Leviticus 11. The worst instincts of humanity are expressed when satisfaction of the "lust of the flesh, the lust of the eye, and the pride of life" (1 John 2:16) is sought through the mortality of some living creature. This leads to a focus on the ethics of animal "products" that do not require the creature's death. This cannot be explored fully here and has many variables. The example of camel's hair seems to fall into this category. John the Baptist's apparel as described in the fifth-century Codex Beza, which uses the Greek term *derris*,[12] or "skin" (of the camel), could put him at odds with Leviticus 11:8—"of their flesh you shall not eat, and their carcass [obviously including the skin] you shall not touch." The Ebionite gospel account of John's prophetic witness[13] tends toward a vegan Jewish Christian correction of his diet, but his clothing is not otherwise addressed. The Slavonic text of Josephus reinforces the reflection of Jesus in Matthew 11:8 that John's clothing was not "soft [or delicate] raiment."

Animals in the families Canidae (dog), Felidae (cat), and Ursidae (bears) generally have thick coats of fur or hair. In the Old Testament many of these larger animals (lions, bears, wolves, leopards) were agents of the Lord's judgment for Israel's sin. The lesson from the Lord to Job in Job 38–39 regarding animals such as the crocodile, hippo, and leviathan, even the "wild ass," was that His creation was not ultimately intended for human use. A pattern of relationships has evolved within nature that limits the extent of interaction between species, for mutual benefit and freedom. Humans have developed attitudes toward many animals that are culturally reinforced but often misleading and not based on direct personal experience. Religious traditions have at their core a message of "righteousness, peace, and joy in the holy spirit" (Romans 14:17) a remedy for the abuse of animals. Human institutions often provide little or no immersion in nature that reveals this truth. The instruction "Love not this world, nor the things of this world"[14] does not cast aspersions on the created order but reflects on the character of human society. When asked where the kingdom could be found, Jesus said (according to the Gospel of Thomas), "If your leaders say to you, 'Behold, the kingdom is in heaven,' then the birds of heaven will precede you. If they say to you, 'It is in the sea,' then the fish will precede you. Rather, the kingdom is within you and it is outside you. When you know yourselves, then you will be known, and you will understand that you are children of the living Father." Also in Thomas, Jesus said, "Know what is before your face . . . "[15] This is the *parousia* (the "presence") in nature that one experiences with living animals.

Cultural heritage presents a variety of responses to naturally occurring species in different parts of the world, with its geographic panorama of species. Often there is a deep thread of collective consensus about any given species due to either familiarity or xenophobia experienced by human and animal. This may be real or imagined, often involving stories and myths. The taxonomic and evolutionary boundaries for interaction and coexistence are historic and innate. Yet the consequences of their human transgression are rarely explored. It is only when such transgression results in great changes, loss, or failure that such a religious response as one sees in the Mosaic animal texts of Leviticus 11 appears. This response gives expression to the awareness presumed from archaeology in Canaan registered as early as the third millennium BC. According to French excavators in Sidon over the past fifteen years, fragmentary bone deposits demonstrate the transition from an era of hunting large animals (carnivores such as lions and bears but also Mesopotamian fallow deer, aurochs, swine, and even hippopotamuses!) to a sharp decline when their presence was no longer attested.[16] When domestication of the ox, sheep, goat, and donkey became widespread within the broader cultural framework, the collective consciousness of familiarity in the natural world was altered.

The restrictions of Leviticus 11 are comprehensive even as they appear, but it is also apparent that their perfection required a priestly mitigation. References to the importance of deceased animals in terms of human interaction denote the measure of "divine holiness" involved in the spiritual dimension of a fellow creature's death, the absent referent. The terms of corpse contact are distinct across taxonomic categories, and none of the fur-bearing animals are permitted, either as food or in terms of contact with their "corpse" (in Hebrew, *Na-Bhe-La-H*).[17] This much is in the Levitical text. The usual remedy for contact is to "wash one's self in water," and "you will be unclean until evening." The additional requirement for one who "picks up the carcass" (Jerusalem Bible trans.), who must "wash his clothes" as well, is included in verse 28. This is not just a tidy deference to occasional inevitabilities (though it is at least that). As with any prescribed ritual, it intends a deeper awareness.

In the eighteenth century, Elijah, the Gaon of Wilna, clarified that "no creatures having life convey or contract uncleanness, except man."[18] The Hebrew terms relate only to the animal's death and contact with its corpse. "As I live, saith the Lord!" is an interjection that directs attention to life as residing in the victorious God of Israel. A look at the animals of the Bible who fall within the boundaries of the modern commercial fur trade seems warranted. Foxes, hares, ferrets, weasels, wolves, lions, leopards, hyrax, river otters, dogs, jackals, and hyenas are all mammals indigenous to Israel, but there is no record of their being commercially exploited for "fur." (The modern Hebrew term is *Pa-R-Wa-H*.[19] It does not appear in the biblical Old Testament or in the Mishnah.) The difference between the "animals that walk on the palms of their feet" (Lev. 11:27–28) and the smaller "creeping things on the ground" (vv. 29–30) plays a significant part in the amount of their corpse that effects contamination by contact in the Mishnah: an olive's bulk for the former and a lentil's bulk for the latter.

Even though uses for fur in the modern sense do not seem to be present, several animals in both taxonomic categories previously mentioned, even mice, are evaluated in reference to corpse contact, in which their skins become an issue (cf. *Mishnah*, Hullin 9:1ff).[20] A majority of fur-bearing animals exploited commercially for fur in the present day fall into these two categories, perhaps all except the aquatic species. Fur seals would be considered aquatic and subject to Deuteronomy 14:9–10 and Leviticus 11:9–12, where the term *She-Qe-Ts* (in KJV, "abomination")[21] first appears in the lists, a rather pejorative term in modern usage in view of the goodness of all creatures described in Genesis 1. An Assyrian cognate for "impure" is also offered, but even there, the collective use of the term, absorbing much of the definition of *Ṯa-Me-A* in all prohibitions across taxonomic categories, suggests a separation between humankind and those species whose postmortem use (either in diet or in other corpse contamination) can have a detrimental influence on one's own human soul (Lev. 11:43–46). To *promote* the death of fur-bearing creatures, or indeed any *permitted* animal in the lists of these two chapters, seems totally contrary to a Jewish or Christian animal ethic.

The skins of so-called clean animals who were permitted as edible were sometimes used as clothing and for other purposes (e.g., scrolls for writing materials). Examples are common in the Bible. Elijah's cloak (possibly made of goatskin) even had miraculous properties and was passed on to his successor Elisha when Elijah was taken up to heaven in a whirlwind. The exclusionary anomalies of the camel and the swine are notable. Both are "unclean" in terms of edibility and corpse contamination. The camel "skin" mentioned earlier for John the Baptist (Mark 1:6) in Codex Beza is a rare translation, and it does not appear in the parallel synoptic passage Matthew 3:4. All other major manuscripts have "hair" (in Greek, *thrix* or *trichas*) in both books, and like wool, this term would not presume a hide with the hair on it. The NEB describes a "rough coat of camel's hair," but there is no textual variation for the "leather girdle [or belt]," which is presumed to be made from the skin of a "clean" animal.

Any ethical approach to commercial items needs to focus on the identity of the source (i.e., the dead animal) rather than the finished product, whose assiduous preparation often obscures moral concern. It is this alienation of knowledge and sensitivity that a religious approach must disallow. The modern fashion usage of mink, chinchilla, fox, ermine, sable, and other furs is tailored to luxury, rarely employed for a practical need with no other option. The older trade in furs and pelts included sea otters and beavers, whose furs fell out of popular use only when the times changed and when supplies were depleted. As a fur-bearer, the river otter was identified as indigenous to Palestine by H. B. Tristram in the late nineteenth century.[22]

Perhaps the most egregious assault on a species for its hide in recent history was that of the American bison, which was driven to near extinction in the late nineteenth century. The original motivation was to clear the landscape of the species *and* eliminate Native American culture with it: animals were skinned, and their carcasses were left to rot on the prairie. But when their massive thick hides became commercially useful in the Industrial Revolution, their fate was sealed. Bison do have extremely soft "wool" that is shed on an annual basis, often as large intact patches left lying on the ground. This raises the question, again, of non-domesticated animal products such as deer antlers, which are also shed annually. But the question of wool, whose shearing over time changes the nature of the species, would seem even more ethically suspect than such annual deposits of natural processes. This criticism is also true of animals used for dairy and other purposes, even if the animal's corpse is not immediately involved. In terms of "products" from naturally deceased animals, however, even those animals permitted for food who die of themselves, subject one to corpse contamination under the Mosaic law if there is contact or handling (Lev. 11:39–40).

Modern research has ushered in changes to several terms and translations of biblical references to animal identity. The older "badgers' skins" (KJV) that were claimed for use as curtains and to cover the sacred items of the wilderness tabernacle in transit are no longer a popular translation for the Hebrew term *Ta-H̱a-Sh-I-M.*[23] This reveals an opening into inconsistencies in the translation. Badgers would be "unclean" for both food and corpse contact according to Leviticus 11, but so would be the Revised Standard Version replacement, "seal skins," or even the "dugong" skin used for sandals. In the Mishnah, Rabbi Judah deferred to "preparation for use" as a change in contact status for such animals.[24] Samson's "foxes" are *Shu-`a-L-I-M*, a Hebrew term (perhaps via Turkish or Persian) from which comes the word "jackal." The "foxes, the little foxes" in the Song of Solomon 2:15 are described using this same term, but in a very different context of historic impression. Even so, there the NEB has "jackals, little jackals." Of the eight "creeping things on the ground" (Lev. 11:29–30), the meaning of several terms is disputed, which is extraordinary given the specificity (and scope) of the contamination that can result from even a lentil's bulk of the referenced animal's corpse, as in the Mishnah. A recent tendency in translation sees more reptiles in the list, but the weasel, the mouse, the ferret, and the mole are all historic mammals with fur that are ensconced in Greek and Latin translation. Since the Mishnah is concerned with volume of the corpse for contamination, the question is whether or not the "skin" (*`-O-R*) of these animals should be considered together with their flesh in this bulk determination.[25] In that context Rabbi Judah stated that "the weasel is like to the lizard" for such a purpose. Both animals appear in the list of eight. The Rabbis' discussion in Hullin 9:2 evolves into a physical investigation of certain animal features, regarding where the skin can, or cannot, be easily separated from the underlying flesh.

ETHICAL CONCERNS FOR PURITY IN BIBLICAL REFERENCE

The concepts of purity and holiness are of primary interest throughout the Bible. (Note the Holy One of Israel in Isaiah.) The understanding of world creation and human history had an ethical basis that always included animals, even if within the sacrificial context. The call of Abraham and the promises to Israel were never bereft of animal relevance. The animal covenants made within the scriptures are often overlooked[26] in deference to the successful physical inheritance of the "promised land," but that promise was never unconditional. Older Middle Eastern religious traditions of the sacrificial system in some form preceded the Mosaic covenant, reflecting on what the priestly Bible account of the Flood would suggest was a world where the consequences of permission to eat flesh (Genesis 9:3–6), apparently never endorsed before the Flood, were fully on display. Thus, the accounts in the Mosaic law of the Lord's "holiness" appear to be a statutory basis for awareness of the unsettled enmity between human and animal, an ethical demarcation providing taxonomic awareness toward peaceful reconciliation. Ritual animal sacrifice to the deity was narrowed to a focus that called into question its very existence. Its eventual conclusion is revealed prophetically in the messianic texts and in the wisdom literature, in which the chosen people are ever more invested in its symbolic spiritual transformation. The Mishnah reflects this transitional legal response in rabbinic Judaism, and the essential Christian frame of reference in the person of Jesus sought vindication and understanding of ethical implications for the animals. They were based on the same textual heritage.

Jesus was not focused on fashion: "Don't worry about what you will eat, or what you will wear."[27] The outward appearance, if anything, often reflected hypocrisy. Ostentation, opulence, and grandeur from the Roman influence on Herod the Great were rejected, and the temple in which sacrificial activities occurred only magnified animal injustice as a cruel spectacle. According to apocryphal sources, Jesus was invested in a communion with the natural world's animals at birth.[28] When he came for his baptism, John said, "Behold the Lamb of God."[29] A dove rested on his head afterward.[30] Jesus said, "Not a sparrow falls from heaven without the Father's knowledge," even as the price of the little bird was rehearsed for sacrificial purposes in two

Gospel accounts.[31] The apostles were to be "wise as serpents, and innocent as doves."[32] Jesus said, "I send you forth as sheep among the wolves."[33] He marveled at the faith of the Canaanite woman who implored him that even the little dogs ate the crumbs from the master's table.[34] The fishermen were transformed into "fishers of men."[35] "Foxes have holes, and birds of the air have nests, but the Son of Man has no place to lay his head."[36] He referred to Herod Antipas as "that fox,"[37] and there the Greek text has *alopex*, with the assumption that it was not referring to the "jackal" (though the Hebrew or Aramaic term could have been mistaken in translation). He offered himself as a mother hen protecting her chicks.[38] He rode into Jerusalem on a donkey.[39] His "cleansing" the temple of animal victims and those who purveyed them was central to his running afoul of the priestly rulers.[40] His crucifixion occurred on the day of the Passover lamb's sacrifice;[41] he was "lifted up" as was the brazen serpent in the wilderness.[42] The list could go on. In John's Apocalypse he is "the Lion of the Tribe of Judah"[43] who is worthy to open the scroll and its seven seals.

One has to rely on these Biblical examples, as well as the writings of his followers, to get a real sense of his animal ethic. His engagement with the religious leaders gives us a glimpse into the conflicts that involved principles and interpretations that are revealed in the Mishnah.[44] Yet he does not seek a detailed casuistic approach to the satisfaction of those problems. He inserts his own personal existence into the equation. In the *Epistle of Barnabas*, he is not only the Passover lamb, but also the red heifer who was immolated for her ashes in the water of purification and also the "scape-goat" who bore the sins of the people out into the wilderness.[45] The Qumran documents offer a wealth of evidence as background material to bridge rabbinic Judaism and Christianity. Yet some principles are never fully aligned. The question of whether one should "violate" the Sabbath rest by pulling one's ox out of a ditch is answered no in the Qumran community,[46] whereas Jesus is fully sympathetic, saying yes even to the activity of satisfying the thirst of an ox or donkey, despite the day's sanctity, in Luke 13:15.

As for Old Testament texts related to some smaller animals, we observe that the Qumran manuscripts of the book of Leviticus have very little variation from the (un-pointed) Hebrew text as we still have it. Two paleo-Hebrew fragments of Leviticus 11 (2QpaleoLev and 11QpaleoLev) do have slight variants that favor the Samaritan and LXX (Greek) texts, and 11QpaleoLev has animals who "go on their *bellies*" (*Ga-H-O[-N]*),[47] such as the "serpent" (in verse 42 of the MT), appearing before the "animals that walk on their paws," in verse 27. Of even more significance is the reconstructed "Halakhic Letter" (4QMMT) in which "concerning the hid[es and the bones of the unclean animals; they shall not make] [from their bones] and from their hides, handles of ves[sels]."[48] This would seem to apply to all "unclean" categories in the chapter, expressing further clarity than merely lifting up or moving the remains, in terms of items made from their corpse or their skins. These texts may cause us to reassess Peter's visit to Simon "the tanner" in Acts 10, Peter's vision of the sheet let down from heaven with the "unclean" animals (which he did *not* kill and eat), and his report to the Jerusalem church in Acts 11.

To summarize Native American experience relative to this rarified Near Eastern tradition, one has to note the ambiance within nature as opposed to the mores of a highly structured and urbanized civilization. The longer one engages in abstract explanations, the greater likelihood there is of estrangement from the mysteries informed by the Spirit in the natural environment. The attire of the shaman, or medicine man, was a communicative reminder of the animals that the tribe had a duty to respect. A Blackfoot medicine man was described by the artist George Catlin in the nineteenth century as being adorned "with tails and tips of almost everything that swims, flies, or runs."[49] The bear is generally credited with the greatest healing medicine, not as a talisman but from within his living spirit. Also, in the portrait of prairie Native Americans in full wolf-skin coverings who (before the horse culture dominated) could sneak up on bison without alarm, what is remarkable is that the buffalo were more apt to fear an actual human than they would a wolf.[50] Instead of a "wolf in sheep's clothing," we have natives as "sheep in wolves' clothing." The necessary items and dress for ritual dance often include remains of various animals, but rarely live ones. For the Hopi Snake Dance, a ceremony of purification and renewal in late August, the dancers wear feathered headdress, kilts, and sticks painted like lightning, fox skins tied on the back, shell necklaces, a "snake whip" made of eagle feathers, turtle-shell rattles below the knees, and a pouch of sacred cornmeal. Live snakes are gathered up in the first four days from the desert and kept in a kiva, and after the nine-day ceremony and dance (with the live snakes), they are returned to the desert.[51]

It is difficult to fault one's ancestors in the communicative use of nature's remnants to inform respect for the living. One may question the understanding of the statement in Genesis 3:21 where God made "animal skins" for the first couple's clothing, even after they had fashioned fig leaves together to cover their nakedness. This may be part of a lost hermeneutic in the earliest sources, or it may simply reflect a glimpse into the ancient reality of prehistory. A look at the tradition of the Rechabites and the Nazirites of the Old Testament would substantiate the view of civilization as an alienation from the natural processes and pure ethic of God's creation. Several examples are striking in the kind of biblical ethic that later applied to the traders and consumers of "luxury" goods like animal furs. One is that of ivory and the elephants. Solomon is said to have had an ivory throne,[52] and Ahab had a house made of ivory,[53] but the prophet Amos railed against this abuse.[54] In

Ezekiel's day the commerce of ivory in Tyre fell under similar prophetic condemnation,[55] a precursor of Babylon; and in the book of Revelation, ivory was implicated in the same fateful activity laid at the doorstep of Rome.[56] A second item is silk, a foreign product capable of seducing the daughters of Jerusalem for the wrong purpose.[57]

One also may call attention to Canaan's trade in royal "purple" (from a sea mollusk, whose shells, after extraction, were heaped up at Sidon).[58] The Roman soldiers put a purple robe on Jesus, mocking him as king before his torture and crucifixion.[59] Fur, ivory tusks, rhino horn, tiger parts, and other "rare" items from animals' bodies should have no sanction or approval in Jewish, Christian, or any other ethics, and that awareness has to be sustained even more diligently in the modern world of commerce. No little creature deserves the wretched fate that the fur industry offers. "Respect Mother Earth and her giving ways, or trade away our silvan days," says a modern Native American song.[60] I cared for an arctic fox years ago. His soul was as pure as his white coat in the winter snow. He would take a caramel from between my fingers and never touch them. This essay is dedicated to his memory.

NOTES

1. Bob Dylan, "Blowin' in the Wind," in *The Lyrics: 1961–2012* (New York: Simon & Schuster, 2016), 53.

2. Ian Barnes, *The Historical Atlas of Native Americans* (New York: Chartwell Books, 2015), 29.

3. Barnes, *Historical Atlas*, 52.

4. Barnes, *Historical Atlas*, 37.

5. Barnes, *Historic Atlas*, 88.

6. Barnes, *Historical Atlas*, 153.

7. Barnes, *Historical Atlas*, 179.

8. *The American College Dictionary* (New York: Random House, 1960), first published 1947, s.v. "fur."

9. *Biblia Hebraica Stuttgartensia*, 4th ed., ed. K. Elliger and W. Rudolph (Stuttgart: Deutsche Bibelgesellschaft, 1990).

10. David Burnie and Don E. Wilson, eds., *Animal: The Definitive Visual Guide to the World's Wildlife* (New York: DK Publishing, 2001). I have used this publication of the Smithsonian for taxonomy throughout.

11. Francis Brown, S. R. Driver, and Charles A. Briggs, eds., *A Hebrew and English Lexicon of the Old Testament*, based on Gesenius's *Lexicon* and *Thesaurus*, trans. Edward Robinson (Oxford: Clarendon Press, 1951), s.v. *`-O-R.*

12. Mark 1:6, *The Greek New Testament*, ed. Barbara Aland et al., 4th rev. ed. (Stuttgart: Deutsche Bibelgesellschaft, 1994), Apparatus. Cf. Matt. 3:4.

13. Keith Akers, *The Lost Religion of Jesus: Simple Living and Nonviolence in Early Christianity* (New York: Lantern Books, 2000).

14. 1 John 2:15–16.

15. *The Gospel According to Thomas*, Coptic text established and trans. A. Guillaumont et al. (Leiden, the Netherlands: E. J. Brill, 1976), 2–5.

16. Claude Doumet-Serhal, "Sidon—Canaan's Firstborn," *Biblical Archaeology Review* 43, no. 4 (July–August 2017): 22, 25n.

17. Brown, Driver, and Briggs, *Hebrew and English Lexicon*, s.v. *Na-Bhe-La-H.*

18. Elijah, the Gaon of Wilna (1720–97), "The Rules of Uncleanness," in Herbert Danby, trans., *The Mishnah: Translated from the Hebrew with Introduction and Brief Explanatory Notes* (1933; Oxford: Oxford University Press, 1992), appendix IV, 18(c), 803.

19. *Oxford English–Hebrew Dictionary* (Oxford: Oxford University Press, 1998), s.v. "fur."

20. Danby, *The Mishnah*, "Kodashim," Hullin 9:1ff.

21. Brown, Driver, and Briggs, *Hebrew and English Lexicon*, s.v. *She-Qe-Ts.*

22. Henry Baker Tristram, *The Fauna and Flora of Palestine: The Survey of Western Palestine* (London: Committee of the Palestine Exploration Fund, 1884), with illustrations, in the Sackler Library, Oxford University.

23. Cf. *Biblia Hebraica Stuttgartensia. `-O-R Ta-Ha-Sh* was used for temple drapes and coverings in Exod. 25, 26, 35, and 36 and also in Num. 4. But in Ezek. 16:10, it was material for footwear. NEB has "porpoise" hides.

24. Danby, *The Mishnah*, "Kodashim," Hullin 9:2.525.

25. Danby, *The Mishnah*, "Kodashim," Hullin 9:2.525.

26. For example, in Hosea 6:6–7, Ephraim's "transgression of the covenant" is described as desiring (animal) sacrifice and burnt offerings more than mercy and the "knowledge of God."

27. Matt. 6:25ff.

28. J. K. Elliott, ed., *The Apocryphal New Testament: A Collection of Apocryphal Christian Literature in English Translation* (Oxford: Clarendon Press, 1993), many examples. Cf. William Hone, comp., *The Lost Books of the Bible* (New York: Bell Publishing, 1979).

29. John 1:29.

30. Matt. 3:16; Mark 1:10; Luke 3:22; John 1:32. For massive construction of *columbaria* in Herodian Jerusalem, cf. Boaz Zissu, "New Testament Tower? This Place Is for the Birds," *Biblical Archaeology Review* 35, no. 3 (May–June 2009): 30–37, 66–67.

31. Of the sparrow, "not one falls to earth without the Father" (two sold for an *assarion*), Matt. 10:29; in Luke 12:6, "not one is lost from God's presence" (five sold for two *assaria*).

32. Matt. 10:16; also in the Gospel of Thomas.

33. Matt. 10:16; Luke 10:3.

34. Matt. 15:27; Mark 7:28 has little dogs beneath the table eating crumbs from the children.

35. Matt. 4:19; Mark 1:17.

36. Matt. 8:20; Luke 9:58.

37. Luke 13:32.

38. Matt. 23:37. Cf. the male eagle's activity with its young in Deut. 32:11.

39. Matt. 21:4–7; John 12:14–15.

40. Matt. 21:12–13; Mark 11:15–17; Luke 19:45–46; and John 2:13–17, early in his ministry.

41. This specific timing is assumed from John's gospel.

42. Direct reference to Moses and the "brazen serpent" in John 3:14; also "when I [the Son of Man] am lifted up" in John 8:28; 12:32, 34.

43. Rev. 5:5.

44. For example, Mark 7:1–23, on washing the hands before a meal and the meaning of "Corban."

45. *Epistle of Barnabas*, in *The Apostolic Fathers*, trans. Kirsopp Lake (Cambridge, MA: Harvard University Press, 1966), vol. 1, chaps. 7, 8, 10, and 12.

46. "Damascus Document" (column xi), in Florentino Garcia Martinez, *The Dead Sea Scrolls: The Qumran Texts in English*, 2nd ed., trans. Wilfred G. E. Watson (Leiden, the Netherlands: E. J. Brill, 1996), 42.

47. "2QpaleoLev" and "11QpaleoLev" in Robert A. Kugler and Kyung S. Baek, *Leviticus at Qumran: Text and Interpretation*, supplement to *Vetus Testamentum* 173 (Leiden, the Netherlands: Brill, 2017), 20–21.

48. "Halakhic Letter 4QMMT," composite text in Martinez, *Dead Sea Scrolls*, 77.

49. James A. Maxwell, ed., *America's Fascinating Indian Heritage: The First Americans, Their Customs, Art, History and How They Lived* (Pleasantville, NY: Reader's Digest Association, 1978), 188.

50. Maxwell, *Fascinating Indian Heritage*, 159.

51. Maxwell, *Fascinating Indian Heritage*, 212–13. It is not public; only Hopi tribal members and participants from the Snake and Antelope religious societies attend.

52. 1 Kings 10:18, 2 Chron. 9:17.

53. 1 Kings 22:39.

54. Amos 3:15; 6:4.

55. Ezek. 27:6, 15.

56. Rev. 18:12.

57. Ezek. 16:10, 13; cf. Rev. 18:12. But note Prov. 31:22, where (in the KJV) along with "purple," silk is a material in the wardrobe of the "virtuous woman." The Hebrew term has been subject to revision.

58. C. L. Wickwire, "Purple," *The Interpreter's Dictionary of the Bible* (Nashville, TN: Abingdon Press, 1962), 3:969–70. Cf. A. S. Kapelrud, "Sidon," *Interpreter's Dictionary*, 4:343–44.

59. Mark 15:17, 20; John 19:2, 5.

60. Walela and Joanne Shenandoah, "Mother Earth," performed on CD *Sacred Ground: A Tribute to Mother Earth* (Boulder, CO: Silver Wave Records, 2005).

REFERENCES

Akers, Keith. *The Lost Religion of Jesus: Simple Living and Nonviolence in Early Christianity.* New York: Lantern Books, 2000.

Aland, Kurt. *Synopsis Quattuor Evangeliorum: Locis parallelis Evangeliorum Apocryphorum et Patrum adhibitis edidit. Editio tertia decima revisa.* Stuttgart: Deutsche Bibelgesellschaft, 1990.

Barnes, Ian. *The Historical Atlas of Native Americans.* New York: Chartwell Books, 2015.

Biblia Hebraica Stuttgartensia. Edited by K. Elliger and W. Rudolph. 4th ed. Stuttgart: Deutsche Bibelgesellschaft, 1990.

Brown, Francis, S. R. Driver, and Charles A. Briggs, eds. *A Hebrew and English Lexicon of the Old Testament.* Based on Gesenius's *Lexicon* and *Thesaurus.* Translated by Edward Robinson. Oxford: Clarendon Press, 1951.

Burnie, David, and Don E. Wilson, eds. *Animal: The Definitive Visual Guide to the World's Wildlife.* New York: DK Publishing, 2001.

Danby, Herbert, trans. *The Mishnah: Translated from the Hebrew with Introduction and Brief Explanatory Notes.* 1933. Oxford: Oxford University Press, 1992.

Doumet-Serhal, Claude. "Sidon—Canaan's Firstborn." *Biblical Archaeology Review* 43, no. 4 (July–August 2017): 20–29.

Dylan, Bob. "Blowin' in the Wind." In *The Lyrics: 1961–2012.* New York: Simon & Schuster, 2016.

Elliott, J. K. *The Apocryphal New Testament: A Collection of Apocryphal Christian Literature in an English Translation.* Oxford: Clarendon Press, 1993.

Epistle of Barnabas. In *The Apostolic Fathers*, translated by Kirsopp Lake, vol. 1. Loeb Classical Library. 1912. Cambridge, MA: Harvard University Press, 1966.

Gospel According to Thomas. Coptic text established and translated by A. Guillaumont, H.-Ch. Puech, G. Quispel, W. Till, and Yassah `Abd Al-Masih. Leiden, the Netherlands: E. J. Brill, 1976.

The Greek New Testament. Edited by Barbara Aland, Kurt Aland, Johannes Karavidopoulos, Carlo M. Martini, and Bruce M. Metzger. 4th rev. ed. Stuttgart: Deutsche Bibelgesellschaft, 1994.

Kapelrud, A. S. "Sidon." *Interpreter's Dictionary of the Bible.* Vol. 4. Nashville, TN: Abingdon Press, 1962.

Kugler, Robert A., and Kyung S. Baek. *Leviticus at Qumran: Text and Interpretation.* Supplement to *Vetus Testamentum* 173. Leiden, the Netherlands: Brill, 2017.

Martinez, Florentino Garcia. *The Dead Sea Scrolls Translated: The Qumran Texts in English.* 2nd ed. Translated by Wilfred G. E. Watson. Leiden, the Netherlands: E. J. Brill, 1996.

Maxwell, James A., ed. *America's Fascinating Indian Heritage: The First Americans, Their Customs, Art, History and How They Lived.* Pleasantville, NY: Reader's Digest Association, 1978.

Tristram, Henry Baker. *Fauna and Flora of Palestine: The Survey of Western Palestine.* London: Committee of the Palestine Exploration Fund, 1884. Sackler Library, Oxford University.

Walela and Joanne Shenandoah. "Mother Earth." Performed on CD *Sacred Ground: A Tribute to Mother Earth.* Boulder, CO: Silver Wave Records, 2005.

Wickwire, C. L. "Purple." *Interpreter's Dictionary of the Bible.* Vol. 3. Nashville, TN: Abingdon Press, 1962.

Zissu, Boaz. "New Testament Tower? This Place Is for the Birds." *Biblical Archaeology Review* 35, no. 3 (May–June 2009): 30–37.

Chapter 6

Of Ermines, Cats, and "the Best-Dressed Pontiff Ever"

The Ethics of Fur-Trimmed Clerical Garb

Kurt Remele

In an article titled "Benedict, the Best-Dressed Pope" in the *Los Angeles Times* in February 2013, Charlotte Allen, a renowned journalist and a stoutly conservative Catholic, contended, "When Pope Benedict XVI announced his pending resignation, my first thought wasn't religious. It was in fact downright superficial. 'There goes the best-dressed pontiff ever!'"[1]

IN PRAISE OF BENEDICT

"The best-dressed pontiff ever": According to Charlotte Allen, during his nearly eight years on the throne of St. Peter, Benedict "always looked absolutely perfect . . . whether garbed in elaborate vestments for an Easter liturgy or clad in the simple but meticulously tailored white caped cassock (it's called a 'simar' in church lingo) that he wears on more ordinary occasions."[2] She was lavish in her praise for Joseph Ratzinger and called him "the pope of aesthetics" and "the Duke of Windsor of popes."[3] The Duke of Windsor, the former King Edward VIII, in case you do not know, was regarded as one of the most elegant men of the twentieth century.

For Catholics like Charlotte Allen, who enjoy the higher clergy's sartorial elegance, Pope Benedict's pontifical garb looked virtually perfect and outstandingly beautiful. She even interpreted it as a reflection of "the beauty of the faith" and as reference to "a beauty that is beyond earthly things."[4] Curiously enough, Benedict's fondness for "more traditional, even baroque, elements of papal dressing"[5] was applauded not only by conservative Catholics but also by English fashion journalist, socialite, and party promoter Henry Conway. His summary of Benedict's pontificate reads as follows: "Papal rings, diamond, sapphire and ruby pectoral crosses, the all-important golden mitres . . . he was a truly bling pope."[6] To illustrate these astounding papal qualities, Conway recounts the story of a young priest who was lucky to be present in the sacristy of St. Peter's Basilica shortly before a pontifical mass. "Pope Benedict came down to the sacristy in a lift, as usual, and had three sets of vestments and mitres set out to choose from. He went straight for the most elaborate."[7]

For both Allen and Conway, "beauty and dignity reflect the splendour and mystery of liturgy."[8] They therefore united in praising Pope Benedict, who enjoyed wearing glamorous vestments for liturgical functions. What splendor and mystery, one might ask, did the pope's other noble garments, those he wore for non-liturgical purposes, reflect?

In Disapproval of Benedict

This praise of Benedict was far from universal, though. Many people, both Catholics and those of other persuasions or none, did not regard Benedict's traditional and stylish pontifical garb as an expression of earthly or heavenly beauty. They rather interpreted it as a sign of nostalgia, pomposity, and vanity, even ruthlessness, because some of the papal garments reintroduced by Benedict included fur.

The best-known of these items is called a *camauro*.[9] At a general papal audience on St. Peter's Square a few days before Christmas in 2005, Pope Benedict wore the so-called winter camauro, a cap or bonnet made of red velvet and ornamented with white ermine fur on the brim. The red camauro gave the Pope a Santa Claus-like appearance that skyrocketed his media presence. There are three types of papal camauro, all of them with ermine fur trimming: a summer camauro in amaranth red silk, an Easter camauro in white damask silk, and as stated previously, a winter camauro. Apparently, the latter kind is the only one Pope Benedict wore, and he did it only once—for the camauro did not produce respect and awe but rather entertainment and ridicule.

Quite frequently, however, Benedict XVI wore the papal *mozzetta*, a waist-length cape with a small hood. There are five types of papal mozzetta, three of which have ermine trimming and two of which, if I am correct, were worn by Pope Benedict: the winter mozzetta made from red velvet with white ermine fur on the fringes and the Easter or Paschal mozzetta made from ermine-trimmed white damask silk. The use of both the winter mozzetta and the Easter mozzetta was abandoned during the pontificate of John Paul II (1978–2005) but restored by Pope Benedict XVI. Pope Francis did away with it once again, this time hopefully for good.

The pain and suffering of ermines, also called stoats, in steel-jaw leghold, or gin, traps (banned in the EU since 1995 but legal in the United States) and so-called fur farms did not deter the pope from desiring to present a fur-trimmed *bella figura*. Animal protection advocates both in Italy and around the world urged Pope Benedict to stop wearing fur on his head and his body. His use of ermines, animals long favored by kings and queens, judges, and actresses, was severely condemned by the Italian Association for the Defence of Animals and the Environment, which gathered signatures for an internet petition to the pope. The head of the organization, Lorenzo Croce, explained, "The pope has often talked about protecting the environment and we are asking that he acknowledges that animals, as God's creation, also deserve respect."[10] Well put. In fact, Pope Benedict had already voiced his opinion on respecting animals when he was still Cardinal Joseph Ratzinger and the head of the Congregation for the Doctrine of Faith. In an interview with Peter Seewald, a German journalist with close ties to Ratzinger, the future pope was asked about human duties to animals. Ratzinger replied:

> That is a very serious question. At any rate, we can see . . . that we cannot do whatever we want with them. Animals, too, are God's creatures. . . . Certainly, a sort of industrial use of creatures, so that geese are fed in such a way as to produce as large a liver as possible, or hens live so packed together that they just become caricatures of birds, this degrading of living creatures to a commodity seems to me in fact to contradict the relationship of mutuality that comes across in the Bible.[11]

As soon as he became pope, both Catholics and non-Catholics urged Joseph Ratzinger to repeat this statement in a more formal and official manner, but to no avail.

VICARIOUS CONSUMPTION? CONSPICUOUS CONSUMPTION!

One legitimately wonders why a person—and on top of that, one who is regarded as the successor to the Apostle Peter by 1.2 billion Roman Catholics—seems to have no qualms wearing fur, an animal product that was ripped off ermines who died a wretched death. This becomes even more mystifying when one is aware that the person in question is very fond of cats and voiced his aversion to the force-feeding of geese and factory farming of hens.

It is safe to say that the ermines whose fur was used to embellish the pope's robes suffered extended and crucial pain either in steel-jaw leghold traps, which cause "injuries such as torn flesh and broken bones,"[12] or on fur factory farms, which are "dismal, often filthy places where thousands of animals are usually kept in wire cages for their entire lives."[13] It should be added that all traps are indiscriminate since they are triggered by the first animal who steps into them. This might be an ermine, a fox, a member of an endangered species, or a companion animal.

Some might argue that contrary to pâté de foie gras and tender chicken breast, which merely satisfy the refined taste of wealthy connoisseurs, ermine fur is a symbol of purity, innocence, and nobility. It therefore incorporates an additional symbolic value, which makes it eminently suitable to be worn to glorify God in the liturgy. In his influential 1899 book, *The Theory of the Leisure Class*, US sociologist and economist Thorstein Veblen argued just that. He noted that in a consumer society, the preeminent function of clothes no longer is protection from environmental adversity. Its main role consists in characterizing its wearer as a member of the privileged social class: members of the elite are engaged in continuous public demonstration of their status, a process that Veblen terms "conspicuous consumption.[14]" According to Veblen, priests wearing precious vestments are exempt from this label, though, for the social role of the priest resembles the role of a servant. His attire—or as Veblen calls it, livery—might be of a very expensive character, yet wearing it enhances neither the physical comfort nor the personal prestige of its wearer. Non-liturgical garments of the priest and, even more so, liturgical vestments are not to be interpreted as manifestations of the wearer's wealth, power, and fame. In Veblen's terminology, they do not represent items of "conspicuous consumption." Quite the opposite: liturgical vestments, in particular, are to be understood as "item[s] of vicarious consumption, and the repute that accrues from [their] consumption is to be imputed to the absent master, not to the servant."[15] Thus, by donning exquisite vestments, the clergyman sets forth "in a beseeming manner the dignity of his exalted master,"[16] not that of himself. The priestly servant's beauty acts nothing but vicariously: it solely points at and reflects the beauty of God, the master.

Thorstein Veblen's distinction between vicarious and conspicuous consumption with regard to clerical garb rather well reiterates a popular traditional argument for the defense of ecclesial luxury and grandiosity. Taking up Charlotte Allen's contentions on exquisite papal garb, which were cited at the beginning of this essay, some might argue that the beauty of the dead animal's fur points to "a beauty that is beyond earthly things"—that is, God's beauty. According to the logic of a certain kind of "theological aesthetics,"[17] the sacrifice of the ermine for a higher spiritual purpose is regarded as justified. It would go beyond the scope of this chapter to address the question of whether fur lining of liturgical vestments was ethically justified in former times when worn by clergymen who were in danger of freezing to death in an icy cold church. Neither can I go into the complex theological and moral questions about animal sacrifice, atonement, and the historical contexts of the human construction of the concept of God. Suffice it to say that, as Andrew Linzey put it, "the inner logic of the sacrifice of Christ is not the sacrifice of the lower to the higher but the higher to the lower."[18] God became flesh in Jesus Christ so that his gospel of love, liberation, compassion, and inclusion could be proclaimed to all creatures. It is an abhorrent idea to argue that God approves of sentient animals such as ermines being tortured and killed in order to point to and represent his or her everlasting glory. One should also remember that neither the prophets of the Hebrew Bible nor Jesus Christ himself spoke generously or kindly of sacrificial religion. On the contrary, in Matthew 9:13 Jesus said to his opponents: "Go and learn the meaning of the words, 'I desire mercy not sacrifice.'"

The belief that pompous liturgical vestments and fur-trimmed clerical garb point to or represent God's transcendent beauty is a mélange of clerical ideology and an outdated concept of God; simply put, it is a case of bad theology. A look at the baroque vestments that archconservative Cardinal Raymond Burke, the former prefect of the Supreme Tribunal of the Roman Curia, is fond of wearing makes this contention plain. Is Burke in all his extravagance—the cappa magna (great cape) with a five-meter-long train held up in the back by an altar server or young cleric and the cappa parva (little cape, mozzetta) made of ermine fur—really the vicarious and humble servant who sets forth the dignity of his exalted master, the Lord God Almighty? Would it be unfair to suspect that His Eminence rather likes to see *himself* as a divinely appointed lord and master of the faithful? Would it be wrong to interpret his magnificent vestments as demonstrations of his exalted rank, his superior status in the Catholic hierarchy? Would not this be a rather obvious case of, to use Veblen's sociological jargon, "conspicuous consumption"?

Among the numerous Catholics who have experienced a traditional Pontifical High Mass with serious qualms, the Trappist monk and writer Thomas Merton is one of the most renowned. In his 1966 book *Conjectures of a Guilty Bystander*, an edited collection of his journal entries over several years, he lucidly recounted his experience on one such occasion in his abbey church:

> The less said about the Easter morning Pontifical Mass the better. . . . Purple zucchetto [clerical skullcap] and cappa magna and of course, it had to be our Mexican novice who was appointed to carry the long train (this inwardly made me furious and practically choked any desire I may have had to sing alleluias). The church was stifling with solemn, feudal, and unbreathable fictions. This

taste for plush, for ornamentation, for display strikes me as secular, no matter how much it is supposed to be "for the glory of God." The spring outside seemed much more sacred.[19]

THE BEAUTY OF THE "BEAST"

Ermine fur and ermine fur–trimmed capes and coats have traditionally been regarded as luxury items for "sovereigns, princes, popes and the wives of some of the wealthiest men on earth."[20] With regard to popes wearing articles of luxury such as fur, the Catholic Church became more self-critical in the wake of Vatican II. In the 1971 document *De iustitia in mundo*[21] (*On Justice in the World*), the Roman Synod of Bishops declared that "action on behalf of justice and participation in the transformation of the world . . . [are] a constitutive dimension of the preaching of the Gospel."[22] Yet precisely because "the Church is bound to give witness to justice," the bishops conclude, "she recognizes that anyone who ventures to speak to people about justice must first be just in their eyes. Hence, we must undertake an examination of the modes of acting and of the possessions and life style found within the Church herself."[23]

When Pope Benedict was asked why he wore the ermine fur–trimmed camauro on St. Peter's Square shortly before Christmas of 2005, he downplayed the event. "I only wore it once," he said, defending himself. "I was freezing and my head is prone to colds. And I said to myself, if we just have the camauro, then we should also wear it."[24] This may be a bit unkind to an old man, but with a nod to the well-known PETA slogan "I'd rather go naked than wear fur," one might describe the preferential papal choice as follows: "I'd rather wear a fur-trimmed cap than have a bare head." Or to be more precise: "I'd rather wear a fur-trimmed cap than have Monsignor Gänswein, my secretary, look for some other headgear without fur."

Peter Seewald, a German journalist who conducted the interview with Benedict, accurately observed that a pope always speaks in symbols, signs, and gestures. The symbol of ermine fur was interpreted by some people, as has been shown, as a welcome return to a religious and cultural past. For others, it was seen as a downright positive acknowledgment that wearing animal fur is morally acceptable. Still others, and this might be the majority of Catholics, did not even comprehend why and for which reasons wearing fur could ever be an issue of ethical debate.

Using the example of a certain Cardinal Andrea Cordero Lanza di Montezemolo, one could assume that the positive interpretation of furry papal clothes was the predominant one in the Vatican. Lanza di Montezemolo pushed back against the opponents of Benedict by downplaying the incident and recalling traditional Catholic doctrine: "Aren't there more important battles to wage?" the Cardinal asked. "There are human beings who merit more urgent assistance that no one is taking care of. And if we eat animals, we can wear them."[25] There is a simple reply to this pompous yet somewhat consistent defense of pompous papal garments: "If you defend cruel trapping, breeding, and killing of animals for fur by pointing to cruel trapping, breeding, and killing of animals for food, it is high time to stop both."

In a remarkable little book written by Italian Franciscan friar Nazareno Fabbretti, in which nonhuman animals voice their complaints toward human animals in fictional letters, an ermine mother states the tragic fate of her many children in a nutshell: "Our beauty is our death sentence." She continues: "You rob us of our beauty to create a luxury market. This theft feeds the pride and the exhibitionist tendencies of the selfish privileged classes . . . the ermine-clad sovereigns [and] the old and powerful clergy."[26]

As far as the Catholic Church is concerned, Pope Frances has introduced a reversal of trend, with regard both to animals and to papal pomp. Yet there is still a lot more to change and to do. It is high time to get rid of all the papal and episcopal furs and donate them to animal rehabilitation centers, where they will be used as bedding and warm cushioning for orphaned and injured free-living animals. Another possibility is to give fur coats to homeless and freezing people at home and abroad. "We can't bring the animals who were slaughtered to make these coats back to life," explained PETA president Ingrid E. Newkirk, "but we can send a message that only people truly struggling to survive have any excuse for wearing fur."[27]

The pope and the Catholic bishops, as a rule, do not belong to the people who are struggling to survive. There are no excuses for them and no extenuating circumstances for their wearing fur.

NOTES

1. Charlotte Allen, "Benedict XVI, the Best-Dressed Pope," *Los Angeles Times*, February 17, 2013, accessed August 10, 2018, articles.latimes.com/2013/feb/17/opinion/la-oe-allen-pope-fashion-20130217.
2. Allen, "Benedict XVI."
3. Allen, "Benedict XVI."
4. Allen, "Benedict XVI."
5. Henry Conway, "Pope Benedict: His True Legacy Is His Fashion Sense," *Guardian*, March 3, 2013, accessed August 13, 2018, www.theguardian.com/fashion/fashion-blog/2013/mar/03/pope-benedict-true-legacy-fashion-sense.
6. Conway, "Pope Benedict."
7. Conway, "Pope Benedict."

8. Conway, "Pope Benedict."

9. A helpful general introduction to the topic of clerical vestments is Sarah Bailey, *Clerical Vestments* (Oxford/New York: Shire Publications, 2013). On the vestments of Pope Benedict XVI, cf. Russell Godman, "The Pope's Wardrobe," *ABC News*, March 4, 2013, accessed August 13, 2018, abcnews.go.com/US/popes-wardrobe/story?id=18650986; ZENIT, "Benedict XVI's Novel Traditions," January 8, 2010, accessed August 13, 2018, www.ewtn.com/catholicism/library/benedict-xvis-novel-traditions-4987.

10. Tom Kington, "Vatican: Pope Makes Fur Fly over Revival of Ermine Robes," *Guardian*, August 13, 2008, accessed August 13, 2018, www.theguardian.com/world/2008/aug/14/catholicism.religion.

11. Joseph Ratzinger, *God and the World: A Conversation with Peter Seewald* (San Francisco: Ignatius Press, 2002), 78–79.

12. Mark Glover and Andrew Linzey, "The Fur Trade," in *The Global Guide to Animal Protection*, ed. Andrew Linzey (Urbana: University of Illinois Press, 2013), 103–4.

13. PETA, "Fur Farms," accessed August 13, 2018, www.peta.org/issues/animals-used-for-clothing/fur/fur-farms/.

14. Thorstein Veblen, *The Theory of the Leisure Class* (1899), Kindle e-book, 51.

15. Veblen, *Theory*, 136.

16. Veblen, *Theory*, 136.

17. Frank Burch Brown, "Aesthetics," in *The New SCM Dictionary of Christian Spirituality*, ed. Philip Sheldrake (London: SCM Press, 2005), 88.

18. Andrew Linzey, *Animal Theology* (London: SCM Press, 1994), 105.

19. Thomas Merton, *Conjectures of a Guilty Bystander* (Garden City, NY: Image Books, 1968), 295.

20. Nazareno Fabbretti, *Animals Write . . . Dear Humans* (Middlegreen, UK: St. Paul Publications, 1990), 45.

21. "Justice in the World (Synod of Bishops, 1971)," in *Catholic Social Thought: Encyclicals and Documents from Pope Leo XIII to Pope Francis*, ed. David O'Brien (Maryknoll, NY: Orbis Books, 2017), Kindle e-book.

22. "Justice in the World," para. 6.

23. "Justice in the World," para. 40.

24. Benedikt XVI, *Licht der Welt. Der Papst, die Kirche und die Zeichen der Zeit* (Freiburg im Breisgau: Herder, 2010), 110 (my translation).

25. Kington, "Pope Makes Fur Fly."

26. Fabbretti, *Animals Write*, 45, 48.

27. PETA, "PETA to Give Away Fur Coats for the Homeless," December 13, 2013, accessed August 13, 2018, www.peta.org/media/news-releases/peta-give-away-fur-coats-homeless/.

REFERENCES

Allen, Charlotte. "Benedict XVI, the Best-Dressed Pope." *Los Angeles Times*, February 17, 2013. Accessed August 10, 2018. articles.latimes.com/2013/feb/17/opinion/la-oe-allen-pope-fashion-20130217.

Bailey, Sarah. *Clerical Vestments.* Oxford/New York: Shire Publications, 2013.

Benedikt XVI. *Licht der Welt. Der Papst, die Kirche und die Zeichen der Zeit.* Freiburg im Breisgau: Herder, 2010.

Brown, Frank Burch. "Aesthetics." In *The New SCM Dictionary of Christian Spirituality*, edited by Philip Sheldrake, 88–89. London: SCM Press, 2005.

Conway, Henry. "Pope Benedict: His True Legacy Is His Fashion Sense." *Guardian*, March 3, 2013. Accessed August 13, 2018. www.theguardian.com/fashion/fashion-blog/2013/mar/03/pope-benedict-true-legacy-fashion-sense.

Fabbretti, Nazareno. *Animals Write . . . Dear Humans.* Middlegreen, UK: St. Paul Publications, 1990.

Glover, Mark, and Andrew Linzey. "The Fur Trade." In *The Global Guide to Animal Protection*, edited by Andrew Linzey, 103–4. Urbana: University of Illinois Press, 2013.

Godman, Russell. "The Pope's Wardrobe." *ABC News*, March 4, 2013. Accessed August 13, 2018. abcnews.go.com/US/popes-wardrobe/story?id=18650986.

"Justice in the World (Synod of Bishops, 1971)." In *Catholic Social Thought: Encyclicals and Documents from Pope Leo XIII to Pope Francis*, edited by David O'Brien. Maryknoll, NY: Orbis Books, 2017. Kindle e-book.

Kington, Tom. "Vatican: Pope Makes Fur Fly over Revival of Ermine Robes." *Guardian*, August 13, 2008. Accessed August 13, 2018. www.theguardian.com/world/2008/aug/14/catholicism.religion.

Linzey, Andrew. *Animal Theology*. London: SCM Press, 1994.

Merton, Thomas. *Conjectures of a Guilty Bystander.* Garden City, NY: Image Books, 1968.

PETA. "Fur Farms." Accessed August 13, 2018. www.peta.org/issues/animals-used-for-clothing/fur/fur-farms/.

———. "PETA to Give Away Fur Coats for the Homeless." December 13, 2013. Accessed August 13, 2018. www.peta.org/media/news-releases/peta-give-away-fur-coats-homeless/.

Ratzinger, Joseph. *God and the World: A Conversation with Peter Seewald.* San Francisco: Ignatius Press, 2002.

Veblen, Thorstein. *The Theory of the Leisure Class.* 1899. Kindle e-book.

ZENIT. "Benedict XVI's Novel Traditions." January 8, 2010. Accessed August 13, 2018. www.ewtn.com/catholicism/library/benedict-xvis-novel-traditions-4987.

PART TWO

Ethical and Cultural Perspectives

Chapter 7

A Case of Wrongful Use

An Ethical Analysis of the Use of Animal Fur

Frances M. C. Robinson

THE HUMAN TRADE IN ANIMAL FUR

The trade in animal fur has had substantial economic and political consequences for the human cultures involved. Although the roots of the trade lie in prehistory, a substantial growth in the trade occurred during the medieval and early modern periods. The driving forces behind that growth were numerous and included the following: financial incentives, status or class, the relationship between demand and supply, and fashion.

1. The wearing of fur was seen to be symbolic of one's status or class within society, and thus, it is highly likely that there would have been many people who wished to wear fur. However, in terms of both quality and quantity of fur, the wealthy and the powerful certainly had an advantage with regard to access. Indeed, the wearing of fur was used by the wealthy and the powerful to reinforce their elevated position within society.[1]
2. In addition, the relationship between demand and supply was an important factor in the development of the transatlantic exchange trade. It so happens that the early European pioneers who arrived on North American land also found an abundant supply of fur-bearing animals there at a time when the supply of fur was dwindling in Europe. The relationship between the abundant supply of fur in North America and the demand for fur in Europe gave rise to the development of trade

between Native Americans who could supply the furs and Europeans who could produce and supply the goods needed by Native Americans, one example of this being cloth. The trade between Native Americans and Europeans also gave rise to an element of competition between different European nation-states.[2]

3. Fashion was also a contributing factor, and a notable example of this is the popularity of the beaver felt hat (also called simply a "beaver"). Indeed, the hat was so popular that the fashion contributed to a rapid decline in the population of beavers not only in Europe but also in North America. The human demand for beaver skins not only proved absolutely disastrous for beavers but also had a serious environmental impact, through the effect of the decline in the beaver population on watercourses, wetlands, flora and fauna, and flooding.[3]

INTRA-SPECIES CONCERNS AND INTER-SPECIES CONCERNS

It is necessary to distinguish between *intra*-species concerns and *inter*-species concerns. If one examines the patterns of human behavior that contributed to the acquisition, trading, and wearing of fur, one can determine the consequences of that behavior—not only for those individuals involved in the business of fur and for those human cultures to which they belonged, but also for other human individuals and for other human cultures that may have been affected either directly or indirectly by the process. Indeed, by taking a global perspective, one may discover that the consequences of those patterns of human behavior were beneficial for some humans but detrimental—even harmful—for other humans. However, there are other consequences resulting from this human behavior: the effects of that behavior on the members of other species. Once again by taking a global perspective, one can see that the consequences for other animals were mainly harmful, and those harmful consequences can be categorized as follows: (1) the mental suffering of individual animals, (2) the physical suffering of individual animals, and (3) the loss of species.

We now know that animals have emotions, that they experience anger, fear, anxiety, joy, and love. Animals form close social bonds, and there is evidence that animals grieve.[4] There is also physiological evidence to indicate that animals can experience both stress and distress.[5] Thus, it is reasonable to argue that when we think about the mental suffering of individual animals, we need to consider not only the mental suffering of the individual victims but also the mental suffering of those animals who are affected detrimentally either through the loss of a close associate or through the witnessing of the mental and/or physical suffering of a close associate.

One also needs to consider the physical suffering of the individual victims, which often occurs at the time of capture for free-ranging animals. Free-ranging animals may be caught in leghold traps, snares, nets, or pits. The animals may be shot, stabbed, clubbed, or poisoned to death. Animals can suffer horrific injuries before death comes as a merciful release. In addition to the hunting of fur-bearing animals, humans breed different species of animals in captivity in order to obtain the animals' fur. Captive animals may suffer both physically and mentally from being reared in poor environmental conditions, which include both physical deprivation and either social deprivation or overcrowding. The animals who are reared in captivity are killed so that people can obtain their fur, and the methods by which they are killed tend to be geared to protecting the fur rather than protecting the welfare of the animal. One example of this is the electrocution of farmed foxes (ages six months plus). It is pertinent to note that the Canadian regulations for the welfare of farmed foxes specify that the electrocution of a fox should not be witnessed by other foxes.[6] Thus, it would appear that there is at least some recognition by some humans that other animals can and do associate themselves with the victims and that those animals can be detrimentally affected as a result.

Another harm is the loss of species. It is a terrible indictment of the human species that humans would hunt another species of animal to the point of extinction. However, historically this has been shown to be the case, and it is indeed an extremely serious problem in the present day. The hunting of a species to the point of extinction is not only absolutely disastrous for the species; this action also may have a detrimental effect on the ecological networks to which that species belongs. Indeed, Edward Wilson points out, "In order to save biodiversity it is necessary to understand how species interact with one another to form ecosystems. Yet so poor is our knowledge of the interactions that ecosystems studies remain an underdeveloped science."[7] Wilson later continues,

> The history of each species can be considered an epic. The entire biology of one species can consume the lifetime of a scientist. Even with a hundred scientists focused on the species, our knowledge of it remains incomplete. There is the niche, where the species lives intimately with other species—prey, predator, inside and outside symbionts, engineers of soil and vegetation. Therein, we can find no species that lives alone. When we allow one species to die, we erase the web of relationships it maintained in life, with consequences that scientists seldom understand.[8]

Thus, the loss of a species erases the web of relationships that the species maintained in life, and scientists have very little idea of what the consequences of that will be. Therefore, the removal of a species has the potential to cause harm, and if an action has the potential to cause harm, then the very least that is required is that one be able to morally justify that action.

Animal ethicists acknowledge that causing harm to a living sentient being is of moral concern. Environmental ethicists argue that causing harm to a species is of moral concern and that causing harm to an ecosystem is of moral concern. Notably, the moral decision-making process necessarily precedes the morally justifiable action. A commonly used method in the ethical decision-making process is the use of a cost–benefit analysis. A cost–benefit analysis is the practical application of the utilitarian moral theory. The central idea is to try to balance potential harm against potential benefit and to somehow arrive at a "best" choice of action. The pertinent point is that to be able to do this, it is necessary to consider both *intra*-species considerations and *inter*-species considerations. More explicitly:

- Even if one considers just the interactions that take place between members of the human species, one can see that there is a high level of complexity.
- There is also likely to be a high level of complexity in both the relationships and the interactions that occur between the victim and other members of his or her own species.
- When one starts to consider *inter*-species interactions, that level of complexity multiplies by a factor of *n*, and at least we know that we know very little about them.

Thus, a central problem for the application of a cost–benefit analysis in trying to determine whether or not the human use of fur is morally justifiable is this category distinction between intra-species considerations and inter-species considerations. In addition, there are numerous problems associated with the application of the utilitarian moral theory itself.[9]

There are certainly both animal welfare issues and ecological issues to be considered. However, from an ethical perspective, there is another issue to be considered: the captivity of an animal. Although both free-ranging and captive animals are killed by humans for their fur, humans take over virtually the entire lives of captive animals, since the options that are available to these animals throughout their lives are very much determined by the decisions that humans make.

Indeed, concern over animal welfare, concern over the captivity of animals, and concern over harm to both species and ecosystems are all concerns associated with the practice of obtaining animal fur. Notably, what is not being provided is an ethical justification for the practice. Thus, the question of central importance is: Can one ethically justify the killing of an animal in order to obtain the animal's fur?

In order to try to answer this particular question, one can use a slightly different ethical approach by starting with the fundamental truth that fur is an integral part of an animal's body, since fur consists not only of hair but also of the skin to which the hair is attached. Thus, unless the animal is already dead, either the removal of fur or the killing of the animal in order to remove the fur will necessarily cause harm to the animal, and causing harm to a living sentient being is of moral concern. It is pertinent to note that both the acquisition and the sale of human body parts by humans, both within and between different human cultures, is also of moral concern, because of the potential harm to humans as well as the potential benefits for humans. Indeed, biomedical ethicists are in the process of developing ethical guidelines for this particular practice—they are in the process of developing *intra*-species ethics. Animal ethicists, on the other hand, are concerned about the acquisition and the sale of nonhuman body parts by humans—their concerns are thus *inter*-species concerns. The relevant question to ask is: Can biomedical ethics (intra-species ethics) be of help in the development of inter-species ethics? There are reasons to believe that biomedical ethics can help.

DEVELOPING ETHICAL GUIDELINES

The following approach may be used in the development of ethical guidelines:

- *One needs to clarify the concepts that one wishes to use.*
  It is so easy to use a concept without fully appreciating the meaning that is being conveyed through the use of that concept. Indeed, the use of even one word in slightly different contexts can result in radically different meanings, and people can interpret texts slightly differently depending on the information that is gleaned from their particular background. Therefore, it is extremely important to clarify the concepts that one wishes to use in order to minimize ambiguity.
- *One needs to provide sound arguments.*
  A sound argument is a valid argument, one in which the conclusion follows logically from the premises, and the premises must be true. If one or more of the premises is false and/or if the argument is an invalid argument, then the argument is of no use. Sound arguments can be used to develop ethical guidelines in order to protect the members of other species, as well as the members of our own species.
- *Ethics is both a continually evolving process and an iterative process.*

It is important to acknowledge that ethics is both a continually evolving process and an iterative one. This is important because the best that one can hope to achieve at any particular moment in time will depend on the information that is available at that particular moment in time; and as more information becomes available, it is absolutely necessary to go back and check the arguments in order to determine whether or not the premises can still be considered true in light of the new information.

Clarifying the Relevant Concepts

In order to establish whether or not the killing of an animal to obtain the animal's fur is morally justifiable, one can start by clarifying the relevant concepts. The first concept to be considered is the concept of person.

Person

There is a distinction to be made between an animate system and an inanimate system, where the term "animate" means having the capacity to be a living system. In light of present information, one can say that having the capacity to be a living system entails that the system is a biological system containing genetic material and that the biological system functions according to patterns of gene expression. There are some biological systems that lie on the borderline between animate and inanimate, one example being a virus. A virus lies on the borderline because it is necessary for the virus to use the services of a host cell in order to function properly and to reproduce.[10] Nevertheless, one can state categorically that all fur-bearing animals are, without exception, animate. Thus, the question arises as to why humans treat fur-bearing animals as if they were inanimate. A case in point concerns the distinction between the concept of person and the concept of property.

Gary Francione has pointed out that animals are treated as property by the law in the United States; he claims that animals are treated as if they were inanimate.[11] This would imply that there is something wrong in the way animals are treated by the US legal system. One of the roles of a legal system is to protect social bonds (in relation to the rest of humanity)—for example, giving legal protection with regard to the sanctity of marriage or giving legal protection with regard to the rights of a child. Social bonds also exist between human animals and animals of different species. It is reasonable to argue that there should be some legal redress to prevent a human from stealing the companion animal of another human. However, the main concern with regard to both the law and human–animal relationships is the existence of a deep-seated problem within legal systems globally—not just within the legal system of the US. This deep-seated global problem is the inappropriate use of the concept of property by legal systems.

The German philosopher Immanuel Kant (1724–1804) argued that one cannot be both a person and a property, and he based his argument on the ethical principle that persons should be treated as ends in themselves and not just as means to another's ends. Kant's moral theory is known as deontology, and this particular moral theory underpins the concept of human rights. However, according to Kant,

> Beings whose existence depends, not on our will, but on nature, have none the less,if they are non-rational beings, only a relative value as means and are consequently called *things*. Rational beings, on the other hand, are called *persons* because their nature already marks them out as ends in themselves—that is, as something which ought not to be used merely as a means—and consequently imposes to that extent a limit on all arbitrary treatment of them (and is an object of reverence).[12]

Thus, one can see that even though Kant argued that persons should be treated as ends in themselves, he qualified his argument by saying that only rational beings are to be called persons. As a consequence of applying Kant's argument in practice, potentially serious problems could emerge for those individuals who behave irrationally within our own species—such as very young children, the mentally challenged, and the elderly. This is because Kant's argument implies that very young children, the mentally challenged, and the elderly are not persons, and therefore they can be used merely as a means to another's ends. On the contrary, most people argue that such individuals are persons and should be morally considered. Tom Regan refers to such individuals as moral patients as opposed to moral agents.[13] However, extremely serious problems have indeed emerged for the members of other species not only as a consequence of Kant's argument, but also as a consequence of the dominant line of thought in Western philosophy.

This line of thought has been as follows: (1) only humans have the capacity for reason, and (2) only humans have the capacity for language. Notably, this line of thought can be traced back to a medical writer known as Alcmaeon (fifth century[14] BCE),[15] and later was adopted by the Greek philosopher Aristotle (384–322 BCE). Aristotle is not only a towering figure in moral philosophy, he also is considered to be the father of biology. The Stoic philosophers, including Chrysippus (280–206 BCE), also thought along the same lines.

The fundamental problem with this line of thinking is that both of those premises are *false*.

There is now a considerable amount of empirical evidence to indicate that animals of many different species have the capacity for reason and that intraspecies communication is widespread, even though interspecies communication remains vastly more difficult. Nevertheless, *The Concise Oxford Dictionary* still equates the term "person" with a human animal, and the English common law (also known as the Anglo-American law) has been very reluctant to class nonhuman animals as persons.

David Favre points out, "The common law legal system has its conceptual roots in the Roman law period. The Roman view of the world produced two fundamental categories: persons and things. Persons had access to the law, and property law was written about things."[16] He notes that within property law there are three basic categories of property—(1) real property, (2) personal property, and (3) intellectual property[17]—and that "some animals are, and have always been, categorized as personal property."[18] In addition, he writes, "as the English common law developed, not all animals had equal presence or status within the law: the common law regards and gives the greatest protection to those designated as 'useful,' and the least protection to those *ferae naturae*."[19]

Favre explains that "the concept of property exists and is well-entrenched in our legal thinking.[20] and that "property law is an institution with four component parts: the persons who hold the rights, the relationships between persons, the objects to which property concepts attach, and sanctions for violations of the rules."[21] However, as animals are persons and not things, the crucial question is: Why are animals categorized as personal property by the US legal system?

Favre continues:

> Animals are like infant children in that they can be recognized as legal persons, but do not have the capacity to understand or knowingly exercise any legal rights allocated to them. This has been particularly difficult for the animals as, unlike children, they are property and one of the legal mantras often repeated is that property cannot be the holder of legal rights.[22]

Thus, the question remains: Why are animals categorized as property by the US legal system?

The English philosopher John Locke (1632–1704) established that private property is absolutely essential for liberty, and the key to understanding Locke's point is understanding what he meant by the concept of private property. Locke writes:

> Every man has a "property" in his own "person." This nobody has any right but to himself. The "labor" of his body and the "work" of his hands, we may say, are properly his. . . . [23]
>
> [T]he supreme power cannot take from any man any part of his property without his own consent.[24]
>
> The reason why men enter into society is the preservation of their property; and the end while they choose and authorise a legislative is that there may be laws made, and rules set, as guards and fences to the properties of all the society, to limit the power and moderate the dominion of every part and member of the society.
>
> [W]henever the legislators endeavour to take away and destroy the property of the people, or to reduce them to slavery under arbitrary power, they put themselves into a state of war with the people, who are thereupon absolved from any farther obedience, and are left to the common refuge which God hath provided for all men against force and violence. Whensoever, therefore, the legislative shall transgress this fundamental rule of society, and either by ambition, fear, folly or corruption, endeavour to grasp themselves, or put into the hands of any other, an absolute power over the lives, liberties and estates of the people, by this breach of trust they forfeit the power the people had put into their hands for quite contrary ends, and it devolves to the people, who have a right to resume their original liberty, and by the establishment of a new legislative (such as they shall think fit), provide for their own safety and security, which is the end for which they are in society.[25]

Thus, Locke highlights the importance of the individual person, not only in terms of the person's contribution and therefore his or her entitlement, but also, importantly, in terms of the correct relationship between the governed and the governing. Locke's radical view at the time was that government is morally obliged to serve persons—by protecting life, liberty, and property. In his *Second Treatise on Civil Government* (1689), Locke argued that government rests in the will of the people, and thus the people have a right to challenge and change their rulers and government. He was critical of the relationship between the structures of power and the protection (or indeed the lack of protection) of individual subjects. More recently, feminist philosophers have noted that evolving power structures within a network of relationships can render the less powerful individuals within that network more and more vulnerable, and an extreme example of this is the "owning" of a slave. Indeed, Catriona Mackenzie points out that "many kinds of vulnerability are primarily the result not of unavoidable biological processes but of interpersonal and social relationships or economic, legal, and political structures."[26] In the twenty-first century the "owning" of a human animal by another human animal would be of considerable *intra*-species moral concern. However, this raises the question of whether a human animal should "own" an animal of a different species—and indeed whether this should be of considerable *inter*-species moral concern. There are reasons to believe that it should be.

There is certainly a need to balance power within a network of relationships, and this balance can be achieved via either ethics or politics. If one takes an ethical approach, then the balance of power may be achieved through the development of ethical principles and ethical guidelines. Of central importance within ethics are the concepts of equality and justice, and the goal of ethics is to achieve both individual justice and social justice. The balancing of power via the political approach is possible only in a democratic process, and ideally within that democratic process, everyone should have a voice, everyone should be heard, and everyone should be justly represented. The political process involves discussion, debate, voting, and sometimes demonstrations. Notably, an imbalance of power within a network of relationships may occur when there is a communication problem—when one party has no voice, is not being heard, or is not being justly represented.

Problems arise for nonhuman animals from at least two fundamental sources. First, all animals are animate, but humans often treat nonhuman animals as if they were inanimate. Thus, humans' treatment of animals can be based on humans' false beliefs. Second, animals effectively have no voice within the networks of relationships that include humans because of the considerable difficulty in interspecies communication. As a result, the interests of nonhuman animals have insufficient representation both within different human legal systems and within different human political systems.

Autonomy

An important document titled *The Belmont Report* was published in the United States in 1979. The report sets out the three basic ethical principles for the protection of human subjects of biomedical and behavioral research, plus guidelines for the application of those principles. The three basic ethical principles are as follows: 1) respect for persons, 2) beneficence and 3) justice. The first basic ethical principle (respect for persons) states that "individuals should be treated as autonomous agents" and that "persons with diminished autonomy are entitled to protection."[27] Notably, an autonomous agent is defined in *The Belmont Report* as "an individual who is capable of deliberation about personal goals and of acting under the direction of such deliberation."[28]

However, within the concept of capability, there is a distinction to be made between the capacity to act autonomously and the freedom to act autonomously. Indeed, the freedom to act autonomously is determined by the particular power structures that exist within the networks of relationships to which the individual is attached. Thus, even though a nonhuman animal has the capacity to act autonomously, whether or not that nonhuman animal has the freedom to do so will be very much context-dependent.

Exploitation

Stephen Wilkinson points out that the term "exploitation" can be used both in the nonmoral sense and in the moral sense. The term is used in the nonmoral sense when applied to inanimate objects,[29] whereas the term is used in the moral sense when applied to persons. He writes, "The most exploitable people are those who are *both* very useful *and* very vulnerable."[30] Notably, the term "exploitation" is used in the moral sense in two different ways. In the first moral sense, exploitation means "a misdistribution of the benefits of social cooperation," and in this sense exploitation is a "disparity of value."[31] In the second moral sense, exploitation means "wrongful use."[32] He explains that the difference between these two moral senses involve 1) the way in which they relate to consent and 2) the way in which they relate to taking advantage of people's vulnerabilities.[33]

Wilkinson later notes that "both commodification and wrongful use are particular types of objectification."[34] Thus the two issues of central importance in determining whether or not exploitation is wrongful are 1) consent and 2) objectification. If two individuals agree to behave in a particular way, and their behavior has no detrimental effect on anyone else, then it is reasonable to argue that no one else has the right to interfere. However, on closer examination, one may discover that one of those individuals is being coerced, however subtly, into participating—participation may be the best of the available options. The nature of consent is of central importance in ethics, and that which is considered to be valid consent is voluntary informed consent. Voluntary informed consent is the application of the first basic ethical principle (respect for persons) in *The Belmont Report* and requires the following: (1) that the individuals involved receive the relevant information in advance, (2) that the individuals involved fully understand that information, and (3) that the individuals involved voluntarily agree to participate without any coercion or undue influence. A significant problem arises in relation to the interactions between human animals and animals of different species as a direct consequence of the considerable difficulty in interspecies communication. The problem is that it is not possible to obtain voluntary informed consent with all that it should entail from nonhuman animals. Voluntary informed consent is not the equivalent of learned behavior. This substantial ethical problem implies that when human animals interact with nonhuman animals, human animals should tread extremely carefully.

Objectification

To objectify is to present as an object of perception. The process of objectification concerns not only the way in which the self perceives the "other" but also, and crucially, the way in which the self perceives his or her relationship with the "other." The self may perceive the relationship to be an I-it relationship rather than an I-he or she relationship.

Martha Nussbaum has set out a list of seven characteristics (or features) of objectification,[35] and a useful exercise is to substitute the word "object" in Nussbaum's list with the name of a particular animal from a particular species and to substitute the word "objectifier"' with the word "human." For this purpose, a silver fox is used as an example of a nonhuman animal (the point of the exercise is more poignant if one chooses a personal name for the particular silver fox). Nussbaum's list now reads as follows:

1. *Instrumentality*: The human treats the silver fox as a tool of his or her purposes.
2. *Denial of autonomy*: The human treats the silver fox as lacking in autonomy and self-determination.
3. *Inertness*: The human treats the silver fox as lacking in agency, and perhaps also in activity.
4. *Fungibility*: The human treats the silver fox as interchangeable (a) with other objects of the same type, and/or (b) with objects of other types.
5. *Violability*: The human treats the silver fox as lacking in boundary-integrity, as something that it is permissible to break up, smash, break into.
6. *Ownership*: The human treats the silver fox as something that is owned by another, can be bought or sold, etc.
7. *Denial of subjectivity*: The human treats the silver fox as something whose experience and feelings (if any) need not be taken into account.[36]

All seven characteristics are present in the way in which humans treat nonhuman animals in order to obtain the nonhuman animals' fur. Indeed, it is enlightening to examine two of these characteristics more closely.

The first characteristic is fungibility. The silver fox is treated as interchangeable with other similar silver foxes—the individuality of the particular silver fox (the particular person) is not recognized. In addition, the silver fox is treated as interchangeable with relevantly similar non-silver foxes. Bearing in mind the effort that is required to understand one species, it does seem somewhat flippant to believe that one can just substitute one species for another. Fungibility indicates that the silver fox is being treated merely as a means to the human's goal; the human perceives his or her relationship with the silver fox as an "I–it" relationship rather than an "I–he or she" relationship.

The second characteristic is the denial of subjectivity, in which the human neither recognizes nor regards as significant the experiences of the silver fox. Yet the mental suffering and physical suffering of a silver fox may be recognized and may be regarded as significant by other silver foxes. The relevant question to ask is: Why is there such a difference in perspective between the human and the silver fox? Some insight into the attitude of the human can be gained by looking at parallel situations within biomedical ethics. The following passage is taken from the *Singapore Medical Journal*. Alastair Campbell writes:

> From a medical perspective, the dead human body—or "cadaver"—is easily viewed in an impersonal way, as a source of knowledge of the causes of death or the effectiveness of therapy through autopsy, or as a source of benefits to others, through the "harvesting" of organs and tissue. Such an objectified view of the dead body is, however, a universe of meaning removed from the perceptions of the bereaved family of a dead person. For them, the body of the deceased represents all that they cared for and all they have lost.[37]

Campbell lays the blame for this disjunction between the scientific view of the dead human body and the layperson's view of the dead human body on seventeenth-century French philosopher René Descartes. Descartes was not only a philosopher and a mathematician, he also performed vivisection. Campbell blames Descartes because of the beliefs that Descartes promoted:

1. The mind and the body are separate entities.
2. The uniqueness of the person resides in the mind.
3. The body is effectively just a receptacle for the mind.[38]

Campbell points out that Descartes' view has helped to desacralize the human body—allowing it to be studied as any complex mechanism. However, at the same time, it has predisposed doctors to see patients not as persons but as exemplars of diseases.[39]

This disjunction offers some insight into the problems that have emerged for nonhuman animals as a direct consequence of the contradiction between the reality of animal minds and the dominant line of thought within Western philosophy. The medical writer Alcmaeon believed that only humans have the capacity for reason and that only humans have the capacity for language. Aristotle reinforced those beliefs with his position that it was the external objects of desire that caused the actions of animals *without* there being any free-thinking or deliberation by the animals. As a result of his belief, Aristotle referred to animals as "sensitive souls" as opposed to "rational souls." In addition, Aristotle claimed that animals could not be held morally responsible for their actions and that because animals lacked moral obligations, they must also lack moral rights.[40]

There are many flaws in Aristotle's thinking. The belief that only humans have the capacity for reason[41] and the belief that only humans have the capacity for language[42] are both false. In addition, Aristotle's belief that external objects of desire cause the actions of nonhuman animals without nonhuman animals engaging in any free-thinking or deliberation is also false.[43] All animals, including human animals, can respond to external stimuli, and sometimes that response can be a very rapid response—for example, when one jumps out of the way of a rapidly approaching car. In short, one can respond rapidly when one is threatened by a dangerous or a potentially dangerous situation. However, sometimes it takes much longer to respond—depending not only on the choices that are available but also on the particular choice that is made. There is nothing in the available empirical evidence to indicate that human animals are unique in their ability to respond in those different ways. In addition, Aristotle's conclusion that animals must lack moral rights does not necessarily follow from his premise that animals cannot be held morally responsible for their actions. Very young children cannot be held morally responsible for their actions, but it does not necessarily follow from this premise that very young children must lack moral rights. Indeed, to the contrary, very young children are entitled to protection. Notably, very young children have to learn to act in a morally responsible way.

Nevertheless, Aristotle's line of thought has persisted and has been very influential. The Stoic philosopher Chrysippus (280–206 BCE) argued that humans have no moral obligations toward animals.[44] In the fourth century CE, St. Augustine argued that animals are not in community with us because they lack reason.[45] St. Thomas Aquinas (1225–74) combined Aristotelian philosophy with Christian doctrine and then declared in his *Summa Theologiae* (1260) that humans were unique and that all other animals were incapable of rationality, because they did not possess a mind. Summarizing this view, Vaughan Monamy writes, "Only humans had a soul and the power to reason. Without a soul, animals were merely objects, devoid of personality or rights."[46]

Thus, it is perhaps not too surprising that by the seventeenth century, Descartes believed that animals were just machines. Indeed, he claimed that animals were just like clocks or church organs. If you hold the following beliefs—(1) that the mind is separate from the body, (2) that the uniqueness of the person resides in the mind, (3) that the body is just a receptacle for the mind, and (4) that nonhuman animals have no minds—then it is quite logical to conclude that nonhuman animals are just receptacles or machines.

The problem with Descartes' line of thought is that his argument is *not* sound, because the premises in his argument are false. Descartes was interested in physiology, and in pursuing this interest, he nailed conscious living animals to boards and dissected them. Notably, anesthetics were not discovered until the nineteenth century. Descartes justified his actions to his colleagues by arguing that the screams of the animals were just the squeaking sounds of the mechanisms. This dominant line of thought in Western philosophy has not been the only line of thought, but unfortunately it has been the most powerful, and it has predisposed humans to the view that the suffering of a nonhuman animal is insignificant.

Commodification

Commodification is defined as the action of turning something into, or treating something as, a (mere) commodity. A commodity is defined as an article or raw material that can be bought and sold, especially a product as opposed to a service—a useful thing.[47]

It is pertinent to point out that fur is an integral part of an animal's body, and therefore, the fur belongs to the animal. It is not a commodity for human use. The ethical principle that should underpin our treatment of nonhuman animal subjects is as follows: always treat persons as ends in themselves and never just as a means to one's own ends.

Justice

In his book titled *A Theory of Justice*, John Rawls set out two principles of justice and they are as follows:

"First Principle"

> Each person is to have an equal right to the most extensive total system of equal basic liberties compatible with a similar system of liberty for all.[48]

"Second Principle"

> Social and economic inequalities are to be arranged so that they are both: (a) to the greatest benefit of the least advantaged, consistent with the just savings principle, and (b) attached to offices and positions open to all under conditions of fair equality of opportunity.[49]

Rawls also set out two priority rules and they are as follows:

"First Priority Rule" (The Priority of Liberty)

> The principles of justice are to be ranked in lexical order and therefore liberty can be restricted only for the sake of liberty. There are two cases: (a) a less extensive liberty must strengthen the total system of liberty shared by all; (b) a less than equal liberty must be acceptable to those with the lesser liberty.[50]

"Second Priority Rule" (The Priority of Justice over Efficiency and Welfare)

> The second principle of justice is lexically prior to the principle of efficiency and to that of maximizing the sum of advantages; and fair opportunity is prior to the difference principle. There are two cases: (a) an inequality of opportunity must enhance the opportunities of those with the lesser opportunity; (b) an excessive rate of saving must on balance mitigate the burden of those bearing the hardship.[51]

Rawls recognized that individuals have different capabilities and different interests, and therefore, diversity in achievement is inevitable over time. However, of central importance as far as justice is concerned is that each individual has an equal opportunity to flourish in whichever way that individual can and wishes to flourish. In particular, Rawls highlights not only the priority of justice but also the priority of liberty within justice.

Liberty

Rawls's first principle of justice has top priority, and this first principle concerns liberty. Notably, the philosopher Isaiah Berlin identified two concepts of liberty, and he referred to these concepts as "negative liberty" and "positive liberty." Negative liberty is the entitlement not to be interfered with, although Berlin recognized that a correct balance had to be found between individual freedom and the freedom of individuals within society. Positive liberty is the degree to which individuals or groups act autonomously.[52]

Berlin writes:

> "Who governs me?" is logically distinct from the question "How far does government interfere with me?" It is in this difference that the great contrast between the two concepts of negative and positive liberty, in the end, consists.[53]
>
> For the "positive" sense of liberty comes to light if we try to answer the question, not "What am I free to do or be?," but "By whom am I ruled?" or "Who is to say what I am, and what I am not, to be or do?"[54]

Nonhuman animals are animate, sentient, and have the capacity to act autonomously. Therefore, nonhuman animals are persons and not things. As persons, they are entitled not to be interfered with (liberty in the negative sense). The question is: Does the nonhuman animal have the freedom to act autonomously? (Does the nonhuman animal have liberty in the positive sense?) Notably, having the freedom to act autonomously in the positive sense is context-dependent. Thus, in seeking justice for nonhuman animals, it is absolutely necessary to consider an animal's liberty in terms of both negative liberty and positive liberty.

CONCLUSION

- Fur-bearing animals are animate and sentient and have the capacity to act rationally. Fur-bearing animals should therefore be treated as persons and not categorized as property (as if they were inanimate). Fur-bearing animals should be treated as ends in themselves and not just as means to humans' own ends.
- Fur-bearing animals are autonomous agents; they have the capacity to act autonomously. The relevant question to ask is whether the animal has the freedom to act autonomously, since positive liberty is context-dependent. Based on the ethical principle of respect for persons, fur-bearing animals should be treated as autonomous agents, and those with diminished autonomy are entitled to protection.
- Human animals objectify nonhuman animals in a number of different ways, as illustrated in Nussbaum's list. This is a direct consequence of the dominant line of thought in Western philosophy, and this line of thought is based on false premises and an unsound argument.
- Nonhuman animals are treated unjustly by humans within the networks of relationships that include both human and nonhuman animals. The injustice arises through insufficient representation of the interests of nonhuman animals both within different human legal systems and within different human political systems. Injustice also arises through insufficient protection of both the negative liberty and the positive liberty of individual nonhuman animals.
- Humans exploit nonhuman animals in the moral sense—since fur-bearing animals are animate. The killing of a nonhuman animal by a human in order for the human to obtain the nonhuman animal's fur is a case of wrongful use. This conclusion is justified by the lack of valid consent (the lack of voluntary informed consent), by the objectification of the nonhuman animal subject, and by the harm that is caused to the nonhuman animal both through injury and through death.

NOTES

1. Eric Jay Dolin, *Fur, Fortune and Empire: The Epic History of the Fur Trade in America* (London: W. W. Norton, 2010), 6–8.

2. Dolin, *Fur, Fortune and Empire*, 8–12.

3. Dolin, *Fur, Fortune and Empire*, 18.

4. Jeffrey Masson and Susan McCarthy, *When Elephants Weep: The Emotional Lives of Animals* (London: Vintage, 1996), 120–36.

5. National Research Council of the National Academies, *Recognition and Alleviation of Distress in Laboratory Animals* (Washington, DC: National Academies Press, 2008), 2, 15–16.

6. National Farm Animal Care Council, *Code of Practice for the Care and Handling of Farmed Fox (Vulpes vulpes)* (Canada Fox Breeders Association and National Farm Animal Care Council, 2013), 28, www.nfacc.ca/pdfs/codes/Farmed_Fox_Code .pdf.

7. Edward O. Wilson, *Half-Earth: Our Planet's Fight for Life* (London: W. W. Norton, 2016), 101.

8. Wilson, *Half-Earth*, 106.

9. (1) There is a risk of tyranny by the majority. (2) There is a lack of restrictions on actions. (3) The theory is impersonal. (4) It is questionable that all of the consequences are predictable. (5) There is a lack of protection for the individual subject.

10. "Unlike cellular organisms, which 'grow' from an increase in the integrated sum of their components and reproduce by division, virus particles are produced from the assembly of preformed components. Once manufactured, virus particles (virions) do not grow or undergo division . . .

[T]he type of host cell infected by the virus has a profound effect on the replication process. There are many examples of viruses undergoing different replicative cycles in different cell types. However, the coding capacity of the genome determines the basic replication strategy used by different viruses. This strategy may involve heavy reliance on the host cell, in which case the virus genome can be very compact and need only encode the essential information for a few proteins, for instance, in parvoviruses. Alternatively, large and complex virus genomes, such as those of poxviruses, encode most of the information necessary for replication, and the virus is only reliant on the cell for the provision of energy and the apparatus for macromolecular synthesis, such as ribosomes."

Alan J. Cann, "Replication of Viruses," in *Encyclopedia of Virology* 3rd edition, ed. Brian W. J. Mahy and Marc H. V. Van Regenmortel (Academic Press, 2008), 407.

www.sciencedirect.com/referencework/9780123744104/encyclopedia-of-virology

11. Gary L. Francione, *Animals as Persons: Essays on the Abolition of Animal Exploitation* (New York: Columbia University Press, 2008), 3.

12. Immanuel Kant, *The Moral Law: Groundwork of the Metaphysic of Morals*, trans. Herbert J. Paton (London: Routledge, 1991), 90–91.

13. Tom Regan, *The Case for Animal Rights* (London: Routledge, 1988), 152–55.

14. Note: Richard Sorabji dates Alcmaeon to the late sixth century B.C.E.

Richard Sorabji, *Animal Minds and Human Morals:The Origins of the Western Debate* (London: Gerald Duckworth & Co. Ltd., 1993), 9.

15. Monica Libell, "A Mirror of Myself? Monist and Dualist Views of Animals," in *Animal Bioethics: Principles and Teaching Methods*, ed. Michel Marie et al. (Wageningen, the Netherlands: Wageningen Academic, 2005), 22.

16. David Favre, "Living Property: A New Status for Animals within the Legal System," in *Marquette Law Review* 93, no. 3 (2010): 1024.
scholarship.law.marquette.edu/mulr/vol93/iss3/3.

17. Favre, "Living Property," 1025

18. Favre, "Living Property," 1026.

19. Favre, "Living Property," 1026.

20. Favre, "Living Property," 1025.

21. Favre, "Living Property," 1024.

22. Favre, "Living Property," 1032.

23. John Locke, *The Second Treatise on Civil Government*, (New York: Prometheus Books, 1986), 20.

24. Locke, *The Second Treatise on Civil Government*, 77.

25. Locke, *The Second Treatise on Civil Government*, 118–119.

26. Catriona Mackenzie, "The Importance of Relational Autonomy and Capabilities for an Ethics of Vulnerability," in *Vulnerability: New Essays in Ethics and Feminist Philosophy*, ed. Catriona Mackenzie, Wendy Rogers, and Susan Dodds (Oxford: Oxford University Press, 2014), 38.

27. National Commission for the Protection of Human Subjects of Biomedical and Behavioral Research, *The Belmont Report: Ethical Principles and Guidelines for the Protection of Human Subjects of Research* (US Department of Health and Human Services, April 18, 1979), 4, www.hhs.gov/ohrp/regulations-and-policy/belmont-report/index.html.

28. National Commission, *Belmont Report*, 4.

29. Stephen Wilkinson, *Bodies for Sale: Ethics and Exploitation in the Human Body Trade* (Abingdon, UK: Routledge, 2003), 11.

30. Wilkinson, *Bodies for Sale,* 24.

31. Wilkinson, *Bodies for Sale,* 15.

32. Wilkinson, *Bodies for Sale,* 15.

33. Wilkinson, *Bodies for Sale*, 26.

34. Wilkinson, *Bodies for Sale*, 27.

35. Martha C. Nussbaum, "Objectification," *Philosophy and Public Affairs* 24, no.4 (Fall 1995):257. www.mit.edu/~shaslang/mprg/nussbaumO.pdf

36. Nussbaum, "Objectification," 257.

37. Alastair V. Campbell, "Why the Body Matters: The Uses and Abuses of the Human Body in Modern Medicine," *Singapore Medical Journal* 50, no. 5 (May 2009): 452.

38. Campbell, "Why the Body Matters," 452. Note: The belief that the mind is separate from the body dates back to early Greek thought. Indeed, Philip Sampson points out, "From a very early period, Greek thought drew a sharp distinction between 'body' and 'soul,' and it came in time to devalue the former in favour of the latter.

By the fourth century BC, this bias was firmly established. So, for Plato, the soul is created first, then embodied." Philip J. Sampson, *Six Modern Myths: Challenging Christian Faith* (Leicester, UK: Inter-Varsity Press, 2000), 117.

39. Campbell, "Why the Body Matters," 452.

40. Gary Steiner, "Descartes, Christianity, and Contemporary Speciesism," in *A Communion of Subjects: Animals in Religion, Science & Ethics*, ed. Paul Waldau and Kimberley Patton (New York: Columbia University Press, 2006), 121.

41. Tomoyuki Furuyashiki, Peter C. Holland, and Michela Gallagher, "Rat Orbitofrontal Cortex Separately Encodes Response and Outcome Information during Performance of Goal-Directed Behaviour," *Journal of Neuroscience* 28, no. 19 (May 7, 2008): 5127–38.

42. Timothy E. Holy and Zhongsheng Guo, "Ultrasonic Songs of Male Mice," *PLoS Biology* 3, no. 12 (December 2005): 2177–86; Charlotte Uhlenbroek, *Talking with Animals* (London: Hodder and Stoughton, 2002).

43. Note the following from Giovanni Pezzulo, Paul F. M. J. Verschure, Christian Balkenius, and Cyriel M. A. Pennartz, "The Principles of Goal-Directed Decision-Making: from Neural Mechanisms to Computation and Robotics," *Philosophical Transactions of The Royal Society B* [*Biological Sciences*] 369, no. 1655 (November 2014): 1.

> A recent trend of research is to focus on goal-directed choice mechanisms that select among anticipated action outcomes in a context-dependent way. These goal-oriented processes provide the foundations of many everyday human and animal decisions. Goal-directed decision-making relies on multiple sources of information beyond immediately available sensory stimuli, such as representations of (proximal and distal) goal states and their utility, memory and predicted future states. . . . We need to understand the specific contributions of goals, episodic memory, working memory and cognitive control to decisions, and to analyse the neural substrates of these brain processes and how they link to flexible forms of computation (e.g. model-based methods of reinforcement learning, which consider specific action outcomes and not only stimulus-response pairs).

44. Steiner, "Descartes, Christianity, and Contemporary Speciesism," 121.

45. Steiner, "Descartes, Christianity, and Contemporary Speciesism," 122.

46. Vaughan Monamy, *Animal Experimentation: A Guide to the Issues*, 2nd ed. (Cambridge: Cambridge University Press, 2009), 10.

47. Della Thompson, ed., *The Concise Oxford Dictionary*, 9th ed. (Oxford: Clarendon Press, 1995).

48. John Rawls, *A Theory of Justice* (Oxford: Oxford University Press, 1973), 302.

49. Rawls, *A Theory of Justice*, 302.

50. Rawls, A *Theory of Justice*, 302

51. Rawls, *A Theory of Justice*, 302–3.

52. Isaiah Berlin, "Two Concepts of Liberty," in *Liberty: Oxford Readings in Politics and Government*, ed. David Miller (Oxford: Oxford University Press, 1993).

53. Berlin, "Two Concepts of Liberty," 42

54. Berlin, "Two Concepts of Liberty," 43.

REFERENCES

Berlin, Isaiah. "Two Concepts of Liberty." In *Liberty: Oxford Readings in Politics and Government*, edited by David Miller, 33–57. Oxford: Oxford University Press, 1993.

Campbell, Alastair V. "Why the Body Matters: The Uses and Abuses of the Human Body in Modern Medicine." *Singapore Medical Journal* 50, no. 5 (May 2009): 451–55.

Cann, Alan J. "Replication of Viruses." In *Encyclopedia of Virology* 3rd edition. Brian W. J. Mahy and Marc H. V. Van Regenmortel, eds., (Academic Press, 2008), 406–412. www.sciencedirect.com/referencework/9780123744104/encyclopedia-of-virology

Dolin, Eric Jay. *Fur, Fortune and Empire: The Epic History of the Fur Trade in America*. London: W. W. Norton, 2010.

Favre, David. "Living Property: A New Status for Animals within the Legal System." *Marquette Law Review* 93, no. 3 (2010). scholarship.law.marquette.edu/mulr/vol93/iss3/3

Francione, Gary L. *Animals as Persons: Essays on the Abolition of Animal Exploitation*. New York: Columbia University Press, 2008.

Furuyashiki, Tomoyuki, Peter C. Holland, and Michela Gallagher. "Rat Orbitofrontal Cortex Separately Encodes Response and Outcome Information during Performance of Goal-Directed Behaviour." *Journal of Neuroscience* 28, no. 19 (May 7, 2008): 5127–38.

Holy, Timothy E., and Zhongsheng Guo. "Ultrasonic Songs of Male Mice." *PLoS Biology* 3, no. 12 (December 2005): 2177–86.

Kant, Immanuel. *The Moral Law: Groundwork of the Metaphysic of Morals*. Translated and analyzed by Herbert James Paton. London: Routledge, 1991.

Libell, Monica. "A Mirror of Myself? Monist and Dualist Views of Animals." In *Animal Bioethics: Principles and Teaching Methods*, edited by Michel Marie, Sandra Edwards, Gustavo Gandini, Michael J. Reiss, and Eberhard von Borell, 19–32. Wageningen, the Netherlands: Wageningen Academic, 2005.

Locke, John. *The Second Treatise on Civil Government*. New York: Prometheus Books, 1986.

Mackenzie, Catriona. "The Importance of Relational Autonomy and Capabilities for an Ethics of Vulnerability." In *Vulnerability: New Essays in Ethics and Feminist Philosophy*, edited by Catriona Mackenzie, Wendy Rogers, and Susan Dodds, 33–59. Oxford: Oxford University Press, 2014.

Mackenzie, Catriona, Wendy Rogers, and Susan Dodds. Introduction to *Vulnerability: New Essays in Ethics and Feminist Philosophy*, edited by Catriona Mackenzie, Wendy Rogers, and Susan Dodds, 1–29. Oxford: Oxford University Press, 2014.

Masson, Jeffrey, and Susan McCarthy. *When Elephants Weep: The Emotional Lives of Animals*. London: Vintage, 1996.

Monamy, Vaughan. *Animal Experimentation: A Guide to the Issues*. 2nd ed. Cambridge: Cambridge University Press, 2009.

National Commission for the Protection of Human Subjects of Biomedical and Behavioral Research. *The Belmont Report: Ethical Principles and Guidelines for the Protection of Human Subjects of Research.* US Department of Health and Human Services, April 18, 1979. www.hhs.gov/ohrp/regulations-and-policy/belmont-report/index.html.

National Farm Animal Care Council. *Code of Practice for the Care and Handling of Farmed Fox (Vulpes vulpes).* Canada Fox Breeders Association & National Farm Animal Care Council, 2013. www.nfacc.ca/pdfs/codes/Farmed_Fox_Code.pdf.

National Research Council of the National Academies. *Recognition and Alleviation of Distress in Laboratory Animals.* Washington, DC: National Academies Press, 2008.

Nussbaum, Martha C. "Objectification." *Philosophy and Public Affairs* 24, no.4 (Fall 1995): 249–291. www.mit.edu/~shaslang/mprg/nussbaumO.pdf

Pezzulo, Giovanni, Paul F. M. J. Verschure, Christian Balkenius, and Cyriel M. A. Pennartz. "The Principles of Goal-Directed Decision-Making: From Neural Mechanisms to Computation and Robotics." *Philosophical Transactions of the Royal Society B* [*Biological Sciences*] 369, no. 1655 (November 2014): 1–5. dx.doi.org/10.1098/rstb.2013.0470.

Rawls, John. *A Theory of Justice.* Oxford: Oxford University Press, 1973.

Regan, Tom. *The Case for Animal Rights.* London: Routledge, 1988.

Sampson, Philip J. *Six Modern Myths: Challenging Christian Faith.* Leicester, UK: Inter-Varsity Press, 2000.

Sleeper-Smith, Susan, ed. *Rethinking the Fur Trade: Cultures of Exchange in an Atlantic World.* Lincoln: University of Nebraska Press, 2009.

Sorabji, Richard. *Animal Minds and Human Morals: The Origins of the Western Debate.* London: Gerald Duckworth & Co. Ltd., 1993.

Steiner, Gary. "Descartes, Christianity, and Contemporary Speciesism." In *A Communion of Subjects: Animals in Religion, Science & Ethics, edited by Paul Waldau and Kimberley Patton, 117–31. New York: Columbia University Press, 2006.*

Thompson, Della, ed. *The Concise Oxford Dictionary.* 9th ed. Oxford: Clarendon Press, 1995.

Uhlenbroek, Charlotte. *Talking with Animals.* London: Hodder and Stoughton, 2002.

Wilkinson, Stephen. *Bodies for Sale: Ethics and Exploitation in the Human Body Trade.* Abingdon, UK: Routledge, 2003.

Wilson, Edward O. *Half-Earth: Our Planet's Fight for Life.* London: W. W. Norton, 2016.

Chapter 8

If a Fox Could Talk

Wittgenstein and the Calculated Silencing of Animals in Industrial Fur Production

K. York

Ludwig Wittgenstein's famous statement that "if a lion could talk, we could not understand him"[1] seems to be in contradiction with his general understanding of how language works. To show how this is so, I would like to briefly outline Wittgenstein's theory of language and meaning for those who are new to him. First, Wittgenstein's early work more closely reflects his intellectual predecessors such as Frege. Both Frege and the early Wittgenstein held a representationalist view of meaning. Wittgenstein conceived of us representing reality to ourselves by means of pictures: pictures are the definite ways in which the elements within the pictures are related to each other.[2] What the picture shares in common with reality is the logical structure shared by the elements of the picture and the objects that compose what Wittgenstein calls "elementary facts." Whether or not the picture shares such a structure with the world is what renders the picture true or untrue. These truth conditions are what give a picture its meaning.[3]

We can call this view "representationalist" because linguistic meaning is thought of as relying on language's means of representing the world. In this view, expressions have essential meanings because there are definite necessary and sufficient conditions for something to be linguistic and to have meaning. Wittgenstein, however, later changed his views. To roughly see why, consider that we use language (and thought) for a great many things, many of which don't involve reference to a set of conditions in the world. Wittgenstein writes:

> Think of the tools in a tool-box: there is a hammer, pliers, a saw, a screw-driver, a rule, a glue-pot, glue, nails and screws.—The functions of words are as diverse as the functions of these objects. (And in both cases there are similarities.) Of course, what confuses us is the uniform appearance of words when we hear them spoken or meet them in script and print.[4]

Think about the phrase "I now pronounce you man and wife." Austin recognized that this phrase, like many, doesn't represent a set of conditions but is rather a performance that brings about those conditions.[5] But there are also deeper reasons for what was, in Wittgenstein's view, the necessity of a new theory of linguistic meaning.

Kripke argues for this idea by way of a skeptical problem.[6] In order to use language, we rely on rules. For example, when I write "2+2=4," I might think that this sentence is true purely based on the meanings of the terms "2," "4," "+," and "=." I could think, for example, that the meaning of "+" is to be analyzed as a function that takes some number x, when added to y, x numbers higher than y. That this is the function of "+" is just a basic rule of math. But as Wittgenstein notes, "How can a rule show me what I have to do at *this* point?"[7] Every action can be made to accord with myriad rules, and there is no way to ensure that your language act accords with the appropriate rule. Given a schema for the application of rules, "it is quite easy to imagine *a method projection* according to which" this schema can be used in myriad ways.[8] Thus, it is impossible to tell which action the rule was *meant* to accord with.[9] So, for example, when I write "2+2=4," how do I know that I do not mean by "+" some function similar to addition but that tells me to write "5" when calculating "2" + "2"?[10] There is no fact of the matter, for Wittgenstein, as to whether I ever mean this or that, whether I have this or that in my mind. This is why Wittgenstein writes, "If God had looked into our minds he would not have been able to see there whom we were speaking of."[11] The only solution here is to root the answer in pure convention.

In place of a unified set of rules for how language represents the world, we are given a theory of myriad language games. A language game is a particular form of using language, according to a particular set of inarticulable rules, that accompanies and enables a particular activity we engage in. On the face of things, Wittgenstein's theory of language, being rooted in convention and behavior rather than deep structure, poses no criteria that might exclude animal communication. Thus, one might think that although Wittgenstein said, "If a lion could talk, we could not understand him,"[12] this is because we could not understand a lion's language unless we participated in that world.

But is it really required that we participate in the language game and the form of life it accompanies? What if we simply mapped out the behavioral and pragmatic correlates of the lion's expressions? These things are accessible to us. I might observe a tribesperson use a particular word in specific circumstances and be able to reproduce this expression to the satisfaction of the other tribespeople. I would in such a case seemingly grasp the meaning of the term, as we can similarly grasp the meanings of the terms in the imaginary language games with which Wittgenstein illustrates his principles. An obvious objection available here would be that a lion cannot grant that I got the gist of his growl. However, this would mean only that the question of meaning does not arise for the lion. A lion does not need a conception of meaning in order to *mean*. He simply cannot play language games involving the direct affirmation or denial of meaning. It is not a necessary component of a language game that it must include the ability to explicitly assess whether the players understand each other: this can be tacit. In fact, there are no necessary and sufficient conditions for qualification as a language game. They are instead linked by a set of interconnected family resemblances. Moreover, I do not need to engage with an animal in order to understand the animal. Studying him or her will suffice.

This anti-essentialist and prototype-based understanding of language bears some extra consideration. Linguists such as Bloomfield, Chomsky, and Hockett assert that there are properties unique to human language that make it qualitatively different from animal communication.[13] One criterion, for example, is displacement, or the ability to refer to remote points in space and time.[14] Wittgenstein often reflected on this difference between humans and certain animals. For example, Wittgenstein writes, "A dog believes his master is at the door. But can he also believe his master will come the day after tomorrow?—And what can he not do here?"[15] However, as Levvis rightly points out, this should make no difference to whether a lion means as we do, since not all of Wittgenstein's imagined and complete language games feature displacement, and such criteria of difference as displacement at most "point to a non-essential difference between human and nonhuman forms of communication."[16]

One immediate lesson to draw from this is that while there are general differences between language and zoosemiotic (or, if you prefer, animal communication) systems, such differences are not essential differences. Moreover, zoosemiotic systems may differ from each other individually as much as either differs from human language or as much as individual human language games may differ from each other. If this seems a surprising claim, consider by analogy the term "animal." The idea of "nonhuman animals" doesn't form anything resembling a natural kind any more than a set composed of all animals except beavers. It would be surprising to find a case where you could infer something like "species a has trait x, so we have reason to think that all nonhuman species of animal have trait x" without also warranting the inference "all members of the metazoan class (including humans) have trait x."[17]

Nor does the class of nonhuman animals share a distinct common microstructure or underlying causal process. My claim is that the same fact might very well hold in the case of distinguishing human from animal languages. We can distinguish human language in any single case, but there is no use in trying to distinguish it from a class composed by the communication of all other animals, at least according to some researchers.[18] There is reason to think that we share with the honeybee communication the capacity for discreteness (being composed of smaller units that can be rearranged to change meaning) and displacement (the ability to communicate about things that are not here and now), with certain crabs a duality of patterning (the capacity to form meaningful units of communication from nonmeaningful units such as phenomes or claw-waves), with seagulls openness or productivity, with songbirds learnability and tradition,[19] with crows prevarication or the capacity to mislead,[20] and with dogs (during play) the capacity for meta-symbolic reference.[21]

Whether or not we decide to use different terms to refer to language and forms of animal communication seems to me a matter of what Burgess and Plunkett call "conceptual ethics," which asks, what "concepts should we use to think and talk about the world and to do all of the other things that mental and linguistic representation facilitates?"[22] More importantly, Wittgenstein's theory of meaning isn't an account of language but an account of semiotic (or, if you prefer, "communicative") systems in general. That Wittgenstein failed to recognize this, I attribute to the fact that he was working in a tradition whose concern was language and not sign systems more broadly. Thus, there is no apparent reason that we should not refer to zoosemiotic activities as "language (or communication) games."

A final remaining reason that we might not understand a lion is the foreignness of a lion's facial expressions. However, as Levvis shows, Wittgenstein recognized that facial expressions gain meaning by virtue of systematic interrelation.[23] Thus, my previous point about the sufficiency of studying animals for understanding what they mean when they bark and tweet should also apply here.

Levvis goes on to assert his own reading of Wittgenstein's assertion that we could not understand a lion. According to Levvis, the important part of Wittgenstein's philosophy to pay attention to here is in Wittgenstein's treatment of predictability. Levvis thinks that for Wittgenstein, the ability to make predictions based on behavioral and linguistic observations is a requisite for understanding them (if I cannot predict any possible moves in a language game, I cannot be thought to understand it). However, after a certain threshold of predictability is exceeded, the comprehensibility actually goes down. Wittgenstein writes, "Life's infinite variations are essential to our life. And so to even the habitual character of life. What we regard as expression *consists* in incalculability. If I knew exactly how he would grimace, move, there would be no facial expression, no gesture."[24] Levvis outlines a distinction that Wittgenstein draws between two kinds of comprehensibility. Wittgenstein asserts, "We speak of understanding a sentence in the sense in which it can be replaced by another which says the same; but also in the sense in which it cannot be replaced by any other. (Anymore than one musical theme can be replaced by another.)"[25] It's worth noting at this point that such understandings don't exhaust the concept of "understand," since understanding and attributions of meaning vary according to different language games.

Levvis then tries to show how animal behavior is incomprehensible on both counts. The predictability of animal behavior, Levvis argues, renders it incomprehensible in the second sense. As Levvis writes, "The unpredictability which is the earmark of human behavior is not found in our interactions with animals."[26] This is supposed to imply, I presume, that the irreplaceability of comprehensible behavior is lacking in the case of animals. Levvis's statement seems *prima facie* doubtable to anyone who has spent any time around animals, which makes it all the more puzzling that it's glazed over as an obvious truth without any evidentiary support. The closest Levvis comes to arguing for this fact is in stating that in human communication, "speakers vary their form of expression to locate themselves (and allow themselves to be located) in . . . a position within social space."[27] But the fact that humans do this is no reason to suppose that nonhumans don't. Moreover, communicative signaling in animals indeed greatly varies according to unique context.[28] At any rate, it's not clear that such a fact, even if true, would establish Levvis's points, since it leaves open the possibility that even human behavior is completely predictable once given the proper context of prediction (the social space).

Levvis's other argument is more interesting. He notes Wittgenstein's argument that animals also fail to meet the first sense of comprehensibility (grouping together here predictability and generalizability) as the reason we cannot understand them: "the uncertainty one feels as to whether animals, like flies and spiders, feel pain does not arise from not knowing what to expect, but from the fact that one does not know *how* to react (or *whether* to react) in the presence of their behavior."[29] Participation in a language game entails not only knowing how the speaker will go on but knowing how you, the listener, will go on as well. Levvis here accurately locates a theoretical basis from which to understand Wittgenstein's point about the comprehensibility of animals. It explains why dogs are more comprehensible to us than foxes. It's not just that we spend more time around dogs. It's that we have established more language games with dogs and more coordinated forms of life (feeding them, playing fetch, calling them, etc.) However, Levvis seems to misunderstand this point.

Levvis goes on: "If Wittgenstein's view is correct, then the assignment of rights to animals becomes tricky. I would suggest that before an individual can be assigned rights it is necessary for that individual to be understood."[30] This would seem to place us into a viscious circle, since any "understanding" of an animal's pain would by this theory require some established normative approach to that animal's pain expression. So, to suggest that a new normative approach would first require understanding would be to put the cart before the horse. When Wittgenstein noted that we did not know how to respond to the pains of a spider,[31] he was not pointing to an eternally insurmountable epistemic problem but was rather outlining our conventional form of life as it now stands. This is not a case where philosophy must leave "everything as it is,"[32] because the problem is not purely philosophical but ethical (Wittgenstein thought of these subjects as at least somewhat distinct). Thus, in this view, for example, a Buddhist monk interested in alleviating the pains of spiders *does* understand their pain expressions simply by virtue of the fact that the monk has set up a system of sympathetic responses to the spiders. Moreover, Levvis is wrong that we have no established conventions regarding responding to the pains of animals. In the case of dogs, these responses are sympathetic and helpful. In the case of animals used in industrial fur and meat production, our convention is to expect and ignore such cries. I will now turn to the case of the industrial farming of animals for fur as a case study of this relationship between ethics and communicative meaning.

FUR, PAIN EXPRESSIONS, AND COMMUNICATION: A CASE STUDY

For Wittgenstein, since communicative meaning is rooted in convention and not in representation, our expressions of internal states should not be thought of as gaining their meaning from some internal experience but rather as gaining meaning from the conventions surrounding the expression. Explaining this idea in clearer terms than Wittgenstein himself, Kripke gives us the example of a child learning how to use the word "'pain." Obviously, if she claims to be in pain only when she is in pain (and not play-acting, etc.), she is using the word correctly. But the parent does not point to some inner state of the child when teaching her the word. "Rather," Kripke writes, "the adult will endorse the child's avowal if the child's behavior (crying, agitated motion, etc.) and, perhaps, external circumstances surrounding the child, indicate that he is in pain."[33] The phrase "I am in pain," then, fulfills the job that the crying used to. Except in very unusual circumstances,[34] claiming to be in pain is not a factual report; instead, it is used for purposes such as receiving aid and sympathy from others. Fittingly, then, my conviction that she is in pain is expressed in my behavioral disposition towards her; if I comfort her or give her medicine, these acts constitute my conviction that she is in pain. The pain cries of animals also have the function of alerting others to danger, calling for help, or requesting care. Even many ants, when endangered, release a pheromone whose function is to call the aid of their cohorts.[35]

It would seem natural to conclude, then, that furriers do not take the cries of fur animals to indicate that they are in pain. After all, they don't seem to respond to the cries of pain in any way. But things may not be quite so simple. When a furrier hears the crying out of a fox, certainly he might imagine that the fox is in the same sort of "help-needing" state that his baby or his dog Fido are in when crying out. As with cases of war, there are times when this "help-needed" sign is taken as something to be ignored. One might hold that an individual's attitude that someone is in pain prototypically involves a predisposition to help them, except in pathological cases. And factory farming might be seen as such a case. Indeed, in the limited literature that exists on the subject of the psychological effects on slaughterhouse workers, the widespread existence of post-traumatic stress disorder and alcohol abuse among such workers indicates strong internal conflict regarding the killing of so-called "livestock."[36] As one worker says, "They have to drink, they have no other way of dealing with killing live, kicking animals all day long. If you stop and think about it, you're killing several thousand beings a day."[37] Since our values and systems of meaning-making can affect what events will lead to the development of PTSD,[38] the recognition of animals as being in pain and worthy of sympathy may indeed conflict with the conventional demands of industrial fur farming in the case of workers who suffer psychological distress.

What we have here, then, is not necessarily evidence for a *lack* of conviction that fur foxes are in pain; there is an observable set of responses on the part of furriers to the pain of these foxes. It's just that these responses, rather than being the straightforward sorts of responses you'd find them having towards Fido's cries of pain, are expressed through indirect and pathological behaviors such as alcohol abuse (and possibly the observable suppression of other reactions).

Still, we can't deny that there is a significant amount of silencing of fur animals going on here. And this silencing indeed feeds into the same vicious cycle of reasoning that is expressed by Levvis when he writes, "before an individual can be assigned rights it is necessary for that individual to be understood." For imagine what distress the furriers might experience if they had to both kill and skin foxes and at the same time sympathetically respond to the foxes' cries of pain (insofar as they could do that while continuing the killing process.) What functionally amounts to a denial of these creatures' capacity to mean eases the process of denying them rights. There are a few reasons for this. First, sincere and warranted pleas or requests for help ordinarily carry an even larger ethical or moral import than mere reports of inner states. Though a utilitarian might deny this on grounds that evidence of suffering is all that matters, pleas or requests for help establish a social or communicative bond that strengthens one's sense of moral duty. Additionally, as we've seen, just as cries might be prototypically read as requests for help, the prototypical response may be to provide help (I mean this only as a suggestion, since this is an empirical question requiring research beyond the scope of this paper). Second, a being who can communicate and mean seems to achieve a higher degree of selfhood. When we hear speech, such speech is conceptualized as coming from *one who* speaks. By contrast, something merely making noises can simply be a *that.* Though it is commonly accepted that animals can communicate, the idea of human language as being essentially different from fox communication opens space for a more Cartesian mechanistic model of animal behavior. Finally, the industrialization of fur production and exportation of killing to a largely invisible class of workers allows for a complete separation between the semiospheres of animals, fur animals, and fur consumers. This certainly makes it easier to think (if unconsciously) of fur animals as mere material; an unheard cry is obviously easier to ignore.

This seems even more apparent when we consider the general public's relationship to fur animals. They are kept out of sight and mind, and probably for very good prudential reason (for fur consumers, anyway). According to one study, 85 percent of meat consumers reported an unwillingness to personally kill to obtain meat.[39] One would imagine at least a comparable percentage if respondents were asked about fur, especially that of the Canidae family. And this may not just be a matter of avoiding the unpleasantries of blood and guts. It may be more important to keep the pleas and cries of pain at a "safe distance." Keeping the fur animals in an isolated semiosphere (or "sphere of communication," if you prefer) where they are only dealt with by a small (and conflicted) group of workers also functions to silence fur animals at a larger scale. To us, unless we are thinking about it, they are the abstract material from which fur comes. This brings to mind Zizek's idea, as expressed by Sharpe, that the "formula describing the operation of ideology today is not 'they do not know it, but they are doing it.' . . . It is 'they know it, but they are doing it anyway.'"[40]

Levvis's claim that "the uncertainty one feels as to whether animals, like flies and spiders, feel pain" arises from the fact that one "does not know *how* to react (or *whether* to react) in the presence of their behavior"[41] does not describe an aporia but a fixable ethical problem. The granting of basic ethical rights to the animals that we currently slaughter for fur would provide a rather straightforward means of extending our conventions regulating requests for help, personal space, and basic freedom to our interactions with foxes. Thus, an ethical transformation on our part would instantly pull fur animals out of silence.[42]

NOTES

1. Ludwig Wittgenstein, *Philosophical Investigations*, trans. G. E. M. Anscombe, 50th anniv. ed. (Oxford: Blackwell, 2001), sec. 223.

2. Ludwig Wittgenstein, *Tractatus Logico-Philosophicus* (Mineola, NY: Dover, 1999).

3. Wittgenstein, *Tractatus*, xxxi. See also Saul Kripke, *Wittgenstein on Rules and Private Language: An Elementary Exposition* (Oxford: Blackwell, 2007), 62.

4. Wittgenstein, *Philosophical Investigations*, sec. 11.

5. John L. Austin, *How to Do Things with Words*, ed. J. O. Urmson and Marina Sbisà (Oxford: Clarendon, 1975).

6. Kripke, *Wittgenstein on Rules and Private Language*, 7. It's worth noting that Kripke's reading of Wittgenstein, while being exceptionally clear, is nonstandard (to the extent that these views are often refered to as "Kripkinstenian."

7. Wittgenstein, *Philosophical Investigations*, sec. 198.

8. Wittgenstein, *Philosophical Investigations*, sec. 139.

9. Note that if we consider using a word as following a system of rules, then the meaning of the word is supposedly tied to the speaker's intention regarding what rule the use of the word was supposed to follow. For example, is one following the rule of an earnest or an ironic apology?

10. Example from Kripke, *Wittgenstein on Rules and Private Language.*

11. Wittgenstein, *Philosophical Investigations*, sec. 217.

12. Wittgenstein, *Philosophical Investigations*, sec. 223.

13. Donald Griffin, *The Question of Animal Awareness: Evolutionary Continuity of Mental Experience* (New York: Rockefeller University Press, 1981), 73–83.

14. Although, as Griffin notes, this criterion does not accomplish the distinction between human language and animal communication that it sets out to (honeybees, for example, indeed use displacement in their symbols), it still might distinguish our languages from the communication of most animals.

15. Wittgenstein, *Philosophical Investigations*, sec. 174.

16. Gary Levvis, "Why We Would Not Understand a Talking Lion," *Between the Species: An Online Journal for the Study of Philosophy and Animals* 8, no. 3 (1992): 157, doi:10.15368/bts.1992v8n3.7.

17. This is not to say you couldn't make inferences about people that won't apply to non-humans. But this is not special to humans; one could do the same with beavers. One might object by pointing to animals' deficient linguistic capabilities, assuming this to be a natural property perhaps rooted in neurology. When we consider the linguistic deficiencies of a mouse compared with an octopus, certainly the neurology of these creatures is so different that this inference would likely just be right by chance rather than reflecting an underlying structure in either animal. The main problem here is that the common traits of metazoans are so basic that inference between members of this class would not allow us to exclude humans as a unique species.

18. See below.

19. See Griffin, *The Question of Animal Awareness*, for a more detailed treatment of this topic, countering in particular Hockett's set of criteria for the uniqueness of human language.

20. It's worth noting here Temple Grandin's psychological comparison of autism and animal experience. For Grandin, the inability to form sufficiently abstract representations of the world serves to explain why autistic children and animals react so strongly to changes in their environments and why autistic children have difficulty developing language. The point to keep in mind here is that even if this is a general linguistic prerequisite in humans, it doesn't serve to deny thought or (quasi-)linguistic capacities to animals. Moreover, not all human language games involve abstract representation, even if our own species' neurological wiring closely relates linguistic capabilities with abstract representational capabilities. Nevertheless, further exploration of the implications of Grandin's work in regard to animal communication is desirable. Some evidence suggests that (at least) abstract reasoning occurs in animals as simple as the betta fish. See: Temple Grandin and Catherine Johnson, *Animals in Translation: Using the Mysteries of Autism to Decode Animal Behavior* (London: Bloomsbury, 2006).

21. Timo Maran, "Mammal Zoosemiotics" (lecture, University of Tartu, Estonia, 2017).

22. Alexis Burgess and David Plunkett, "Conceptual Ethics II," *Philosophy Compass* 8, no. 12 (2013): 1, doi:10.1111/phc3.12085.

23. Levvis, "Why We Would Not Understand," 159.

24. Wittgenstein, *Philosophical Investigations*, sec. 203; cited in Levvis, "Why We Would Not Understand," 160.

25. Wittgenstein, *Philosophical Investigations*, sec. 531; cited in Levvis, "Why We Would Not Understand," 160.

26. Levvis, "Why We Would Not Understand," 160.

27. Levvis, "Why We Would Not Understand," 160.

28. Erik Thomas Frank et al., "Saving the Injured: Rescue Behavior in the Termite-Hunting Ant *Megaponera analis*," *Science Advances* 3, no. 4 (2017), doi:10.1126/sciadv.1602187.

29. Levvis, "Why We Would Not Understand," 161.

30. Levvis, "Why We Would Not Understand," 161.

31. Wittgenstein, *Philosophical Investigations*, sec. 564.

32. Wittgenstein, *Philosophical Investigations*, sec. 124.

33. Kripke, *Wittgenstein on Rules*, 99–100.

34. For example, in the case of a man with paralysis in his leg visiting a doctor, who prods his leg with a needle and asks, "Does that hurt?"

35. Timo Maran, "Insect Zoosemiotics" (lecture, University of Tartu, Estonia, 2017).

36. Jennifer Dillard, "A Slaughterhouse Nightmare: Psychological Harm Suffered by Slaughterhouse Employees and the Possibility of Redress through Legal Reform," *Georgetown Journal on Poverty Law & Policy* 15, no. 2 (2008): 391–92.

37. Dillard, "A Slaughterhouse Nightmare," 397.

38. Julia Rae Harper, "PTSD: A Situated Look at the Semiotic Process and Role of Individual Umwelts in Human Existence/Function," *Semiotica*, no. 175 (2005): 337–85.

39. Melanie Joy, "Psychic Numbing and Meat Consumption: The Psychology of Carnism" (PhD diss., Saybrook Graduate School, 2002), 137.

40. Matthew Sharpe, "Žižek, Slavoj," *Internet Encyclopedia of Philosophy*, accessed April 1, 2017, www.iep.utm.edu/zizek/.

41. Levvis, "Why We Would Not Understand," 10–11.

42. This is, of course, not to say that these foxes are silent to each other but rather only to us.

REFERENCES

Austin, John L. *How to Do Things with Words*. Edited by J. O. Urmson and Marina Sbisà. Oxford: Clarendon, 1975.

Burgess, Alexis, and David Plunkett. "Conceptual Ethics II." *Philosophy Compass* 8, no. 12 (2013).

Dillard, Jennifer. "A Slaughterhouse Nightmare: Psychological Harm Suffered by Slaughterhouse Employees and the Possibility of Redress Through Legal Reform." *Georgetown Journal on Poverty Law & Policy* 15, no. 2 (2008): 391–409.

Dorovskikh, Anna. "Killing for a Living: Psychological and Physiological Effects of Alienation of Food Production on Slaughterhouse Workers." Undergraduate honors thesis, University of Colorado at Boulder, 2015.

Frank, Erik Thomas, Thomas Schmitt, Thomas Hovestadt, Oliver Mitesser, Jonas Stiegler, and Karl Eduard Linsenmair. "Saving the Injured: Rescue Behavior in the Termite-Hunting Ant *Megaponera analis*." *Science Advances* 3, no. 4 (2017).

Grandin, Temple, and Catherine Johnson. *Animals in Translation: Using the Mysteries of Autism to Decode Animal Behavior*. London: Bloomsbury, 2006.

Griffin, Donald R. *The Question of Animal Awareness: Evolutionary Continuity of Mental Experience*. New York: Rockefeller University Press, 1981.

Harper, Julie Rae. "PTSD: A Situated Look at the Semiotic Process and Role of Individual Umwelts in Human Existence/Function." *Semiotica*, no. 175 (2005): 337–85.

Joy, Melanie. "Psychic Numbing and Meat Consumption: The Psychology of Carnism." PhD diss., Saybrook Graduate School and Research Center, 2002.

Kripke, Saul A. *Wittgenstein on Rules and Private Language: An Elementary Exposition*. Oxford: Blackwell, 2007.

Levvis, Gary W. "Why We Would Not Understand a Talking Lion." *Between the Species: An Online Journal for the Study of Philosophy and Animals* 8, no. 3 (1992).

Maran, Timo. "Insect Zoosemiotics." Lecture, University of Tartu, Tartu, 2017.

———. "Mammal Zoosemiotics." Lecture, University of Tartu, Tartu, 2017.

Sharpe, Matthew. "Žižek, Slavoj." *Internet Encyclopedia of Philosophy*. Accessed April 1, 2017. www.iep.utm.edu/zizek/.

Wittgenstein, Ludwig. *Philosophical Investigations*. Translated by G. E. M. Anscombe. 50th anniv. ed. Oxford: Blackwell, 2001.

———. *Tractatus Logico-Philosophicus*. Mineola, NY: Dover, 1999.

Chapter 9

"All Fur Coat and No Knickers!"

The Speciesism of Fur in Disney Media

Rebecca Rose Stanton

In 2010, pop star Lady Gaga famously, or rather infamously, wore a dress made of raw beef, often dubbed the "meat dress."[1] The meat dress attracted a lot of negative criticism from the public and animal rights groups such as PETA,[2] but why? What was so offensive about Gaga's meat dress? After all, Gaga frequently wears leather, a material that comes from the same animal as her controversial "meat dress," yet when Gaga wears leather, she attracts no criticism, outrage, or attention. It is as if the ethics of wearing meat and leather are separate moral issues, despite both being dead animal flesh. A similar inconsistency is evident when discussing the ethics of fur and leather.

Celebrated fashion designer Karl Lagerfeld says, "In a meat-eating world, wearing leather for shoes and clothes and even handbags, the discussion of fur is childish."[3] By "childish," Lagerfeld is implying that the public's reaction to fur is undercut by a lack of critical reflection on other forms of animal cruelty, such as the production of leather. Is Lagerfeld right? Is the public's outrage over fur "childish" because it is often ignorant of similar animal welfare issues? A look at Disney media indicates that Lagerfeld is right: the discussion of fur *is* "childish."

This essay will discuss the inconsistencies of the fur debate, looking specifically at Disney media to do so. The wearing of fur has been a well-discussed issue in the West, but other animal welfare issues, such as wearing leather, have not yet received the same attention. This inconsistency exists because of speciesism, the practice of treating animals differently because of their species.[4]

DISNEY MEDIA

Many of Walt Disney's biographies suggest that Walt[5] was an animal lover who vocally sympathized with abused animals. This is frequently evident within early Disney media, such as *Dumbo* (1941) and *Bambi* (1942).[6] While some of the ways that Walt used animals at Disney would invite criticism today, there is much evidence to suggest that he genuinely did care for the reputation and representation of the animals used by his company. For example, during the making of *Bambi*, Walt insisted that his animators intensely study the bodies and movements of deer and other woodland creatures in order to depict them accurately.[7] This significant attention to detail gave Disney an artistic edge over its animation competitors, such as Warner Brothers, a reputation that still stands with the company today.[8] However, Walt's reason for doing this extra work was not purely for the creative credentials it gave him; it was also because he wanted to be fair to the species of animals that his company animated.[9]

In the 1950s, Disney produced the live-action television series *Disneyland*, which featured the character of iconic American frontiersman Davy Crockett. In this show, Crockett (played by Fess Parker) usually wore his leitmotif, a prominent "coonskin" hat made from real raccoon skin and fur. Given the success of Crockett's show, many sequels were made, and they always featured this iconic fur hat. This led to the hat becoming hugely popular, especially with young boys.[10] During this craze, it was estimated that five thousand of these coonskin caps were sold every day.[11] The mass-market version was made using fake fur, but with a real raccoon tail. This use of fur was not criticized by the public, even though the scale of racoon deaths necessitated for the hat production seemed to be at odds with Walt's "animal-loving" outlook. Disney even cashed in on this lucrative trend by depicting the fur cap on other popular Disney characters, such as Mickey Mouse and Donald Duck.[12] Traces of the Davy Crockett craze can still be seen in Disney today, especially in the company's merchandise and at the Disney parks. However, now the caps officially sold as merchandise are made entirely from fake fur, with a replica raccoon tail. What is interesting about the Davy Crockett craze is that Disney would soon after be involved in another movement involving fur, one that would become a defining moment of change for the fur industry.

Prior to 1961's *One Hundred and One Dalmatians*, Disney had successfully challenged other animal welfare issues such as hunting and circuses. For example, Disney's *Bambi* (1942) is widely credited with contributing to the modern decline in hunting.[13] The editor of *Outdoor Life* magazine, Raymond Brown, even angrily claimed that *Bambi* was "the worst insult ever offered in any form to American sportsmen."[14] Furthermore, the mass media in general have a strong history of influencing public perception of animal welfare. For example, it has been suggested that Anna Sewell's 1877 classic novel, *Black Beauty*, greatly changed attitudes toward working horses in England, leading to the widespread removal of a leather strap that held working horses' heads unnaturally high.[15] Therefore, it is no great surprise that Disney's 1961 classic anti-fur animation, *One Hundred and One Dalmatians*, is frequently credited as the catalyst for fur's Western decline in popularity.[16]

One Hundred and One Dalmatians

After *Dalmatians*' 1961 release, real fur became noticeably less popular as a fashion item.[17] The film was even bitterly described by the now-defunct pro-fur publication *Fur Age Weekly* as giving children "a gruesome picture" of the fur industry, which perhaps highlights just how strong the film's influence was on the fur business.[18] The anti-fur trend exploded in the 1980s thanks to the birth of PETA, which focused many of its eye-catching campaigns on the cruelty of fur production: "Almost overnight, wearing fur became unfashionable and designers couldn't wait to shout about how they were fur-free and fabulous. Retailers such as Selfridges and Liberty brought in strict no-fur policies."[19] The anti-fur message of Disney's *Dalmatians* clearly worked and is still widely used today in anti–animal abuse campaigns. For example, a set of 2014 graphic designs by artist Saint Hoax titled "Furry Tales" depict various popular Disney characters, such as the Dalmatian puppies and Bambi, as skinned, bleeding, and in distress, to highlight the suffering involved in fur production.[20]

Cruella De Vil is by far the most famous character from *Dalmatians*. In fact, she is one of the most famous Disney characters and film villains ever.[21] However, the nastiness of Disney's 1961 Cruella pales in comparison to the very first Cruella depicted in Dodie Smith's original novel, *The Hundred and One Dalmatians* (1956). For example, when discussing her unloved Persian cat, Smith's Cruella boasts, "I've drowned dozens and dozens of my cat's kittens. She always chooses some wretched alley-cat for their father. So they're never worth keeping."[22] Smith's original text contains much more overt animal abuse than Disney's first *Dalmatians* adaptation does. It includes stray dogs, abused cats, drowned kittens, and even more danger for the hunted Dalmatian puppies. Much of this animal abuse was adapted out, attenuated, or humorized by Disney, which chose not to show the worst of Cruella's cruelty, despite the animals being animated and, of course, fictional. These character and storyline changes gave Disney's Cruella a comic edge over Smith's original. Like many other comical Disney villains, such as Captain Hook (*Peter Pan*) and Ursula (*The Little Mermaid*), Cruella's success arises from the way that she makes the audience love to hate her. As if she were a melodramatic pantomime dame, the audience eagerly awaits her dramatic demise and cheers her comical comeuppance. When discussing Disney villains, classic Disney animators Ollie Johnston and Frank Thomas remarked, "You can't make the character too evil, ugly or stupid because the audience won't accept him."[23] Johnston and Thomas's comment shows that Disney knew that its Cruella had to be less harsh than Dodie Smith's was. As their quote highlights, the audience might not have accepted her otherwise. In addition to her "pantomime dame" traits, Cruella is styled according to the classic Disney formula of other female villains before her. She is ugly, old, skinny, and posh and has few friends.[24] However, despite Cruella's vocally violent intentions, she does not actually ever kill or physically harm any animals in any Disney adaptation she features in. This keeps her famous spark of humor, and thus hilarious character, alive.

Dalmatians is not the first or last Disney text to make a joke out of animal suffering. Another notable example is 1933's *The Three Little Pigs*, which darkly jokes about the meat industry. Inside the house of the pig characters, there is a hanging picture of a string of sausages with the name "Father" underneath, a background joke about the use of pigs in the meat industry. Another example is 2012's *Partysaurus Rex*, a Pixar short that jokes about making a furry toilet seat from monster fur. Earlier, in 2001's feature film *Monsters, Inc.*, the antagonist Randall intimidates the film's protagonist Sully, a furry monster, by telling him that "humans skin monsters and make toilet covers out of their fur."[25] This is a jokey reference to how some furry animals are used by humans in fur production. The Disney theme parks also make sly jokes about animal abuse. For example, Disneyland's Country Bear Jamboree, a musical animatronic attraction featuring singing country bears, has several (fake) bear pelts and hunting trophies hung throughout the attraction. Furthermore, the bear band is jokingly named "The Five Bear Rugs."[26] Interestingly, this attraction was actually created from an idea by Marc Davis, the same animator who brought Cruella to life and transformed her into a comical animal abuser.[27] These jokes may seem like harmless fun, but they make a mockery of animal abuse.

In 1996, Cruella's character was brought to life in the hugely successful live-action *Dalmatians* remake. As with the 1961 adaptation, Cruella's puppy kill count remained at zero. In fact, the ethical treatment of the canine performers used during filming was even used to promote the film.[28] Moreover, in addition to having the standard American Humane Association approval message, Disney encouraged its viewers to adopt dogs responsibly during the film's credits.[29] More recently, Cruella came to life in the Disney Channel's *Descendants* movie (2015), which features Cruella as a stand-alone character in an entirely new story, which again highlights the character's popularity compared with the story's other characters.

Interestingly, in all her adapted forms, Cruella is modeled after Disney's 1961 Cruella, not Dodie Smith's.[30] Furthermore, the actors who have portrayed Cruella in live-action films all have been keen to demonstrate their love of dogs in real life, which seems incompatible with the character of Cruella yet is often essential for the actor's public relations.[31] It seems clear that Cruella's comical animal abuse must be fake for the character to be enjoyable, which also may help explain why Dodie Smith's much crueler Cruella is far less popular than Disney's. However, this strange actor clause seems limited to the Cruella character: after all, actors playing serial killers are not routinely asked to confirm that they are not really serial killers. Ted Levine, who played the sadistic "Buffalo Bill" in *The Silence of the Lambs*, did not feel the need to publicly confirm that he did not approve of abducting women or wearing human skin, even though his character is seen committing such acts within the film. In fact, it seems insulting to question actors in this manner.

Cruella is a character famous for attempting to abuse animals, but she does not fit the profile of a typical direct animal abuser. While some of Cruella's character traits, such as her lack of empathy[32] and her choice of animal to abuse,[33] are also frequently evident in real direct animal abusers, most of her character is not typical of a direct animal abuser. Recent research into direct animal abusers has claimed that direct animal abuse is overwhelmingly committed by individual teenage males from lower socioeconomic backgrounds as a result of mental instability.[34] Cruella, as an older rich female, clearly does not fit the statistical portrait of a direct animal abuser, but she does perfectly epitomize the characteristics of *indirect* animal abusers—that is, fur wearers.

Cruella does not murder any animals across her many Disney adaptations, even though she has had many chances to do so. In contrast, the fur industry murders so many animals that the numbers can only be estimated to the nearest million.[35] The real fur industry is not fictional, animated, or exaggerated. If anything, its existence is minimized within mainstream media such as *Dalmatians*. Furthermore, real fur wearers are normal, everyday people, nothing like the highly dramatized Cruella. Unlike Cruella, real fur wearers rarely have to hunt the animals they are wearing because most fur comes ready-made from fur farms, notorious for their inattention to animal welfare.[36] The horrific realities of fur production have not, of course, been shown by Disney, despite the company's numerous adaptations of this fur-centered story. Moreover, Disney arguably never shows the reality of animal abuse in any of its many animal-focused films, although this criticism also applies to Western mainstream media more broadly. If anything, *Dalmatians* and its many adaptations could be seen as a compliment to the fur industry because it places the blame of fur onto direct animal abusers rather than the more indirect (but much larger) fur farms.

However, Disney's wholesome, funny animation was effective and popular precisely *because* it did not contain violence or animal cruelty. If it had contained animal violence or abuse, it likely would have received a different reaction and legacy, as other films demonstrate. For example, *Watership Down* (1979), an animated adaptation of Richard Adams's acclaimed novel, has become more famous for its bloody animal-fight scenes than for its artistic merits. In fact, the British Board of Film Classification reports that it has received so many complaints about the film's gruesome violence that *Watership Down* is now the most-complained-about film of all time in the UK.[37] Similarly, PETA's shocking exposé films often receive negative reactions from both critics and viewers.[38] As a result, it is often argued that the grisly violence of PETA's campaigns actually turns people away from animal rights issues, which is the opposite of PETA's aim.[39] This demonstrates that media containing bloody, realistic animal abuse are usually unpopular, their messages overshadowed by their violence.[40] In contrast, the 1961 version of *Dalmatians* and its many adaptations are cute, funny, films with happy endings.[41]

Despite adopting a seemingly anti-fur stance with *Dalmatians*, after 1961, Disney continued to dress its animated characters in fur. For example, in 1977's *The Rescuers*, fur is a symbol of culture and elegance for the film's charming heroine, Ms. Bianca. Furthermore, in 1988's *Oliver and Company*, the cat-hating posh poodle, Georgette, lavishly drapes herself in leopard fur to establish her dominance as "top dog": for her, fur is a symbol of her wealth and prestige. Another example is 1991's *Beauty and the Beast*, in which a regal fur-trimmed cloak personifies Belle as an elegant, ladylike, civilized character, similar to Ms. Bianca in *The Rescuers*. In contrast to Belle's fur, the Beast's fur establishes him as a "wild" animal and not the human he so longs to be. In one scene, after having a bath, the Beast shakes his fur to dry himself, similar to a bear or dog. Unlike the other characters mentioned, who have presumably chosen to wear fur, the Beast has no choice but to wear fur because it is a part of him.

Additionally, Disney often depicts fur on its nomadic and historical male characters, for which the company also receives no criticism. In *Hercules* (1997), Hercules is shown wearing the dead carcass of the lion Scar from *The Lion King* (1994). This is an intentional historical reference to the legendary killing of the Nemean lion, who, according to ancient Greek mythology, was killed by Hercules.[42] This is yet another example of Disney making subtle jokes about animal abuse. In another example of nomadic fur-wearing,

Brother Bear (2003) depicts indigenous tribe members wearing fur to keep warm. However, it is notable that the animals used for fur in these historical films are always "free-range" animals and not fur-farmed. As highlighted earlier, fur farms kill many more animals than direct animal abusers do. However, media representations rarely depict this truth and instead focus on the smaller issues within animal welfare.

Disney's various depictions of animals and inconsistent approaches to issues such as utilizing animal skin for clothing imply that it is acceptable to abuse only specific species, such as "livestock." These speciesist attitudes are demonstrated daily by the common outrage many people feel toward the fur trade. The fur trade is one of the most frequently criticized areas of global animal abuse even though it has far fewer victims than other areas of animal abuse, such as the meat and dairy industries.[43] If Disney really wanted to improve animal welfare, then surely it could make a film equivalent to *Dalmatians* that focuses on the meat industry?

It is clear that with the notable exception of the *Dalmatians* franchise, fur is often used by Disney to establish character roles or context. From 1937's *Snow White* to 2016's *Moana*, fur appears in thirty-three of fifty-six Walt Disney Animation Studios (WDAS) films.[44] However, fur is most often just background clothing, with no further comment or criticism given, just as it was during the Davy Crockett craze. Similarly, in the same group of films, leather appears forty-seven times, and unlike fur, the use of leather is always presented without comment or criticism. Meat appears in thirty of these fifty-six films, again without depiction of the processes of meat production and without comment on its cruelty or the lives of the animals involved.[45] This proves that WDAS is discerning with its animal welfare issues. Animal abuse is a frequent topic in WDAS films but is explored only selectively. For example, of the fifty-six WDAS films studied, zoos were featured four times and "pet shops" three times.[46] In contrast to this, slaughterhouses and fur farms have never been depicted. Furthermore, the animal welfare issues raised in these films usually relate only to more popular animal species, such as elephants, dogs, and cats. However, this inconsistency is reflective of real reactions to animal welfare issues. In reality, people are speciesist and tend to care more about animal welfare issues that affect the species with whom they are more familiar. It has been claimed that speciesist attitudes work on a "socio-zoological scale."[47] This scale determines how important a species is—or is not—to humans. A species' rank is determined by the following criteria: usefulness, human relationship, appearance, danger factor, and how demonic the animal seems to humans.[48] For example, cats score very highly on this scale, whereas cockroaches do not. It seems clear that species who rank high on the socio-zoological scale are also much more likely to appear in WDAS films and have their welfare issues raised.

Leather

Disney has never critiqued the use of leather. In fact, the company even sells it in many of its parks and stores. Furthermore, the cruelty that leather production entails has never been the topic of a Disney film, whereas animal cruelty involving more popular animals, such as in the cases of fur and circuses, has been. This inconsistency is reflective of how people view the production of fur and leather in real life. A 2011 estimate found that 95 percent of British people oppose the production of fur.[49] Furthermore, in 2000, the UK proudly banned fur farming.[50] However, the UK has numerous slaughterhouses, "pet shops," factory farms, dairy farms, and even fur shops. Ninety-five percent of the British population evidently oppose fur production, but just 2 percent of the same group of people questioned opposed using leather. Leather is widely used across Western culture, with little criticism. This seems to connect to the points raised earlier by Karl Lagerfeld, in that the discussion of fur lacks critical thinking. It seems clear from both Disney depictions and public attitudes that wearing fur is morally unacceptable, whereas wearing leather is permissible. So, what is the difference between fur and leather that causes this difference in acceptance?

Is it the cost? Fur generally costs much more than leather. Therefore, the two attract different types of customers. This is accurately reflected in Disney through the types of characters who often wear fur and leather. For example, in WDAS films set in modern narratives, fur is more often worn by rich women, such as Ms. Bianca (*The Rescuers*) and Cruella (*Dalmatians*). However, leather often appears to be worn by poorer, more common characters, such as Amos from *The Fox and the Hound*.

Might it be their differing appearance? Fur often looks similar to how it looked upon the animal from whom it came, which Cruella famously loved. Cruella wanted a coat made of Dalmatian puppies specifically because of their attractive signature spots. In contrast, leather usually looks unrecognizable from the animal that it came from. In fact, in one scene in 1961's *Dalmatians*, the Dalmatian puppies are placed on what appears to be a brown leather sofa. This is where Gaga's "meat dress" becomes interesting. As noted earlier, the dress was made from raw beef, which comes from cows, just as leather usually does. However, the meat dress was controversial because of its grotesque "meaty" appearance. If Gaga had worn a leather dress, this would have been unlikely to provoke outrage since leather does not look like the animal it came from.

Further to their differences in appearance, the terms "fur" and "leather" perhaps also support the divide between the two. "Fur" keeps the same name from animal to clothing. For example, a Dalmatian's fur can become a Dalmatian fur coat. In contrast, "animal skin" and "leather" (or "suede") are vastly different terms with no linguistic connection to each other. This difference in name allows consumers to separate the abused animal from the end product when buying leather, something that is much harder to do when buying fur.

However, the main difference between fur and leather—the difference that causes the wide contrast in public attitudes—is, of course, the animals from whom fur and leather are made. Speciesism is what causes this division. Fur comes from fluffy, familiar animals such as foxes who score high on the socio-zoological scale. In contrast, leather comes from farmed animals, so-called "livestock" such as cows, who score lower on the socio-zoological scale. Resultantly, leather is frequently defended as a "by-product" of the meat industry.[51]

CONCLUSION

Despite the past backlash against fur, it is making a steady comeback.[52] Moreover, this time, the media seem far less interested in fighting it, and the fur industry seems to know that it needs the media firmly on its side. Evidence clearly suggests that the fur industry has learned a lesson from the reputational damage caused by 1961's *Dalmatians*.[53] Interestingly, fur continues to be a common type of clothing for characters in animated Disney films. It was recently featured in *The Princess and the Frog* (2009), *Tangled* (2010), and *Frozen* (2013) with no criticism or comment. It is merely background clothing used to convey context or character personality.

It is clear the media can reflect changes in animal welfare issues, as has been demonstrated with *Dalmatians* and other anti–animal abuse media. Animal abuse, which is the largest form of violence globally, is increasing.[54] However, exposure to it is decreasing, despite the expansion of the global media.[55] *Cruella* (2021), the most recent Disney *Dalmatians* adaptation, focuses on Cruella's back story with themes of fashion, music, and human rivalries. Thus, the anti-fur message of the original text has been attenuated in favor of Cruella's character. As demonstrated here, Disney clearly has limits to its concern for animal welfare. Luckily for Disney, these concerns are matched by the public.

NOTES

1. Katie Baron, "Fashion's Greatest Pop Hits—From Gaga's Meat Dress to Grace Jones's Armani Suit," *Guardian*, August 16, 2016, www.theguardian.com/fashion/2016/aug/16/fashions-greatest-pop-hits-from-gagas-meat-dress-to-grace-joness-armani-suit.

2. Ingrid E. Newkirk, "Lady Gaga's Meat Dress," *PETA*, September 13, 2010, www.peta.org/blog/lady-gagas-meat-dress/.

3. Stephen Adams, "Karl Lagerfeld Defends Fur Industry Saying 'Beasts' Would Kill Us If We Didn't Kill Them," *Telegraph*, January 2, 2009, fashion.telegraph.co.uk/news-features/TMG4075783/Karl-Lagerfeld-defends-fur-industry-saying-beasts-would-kill-us-if-we-didnt-kill-them.html.

4. An in-depth discussion of speciesism and its meaning can be found in O. Horta, "What Is Speciesism?," *Journal of Agricultural and Environmental Ethics* 23, no. 3 (2010): 243–66.

5. This essay will refer to Walt Disney as Walt in order to avoid confusion between Walt Disney the person and the Walt Disney Company.

6. Bob Thomas, *Walt Disney: An American Original* (New York: Simon and Schuster, 1976).

7. Ralph H. Lutts, "The Trouble with *Bambi*: Walt Disney's *Bambi* and the American Vision of Nature," *Forest & Conservation History* 36, no. 4 (1992): 163.

8. It is often noted that Warner Brothers placed more importance on an animation's jokes than on the quality of animation. Amy M. Davis, *Good Girls and Wicked Witches: Changing Representations of Women in Disney's Feature Animation* (Barnet, UK: John Libbey, 2007), 59.

9. Chris Pallant, *Demystifying Disney: A History of Disney Feature Animation* (London: Continuum, 2011), 41.

10. Additionally, to attract the attention of female fans, a "female" version of the hat, the "Polly Crockett" hat (named after Crockett's wife), was also produced using white rabbit fur.

11. John Johnson, "Coonskin Cap Clings to 'Crockett,'" *Los Angeles Times*, August 23, 2002, articles.latimes.com/2002/aug/23/local/me-fess23.

12. J. P. Walker, *The Legendary Mountain Men of North America* (Morrisville, NC: Lulu Books, 2015), 24.

13. Lutts, "The Trouble with *Bambi*," 162–63.

14. Matt Cartmill, *A View to a Death in the Morning: Hunting and Nature through History* (Cambridge, MA: Harvard University Press, 1996), 178.

15. Gina Marlene Dorré, "Horses and Corsets: 'Black Beauty,' Dress Reform, and the Fashioning of the Victorian Woman," *Victorian Literature and Culture* 30, no. 1 (2002): 157–78.

16. Sidney Urquhart, "What Becomes a Legend Least?," *Time*, August 19, 1991, content.time.com/time/magazine/article/0,9171,973656,00.html.

17. Richard D. North, *Fur and Freedom: In Defence of the Fur Trade* (London: Institute of Economic Affairs, 2000), 17–18.

18. Urquhart, "What Becomes?"

19. Tracy McVeigh, "Animal Rights Campaigners Protest as Fur Comes Back into Fashion," *Guardian*, March 1, 2014, www.theguardian.com/fashion/2014/mar/01/animal-campaigners-protest-fur-fashion.

20. Lizzie Dearden, "Simba, Bambi and Other Disney Characters Shown Skinned and Bleeding in Anti-Fur Campaign," *Independent*, December 1, 2014, www.independent.co.uk/arts-entertainment/art/news/simba-bambi-and-disney-characters-shown-skinned-and-bleeding-in-anti-fur-campaign-9896355.html.

21. Eliana Dockterman and Kelly Conniff, "*Maleficent* and 16 Other Famous Queens of Mean," *Time*, May 31, 2014, time.com/2801704/maleficent-villains-wicked-witch-catwoman/.

22. Dodie Smith, *The Hundred and One Dalmatians* (London: Egmont UK, 2010), 14.

23. Ollie Johnston and Frank Thomas, *The Disney Villain* (New York: Hyperion Press, 1993), 18–19.

24. Davis, *Good Girls and Wicked Witches*, 215.

25. Susanna Lazarus, "Has Sully from *Monsters Inc* Been Turned into a Toilet Seat Cover?," *Radio Times*, August 12, 2015, www.radiotimes.com/news/2015-08-12/has-sully-from-monsters-inc-been-turned-into-a-toilet-seat-cover/.

26. Brooks Barnes, "Despite Fans' Fears, Disney's Country Bears Remain Corny," *New York Times*, October 19, 2013, www.nytimes.com/2012/10/20/arts/country-bear-jamboree-at-walt-disney-world.html?mcubz=1.

27. Barnes, "Despite Fans' Fears."

28. Erica Sheen, "101 and Counting: Dalmatians in Film and Advertising," *World-views: Global Religions, Culture, and Ecology*, no. 9 (2005): 247.

29. Sheen, "101 and Counting," 237.

30. In 1967, six years after the first *Dalmatians* film, Dodie Smith released a sequel novel: *The Starlight Barking*. The sequel resumes where the previous novel finished, but during Cruella's miniscule appearance, she is asleep. Unsurprisingly, Disney has yet to show any interest in adapting Smith's dog-focused sequel, most likely because of Cruella's fleeting appearance. However, Disney has written its own sequels to the *Dalmatians* story, all of which heavily feature the company's own 1961 Cruella character, rather than Smith's much crueller one.

31. Rebecca Rose Stanton, "Speak of the Devil! The Keys to Cruella's Success," *Animation Studies*, June 12, 2017, blog.animationstudies.org/?p=2049.

32. Lori Marino and Michael Mountain, "Denial of Death and the Relationship between Humans and Other Animals," *Anthrozoos* 28, no. 1 (2015): 5–21.

33. Clifton P. Flynn, *Understanding Animal Abuse: A Sociological Analysis* (New York: Lantern Books, 2012), 23.

34. Flynn, *Understanding Animal Abuse*, 10–30.

35. Humane Society International, "The Fur Trade," accessed January 31 2022, www.hsi.org/news-media/fur-trade/.

36. Charlotte Meredith, "Animals Electrocuted, Strangled and Skinned Alive: The True Face of China's Fur Farms," *Express*, March 1, 2013, www.express.co.uk/news/world/381117/Animals-electrocuted-strangled-and-skinned-alive-The-true-face-of-China-s-fur-farms.

37. Noel Brown, *British Children's Cinema: From the Thief of Bagdad to Wallace and Gromit* (London: I. B. Tauris, 2017).

38. Jonathan Burt, *Animals in Film* (Islington, UK: Reaktion Books, 2002), 171.

39. A brief overview of some of PETA's controversial campaigns can be found in Lisa Yount, *Animal Rights* (New York: Infobase, 2008), 15–17.

40. Burt, *Animals in Film*, 141.

41. Interestingly, the 1961 *Dalmatians* film did receive criticism and complaints for a scene in which the Dalmatian puppies nurse from some happy free-range dairy cows. This scene was cut from the film's theatrical release in many countries because the sight of animated cow teats was deemed offensive. Emma Cochrane, Rev. of *101 Dalmatians*, *Empire*, January 1, 2014, www.empireonline.com/movies/101-dalmatians/review/.

42. Emma Stafford, "Hercules' Choice: Virtue, Vice and the Hero of the Twentieth Century Screen," in *The Reception of Ancient Virtues and Vices in Modern Popular Culture: Beauty, Bravery, Blood and Glory*, ed. Eran Almagor and Lisa Maurice (Leiden, the Netherlands: Brill, 2017), 140.

43. Jonathan Safran Foer, *Eating Animals* (London: Penguin Books, 2009), 1.

44. Rebecca Stanton, *The Disneyfication of Animals* (Basingstoke, England: Palgrave Macmillan, 2021), 177.

45. Stanton, *The Disneyfication of Animals*, 172.

46. Stanton, *The Disneyfication of Animals*, 127, 186.

47. Arnold Arluke and Clinton R. Sanders, *Regarding Animals* (Philadelphia: Temple University Press, 1996), 167–86.

48. Arluke and Sanders, *Regarding Animals*, 167–86.

49. McVeigh, "Animal Rights Campaigners Protest."

50. Paul Brown, "Last Mink Fur Farms Must Close by 2003," *Guardian*, December 28, 2001, www.theguardian.com/uk/2001/dec/28/immigrationpolicy.

51. Kate Carter, "Don't Hide from the Truth," *Guardian*, August 27, 2008, www.theguardian.com/lifeandstyle/2008/aug/27/ethicalfashion.leather.

52. McVeigh, "Animal Rights Campaigners Protest."

53. Richard Conniff, "Why Fur Is Back in Fashion," *National Geographic Magazine*, September 2016, www.nationalgeographic.com/magazine/2016/09/skin-trade-fur-fashion/.

54. Catherine Tiplady, *Animal Abuse: Helping Animals and People* (Oxford: CABI, 2013), 14.

55. Shea Bennett, "The Numbers Just Keep On Getting Bigger: Social Media and the Internet 2011 [Statistics]," *Adweek*, January 23, 2012, www.adweek.com/digital/social-media-internet-2011/.

REFERENCES

Adams, Stephen. "Karl Lagerfeld Defends Fur Industry Saying 'Beasts' Would Kill Us If We Didn't Kill Them." *Telegraph*, January 2, 2009. fashion.telegraph.co.uk/news-features/TMG4075783/Karl-Lagerfeld-defends-fur-industry-saying-beasts-would-kill-us-if-we-didnt-kill-them.html.

Arluke, Arnold, and Clinton R. Sanders. *Regarding Animals*. Philadelphia: Temple University Press, 1996.

Barnes, Brooks. "Despite Fans' Fears, Disney's Country Bears Remain Corny." *New York Times*, October 19, 2013. www.nytimes.com/2012/10/20/arts/country-bear-jamboree-at-walt-disney-world.html?mcubz=1.

Baron, Katie. "Fashion's Greatest Pop Hits—From Gaga's Meat Dress to Grace Jones's Armani Suit." *Guardian*, August 16, 2016. www.theguardian.com/fashion/2016/aug/16/fashions-greatest-pop-hits-from-gagas-meat-dress-to-grace-joness-armani-suit.

Bennett, Shea. "The Numbers Just Keep On Getting Bigger: Social Media and the Internet 2011 [Statistics]." *Adweek*, January 23, 2012. www.adweek.com/digital/social-media-internet-2011/

Brown, Noel. *British Children's Cinema: From the Thief of Bagdad to Wallace and Gromit*. London: I. B. Tauris, 2017.

Brown, Paul. "Last Mink Fur Farms Must Close by 2003." *Guardian*, December 28, 2001. www.theguardian.com/uk/2001/dec/28/immigrationpolicy.

Burt, Jonathan. *Animals in Film*. Islington, UK: Reaktion Books, 2002.

Carter, Kate. "Don't Hide from the Truth." *Guardian*, August 27, 2008. www.theguardian.com/lifeandstyle/2008/aug/27/ethicalfashion.leather.

Cartmill, Matt. *A View to a Death in the Morning: Hunting and Nature through History*. Cambridge, MA: Harvard University Press, 1996.

Cochrane, Emma. Review of *101 Dalmatians*. *Empire*, January 1, 2014. www.empireonline.com/movies/101-dalmatians/review/.

Conniff, Richard. "Why Fur Is Back in Fashion." *National Geographic Magazine*, September 2016. www.nationalgeographic.com/magazine/2016/09/skin-trade-fur-fashion/.

Davis, Amy M. *Good Girls and Wicked Witches: Changing Representations of Women in Disney's Feature Animation*. Barnet, UK: John Libbey, 2007.

Dearden, Lizzie. "Simba, Bambi and Other Disney Characters Shown Skinned and Bleeding in Anti-Fur Campaign." *Independent*, December 1, 2014. www.independent.co.uk/arts-entertainment/art/news/simba-bambi-and-disney-characters-shown-skinned-and-bleeding-in-anti-fur-campaign-9896355.html.

Dockterman, Eliana, and Kelly Conniff. "*Maleficent* and 16 Other Famous Queens of Mean." *Time*, May 31, 2014. time.com/2801704/maleficent-villains-wicked-witch-catwoman/.

Dorré, Gina Marlene. "Horses and Corsets: 'Black Beauty,' Dress Reform, and the Fashioning of the Victorian Woman." *Victorian Literature and Culture* 30, no. 1 (2002): 157–78.

Flynn, Clifton P. *Understanding Animal Abuse: A Sociological Analysis*. New York: Lantern Books, 2012.

Foer, Jonathan Safran. *Eating Animals*. London: Penguin Books, 2009.

Humane Society International. "The Fur Trade." Accessed January 31 2022. www.hsi.org/news-media/fur-trade/.

Horta, O. "What Is Speciesism?" *Journal of Agricultural and Environmental Ethics* 23, no. 3 (2010): 243–66.

Johnson, John. "Coonskin Cap Clings to 'Crockett.'" *Los Angeles Times*, August 23, 2002. articles.latimes.com/2002/aug/23/local/me-fess23.
Johnston, Ollie, and Frank Thomas. *The Disney Villain*. New York: Hyperion Press, 1993.
Lazarus, Susanna. "Has Sully from *Monsters Inc* Been Turned into a Toilet Seat Cover?" *Radio Times*, August 12, 2015. www.radiotimes.com/news/2015-08-12/has-sully-from-monsters-inc-been-turned-into-a-toilet-seat-cover/.
Lutts, Ralph H. "The Trouble with *Bambi*: Walt Disney's *Bambi* and the American Vision of Nature." *Forest & Conservation History* 36, no. 4 (1992): 160–71.
Marino, Lori, and Michael Mountain. "Denial of Death and the Relationship between Humans and Other Animals." *Anthrozoos* 28, no. 1 (2015): 5–21.
McVeigh, Tracy. "Animal Rights Campaigners Protest as Fur Comes Back into Fashion." *Guardian*, March 1, 2014. www.theguardian.com/fashion/2014/mar/01/animal-campaigners-protest-fur-fashion.
Meredith, Charlotte. "Animals Electrocuted, Strangled and Skinned Alive: The True Face of China's Fur Farms." *Express*, March 1, 2013. www.express.co.uk/news/world/381117/Animals-electrocuted-strangled-and-skinned-alive-The-true-face-of-China-s-fur-farms.
Newkirk, Ingrid E. "Lady Gaga's Meat Dress." *PETA*, September 13, 2010. www.peta.org/blog/lady-gagas-meat-dress/.
North, Richard D. *Fur and Freedom: In Defence of the Fur Trade*. London: Institute of Economic Affairs, 2000.
Pallant, Chris. *Demystifying Disney: A History of Disney Feature Animation*. London: Continuum, 2011.
Sewell, Anna. *Black Beauty*. London: Penguin Classics, 1995.
Sheen, Erica. "101 and Counting: Dalmatians in Film and Advertising." *Worldviews: Global Religions, Culture, and Ecology*, no. 9 (2005): 236–54.
Smith, Dodie. *The Hundred and One Dalmatians*. London: Egmont UK, 2010.
———. *The Starlight Barking*. London: Egmont UK, 2006.
Stafford, Emma. "Hercules' Choice: Virtue, Vice and the Hero of the Twentieth Century Screen." In *The Reception of Ancient Virtues and Vices in Modern Popular Culture: Beauty, Bravery, Blood and Glory*, edited by Eran Almagor and Lisa Maurice, 140–66. Leiden, the Netherlands: Brill, 2017.
Stanton, Rebecca Rose. "Speak of the Devil! The Keys to Cruella's Success." *Animation Studies*, June 12, 2017. blog.animationstudies.org/?p=2049.
———. *The Disneyfication of Animals*. Basingstoke, England: Palgrave Macmillan, 2021.
Thomas, Bob. *Walt Disney: An American Original*. New York: Simon and Schuster, 1976.
Tiplady, Catherine. *Animal Abuse: Helping Animals and People*. Oxford: CABI, 2013.
Urquhart, Sidney. "What Becomes a Legend Least?" *Time*, August 19, 1991. content.time.com/time/magazine/article/0,9171,973656,00.html.
Walker, J. P. *The Legendary Mountain Men of North America*. Morrisville, NC: Lulu Books, 2015.
Yount, Lisa. *Animal Rights*. New York: Infobase, 2008.

FILMS REFERENCED

Bambi. Directed by David Hand. 1942. Burbank: Walt Disney Animation Studios, 2007. DVD.

Beauty and the Beast. Directed by Gary Trousdale and Kirk Wise. 1991. Burbank: Walt Disney Animation Studios, 2002. DVD.

Brother Bear. Directed by Aaron Blaise and Robert Walker. 2003. Burbank: Walt Disney Animation Studios, 2004. DVD.

Cruella. Directed by Craig Gillespie. 2021. Burbank: Walt Disney Studios Motion Pictures, 2021. DVD.

The Fox and the Hound. Directed by Ted Berman, Richard Rich, and Art Stevens. 1981. Burbank: Walt Disney Animation Studios, 2000. DVD.

Hercules. Directed by John Musker and Ron Clements. 1997. Burbank: Walt Disney Animation Studios, 1999. DVD.

The Little Mermaid. Directed by Ron Clements and John Musker. 1989. Burbank: Walt Disney Animation Studios, 1999. DVD.

Oliver & Company. Directed by George Scribner. 1988. Burbank: Walt Disney Animation Studios, 2002. DVD.

One Hundred and One Dalmatians. Directed by Wolfgang Reitherman, Hamilton Luske, and Clyde Geronimi. 1999. Burbank: Walt Disney Animation Studios, 2000. DVD.

The Rescuers. Directed by Wolfgang Reitherman, John Lounsbery, and Art Stevens. 1977. Burbank: Walt Disney Animation Studios, 2003. DVD.

The Silence of the Lambs. Directed by Jonathan Demme. 1991. Burbank: Orion Pictures, 2001. DVD.

Snow White and the Seven Dwarves. Directed by David Hand. 1937. Burbank: Walt Disney Animation Studios, 2001. DVD.

Watership Down. Directed by Martin Rosen. 1979. Burbank: Universal Home Entertainment, 2001. DVD.

Chapter 10

Bringing Nonhuman Animals into Anthropologies of Fur

Jen Clements

ANTHROPOLOGY AND FUR

Literature on animals in anthropology has historically been dominated by structuralism and materialism, as evidenced by concerns over linguistic categories, symbolism, value, and economy.[1] Unsurprisingly, such accounts are avowedly anthropocentric. For example, Barbara Noske has highlighted that while biological essentialism has been rejected with regard to explaining social differences between humans on grounds such as race or sex, differences between nonhuman animals are often unquestioningly associated with biological and genetic explanations.[2] In this vein, approaches to fur within anthropology have been predominantly materialist and structural-functionalist, as the following two examples from classic works illustrate.

Edward Evans-Pritchard wrote a seminal ethnography of the Nuer people of Sudan.[3] He famously argued that their social and political organization was acephalous (headless) and nonhierarchical, which was the basis of his segmentary lineage theory. Evans-Pritchard considered the ritual specialist known as the leopard-skin chief a key figure in maintaining the system, particularly by mediating disputes. However, the leopard itself and the acquisition and processing of the animal's skin are barely mentioned. An example of an even more incongruous omission can be taken from Eric Wolf's text *Europe and the People without History*. Wolf considers the fur trade in great detail, particularly with regard to the rise and decline of imperial powers, such as Russia, Iberia, France, and Britain, and the impact of the trade on the lives of native peoples.[4] Yet nonhuman animals are considered only at the level of whole populations—namely, with regard to the growing scarcity of beavers, sea otters, and bison. Wolf's account is a work of Marxist-influenced political economy, and as such, the specific qualities of fur (and the animals from whom it is created) are neglected in favor of the analysis of power. As a result, the material under consideration—fur—easily could be swapped out for another material without undermining the salience of Wolf's argument. A critique of these epistemologies was at the center of later disciplinary turns.

THE MATERIAL AND THE ONTOLOGICAL

Of particular relevance to fur and the experiences of nonhuman animals are the material and ontological turns. The former can be illustrated by Arjun Appadurai's object biographies,[5] Igor Kopytoff's discussion of regimes of value,[6] and Alfred Gell's account of material agency.[7] These material approaches offer a way in which fur can be contextualized as a dynamic object with its own history, including the animal from whom it was taken. But given the origin of fur in the living animal, it is not enough to include material agency without some attempt to account for the subjectivity of the nonhuman animal. Perspectivism and the resulting ontological turn address the issue of how to represent nonhuman subjectivities. These theoretical developments grew out of ethnographies of indigenous peoples, particularly in lowland South America.

A typical example is the work of Lima on the Juruna peccary hunt. For the Juruna, what is a hunt from the human perspective is warfare from the peccary point of view, and hunters must be careful to resist adopting this point of view lest they become prey themselves.[8] As such, personhood and the related categories of natural/cultural are contextual. A similar logic can be found in Rane Willerslev's ethnography of Yukaghir hunters in northeastern Siberia.[9] Using Michael Taussig's conception of mimesis,[10] Willerslev argues that the Yukaghir can maintain multiple ontological perspectives; thus, they can become the prey they hunt while also remaining distinct persons. These examples illustrate that it is possible for anthropological analysis to account for multiple conflicting ontologies, which, when applied to nonhuman agency, is one way of avoiding overt anthropocentrism.

These theoretical developments are the necessary foreground to proposing potential anthropologies of fur that can trace and analyze relationships between multiple agents of different types, regardless of conceptual boundaries such as human–other or nature–culture. Posthumanism offers one possible theoretical frame for such an endeavor—most notably, Donna Haraway's multispecies ethnography and conception of "companion species."[11] This expands upon Michel Foucault's discussion of the "death of man,"[12] wherein he argues that the human is a shifting episteme rather than an objective reality. These arguments have been adopted within anthropology, most notably by Tim Ingold, who was prompted by his work among Sami reindeer herders to argue that species "do not *exist*" but rather "*occur*."[13] Despite the obvious theoretical relevance of posthumanism, I would argue that material semiotics has more to offer anthropologies of fur, at least with regard to a potential methodology. Material semiotics also has the advantage of having a built-in analytical frame for material agents, in this case fur.

Material Semiotics

Material semiotics is a loose body of methodologies that can trace its theoretical ancestry to Claude Lévi-Strauss's notion of the *bricoleur*.[14] Bricolage is a combinational logic; individual objects possess meanings through the ways in which they are bound together by their potential relationships. This is a clear precursor to both Bruno Latour's work on actor-network theory (ANT) and Donna Haraway's suggestion that a multispecies approach must be intersectional.[15]

In his books *We Have Never Been Modern* and *Reassembling the Social*, Latour argues that the modernist distinction between nature and culture never truly existed.[16] Instead, he espouses an approach wherein natural and social phenomena are seen as hybrids rather than as niches for specialists. Latour is best known in the context of science and technology studies and as a key proponent of actor-network theory. The latter aims to remove hierarchy in considering relations between actors, thus weighting each actor (whether human or nonhuman) equally.[17] To what extent this is achieved in practice is certainly up for debate; however, as a theoretical aim it provides fertile ground for future anthropologies of fur.

John Law arguably provides a more approachable and pragmatic discussion of actor-network theory and material semiotics more generally.[18] He makes overt the link between ANT and Thomas Kuhn's work on scientific paradigms,[19] which is an important precursor given the relational and epistemic nature of material-semiotic approaches. For example, one of Law's own concepts—"modes of ordering"—is heavily influenced by a Foucauldian notion of "discourses."[20] In other words, ANT is a way to describe materials, semiotics, and heterogeneity as a precarious process that shapes power, space, and scale. Naturally, this focus is highly compatible with a grounded and critical approach to fur, while the deconstruction of foundational divides such as the human–animal boundary also makes it possible to bring in elements of posthumanism.

The sociologist Leslie Irvine has posited that animal selves or consciousness can be evidenced through observations of behavioral flexibility, which has been observed in both domesticated and free-living animals.[21] This maps well onto a material-semiotic notion of agency and allows the practitioner to proceed without engaging in debates over nonhuman personhood. Thus, anthropologies of fur with roots in material semiotics can acknowledge the interiority of nonhuman animals while still placing material objects, nonhumans, and humans at the same analytical level. In short, the broad agentic focus of material semiotics provides adequate conceptual space for both the changing impact of fur objects and the experiences of living subjects, regardless of the researcher's concern with animal ethics, which within anthropology is highly variable. This has the additional benefit of allowing analysis to take account of both individual subjects and the relevance of species-wide effects, for example, upon demography.

Fur as a Material

As the earlier discussion of the state of the discipline shows, anthropological discussions of fur have widely neglected to consider its specific material qualities. It is first necessary to emphasize the difference between material-semiotic and materialist approaches. York and Longo argue for a critical animal studies that includes analysis of the materiality of animals, rather than simply discussing how they are socially constructed by humans. However, they go on to equate realism with materialism,[22] and privileging the material or physical dimension of animals above their subjectivity and selfhood, as well as the morality of human behavior toward animals, is the antithesis of a "critical animal studies." Indeed, a truly materialist approach to animals would be the Cartesian reduction of animal beings to mindless automata. An approach informed by material semiotics as well as broad anthropological traditions must balance the demands of material qualities, subjectivities, and semiotic signification.

To this end, it is important to highlight in detail a rare anthropological account of what fur actually is and how it is made. In essence, animals must be farmed, trapped, or hunted, and their skins must be removed, prepared, and tanned to prevent rotting, yet most literature makes no mention of these laborious processes. This replicates a consumerist form of commodity fetishism[23] that is socially constructed and further is alien to most cultural contexts. In this regard, many accounts present fur as something that is quick, easy, and clean to harvest, much like the click of a button that represents this process in many popular video games.

In his extensive account of skin clothing in the arctic regions of Eurasia and America, Gudmund Hatt devotes considerable space to a general discussion of the stages of fur processing.[24] In broad terms, after the animal is skinned, the subcutaneous tissue and any attached fat or flesh are removed because these are likely to rot.[25] In the case of fur, the skin is not depilated, but the skin or corium is still tanned in order to increase durability, soften the skin, and protect from moisture and sometimes to alter the color.[26] Tanning materials ultimately originate from these sources—fats, plants, urine, blood, and minerals[27]—although most industrial societies chemically extract or artificially synthesize the desired compounds. Traditional techniques often supplement tanning with smoking, but the final stage is always to stretch the skin out to prevent shrinkage.[28] A discussion of the sociocultural relevance of fur in a specific context cannot be complete without reference to both the experiences of the source animal and the process by which the desired object is produced.

The anthropologist Tim Ingold also has emphasized the importance of considering material processes and qualities, particularly with regard to material culture studies. He contrasts such a discussion with the often nebulous and ill-defined concept of "materiality," which he argues is driven by a desire to "make things 'thingly.'"[29] Material semiotics avoids this problem by analyzing material objects as agents with material qualities that produce effects in the world that change as a result of relationships with other agents, whether objects, nonhumans, or humans.

Fur and Indigenous Communities

Anthropology is concerned with all peoples. However, it is also a discipline with a long history of representing and engaging with indigenous people and communities. As such, anthropologies of fur must not further colonial and exploitative legacies that have been so prevalent both within and outside of the discipline. Furthermore, an approach informed by animal ethics also must critically engage with the rights and reparations due to indigenous peoples. There can be no general guideline for the possible competing demands of these ethical compunctions—and in any case, no one person could be qualified to write one—but it is worth emphasizing understanding, broadcasting indigenous voices, avoiding condemnation, and being aware of positionality. The truth remains that most fur is produced by and for non-indigenous cultures and unilaterally involves more animal suffering than does indigenous fur use. As such, it is important that anthropologies of fur do not disproportionately focus on fur among indigenous communities.

Additionally, fur has become an important source of income for many indigenous peoples and, especially in the case of arctic communities, is of great cultural importance. Larsen et al. have argued that economic success and traditional values are key to the survival and well-being of contemporary indigenous communities.[30] However, global market forces and climate change have made earning a living from hunting animals for fur unstable. As such, anthropologists must balance the demands of multiple kinds of advocacy, ideally improving the lot of the oppressed regardless of species.

CONCLUSIONS

Fur retains cultural and economic value in many world cultures. Anthropological analysis must meet the challenge of understanding and representing a complex material that is shaped by a web of diverse agents, both human and nonhuman. I have proposed that a material-semiotic approach, alongside an engagement with posthumanism, is best equipped to meet this challenge. Advocacy for nonhuman animals remains a fringe viewpoint in anthropology. However, I hope I have shown that an ANT approach to fur has much to offer, regardless of the researcher positionality or their stance on animal ethics.

NOTES

1. An early version of this article was presented at the 2017 Oxford Animal Ethics Summer School and it would not exist without the support of that community.

2. Barbara Noske, "The Animal Question in Anthropology: A Commentary," *Society and Animals* 1, no. 2 (1993): 185–90.

3. Edward Evans-Pritchard, *The Nuer: A Description of the Modes of Livelihood and Political Institutions of a Nilotic People* (1940; Oxford: Oxford University Press, 1969).

4. Eric Wolf, *Europe and the People without History* (1982; Berkeley: University of California Press, 1997), 158–94.

5. Arjun Appadurai, "Introduction: Commodities and the Politics of Value," in *The Social Life of Things: Commodities in Cultural Perspectives*, ed. Arjun Appadurai (Cambridge: Cambridge University Press, 1986).

6. Igor Kopytoff, "The Cultural Biography of Things: Commoditisation as a Process," in *The Social Life of Things: Commodities in Cultural Perspectives*, ed. Arjun Appadurai (Cambridge: Cambridge University Press, 1986), 64–91.

7. Alfred Gell, *Art and Agency* (Oxford: Clarendon, 1998).

8. T. S. Lima, "The Two and Its Many: Reflections on Perspectivism in a Tupi Cosmology," *Ethnos: Journal of Anthropology* 64, no. 1 (1999): 122–24.

9. Rane Willerslev, "Not Animal, Not Not-Animal: Hunting, Imitation and Empathetic Knowledge among the Siberian Yukaghirs," *Journal of the Royal Anthropological Institute* 10, no. 3 (2004): 629–52.

10. Michael Taussig, *Mimesis and Alterity: A Particular History of the Senses* (London: Routledge, 1993).

11. Donna Haraway, *The Companion Species Manifesto* (Chicago: Prickly Paradigm Press, 2003); Haraway, *Cyborg Manifesto* (1985; New York: Routledge, 1991); Haraway, *When Species Meet* (Minneapolis: University of Minnesota Press, 2006).

12. Michel Foucault, *The Order of Things* (1966; New York: Random House, 1994).

13. Tim Ingold, "Anthropology beyond Humanity," *Suomen Anthropologi: Journal of the Finnish Anthropological Society* 38, no. 3 (2013): 21 (emphasis in original).

14. Claude Lévi-Strauss, *The Savage Mind* (London: Weidenfeld and Nicolson, 1966).

15. Haraway, *When Species Meet.*

16. Bruno Latour, *We Have Never Been Modern* (Cambridge, MA: Harvard University Press, 1993); Latour, *Re-assembling the Social: An Introduction to Actor Network Theory* (Oxford: Oxford University Press, 2005).

17. Bruno Latour, "Mixing Humans with Non-Humans: Sociology of a Door-Closer," *Social Problems* 35 (1988): 307–10.

18. John Law, "Actor Network Theory and Material Semiotics," 2007, www.heterogeneities.net/publications/Law2007ANTandMaterialSemiotics.pdf.

19. Thomas Kuhn, *The Structure of Scientific Revolutions* (1962; Chicago: University of Chicago Press, 1970).

20. John Law, "Notes on the Theory of the Actor-Network: Ordering, Strategy, and Heterogeneity," *Systems Practice* 5, no. 4 (1992): 379–93.

21. Leslie Irvine, "The Question of Animal Selves: Implications for Sociological Knowledge and Practice," *Qualitative Sociology Review* 3, no. 1 (2007): 5–16.

22. R. York and S. B. Longo, "Animals in the World: A Materialist Approach to Sociological Animal Studies," *Journal of Sociology* 53, no. 1 (2015): 32–39.

23. Cf. Karl Marx, *Capital*, vol. 1 (1867; London: Lawrence and Wishart, 1970).

24. Gudmund Hatt and K. Taylor, "Arctic Skin Clothing in Eurasia and America: An Ethnographic Study" (1914), *Arctic Anthropology* 5, no. 2 (1969): 3–132.

25. Hatt and Taylor, "Arctic Skin Clothing," 11.

26. Hatt and Taylor, "Arctic Skin Clothing," 11–14.

27. Hatt and Taylor, "Arctic Skin Clothing," 14–19.

28. Hatt and Taylor, "Arctic Skin Clothing," 19–20.

29. Tim Ingold, "Materials against Materiality," *Archaeological Dialogues* 14, no. 1 (2007): 2, 9.

30. J. Larsen, P. Schweitzer, A. Petrov, and G. Fondahl, "Tracking Change in Human Development in the Arctic," *Arctic Social Indicators: ASI II: Implementation*, TemaNord (Copenhagen: Nordic Council of Ministers, 2015).

REFERENCES

Appadurai, Arjun. "Introduction: Commodities and the Politics of Value." In *The Social Life of Things: Commodities in Cultural Perspectives*, edited by A. Appadurai. Cambridge: Cambridge University Press, 1986.

Condon, R. G. "The History and Development of Arctic Photography." *Arctic Anthropology* 26, no. 1 (1989): 46–87.

Cudworth, E. "Killing Animals: Sociology, Species Relations and Institutionalized Violence." *Sociological Review* 63 (2015): 1–18.

Evans-Pritchard, Edward E. *The Nuer: A Description of the Modes of Livelihood and Political Institutions of a Nilotic People*. 1940. Oxford: Oxford University Press, 1969.

Foucault, Michel. *The Order of Things*. 1966. New York: Random House, 1994.

Gell, Alfred. *Art and Agency*. Oxford: Clarendon, 1998.

Haraway, Donna. *The Companion Species Manifesto*. Chicago: Prickly Paradigm Press, 2003.

———. *Cyborg Manifesto*. 1985. New York: Routledge, 1991.

———. *When Species Meet*. Minneapolis: University of Minnesota Press, 2006.

Hatt, Gudmund., and K. Taylor. "Arctic Skin Clothing in Eurasia and America: An Ethnographic Study." 1914. *Arctic Anthropology* 5, no. 2 (1969): 3–132.

Ingold, Tim. "Anthropology beyond Humanity." *Suomen Anthropologi: Journal of the Finnish Anthropological Society* 38, no. 3 (2013): 5–23.

———. "Materials against Materiality." *Archaeological Dialogues* 14, no. 1 (2007): 1–16.

Irvine, Leslie. "The Question of Animal Selves: Implications for Sociological Knowledge and Practice." *Qualitative Sociology Review* 3, no. 1 (2007): 5–16.

Kohn, E. "How Dogs Dream: Amazonian Natures and the Politics of Transspecies Engagement." *American Ethnologist* 34 (2007): 3–24.

Kopytoff, Igor. "The Cultural Biography of Things: Commoditisation as a Process." In *The Social Life of Things: Commodities in Cultural Perspectives*, edited by A. Appadurai, 64–91. Cambridge: Cambridge University Press, 1986.

Kuhn, Thomas. *The Structure of Scientific Revolutions*. 1962. Chicago: University of Chicago Press, 1970.

Larsen, J., P. Schweitzer, A. Petrov, and G. Fondahl. "Tracking Change in Human Development in the Arctic." *Arctic Social Indicators: ASI II: Implementation*. TemaNord. Copenhagen: Nordic Council of Ministers, 2015.

Latour, Bruno. "Mixing Humans with Non-Humans: Sociology of a Door-Closer." *Social Problems* 35 (1988): 298–310.

———. *Re-assembling the Social: An Introduction to Actor Network Theory*. Oxford: Oxford University Press, 2005.

———. *We Have Never Been Modern*. Cambridge, MA: Harvard University Press, 1993.

Law, John. "Actor Network Theory and Material Semiotics." www.heterogeneities.net/publications/Law2007ANTandMaterialSemiotics.pdf.

———. "Notes on the Theory of the Actor-Network: Ordering, Strategy, and Heterogeneity." *Systems Practice* 5, no. 4 (1992): 379–93.

Lévi-Strauss, Claude. *The Savage Mind*. London: Weidenfeld and Nicolson, 1966.

Lima, T. S. "The Two and Its Many: Reflections on Perspectivism in a Tupi Cosmology." *Ethnos: Journal of Anthropology* 64, no. 1 (1999): 107–31.

Marx, Karl. *Capital*. Vol. 1. 1867. London: Lawrence and Wishart, 1970.

Noske, Barbara. "The Animal Question in Anthropology: A Commentary." *Society and Animals* 1, no. 2 (1993): 185–90.

Sandell, H., and B. Sandell. "Polar Bear Hunting and Hunters in Ittoqqortoormiit/Scoresbysund, NE Greenland." *Arctic Anthropology* 33, no. 2 (1996): 77–93.

Taussig, Michael. *Mimesis and Alterity: A Particular History of the Senses*. London: Routledge, 1993.

Viveiros de Castro, E. "Cosmological Deixis and Amerindian Perspectivism." *Journal of the Royal Anthropological Institute* 4 (1998): 469–88.

———. "Exchanging Perspectives: The Transformation of Objects into Subjects in Amerindian Ontologies." *Common Knowledge* 10 (2004): 463–84.

Willerslev, Rane. "Not Animal, Not Not-Animal: Hunting, Imitation and Empathetic Knowledge among the Siberian Yukaghirs." *Journal of the Royal Anthropological Institute* 10, no. 3 (2004): 629–52.

Wolf, Eric. *Europe and the People without History*. 1982. Berkeley: University of California Press, 1997.

York, R., and S. B. Longo. "Animals in the World: A Materialist Approach to Sociological Animal Studies." *Journal of Sociology* 53, no. 1 (2015): 32–46.

Chapter 11

Video Killed the Animal for Fur

An Analysis of the Influence of Pop Music Culture on Perceptions about Fur

Ambrose Tinarwo

Popular music culture is a legitimate candidate for scholarly inquiry into animal ethics on the basis of its penetration into households (e.g., MTV reaches four hundred million subscribers globally across 178 countries[1]) and popular music culture's undertones of anthrozoologic messages within a wider context of an aspirational subculture. June O'Connor[2] acknowledges Gilbert Seldes as an early proponent of including popular culture in ethical scholarship on the basis that popular art forms are not only entertaining (and therefore have a captive audience) but also important subjects of academic interrogation. O'Connor's review of case studies on the impact of popular culture is limited to radio, television shows, and printed media, but similar arguments hold for the role of the music video as a vehicle for ethical discourse. As early as 380 BC, acknowledging that music has an effect of bestowing either virtue or vice on society, Plato wrote in the *Republic*, "For any musical innovation is full of danger to the whole State, and ought to be prohibited. So Damon tells me, and I can quite believe him;—he says that when modes of music change, of the State always change with them."[3] Popular music culture, due to its aspirational outlook, often presents overt and covert messages about animals and the use of animal-derived products as goods that reinforce social status.

Listening to music can increase empathy toward the cultures and people the music portrays,[4] and therefore an inquiry into the impact of the content of popular music culture on animal ethics is a legitimate academic pursuit. Music video, in particular, has shifted the emphasis of music from the semantic and affective aural experience to a visual format that limits the interpretive liberty of the listener and in exchange offers a more theatrical product in which the image of the star is more important than the intrinsic musical value.[5] This means that the visual fashion content of pop music videos is important in analyzing attitudes toward animal fur.

IMPACT OF MUSIC ON MORALITY

There have been several discussions within academia and society at large on the impact of popular music on moral virtue. However, this has largely been confined to the impact of lyrics on violent behavior and gender relations. In considering the impact of music on moral values, it is imperative to distinguish between absolute music (purely instrumental without lyrics) and all the other various parts of music delivery, including lyrics, visuals, and context. Peter Kivy[6] argues that absolute music is devoid of an intrinsic moral value as it lacks semantic or representational content and therefore has no meaning beyond the quasi-syntactical structure of sound. Despite this, there is evidence from neuroimaging that absolute music can modulate activity in brain structures involved in the generation of emotional experiences, such as the amygdala, nucleus accumbens, hypothalamus, hippocampus, insula, cingulate cortex, and orbitofrontal cortex.[7] The link between emotions and morality can be made via the instrumental effects of emotion on behavior, as well as to some extent the intrinsic value of emotion rewarding or punishing our actions.[8]

Ziv et al.[9] demonstrated that music could be used to manipulate and bias moral judgment. Their studies on the use of music as a background to advertisements demonstrated that positive valence music reduced awareness of an unethical message and increased acceptance of a morally questionable product. These effects were achieved not through overt semantic or contextual staging but via the subliminal background effect of music. These findings lend further credence to the interest in studying the impact of typically upbeat pop music on moral judgment regarding the questionable fashion choices presented in videos.

The pop music video is now arguably as important as the music. Pop music videos take the form of either a performance video, which focuses on a recording (live or otherwise) of the artists playing the music, or a conceptual video, which tells a story that may or may not be directly related to the lyrics of the song. Conceptual pop videos tend to present aspirational scenarios full of opulent surroundings, luxurious cars, and exclusive fashion, including designer fur garments, as symbols of success and wealth. The American Academy of Pediatrics Council on Communication and Media reviewed studies on the impact of music, music lyrics, and music videos and concluded in part that pop music videos were associated with violent behaviors, drug and alcohol abuse, and unhealthy relationships within the adolescent populations in Europe and America.[10] They stopped short of claiming a causal relationship, but the implied links are very strong. The focus of this essay is the holistic effect of non-absolute music (pop music videos), acknowledging the impact that visual and semantic elements of music have on social empathy and therefore the construct of moral acceptability of fur as clothing.

Pop Music Culture and Its Influence

There has been, in recent years, an increase in the incidence of pop music on television. This increase has been not only in stand-alone programming but also in the use of pop soundtracks in place of incidental music as stock or background music and in advertisements.[11] This persistence on television has actively captured the attention of adolescent viewers, who translate into a key target group for marketing fashion trends such as fur trim and coats. The influence of pop music artists on modern society can be illustrated by looking at a league table of social media profiles. Such tables can be viewed as a proxy for individuals' level of influence on society through electronic media, and the people on it arguably have a more direct influence on modern-day moral discourse than scholars in academic settings. The Twitter Profiles League Table (see Table 11.1) reveals that six of the top-ten league leaders at the time of these rankings were pop music artists, with four occupying the top five positions. This influence also is acknowledged in *Time* magazine's "100 Most Influential People of 2019" list, which features six pop music artists.

The influence and reach of pop music artists via music video is well illustrated by the figures from Trefis as of June 18, 2017, showing that MTV,

Table 11.1. Twitter Profiles League Table

Rank	*Profile*	*Total Followers*	*Profession*
1	Barack Obama	117,996,775	Politician
2	Justin Bieber	111,774,200	Pop music artist
3	Katy Perry	108,506,239	Pop music artist
4	Rihanna	96,919,196	Pop music artist
5	Taylor Swift	86,139,782	Pop music artist
6	Cristiano Ronaldo	85,011,265	Footballer (soccer)
7	xoxo, Joanne	81,337,454	Pop music artist
8	Ellen DeGeneres	80,170,076	TV host, comedian
9	Donald J. Trump	79,517,737	Politician
10	Ariana Grande	73,725,222	Pop music artist

Source: Created using data from Trackalytics, *The Most Followed Twitter Profiles*, www.trackalytics.com, 27 May, 2020, https://www.trackalytics.com/the-most-followed-twitter-profiles/page/1/.

the pioneer for pop music video, reaches four hundred million subscribers annually, across 178 countries. MTV has a target demographic of twelve- to thirty-four-year-olds, representing a buying power of $12.5 billion.[12] Pop artists regularly feature on other popular polls of societal influence such as the Forbes Celebrity 100 as well as fashion-specific indices, as influencers of societal trends. The combined impact of pop artists' huge social media presence and reach into households via TV and other electronic devices and their apparent influence on adolescents with huge buying power presents a potentially huge impact on fashion trends.

The potential influence of pop music artists on fashion trends has not gone unnoticed by the fashion industry. Before the surge of the music video, iconic artists such as Kurt Cobain created fashion trends such as the flannel shirt and ripped jeans, as hordes of fans tried to dress like their icons. Artists such as Christopher George Latore Wallace (better known by his stage name, Biggie Smalls) started mixing high fashion, such as Versace shirts, and street wear such as Timberland boots, creating an edgy new look that attracted the attention of both fans and the fashion industry. Dressing in flamboyant attire, including exclusive and expensive materials (such as fur), was meant to project wealth and success and appeal to aspirational low- and medium-income consumers. With the advent of high-speed broadband internet and the music video, pop artists realized that they could use their videos and clothing as a means to promote their image or message and increase revenue from merchandising through this de facto free advertising platform. This created a music merchandise business worth hundreds of millions, which not only had the direct benefit of fans buying clothing and accessories worn by stars in their videos, but also increased interest in the artists, their social media profiles, and their music as a result. The trend of name-checking designer brands in songs, while also prominently displaying the fashion labels in music videos, provided an effective platform for advertising fashion trends to music audiences. A marriage of convenience was thus formed between pop artists and fashion labels, which has resulted in several collaborations (Table 11.2).

The collaboration between fashion brands and pop music artists provided a conduit to bring designer clothes to the masses. Some specific collaborations between pop artists and High Street fashion retailers, such as those between Rihanna's Fenty brand and River Island or Beyoncé's Ivy Park and Topshop, were designed to bring affordable pop music–derived designer clothing to a new audience, with free advertising through music videos. Most pop artists further developed their fashion brands into independent labels on the back of their popularity and marketed their clothing merchandise via their music videos and social media profiles.

Table 11.2. Collaborations between Pop Music Artists and the Fashion Industry

Artist	*Fashion Brand*	*Collaborators*
Victoria Beckham	Victoria Beckham	Estee Lauder
Beyoncé Knowles	Ivy Park	Topshop, Adidas
Gwen Stefani	L.A.M.B.	LeSportsac, Coty Inc., Tura Inc
Kanye West	Yeezy	Adidas, Louis Vuitton, Nike
Pharrell Williams	Billionaire Boys Club	Louis Vuitton, Moncler, Uniqlo, Chanel, Adidas, Timberland
Jay Z	Rocawear	Iconix Brand Group
Rihanna	Fenty	Louis Vuitton, LVMH, Armani, River Island
Jennifer Lopez	J.Lo	Sweetface Fashion Co.
Diddy (Sean John Combs)	Sean John	
Drake	October's Very Own	Nike, Canada Goose, Clarks, Alpha Industries
Adam Levine	Adam Levine	Kmart

Source: Compiled by Chapter Author.

Fur in Your Face: Pop Music Culture and Fur

Although fur has traditionally been the preserve of high-fashion purveyors, there has recently been some evidence of a change in attitudes, moving against its use. For example, London Fashion Week became fur-free in 2018 on ethical grounds.[13] However, there appears to be a concurrent increase in the presence of fur or furlike products (faux fur) on the UK's High Streets. A lot of these fur (or faux fur) designs can be traced back to pop stars and their music videos, wherein the distinction between real and fake fur is not clear. The following are some case studies into how pop music videos and pop culture may be influencing attitudes and therefore consumption of fur products by music fans as a sub-sample of society.

Pimp Subculture and Normalization of Fur

Modern rap music includes a subculture called pimp culture. This subculture is characterized by the presentation of males as pimps who control women who are characterized as prostitutes. Laying aside the misogynistic and hegemonic masculinization portrayed by the songs, the music videos present a distinctive fashion style of fur coats and chunky jewelry made from precious metals and stones. Steiner[14] traces this imagery to Iceberg Slim, a real-life pimp turned influential biopic author in the 1960s and 1970s. Pioneers of pimp rap include former real-life pimp, filmmaker, and rapper Ice T, with songs like his 1987 "Somebody Gotta Do It (Pimpin' Ain't Easy)." Pimp rap was carried onto music video and popularized by artists such as Snoop Dogg

(Calvin Broadus) with his hit debut album *Doggystyle*, inspiring a generation of rap artists to follow the pimp rap subculture.

Ronald Weitzer and Charis E. Kubrin[15] argue that the content of rap music is inspired by wider gender relationships, the music industry fraternity, and the neighborhood conditions in which the artists grew up. This is echoed by pimp rap artists who state that their music is reflective of life in their community, where most of them are struggling to get rich quick to improve their lives. Fur coats are presented as aspirational, as status symbols, and as a sign of countercultural identity in a section of low-income African American society. However, the influence of this music transcended racial barriers, inspiring artists such as Macklemore (Benjamin Haggerty), whose song "Thrift Shop" directly references and promotes fur, albeit secondhand old fur. The double Grammy Award–winning song reached number one in the United States of America, the United Kingdom, Ireland, Canada, France, Denmark, the Netherlands, Australia, and New Zealand. The CD sleeve artwork for the song features a scene from the music video, in which actors and Macklemore are all wearing fur. The song's music video has achieved more than 1.4 billion views on YouTube. The video and lyrics are countercurrent to popular hip-hop culture, which is usually about excess and spending; according to the artist, the song is about demonstrating that you can look fresh while saving money. "Thrift Shop" references buying a mink coat and alligator shoes for ninety-nine cents from a thrift (or charity) shop and says that the outfit looks good and attracts compliments. The overwhelming success of this music video is purported to have translated into an increase in business for thrift shops from college students seeking bargain fur products,[16] although there are some reports to the contrary.[17] Whereas the impact of the video on direct sales of fur from thrift shops is debatable, what is clear is that the video captured people's attention to the tune of more than a billion views on YouTube. It became, perhaps inadvertently, an ambassador for normalizing secondhand fur as it gave wearing fur a wide audience as well as "whitewashed" secondhand fur garments. Pimp rap is becoming increasingly unpopular due to its questionable portrayal of gender and intergender relationships, but the associated videos and the fashions they portray have been somewhat influential, if not persistent. The impact of pimp rap on fashion was to normalize the wearing of fur as modeled by the artists.

Fashion, Fur, and R&B

A residual impact of the pimp rap subculture is the carryover of the aspirational fashion culture, including fur in particular, to other pop music subgenres. This is best illustrated by Mary J. Blige, an R&B artist who has courted controversy through her defense of wearing fur. Mary J. Blige was signed to the record label Uptown Records and was closely associated with the pimp/gangsta rap artist Biggie Smalls. Uptown Records pioneered the fusion of rap and R&B with much success, as exemplified through Mary J. Blige's accolades, including nine Grammy Awards, twelve Billboard Music Awards, and the naming of her 1994 album *My Life* as one of *Rolling Stone*'s five hundred best albums of all time. Her success has led to a massive following on social media, with more than 4.5 million followers on Instagram, more than five million on Snapchat, and more than six million on Twitter.

Mary J. Blige is viewed as an advocate for social liberty and female liberation and is associated with several philanthropic causes. However, she is often pictured wearing extravagant fur coats, reminiscent of pimp rap. She was quoted by the *Irish Examiner*,[18] warning PETA activists against throwing paint on her fur coats. In the article she refers to liberty, personal choice, and female liberation. Mary J. Blige has presented the wearing of fur as a mainstream and ethically defensible act on a wide platform through her music videos, appearances in fashion magazines, and red-carpet appearances. Worn by Mary J. Blige, fur can be viewed as a symbol of success, style, and personal choice, all tenets that may leave a positive impression on many of her followers. She has been used as a de facto ambassador by the pro-fur magazine *FurInsider*, which did a spread in its December 2015 edition titled "Mary J. Blige—Divas We Love Series." She is also regularly featured on *FurInsider*'s social media as a fur fashion icon.

Impact of Pop Music Videos on the Ethics of Wearing Fur

The overwhelming impact of pop music videos, as illustrated with the two case studies, is to normalize the wearing of fur. Some pop music videos have become de facto advertisements for fur as fashion, with an extensive reach to a fashion-conscious audience with significant buying power. Pop music videos present fur as an aspirational good, a symbol of success and personal liberty through consumer choice. Pro-fur media present pop music artists as icons for fur fashion—the *FurInsider*'s "Top Five Style Icons of 2014" included Rihanna and Rita Ora, who are pop artists; June Ambrose, a stylist to pop artists such as Mary J. Blige; Kim Kardashian, who is married to pop artist and fashion icon Kanye West; and American socialite and influencer Olivia Palermo.

Pop music videos are also bridging the age gap by introducing younger audiences to their teen pop idols wearing fur fashion. This then translates to High Street fashion through shops such as Topshop and River Island, which have deals with pop stars to translate their fashions into less expensive copies. Increased efficiency in the global fashion supply chains means that pop icons' fashion styles can be translated quickly from music videos or social media and made ready for sale through online shops such as ASOS.com within a short period of time. Websites targeting teens, such as Steal Her Style, present fur fashion as worn by young pop stars to a young audience. These products target young teenagers and preteens who may not yet have been exposed to the ethical discourse on the wearing of fur. An example is a post by the young pop star and idol Ariana Grande, showing off her Tzarina by Ollia Monaco fox fur jacket. This post and other social media posts arguably generated demand for this fur product, spurning the production of several copies online, most of which are sold as faux fur and at a fraction of the cost (£1900 for the original Tzarina versus £54.40 for the replica Aniyah on www.missyempire.com). This publicity and collaboration between pop stars and High Street fashion outlets and the accessible price points partly explain the resurgence of fur on the UK's High Streets and in online fashion shops.

Despite a lot of the replica pop-star fur fashion being made of synthetic (faux) fur, the British Fur Trade Association reported an increase in demand for fur products[19] and cited the decision by Canada Goose (a historic purveyor of fur and feathers, who have since made steps to go fur-free from 2022) to open its first European flagship store in 2017 as evidence of commercially viable demand for fur. In the same document, the British Fur Trade Association highlighted an increased interest in working with fur among young designers and students. Moreover, an investigation by Sky News and the Humane Society International in 2017 revealed several items sold as faux fur in several UK High Street shops, independent retailers, market stalls, and online shops to be actually made of real fur. The Environment, Food and Rural Affairs Committee's report on the fur trade in the UK confirmed this phenomenon and attributed this misrepresentation of fur to the low cost of fur trim, as available through websites such as Alibaba.com. This low price is due to the low production costs afforded by the low-welfare systems in which the fur animals are farmed.[20] This completes the cycle of normalizing the wearing of fur, through promotion via pop music role models, provision of fur at accessible price points, and logistical access via High Street and online shops.

An analysis of the top twenty official pop music videos on MTV's top 100 music videos of the 1990s shows that 25 percent of the videos feature the artists wearing fur or feathers in glamorous settings. The images are usually presented for no more than five seconds at a time, making the presentation a more subliminal rather than explicit promotion of fur and furthering of it as fashion. The messages from pop music icons on the ethics of fur can be inconsistent and confusing. For example, the *Guardian* newspaper reported on December 10, 2013, that Beyoncé Knowles, a pop icon who was following a plant-based diet at the time, wore fur to a vegan restaurant.[21] This behavior may confuse some fans and cause them cognitive dissonance in their attempt to reconcile the perceived ethical standing of role models and admiration of their fashion sense with their own ethical concerns for animal well-being. It fosters doubt about whether perhaps it is okay to wear fur if you help animals in other ways, such as not eating them. Reports such as a piece in *Teen Vogue*[22] that featured Ariana Grande wearing a pink vintage Fendi fur coat, calling it faux fur in the title, do little to help naïve fans of pop music artists when they are making decisions about following the fashion trends set by their icons.

Positive Voices in Pop Music

An increasing number of pop artists are speaking out against animal cruelty and the wearing of fur. Through his vegan music festival, Moby is one of the most influential, if rather niche, artists who have been vocal against wearing fur. The artist Pink and Simon Cowell (a pop music mogul) have famously modeled for PETA on anti-fur campaigns. There is potential to work with similar artists and music industry managers to press for standards on pop music videos' animal ethics messaging. Jemima Webber[23] identified twenty-one top pop-music artists who are vegan, highlighting those who are using their music as well as their celebrity status to spread the message against cruelty to animals. However, Webber's analysis identifies animal welfare as one of several motivations for pop celebrities becoming vegan. Given the magnitude of the platform these artists have via pop music videos and on social media, they present a real prospect for positive messaging in the ethical debate on wearing fur.

CONCLUSION

Pop music videos present artists' fashion choices to a large audience of captive fans who translate what they see in these videos, the fashions worn by their icons, into real-world purchasing decisions. Pop music videos have historically presented wearing fur as an aspirational execution of personal liberty in consumer choice. This messaging helps to normalize the wearing of fur, and the subsequent social and print media can have the effect of whitewashing the ethical implications of wearing fur. Fur fashions worn by pop icons can be directly traced to High Street stores, where not only is there an increase in faux fur copies, but there is also a reported increase in demand for real fur products. Investigations have shown the insidious presence of real fur products sold as faux fur to supply the demand among increasingly younger consumers of fur, who are following trends set by their pop star icons. Despite the negative links between certain genres of music and the fur industry, it is clear that there are positive voices speaking out against the wearing of fur. Therefore, there is great potential to work with pop artists and the music industry at large to use the pop music video for positive animal ethics messaging.

NOTES

1. Trefis, "Viacom In-Depth Analysis," accessed June 18, 2017, www.trefis.com/stock/via/model/trefis?easyAccessToken=PROVIDER_3b9bef29d6015c31339b011faaeeb0682b07d779.

2. June O'Connor, "Ethics in Popular Culture," *Journal of the Society of Christian Ethics* 24, no. 2 (2004): 3.

3. Plato, *The Republic*, trans. Benjamin Jowett (Seattle: Amazon Classics, 2018), book 4, location 5623, Kindle.

4. Jonna K. Vuoskoski, Eric F. Clarke, and Tia DeNora, "Music Listening Evokes Implicit Affiliation," *Psychology of Music* 45, no. 4 (2017): 584–99, doi.org/10.1177%2F0305735616680289.

5. Will Straw, "Music Video in Its Contexts: Popular Music and Post-Modernism in the 1980s," *Popular Music* 4, no. 7 (October 1988): 247–66, www.jstor.org/stable/853024.

6. Peter Kivy, *Antithetical Arts: On the Ancient Quarrel between Literature and Music* (Oxford: Oxford University Press, 2009), 215–34.

7. Stefan Koelsh, "Brain Correlates of Music-Evoked Emotions," *Nature Reviews: Neuroscience* 15 (March 2014): 170–80.

8. Aaron Ben-Ze'Ev, "Emotions and Morality," *Journal of Value Enquiry* 31 (1997): 195–212.

9. Naomi Ziv, Moran Hoftman, and Mor Geye, "Music and Moral Judgment: The Effect of Background Music on the Evaluation of Ads Promoting Unethical Behavior," *Psychology of Music* 40, no. 6 (2011): 738–60.

10. Council on Communications and Media, "Policy Statement: Impact of Music, Music Lyrics, and Music Videos on Children and Youth," *Pediatrics* 124, no. 5 (November 2009): 1488–94, doi.org/10.1542/peds.2009-2145.

11. K. J. Donnelly, "Tracking British Television: Pop Music as Stock Soundtrack to the Small Screen," *Popular Music* 21, no. 3 (2002): 331–43, www.jstor.org/stable/853722.

12. Viacom Inc., "Annual Report Pursuant to Section 13 or 15(D) of the Securities Exchange Act of 1934 for the Fiscal Year Ended September 30, 2016," Form 10-K (New York: United States Securities and Exchange Commission, 2016), commission file number 001–32686.

13. British Fashion Council, "British Fashion Council Champions Positive Fashion: Survey Shows that London Fashion Week September 2018 Will Be Fur Free" (London Fashion Week 2018 press release), September 7, 2018, www

.britishfashioncouncil.co.uk/pressreleases/BFC-Champions-Positive-Fashion-Survey-Shows-that-London-Fashion-Week-September-2018-Will-be-Fur-Free.

14. B. J. Steiner, "The Game Is to Be Sold, Not to Be Told: A Look at Pimp Rap through the Years," *Complex*, last updated October 17, 2014, www.complex.com/music/2014/10/pimp-rap-through-years/.

15. Ronald Weitzer and Charis E. Kubrin, "Misogyny in Rap Music—A Content Analysis of Prevalence and Meanings," *Men and Masculinities* 12, no. 1 (October 2009): 3–29, doi.org/10.1177%2F1097184X08327696.

16. Bridjet Mendyuk, "'Thrift Shop' Opens Students' Eyes to Retail Alternatives," *BG News*, last modified March 3, 2013, www.bgfalconmedia.com/entertainment/thrift-shop-opens-students-eyes-to-retail-alternatives/article_8ecced04-8233-11e2-a242-0019bb2963f4.html.

17. Maya Shwayder, "Macklemore's 'Thrift Shop' Has Had No Effect on Actual Thrift Shop Revenues," *International Business Times*, last modified March 6, 2013, www.ibtimes.com/macklemores-thrift-shop-has-had-no-effect-actual-thrift-shop-revenues-1114394.

18. *Irish Examiner*, "Blige Warns Activists to Leave Her Fur Coat Alone," January 14, 2006, www.irishexaminer.com/breakingnews/entertainment/blige-warns-activists-to-leave-her-fur-coat-alone-239599.html.

19. British Fur Trade Association, "Written Evidence Submitted by the British Fur Trade Association (FUR0053)," accessed December 3, 2018, www.parliament.uk/business/committees/committees-a-z/commons-select/environment-food-and-rural-affairs-committee/inquiries/parliament-2017/fur-trade-in-the-uk-17-19/publications/.

20. Environment, Food and Rural Affairs Committee, "Fur Trade in the UK: Seventh Report of Session 2017–19," HC 823, House of Commons, London, July 22, 2018, publications.parliament.uk/pa/cm201719/cmselect/cmenvfru/823/823.pdf.

21. Hadley Freeman, "Beyonce Wore Fur to a Vegan Restaurant," *Guardian*, December 10, 2013, www.theguardian.com/commentisfree/2013/dec/10/beyonce-fur-vegan-restaurant-veganism-lifestyle-celebrity.

22. Avery Matera, "Ariana Grande Walked Dog Myron in Pink Lipstick and a Matching Faux Fur Coat," *Teen Vogue*, January 3, 2019, www.teenvogue.com/story/ariana-grande-walked-dog-myron-pink-lipstick-faux-fur-coat.

23. Jemima Webber, "Did You Know These 21 Musicians Are All Vegan?," *Live Kindly*, October 11, 2019, www.livekindly.co/vegan-musicians/.

REFERENCES

Ben-Ze'Ev, Aaron. "Emotions and Morality." *Journal of Value Enquiry* 31 (1997): 195–212.

British Fashion Council. "British Fashion Council Champions Positive Fashion: Survey Shows That London Fashion Week September 2018 Will Be Fur Free." London Fashion Week 2018 press release, September 7, 2018. www

.britishfashioncouncil.co.uk/pressreleases/BFC-Champions-Positive-Fashion-Survey-Shows-that-London-Fashion-Week-September-2018-Will-be-Fur-Free.

British Fur Trade Association. "Written Evidence Submitted by the British Fur Trade Association (FUR0053)." Accessed December 3, 2018. www.parliament.uk/business/committees/committees-a-z/commons-select/environment-food-and-rural-affairs-committee/inquiries/parliament-2017/fur-trade-in-the-uk-17-19/publications/.

Council on Communications and Media. "Policy Statement: Impact of Music, Music Lyrics, and Music Videos on Children and Youth." *Pediatrics* 124, no. 5 (November 2009): 1488–94. doi.org/10.1542/peds.2009-2145.

Donnelly, K. J. "Tracking British Television: Pop Music as Stock Soundtrack to the Small Screen." *Popular Music* 21, no. 3 (2002): 331–43. www.jstor.org/stable/853722.

Environment, Food and Rural Affairs Committee. "Fur Trade in the UK: Seventh Report of Session 2017–19." HC 823, House of Commons, London, July 22, 2018. publications.parliament.uk/pa/cm201719/cmselect/cmenvfru/823/823.pdf.

Freeman, Hadley. "Beyonce Wore Fur to a Vegan Restaurant." *Guardian*, December 10, 2013. www.theguardian.com/commentisfree/2013/dec/10/beyonce-fur-vegan-restaurant-veganism-lifestyle-celebrity.

Irish Examiner. "Blige Warns Activists to Leave Her Fur Coat Alone." January 14, 2006. www.irishexaminer.com/breakingnews/entertainment/blige-warns-activists-to-leave-her-fur-coat-alone-239599.html.

Koelsh, Stefan. "Brain Correlates of Music-Evoked Emotions." *Nature Reviews: Neuroscience* 15 (March 2014): 170–80.

Kivy, Peter. *Antithetical Arts: On the Ancient Quarrel between Literature and Music*. Oxford: Oxford University Press, 2009.

Matera, Avery. "Ariana Grande Walked Dog Myron in Pink Lipstick and a Matching Faux Fur Coat." *Teen Vogue*, January 3, 2019. www.teenvogue.com/story/ariana-grande-walked-dog-myron-pink-lipstick-faux-fur-coat.

Mendyuk, Bridjet. "'Thrift Shop' Opens Students' Eyes to Retail Alternatives." *BG News*. Last modified March 3, 2013. www.bgfalconmedia.com/entertainment/thrift-shop-opens-students-eyes-to-retail-alternatives/article_8ecced04-8233-11e2-a242-0019bb2963f4.html.

O'Connor, June. "Ethics in Popular Culture." *Journal of the Society of Christian Ethics* 24, no. 2 (2004): 3.

Plato. *The Republic*. Translated by Benjamin Jowett. Seattle: Amazon Classics, 2018. Kindle.

Shwayder, Maya. "Macklemore's 'Thrift Shop' Has Had No Effect on Actual Thrift Shop Revenues." *International Business Times*. Last modified March 6, 2013. www.ibtimes.com/macklemores-thrift-shop-has-had-no-effect-actual-thrift-shop-revenues-1114394.

Steiner, B. J. "The Game Is to Be Sold, Not to Be Told: A Look at Pimp Rap through the Years." *Complex*. Last updated October 17, 2014. www.complex.com/music/2014/10/pimp-rap-through-years/.

Straw, Will. "Music Video in Its Contexts: Popular Music and Post-Modernism in the 1980s." *Popular Music* 4, no. 7 (October 1988): 247–66. www.jstor.org/stable/853024.

Trefis. "Viacom In-Depth Analysis." Accessed June 18, 2017. www.trefis.com/stock/via/model/trefis?easyAccessToken=PROVIDER_3b9bef29d6015c31339b011faaeeb0682b07d779.

Viacom Inc. "Annual Report Pursuant to Section 13 or 15(D) of the Securities Exchange Act of 1934 for the Fiscal Year Ended September 30, 2016," Form 10-K. New York: United States Securities and Exchange Commission, 2016. Commission file number 001–32686.

Vuoskoski, Jonna K., Eric F. Clarke, and Tia DeNora. "Music Listening Evokes Implicit Affiliation." *Psychology of Music* 45, no. 4 (2017): 584–99. doi.org/10.1177%2F0305735616680289.

Webber, Jemima. "Did You Know These 21 Musicians Are All Vegan?" *Live Kindly*, October 11, 2019. www.livekindly.co/vegan-musicians/.

Weitzer, Ronald, and Charis E. Kubrin. "Misogyny in Rap Music—A Content Analysis of Prevalence and Meanings." *Men and Masculinities* 12, no. 1 (October 2009): 3–29. doi.org/10.1177%2F1097184X08327696.

Ziv, Naomi, Moran Hoftman, and Mor Geye. "Music and Moral Judgment: The Effect of Background Music on the Evaluation of Ads Promoting Unethical Behavior." *Psychology of Music* 40, no. 6 (2011): 738–60.

PART THREE

Political and Legal Perspectives

Chapter 12

Politics, Law, and Grasping the Evidence in Fur Farming

A Tale of Three Continents

Simon Brooman

Farming played a vital role in the development of humankind by freeing up time for hunter-gatherers to develop their intellect and society.[1] However, since the postwar period, intensive farming practices have focused on the production of cheap animal products in great quantity at the cost of sweeping aside concerns for animal welfare.[2] Fur farming sits at the pinnacle of these concerns because it produces luxury items that appeal to human vanity rather than a need. Use of fur neither adds to human intellect nor makes any meaningful contribution to society.

This essay discusses the practice of fur farming through an examination of differing regulatory frameworks and their underpinning socio-legal[3] context across three continental areas. Europe, North America, and Asia/Oceania are responsible for the vast majority of both the production of and the market for fur. Most of this discussion centers on mink because mink is the largest source for fur.

Fur-farming production and the trade in fur products appear to be in a perpetual state of flux, with industry production figures illustrating extreme volatility. However, despite occasional rises due to changes in fashion, the general trend appears to be downward, especially in Europe with bans in 14 countries by 2022 as indicated in Table 12.1.[4]

Despite producing a controversial "luxury" item, fur farming often has escaped regulation in some parts of the globe, even where those jurisdictions have legislated in other areas such as animal experimentation, food production, and slaughter. Restrictions are now possible for the first time in China,

Table 12.1. Worldwide Mink Farming Production

	2013	*2014*	*2015*	*2016*
Global	87 million		72 million	70 million
China	40 million	35 million	18 million	20 million
USA/Canada	6.3 million	6.2 million	7.5 million	7.5 million
Denmark		18 million	18.6 million	18 million
Eastern Europe			16 million	15 million
European Union		41 million	45.4 million	35 million

Notes: Gaps indicate no reliable figures found; Figures are approximate and based on several worldwide sources. Source: Compiled by Chapter Author.

where legislators have been reluctant to protect animal welfare despite evidence of growing concern among the population.[5] Other countries have long since banned fur farming or are about to do so. One question asked here is whether any consistent patterns of regulatory control are emerging in the regulation of fur farming.

Emerging scientific evidence, discussed in detail as this essay continues, indicates that the animals used in fur production suffer to an even greater degree than many other farmed animals—the animals remain inherently "wild" animals, even when in captivity. Is regulation keeping up with emerging scientific evidence regarding free-living animal suffering or environmental damage? Finally, does fur farming suffer from the lack of ethical coherence in terms of free-living animal welfare?[6]

This study aims to reveal the overall regulatory trends in worldwide fur production. It assesses the effectiveness of regulation in light of concerns over the farming of animals who are unsuited to close confinement. In addition, an examination of these areas might reveal how much politics and culture play a part in the extent of regulation and might reveal why further regulatory control has been difficult to enact. What can we learn from an overview of international control? Are previous assumptions—for example, about the chief culprits being fur farmers in China—entirely accurate? Is a consensus approach to regulation likely? What is the best way forward to improve the welfare of these animals?

MAIN CENTERS OF THE FUR TRADE

The first contentious issue that becomes apparent when examining the fur trade is the difficulty in obtaining accurate figures for worldwide production. For example, during research for this essay, the attempt to obtain figures for five years earlier (2015) uncovered differing estimates that varied from the figure given in Table 12.1 by five to fifteen million. Therefore, Table 12.1

shows an approximation based on recent figures available for mink farming, but the numbers' accuracy is doubted in the absence of reliable data in this area. It is troubling that an industry involving so many animals has such an apparent lack of transparency regarding the number of animals involved.

Despite the difficulty in obtaining reliable figures, it is possible to draw some initial conclusions from the available data in Table 12.1. The first is that the overall production of fur fell during 2013–2015. This was due to greater consumer concerns over welfare, particularly in important production areas such as China, where consumer awareness and recognition of animal welfare is growing.[7] Other key observations are the confirmation of the European Union as the growing center of worldwide fur production and the rise of eastern Europe as a major producer of fur. The figures confirm that a relatively small country, Denmark, is a major player in the world fur markets well beyond what might be explained by domestic demand. The aforementioned downward trend may not be continuing, however, since the anti-fur group Fur for Animals estimates that the total number of animals killed for their fur in 2019 was over eighty million.[8] Therefore, an overall downward trend is difficult to establish conclusively.

These basic observations are important because where production takes place in global terms has a bearing on the welfare standards experienced by animals raised in the close confinement conditions of fur farms. For example, Europe has well-established animal welfare standards in comparison to other areas of production such as China, where regulation is in its infancy. Therefore, can we assume that the EU situation is less of a concern than the one in China? The production of fur is a combination of farming, marketing, and markets. Each influences the other, so that production involving suffering occurs only because someone, somewhere in the world, wants to buy fur.

It is not possible to discuss the welfare standards and legal approach of every fur-farming nation in this space. However, looking at regulations in certain areas brings out the overall trends, contradictions, and uncertainties that arise in this contentious area of modern farming. Analysis of worldwide fur-farming production and markets leads to the conclusion that three main "centers" are particularly useful in analyzing the overall socio-legal situation for animals used in fur production.

Europe is the major producer and market for fur production and a continent of stark contrasts in relation to how countries view the moral acceptability of the industry. The UK, Austria, and Croatia have banned fur farming, whereas countries such as Denmark defend the practice vociferously, and new producers are emerging in eastern Europe. As the hub of worldwide fur farming, Europe demands inclusion in this discussion.

The United States and Canada have contrasting approaches and are historical locations of fur farming in traditional "frontier" locations. The USA has introduced novel ways to regulate fur farming such as a "Humane Care award program" and labeling according to origin and species, which aim to allow consumers to choose according to welfare standards. The USA is also notable for high-profile anti-fur activity, as shown by the release of 38,000 mink into nature from the Lang mink farm in Minnesota in July 2017. The USA is worthy of inclusion because it allows for discussion of new approaches to regulation and whether they are successful. Canada is unusual among advanced nations in its apparent historical reluctance to regulate fur farming. It has a long-standing history of trapping, rather than farming, fur animals. Its animal welfare laws are weak in the area of fur farming. Considering the USA and Canada together is useful because of the existence of very different approaches in neighboring countries with large markets for fur and many shared cultural links.

Together the areas comprising Asia and Oceania make up the second-largest area of production and illustrate significant differences in approaches to animal welfare and fur farming in particular. China might have been included in its own right as a discussion point since it has a particularly strong presence in both the production of and the market for fur. However, discussing China along with Australia allows a contrast with Australia, where there is a strong focus on welfare and consumer rights in relation to fur. New Zealand also can be included here because it has effectively dissipated the market for mink by banning the import of these animals, thereby making it almost impossible to farm them with no new animals able to be imported.

THE USE (AND ABUSE) OF SCIENCE IN FUR FARMING

Before any conclusions are drawn about the socio-legal status of worldwide fur farming, it is necessary to summarize the scientific evidence in this area. In recent years, with the call for animal welfare claims to be evidence-based rather than reliant on anthropomorphic views of animal behavior, scientific evidence has burgeoned, answering the call.[12]

The farming of fur animals has, historically, attracted less criticism than the trapping of free-living fur animals.[13] However, the farming of, effectively, undomesticated animals continues to attract significant criticism on the basis that the animals involved are naturally less able to adapt to the necessary conditions of confinement. Confinement seriously compromises their natural behavior and leads to the development of psychological disorders, casting doubt on the morality of using them in intensive confinement farming. A 2001 report on animals kept for fur farming, published by the European Commission's Scientific Committee on Animal Health and Animal Welfare, concluded that "these species, in comparison with other farm animals, have

Table 12.2. Summary of Fur-Farming Regulations and Issues

Country/Region	*Summary of Regulation and Control of Fur Farming*
USA	Regulated at state rather than federal level, so control varies. Most anticruelty laws exempt fur-farmed animals. Regulation is weak in most areas. Exceptions include California, where tight regulation of conditions made production costs prohibitive and a ban on fur trapping was introduced in 2019 (for implementation in 2023). The federal Fur Products Labeling Act requires details of place of origin and species. Controversially, interference with fur farming is considered terrorism under the federal Animal Enterprise Terrorism Act.
Canada	No federal law—but mink and foxes are covered by the National Farm Animal Care Council's Codes of Practice on fur farming.
Europe (including countries not in the EU)	Council of Europe's European Convention for the Protection of Animals Kept for Farming Purposes, adopted in 1976.[9] Animals must be kept according to their species needs according to scientific knowledge. Commentators suggest that this should effectively ban fur farming.
European Union	European Union Directive 98/58/EC of 20 July 1998 concerning the Protection of Animals Kept for Farming Purposes.[10] No animal may be kept for fur farming if it is detrimental to the animal's welfare. It has been suggested that this should effectively ban fur farming. Several countries have banned fur farming, such as the United Kingdom (2000), Austria (2004), the Czech Republic (2019), Croatia (phasing out by 2027), Belgium (by 2023), and the Netherlands (by 2024). In 2019 the Republic of Ireland voted to do likewise, and others are considering doing the same.[11]
China	Regulation is extremely weak. There have been new moves to introduce controls, but these are highly unlikely to match the level of regulation seen in other countries.
New Zealand/ Australia	New Zealand prohibits the import of mink, effectively banning mink farming. Lack of labeling laws. Australia has a very limited market and is a strong campaigner against fur farming.

Source: Compiled by Chapter Author.

been subjected to relatively little active selection, except with respect to fur characteristics. There has thus been only a limited amount of selection for tameness and adaptability to captive environments."[14]

Other studies have looked at the wider environmental impact of fur farming. One study in Canada concluded that as "fur production is intensely polluting, energy-consumptive and an otherwise unnatural process, fur cannot be considered an environmentally friendly product."[15] In Europe, a report by the Eurogroup for Animals concluded that the climate change impact of mink fur is five times that of wool and that fur products contain carcinogens and other hazardous substances potentially detrimental to human health.[16] Therefore, fur farming shares many of the traits identified with animal farming more generally, as a large polluter that unnecessarily increases global emissions in a trade whose major function is the generation of profit.[17]

The fur industry now seeks to use science to defend its practice. For example, the pro-fur lobbying group Fur Europe has championed its "WelFur science-based assessment program," introduced in 2009, which professes to be the "world's most advanced animal welfare assessment program."[18] Its overall claim is that science proves that fur farming in the EU is adequately protected by scientifically monitored welfare standards in areas of concern such as the development of negative emotions, appropriate housing systems, and allowing for natural behavior. The group proposes that clean conditions of care (e.g., lack of flies) and a "nutritious diet" are evidence of good practice and humane conditions.

Tensen suggests that the farming of foxes and mink may decrease illegal poaching.[19] However, Tensen's article does not examine the danger that increased availability of fur products may stimulate demand in the market, leading to more poaching and captures of free-living animals, as witnessed in the case of ivory and rhino horns.[20] Instead, Tensen relies on evidence from a 1937 book concerning the breeding of fur animals.[21]

In response to the "scientific approach" of WelFur, Respect for Animals published *The Case against Fur Factory Farming* in 2015.[22] This report presents evidence that species' needs are not met on fur farms. It suggests that the welfare of animals used in fur farming is severely compromised, and animals remain unable to perform many of their natural behaviors, despite claims that they have improved diets and clean environments. The report's authors maintain that WelFur's approach fails, for example, to address serious limitations of current housing, does not meet existing minimum standards, involves dubious slaughter practices, and would be misleading if used as a basis for a labeling system. The report concludes that it is "impossible for the needs of mink and foxes to be met by the fur industry. A ban is the only viable solution."[23] WelFur's claim that it deals with welfare concerns should be viewed with skepticism as it does not carry the weight of scientific evidence. The same problem may apply in relation to labeling in the United States because labeling as to origin may have a limited impact on the overall welfare of fur-farmed animals.

IS FUR FARMING MORALLY JUSTIFIABLE?

Evidence showing the poor conditions experienced by fur animals has fueled consistent criticism. Perhaps the most shocking evidence arose from film footage of the live skinning of animals in China published by Swiss Animal

Protection in 2005. No one on either side of the debate appears to support these barbaric scenes of suffering. Groups such as WelFur distance themselves from those practices, claiming that their animals have never lived freely, that they are better at coping with captive conditions, thereby allaying moral concerns. The question arises whether different killing techniques make this fur-farming morally acceptable.

This essay takes the position that the weight of scientific evidence leads to an inevitable conclusion that all animals confined and slaughtered for fur will be unable to express natural behaviors—for example, the desire of mink to swim—and that fur farming is a large contributor to environmental damage. When these factors are measured against fur farming's claimed benefits in supplying items for the fashion industry and a limited amount of employment, the practice cannot be considered "essential" in any normal meaning of the word.[24] Given the weight of evidence, the inevitable conclusion is that fur farming is morally unjustifiable in light of its inherent animal suffering and environmental damage, and the question should move to how to phase out its existence.

Counterarguments include Arney and Piirsalu's conclusion that the moral argument is based upon "the rather weak position of not harming furry animals with appealing faces."[25] With the greatest of respect to those authors, it is suggested here that this conclusion runs contrary to a significant body of scientific evidence and the weight of moral discourse.

The basic principles behind concern for animals used in farming generally were elucidated in the 1965 Brambell report. These principles are accepted as the minimum measure of morality in many countries. When the natural instincts and behaviors of animals such as mink are taken into account, this consideration adds weight to the suggestion that fur farming is morally unacceptable:

> Modern, intensive animal production methods most markedly increase the responsibility of those who use them towards the animals in the charge. If any creature is wholly and continuously under control, we believe that this total human responsibility must be acknowledged, and that there is widespread public concern that it be seen to be acknowledged. Changing patterns of husbandry may mean varying degrees of frustration and discomfort to animals whose normal patterns of behavior are still imperfectly understood.[26]

In 2001, the Scientific Committee on Animal Health and Animal Welfare noted that "these species, in comparison with other farm animals, have been subjected to relatively little active selection, except with respect to fur characteristics. There has thus been only a limited amount of selection for tameness and adaptability to captive environments."[27] The weight of evidence is conclusively against there being any moral justification for fur farming. Thus, labeling (as in the USA) and pro–fur farming marketing campaigns such as WelFur do little to change this moral position.

SOME CONCLUSIONS FROM THIS TALE OF THREE CONTINENTS

It Is Time to Implement a "Precautionary Principle" in Relation to Fur-Farming Law

The proponents of animal welfare have always been saddled with a high burden of proof when making the case against fur farming and other misuse of animals. The argument goes something like this (I paraphrase): "If you want to change long-established practice in the use of animals, then you have to prove your case beyond all reasonable doubt. We make our living from it and have been doing this for such a long time that you must adduce strong evidence that irrefutably supports your contention to change the law."

However, studying the nature of the potential harm should lead to a different approach according to studies in the related field of environmental ethics, where it is suggested that the pace of change is often slower than desirable, and that law fails to keep pace with evidence. Kriebel et al. argue that there are areas where there is residual doubt about ultimate proof and that competing science can always reveal a certain ambiguity or uncertainty that often results in no change to the status quo. They suggest the use of a precautionary principle in gray areas where the harm–benefit analysis is uncertain. The burden of proof should fall on those who are engaging in and seeking to continue with a potentially damaging policy or practice.[28]

Using this approach would radically affect fur farming. The introduction of a "science-based" argument such as WelFur clearly has the potential to muddy the waters so that those favoring a ban will find it more difficult to alter dubious practices. However, using the precautionary principle in fur farming is entirely reasonable in light of evidence of significant welfare concern. The reasoning behind applying the principle to cases of environmental concern should surely apply even more so to cases of the suffering of sentient beings. Using the precautionary principle shifts the burden of proof and is highly pertinent in many areas where animal welfare problems persist. It asks those producing fur to prove that the human need to wear animal skins outweighs the evidence of animal suffering in captive fur-farming environments.

A word of caution on the potential use of the principle is that it is likely to come up against the same resistance that is encountered when concerns are raised over the captive housing of undomesticated animals—convincing governments to implement the principle may be difficult. However, it does have the benefit of wide global support that has seen it applied in law in cases of, for example, overfishing, North Sea pollution, and ozone depletion.[29]

The Weight of Animal Welfare and Environmental Evidence Counters Unconvincing Claims of the Industry

The fur trade has been remarkably resilient in the face of evidence of suffering that has caused consumer demand to fall. Figures reveal that demand has often recovered as new markets emerge and regulators fail to take full cognizance of scientific evidence in relation to suffering. It is in some ways remarkable that the industry has survived for so long—a testament to strong lobbying and a willing fashion market.

Whereas markets drive demand, it is widely acknowledged that animal welfare and policy need to be guided by evidence: "Advances in knowledge of animal behavior and biology support the belief that many animals are sentient and have complex social behaviors, a means of communication and some demonstration of self-awareness . . . as a result . . . we are forced to consider the moral implications of our interactions with animals."[30] More recently, the fur industry's moves toward countering science with the pseudo-scientific evidence of WelFur have tended to deflect evidence that undomesticated animals have intrinsic desires, habits, and behaviors that cannot be met in highly confined conditions. A spokesman for WelFur suggests that free-living animals are different from the captive-bred animals used in fur farming[31]—but this does not address continued evidence that the latter animals self-harm and show signs of mental distress. WelFur does not counter a key criticism that fur farms do not cater to any need, nor does the scheme answer concerns regarding environmental damage caused by the industry. WelFur is a marketing strategy created to counter criticism and used to bolster fur's acceptability in the fashion market.

Another problem with the scientific evidence used by the pro-fur lobby is that it is selective in examining welfare concerns. For example, Korhonen et al.'s evaluation of the euthanasia of farmed foxes concludes that electrical stunning is a humane method of euthanasia.[32] While a scientific approach is welcome, this conclusion falls into the common trap of failing to put the whole life cycle of farmed foxes into perspective. Suffering can occur at many stages of an animal's life cycle, from birth to slaughter.

Focusing on only one element of this life cycle may skew moral considerations toward a false result, as seen in the case of religious slaughter.[33] Full ethical evaluation can occur only where all potential areas of concern are considered, such as the conditions in which the animal is raised, how the animal is treated up to slaughter and transported to slaughter, and the way in which the animal was allowed to express his or her natural habits and behaviors. These factors all need consideration in an open and honest evaluation of evidence. Perhaps one solution for evaluating evidence would be to open up fur farming to greater scrutiny by local councils on welfare that would include membership from academic and welfare groups and so extend a system for other farming suggested by Mejdell.[34]

Is Education a Better Tool to Reduce Fur-Farming Than Legislation?

The United Kingdom became the first country in Europe to ban fur farming with the Fur Farming (Prohibition) Act 2000. The time limit imposed for compliance was three years. Thus came an end to the farming of 1.3 million animals for pelts annually in the UK, with only the by-products of meat production exempted. The ban followed a public consultation by the government that confirmed widespread support for the measure. Public awareness of and disquiet at the suffering of fur-farmed animals followed a concerted campaign by groups such as Respect for Animals that managed to gain a commitment to act from an incoming government.

However, the question is whether the same pattern leading to a ban is repeatable in other parts of the world. The United Kingdom has a long history of leading animal welfare regulation, starting with its historic introduction of an Act to Prevent the Cruel and Improper Treatment of Cattle in July 1822 by Richard Martin.[35] Other countries are less open to introducing animal welfare legislation, and considerable work will need to be done.

In China, for example, there are significant cultural barriers and economic imperatives that make complete prohibition difficult to achieve, since there are different priorities.[36] In situations such as this, the best that might be achieved is regulation to significantly reduce suffering.[37] In the EU, there is a much more realistic chance of prohibiting fur farming in the near future. The momentum appears to be swinging conclusively in the direction of countries banning the practice outright, although fluctuations in demand have seen the emergence of new fur-farming production in eastern Europe. There may also be a downside to consider—how would welfare advocates react if all fur were imported from areas with weaker regulation? The answer may lie in the approach of the UK that, in 2021, began consultation to potentially ban fur imports so targeting the market, as well as production.

The fur-fashion industry, from production to sale, is not responding to the evidence that emerges from animal welfare science—even though EU Directive 98/58/EC is clear that conditions need to be adjusted if the keeping of an animal is clearly detrimental to the animal's welfare.[38] However, where law-makers fail to intervene effectively, an educated consumer can alter the future of fur farming by reducing demand for products produced with inherent cruelty. In addition, educating those in the industry may also provide part of the answer. There is a strong moral case not only to exert consumer or legislative pressure, but to educate those in the industry to avoid fur. As Nathaniel Beard suggests,

> ultimately . . . the continuation of ethical fashion lies with the people engaged within it. Education initiatives, such as the establishment of an MA in Ethical Fashion by the University of the Creative Arts, aims [*sic*] to ensure that future generations of fashion professionals and decisions makers develop a prolonged passion for ecofashion to take with them into the industry.[39]

Education has the power to reach where governments fear to tread. In this regard, the emergence of new discipline-based law courses that address issues around animal welfare will also help.[40] These have the potential to educate the next generation of decision makers, generate evidence, create partnerships for action between academia and industry, and examine the issues through networks of academic activity. It will fall on governments to act, but they are likely to be driven to do so by educated voters who demand change.

The European paradox needs to be challenged

The European Union, or perhaps more accurately, Europe, contains perhaps the greatest paradox in the case of fur farming. Europe boasts a host of animal welfare–conscious nations, animal protection laws, and organizations campaigning for animal welfare. The United Kingdom is the birthplace of much animal welfare legislation, as shown by government reactions to the Brambell report, which influenced the introduction of legislation to protect farmed animals in many countries. China attracts attention because of poor conditions in the housing, treatment, and slaughter of fur animals. Although it is suggested that China is the area in need of most improvement, its global influence is not as great as Europe's.[41]

The continent of Europe plays the leading role in the worldwide fur-farming industry. It is home to the highly influential International Fur Federation, which lobbies strongly for the industry, and is the location of a significant percentage of fur production. It is home to the biggest global fur-fashion houses, making it both the crucial hub for designers who create the demand for fur, alongside those who provide the market with pelts.

At the same time, Europe has laws in place that already could have made fur production in Europe obsolete. Chief among these is Article 3 of the European Convention for the Protection of Animals Kept for Farming

Purposes: "Animals shall be housed and provided with food, water and care in a manner which—having regard to their species and to their degree of development, adaptation and domestication—is appropriate to their physiological and ethological needs with established experience and scientific knowledge."[42] This is amended in the case of the EU by a European Union directive (98/58/EC) that gives further detail regarding the protection given to animals in the EU itself: "No animal shall be kept for farming purposes unless it can reasonably be expected . . . that it can be kept without detrimental effect on its health or welfare."[43]

Vaqué suggests that this creates a positive duty to act where animals cannot be kept without detrimental effects on their welfare.[44] But the European Union has failed to enforce existing legislation against fur farming. It appears that the European Court of Justice has ignored scientific evidence on the ability of fur-farmed animals to express their natural behavior. Only consumer demand, affected by evidence of poor animal welfare, appears to halt the market for fur.

In 1997, the EU introduced a protocol to its treaties that stated the following:

> In formulating and implementing the Community's agriculture, transport, internal market and research policies, the Community and the Member States shall pay full regard to the welfare requirements of animals, while respecting the legislative or administrative provisions and customs of the Member States relating in particular to religious rites, cultural traditions and regional heritage.

A failure to act in the case of fur farming may be explained by the fact that the suffering of fur-farmed animals is part of the "cultural tradition" in those countries. If so, this state of affairs could justify almost any treatment, no matter how cruel. It is concluded here that in Europe cruel fashion has not been adequately scrutinized under existing law. This has been recognized for a considerable time.[45]

CONCLUSION

The weight of scientific evidence is against fur farming, despite attempts to confuse decisive science with marketing campaigns such as WelFur. However, fur farming continues to thrive to a large extent because some governments face cultural barriers to introducing legislation, and others are influenced by strong lobbyists. The fashion industry plays an extensive role in driving the global market in fur, its approach fluctuating from occasional consumer-driven distaste and eco-consciousness to blatant championing of fur.

This essay reveals a paradox in that Europe is the originator of the strongest legislation against fur farming yet maintains its undoubted status as the hub of the fur market. It provides a home to the large fashion houses and is the point of origin for fur-production marketing strategies. The paradox is enhanced by the presence of legislation that could, if properly enforced, ban fur farming in Europe. The existence of fur farming appears to be contrary to Council of Europe and EU provisions that specifically require that farming practices take adequate account of the natural habits of the species involved. Those in the industry claim that they take adequate account of species requirements, but convincing evidence that weighs heavily against this claim continues to emerge.

Perhaps it will take something as significant as the global pandemic of 2020 to bring an end to fur farming. It was reported in May 2020 that coronavirus is passed between farm workers and mink, thereby illustrating the dangers we face in interfering with the lives of undomesticated animals for superfluous benefits.[46] Thousands of animals were slaughtered as a result. The move towards banning fur-farming and preventing the suffering of animals in this dubious luxury market is gathering pace, but action to protect human beings happens extremely quickly. If fur-farming affects human health directly it will come under intense pressure. However, if human interest does not reduce the practice, campaigns against fur may follow the experience of previous animal welfare campaigns such as whaling, seal culling, bearbaiting, use of leghold traps, experimentation on higher primates, and foxhunting. Significant change requires education of both consumer and those in the market for fur—to allow the emergence of what is evident and clear—fur-farming is barbaric and needs to stop.

NOTES

1. Richard Leaky and Roger Lewin, *Origins Reconsidered: In Search of What Makes Us Human* (London: Abacus Books, 1992), 351.

2. Simon Brooman and Deborah Legge, *Law Relating to Animals* (London: Cavendish, 1997), 171.

3. "Socio-legal" scholars examine law in context—for example, political, social, and environmental—in order to critique an existing situation.

4. See www.furfreealliance.com/wp-content/uploads/2022/01/Facts-on-fur-farming-legislation_Fact-sheet-3.pdf. Accessed February 17, 2022.

5. Yangzi Sima and Siobhan O'Sullivan, "Chinese Animal Protection Laws and the Globalization of Welfare Norms," *International Journal of Law in Context* 12, no. 1 (2016): 1–23.

6. Gareth Spark, "Protecting Wild Animals from Unnecessary Suffering," *Journal of Environmental Law* 26 (2014): 473–94.

7. Sima and O'Sullivan, "Chinese Animal Protection Laws," 2.

8. Respect for Animals, "Statistics," accessed February 17, 2022, www.respectforanimals.org/statistics/.

9. Council of Europe, European Convention for the Protection of Animals Kept for Farming Purposes (Strasbourg, France, March 10, 1976), 1–6.

10. Council of the European Union, "Council Directive 98/58/EC of 20 July 1998 concerning the Protection of Animals Kept for Farming Purposes," *Official Journal of the European Union, L* 221 (1998).

11. Eurogroup for Animals and Fur Free Alliance, "The Environmental Impact of Fur Farming," 2015, accessed May 19, 2020, http://www.tierschutz.com/pelz/toxic_fur/pdf/environmental_impact_fur_farming.pdf.

12. Brooman and Legge, *Law Relating to Animals*, chap. 1.

13. Robert Garner, *Animals, Politics and Morality* (Manchester: Manchester University Press, 2004), 191.

14. Scientific Committee on Animal Health and Welfare, *The Welfare of Animals Kept for Fur Production* (European Commission, December 12–13, 2001), 185, accessed May 20, 2020, ec.europa.eu/food/sites/food/files/safety/docs/sci-com_scah_out67_en.pdf.

15. Humane Society of the United States, "Toxic Fur: The Impacts of Fur Production on the Environment and the Risks to Human Health," January 29, 2009, 5, accessed May 19, 2020, www.scribd.com/document/38836299/Toxic-Fur.

16. Eurogroup and Fur Free Alliance, "Environmental Impact of Fur Farming."

17. Ramona Ilea, "Intensive Livestock Farming: Global Trends, Increased Environmental Concerns, and Ethical Solutions," *Journal of Agricultural & Environmental Ethics* 22 (2009): 153–67.

18. Fur Europe, "WelFur: Science-Based Animal Welfare Programme," 2017, www.fureurope.eu/video/welfur-science-based-animal-welfare-assessment/.

19. Laura Tensen, "Under What Circumstances Can Wildlife Farming Benefit Species Conservation?," *Global Ecology and Conservation* 6 (2016): 286–98.

20. Elizabeth Bennett, "Legal Ivory Trade in a Corrupt World and Its Impact on African Elephant Populations," *Conservation Biology* 29, no. 1 (2015): 54–60.

21. Frank Ashbrook, *The Breeding of Fur Animals* (Washington, DC: US Government Printing Office, 1937).

22. Heather Pickett and Stephen Harris, *The Case against Fur Factory Farming: A Scientific Review of Animal Welfare Standards and "WelFur"* (Nottingham: Respect for Animals, 2015), accessed May 19, 2020, www.furfreealliance.com/wp-content/uploads/2015/11/Case-against-fur-farming.pdf

23. Pickett and Harris, *The Case against Fur Factory Farming*, 7.

24. Nibedita Jena, "Animal Welfare and Animal Rights: An Examination of Some Ethical Problems," *Journal of Academic Ethics* 15 (2017): 377.

25. David Arney and Peep Piirsalu, "The Ethics of Keeping Fur Animals: The Estonian Context," *Proceedings of the Latvian Academy of Sciences, Section B: Natural, Exact, and Applied Sciences* 71, nos. 1–2 (2017): 80.

26. Francis William Rogers Brambell, *Report of the Technical Committee to Enquire into the Welfare of Animals Kept under Intensive Livestock Husbandry Systems* (1965), para. 46.

27. Scientific Committee, *The Welfare of Animals Kept for Fur Production*, 185.

28. David Kriebel et al., "The Precautionary Principle in Environmental Science," *Environmental Health Perspectives* 109, no. 9 (2001): 871–76.

29. Kriebel et al., "The Precautionary Principle," 871.

30. Carla Brown, "Animal Welfare: Emerging Trends in Legislation," in *Report of the Whale Welfare and Ethics Workshop* (2011), 57, held 22/23 March 2011, Eden Project, Cornwall, United Kingdom, www.awionline.org/sites/default/files/uploads/documents/ml-whalewelfareethicsworkshopreport-101111.pdf#page=57.

31. Cited in Rachel Bale, "Fur Farms Still Unfashionably Cruel, Critics Say," *National Geographic*, August 17, 2016, accessed May 19, 2020, www.nationalgeographic.com/animals/article/wildlife-china-fur-farming-welfare.

32. Hannu Korhonen, Sigitas Cizinauskas, and Ranno Viitmaa, "Evaluation of the Traditional Way of Euthanasia of Farmed Foxes from an Animal Welfare Point of View," *Annals of Animal Science* 9, no. 1 (2009): 73–87.

33. Simon Brooman, "In Search of the Missing Ingredient: Religious Slaughter, Incremental Failure, and the Quest for the Right to Know—A Response to Anna Joseph," *Journal of Animal Ethics* 6, no. 2 (2016): 153–63.

34. Cecilie Marie Mejdell, "The Role of Councils on Animal Ethics in Assessing Acceptable Welfare Standards in Agriculture," *Livestock Science* 103, no. 3 (2006): 292–96.

35. Brooman and Legge, *Law Relating to Animals*, 44.

36. Peter J. Li, "Animal Suffering in China," *Animal Sentience: An Interdisciplinary Journal on Animal Feeling* 1, no. 7 (2016): 8.

37. Sima and O'Sullivan, "Chinese Animal Protection Laws," 21.

38. Council of the European Union, "Council Directive 98/58/EC."

39. Nathaniel Dafydd Beard, "The Branding of Ethical Fashion and the Consumer: A Luxury Niche or Mass-Market Reality?," *Fashion Theory* 12, no. 4 (2008): 464.

40. Simon Brooman, "Creatures, the Academic Lawyer and a Socio-Legal Approach: Introducing Animal Law into the Legal Education Curriculum," *Liverpool Law Review* 38, no. 3 (2017): 243–57.

41. Lesley Peterson, "Summary of Fur Laws and Fur Production," Animal Legal and Historical Center, Michigan State University College of Law, 2010, accessed May 19, 2020, www.animallaw.info/intro/fur-production-and-fur-laws.

42. Council of Europe, European Convention. (The Council of Europe is a pan-European body that encompasses countries within the European Union and those outside it.)

43. Council of the European Union, "Council Directive 98/58/EC."

44. Luis González Vaqué, "The Cloning of Animals for Farming Purposes in the EU: From Ethics to Agri-Food Law," *European Food and Feed Law Review* 9, no. 4 (2014): 223.

45. Andrew Linzey, "The Ethical Case for European Legislation against Fur Farming," *Animal Law* 13 (2006): 147.

46. Helen Briggs, "Coronavirus: Calls to Shut Down 'Dirty Fur Trade,'" *BBC*, May 5, 2020, accessed May 21, 2020, www.bbc.co.uk/news/science-environment-52535075.

REFERENCES

Arney, David, and Peep Piirsalu. "The Ethics of Keeping Fur Animals: The Estonian Context." *Proceedings of the Latvian Academy of Sciences, Section B: Natural, Exact, and Applied Sciences* 71, nos. 1–2 (2017): 78–80.

Ashbrook, Frank. *The Breeding of Fur Animals*. Washington, DC: US Government Printing Office, 1937.

Bale, Rachel. "Fur Farms Still Unfashionably Cruel, Critics Say." *National Geographic*, August 17, 2016. Accessed May 19, 2020. www.nationalgeographic.com/animals/article/wildlife-china-fur-farming-welfare.

Beard, Nathaniel Dafydd. "The Branding of Ethical Fashion and the Consumer: A Luxury Niche or Mass-Market Reality?" *Fashion Theory* 12, no. 4 (2008): 447–67.

Bennett, Elizabeth. "Legal Ivory Trade in a Corrupt World and Its Impact on African Elephant Populations." *Conservation Biology* 29, no. 1 (2015): 54–60.

Brambell, Francis William Rogers. *Report of the Technical Committee to Enquire into the Welfare of Animals Kept Under Intensive Livestock Husbandry Systems*. 1965.

Briggs, Helen. "Coronavirus: Calls to Shut Down 'Dirty Fur Trade.'" *BBC*, May 5, 2020. Accessed February 17, 2022. www.bbc.co.uk/news/science-environment-52535075.

Brooman, Simon. "Creatures, the Academic Lawyer and a Socio-Legal Approach: Introducing Animal Law into the Legal Education Curriculum." *Liverpool Law Review* 38, no. 3 (2017): 243–57.

———. "In Search of the Missing Ingredient: Religious Slaughter, Incremental Failure, and the Quest for the Right to Know—A Response to Anna Joseph." *Journal of Animal Ethics* 6, no. 2 (2016): 153–63.

Brooman, Simon, and Deborah Legge. *Law Relating to Animals*. London: Cavendish, 1997.

Brown, Carla. "Animal Welfare: Emerging Trends in Legislation." In *Report of the Whale Welfare and Ethics Workshop*, 57. 2011, held 22/23 March 2011, Eden Project, Cornwall, United Kingdom. www.awionline.org/sites/default/files/uploads/documents/ml-whalewelfareethicsworkshopreport-101111.pdf#page=57.

Council of Europe. European Convention for the Protection of Animals Kept for Farming Purposes. Strasbourg, France, March 10, 1976.

Council of the European Union. "Council Directive 98/58/EC of 20 July 1998 concerning the Protection of Animals Kept for Farming Purposes." *Official Journal of the European Union, L* 221 (1998).

Eurogroup for Animals and Fur Free Alliance. "Overview of National Legislation on Fur Farming in Europe." 2015. Accessed February 17, 2022. www.furfreealliance.com/wp-content/uploads/2016/11/Overview-of-national-legislation-on-fur-farming-in-Europe-1.pdf.

———. “The Environmental Impact of Fur Farming.” 2015. Accessed February 17, 2022. www.tierschutz.com/pelz/toxic_fur/pdf/environmental_impact_fur_farming.pdf.

Fur Europe. “WelFur: Science-Based Animal Welfare Programme.” 2017. See www.sustainablefur.com/animal-welfare/.

Garner, Robert. *Animals, Politics and Morality*. Manchester: Manchester University Press, 2004.

Humane Society of the United States. “Toxic Fur: The Impacts of Fur Production on the Environment and the Risks to Human Health.” January 29, 2009. Accessed February 17, 2022. www.scribd.com/document/38836299/Toxic-Fur.

Ilea, Ramona. “Intensive Livestock Farming: Global Trends, Increased Environmental Concerns, and Ethical Solutions.” *Journal of Agricultural & Environmental Ethics* 22 (2009): 153–67.

Jena, Nibedita. “Animal Welfare and Animal Rights: An Examination of Some Ethical Problems.” *Journal of Academic Ethics* 15 (2017): 377–95.

Kriebel, David, Joel Tickner, Paul Epstein, John Lemons, Richard Levins, Edward L. Loechler, Margaret Quinn, Ruthann Rudel, Ted Schettler, and Michael Stoto. “The Precautionary Principle in Environmental Science.” *Environmental Health Perspectives* 109, no. 9 (2001): 871–76.

Korhonen, Hannu T., Sigitas Cizinauskas, and Ranno Viitmaa. “Evaluation of the Traditional Way of Euthanasia of Farmed Foxes from an Animal Welfare Point of View.” *Annals of Animal Science* 9, no. 1 (2009): 73–87.

Leaky, Richard, and Roger Lewin. *Origins Reconsidered: In Search of What Makes Us Human*. London: Abacus Books, 1992.

Li, Peter J. “Animal Suffering in China.” *Animal Sentience: An Interdisciplinary Journal on Animal Feeling* 1, no. 7 (2016): 8–11.

Linzey, Andrew. “The Ethical Case for European Legislation against Fur Farming.” *Animal Law* 13 (2006): 147.

Mejdell, Cecilie Marie. “The Role of Councils on Animal Ethics in Assessing Acceptable Welfare Standards in Agriculture.” *Livestock Science* 103, no. 3 (2006): 292–96.

Pickett, Heather, and Stephen Harris. *The Case against Fur Factory Farming: A Scientific Review of Animal Welfare Standards and “WelFur.”* Nottingham: Respect for Animals, 2015. Accessed February 17, 2022. www.furfreealliance.com/wp-content/uploads/2015/11/Case-against-fur-farming.pdf.

Peterson, Lesley. “Summary of Fur Laws and Fur Production.” Animal Legal and Historical Center, Michigan State University College of Law, 2010. Accessed February 17, 2022. www.animallaw.info/intro/fur-production-and-fur-laws.

Respect for Animals. “Statistics.” Accessed May 19, 2020. www.respectforanimals.org/statistics/.

Scientific Committee on Animal Health and Welfare. *The Welfare of Animals Kept for Fur Production*. European Commission, December 12–13, 2001. ec.europa.eu/food/system/files/2020-12/sci-com_scah_out67_en.pdf. Accessed February 17, 2022.

Sima, Yangzi, and Siobhan O'Sullivan. "Chinese Animal Protection Laws and the Globalization of Welfare Norms." *International Journal of Law in Context* 12, no. 1 (2016): 1–23.

Spark, Gareth. "Protecting Wild Animals from Unnecessary Suffering." *Journal of Environmental Law* 26 (2014): 473–94.

Tensen, Laura. "Under What Circumstances Can Wildlife Farming Benefit Species Conservation?" *Global Ecology and Conservation* 6 (2016): 286–98.

Vaqué, Luis González. "The Cloning of Animals for Farming Purposes in the EU: From Ethics to Agri-Food Law." *European Food and Feed Law Review* 9, no. 4 (2014): 223–32.

Chapter 13

Legislation against Animals Reared for Fur in Brazil

Letícia Albuquerque and Gabriela Franziska Schoch Santos Carvalho

Fur, unlike leather, is neither widely used nor popular in Brazilian fashion. This is exemplified by the case of Arezzo, a leading Latin American shoe, bags, and accessories brand founded in 1972. In 2011, for the first time in its almost forty-year history, Arezzo included some items appareled with fox, sheep, and rabbit pelt in its winter collection. According to the company's founder, the idea was to "put [Arezzo] on par with international brands, with great designer brands that include fur in their collections." The collection, named *pelemania* ("fur mania"), became the object of criticism and protest on social media. This rejection led Arezzo to withdraw the collection.[1]

Nevertheless, animals are reared in Brazil for their fur—mostly chinchillas but also foxes, rabbits, mink, badgers, seals, coyotes, and squirrels.[2] Chinchilla pelts are mainly exported and sold to international markets, primarily China. According to the newspaper *O Estado de São Paulo*, "Brazil stands amongst the biggest producers of chinchilla fur and is its second biggest exporter in the world, second only to Argentina."[3]

Since chinchillas are not a species native to Brazil and are considered domesticated animals and not "wildlife," the exportation of their pelts is legal. According to Brazilian law, the exportation of skin and pelts of species considered "wildlife" is illegal or subjected to stricter rules than the exportation of products made from domesticated animals.

The purpose of this essay is to provide an overview of Brazil's regulatory framework for the welfare of animals reared for fur. The first section outlines the general legal provisions regarding animals in Brazilian law; the second section looks at legislation that specifically addresses the issue of animals farmed for fur.

LEGAL FRAMEWORK FOR ANIMAL ISSUES IN BRAZIL

Unlike the United Kingdom and Switzerland, for instance, Brazil does not have an "Animal Protection Act" or "Animal Welfare Act." There are, however, a number of legal provisions regarding animals—most importantly, the Brazilian Federal Constitution and the federal law on environmental crimes. Moreover, since Brazil is a federal state, the constitution of which confers jointly on the federal government, the states, and the municipalities the authority and duty to protect the fauna, legal rules that regulate the human–animal relationship are scattered in federal, state, and municipal law.[4] This first section aims at providing a brief overview of this general legal framework for animals in Brazil by looking at the Federal Constitution and the federal Environmental Crimes Law.

Constitution of the Federative Republic of Brazil of 1988

Brazil is one of the few countries that mention animals in their constitutions. The Brazilian Federal Constitution, promulgated in 1988, emerged in the context of the country's re-democratization after the military ruled from 1964 to 1985. Influenced by the global tendency toward protecting the environment and the Declaration of the United Nations Conference on the Human Environment, held in Stockholm in 1972, to which Brazil was a signatory, the constituents decided to dedicate a whole chapter to the protection of the environment.[5]

Article 225 of the Brazilian constitution states that everybody has a right to an ecologically balanced environment and that "both the Government and the community shall have the duty to defend and preserve it for present and future generations."[6] Therefore, both the federal government and the states and municipalities are called to protect the environment and the Brazilian fauna and flora. While this section of the Federal Constitution is primarily preoccupied with ecological concerns, it also addresses cruelty toward animals. The last sentence of article 225 describes the state's duty "to protect the fauna, prohibiting any actions that would risk the animals' ecological function, cause their extinction, *or subject animals to cruelty*" (emphasis added). This provision authorizes and obligates the state to deal with cruelty against any kind of animal, not only free-living animals but also domesticated animals. By elevating the protection of animals against cruelty to the constitutional sphere by means of article 225, paragraph 1, section VII, the state has acknowledged the intrinsic value of nonhuman animals and their lives and freedom.

Federal Environmental Crimes Law (Law No. 9.605/98)

To complement this provision established by the Federal Constitution and to impose criminal liability for damages to the environment and fauna, the Brazilian Congress enacted, in 1998, the federal Environmental Crimes Law (law no. 9.605/98).[7] This law implements criminal penalties in cases of actions that may damage the environment, including crimes against fauna. Article 32 of the federal Environmental Crimes Law prohibits the abuse, mistreatment, or mutilation of domesticated animals or free-living animals, including exotic animals, as well as domesticated fauna (previously free-living animals who have been captured and tamed). This provision safeguards all animals from aggression and mistreatment, making cruelty against all animals (exotic, free-living, and domesticated, including farmed animals) a crime with penalties ranging from three months to one year of imprisonment and fines.

The federal Environmental Crimes Law does not provide a clear and actual definition of crimes against animals. Definitions of acts of maltreatment and abuse can be found, however, in Federal Decree no. 24.645, promulgated in 1934 (revoked in 1991). For example, confining an animal in a cruel manner is among the behaviors that were listed as abusive and as mistreatment of animals.[8]

The Brazilian environmental protection law has been described in a United Nations report as "one of the world's most modern and comprehensive legal texts focusing on environmental crime."[9] Although it is considered an improvement for animal protection in Brazil, it is not strictly enforced, and penalties might not be severe enough to deter crimes against animals.

Animal Protection Development in Brazil: Steps Forward and Setbacks

The problem is not only legislation and its enforcement but also the attitude toward animals in general. Carlos Naconecy has pointed out a series of factors that contribute to why the discourse on the protection of animals has had less support in Latin America than in other parts of the world, such as Europe and the United States. He explains, for example, that "the myth of overabundance of nature weakens the notion that nonhuman lives are intrinsically valuable"; furthermore, "the low standards of living conditions in developing countries" and violence against humans "deflect moral attention away from the conditions in which animals live."[10]

Brazil is a country marked by contrasts between different regions and climates, urban and rural lifestyles, and socioeconomic and cultural realities, which makes it difficult to characterize the nature of the human–animal relationship in a general fashion. Over the past decades, changes in behavior toward animals by society in general, including the legal system and public policies, have been observed.

For example, in 1997, in what was a "historic landmark in animal protection development in Brazil,"[11] the Brazilian Supreme Court ruled that the popular Oxen Festival, Farra do Boi, violated the rule of article 225 of the Federal Constitution, which forbids cruelty toward the animals.[12] The Oxen Festival is a popular annual tradition practiced in the south of Brazil; it "involves crowds of villagers brandishing weapons such as sticks, knives, whips, or stones, as they chase an ox through the streets while inflicting their blows upon the animal."[13] Animal protection associations had brought a public-interest civil action against the state of Santa Catarina, alleging that although it is the duty of the state to guarantee the expression of cultural rights, the Oxen Festival should be banned because the animals suffered cruelty and maltreatment. The first-instance judge ruled against the plaintiffs, claiming a lack of legal basis to put an end to the tradition. On appeal to the Federal Supreme Court, the tradition was ruled to be prohibited by article 225 of the Federal Constitution and therefore unconstitutional.[14]

In 2005, 2007, and 2011, the Brazilian Federal Supreme Court declared cockfighting unconstitutional because of its cruelty toward animals.[15]

Another case that was examined by the judiciary is worth mentioning. It was put forward by Sea Shepherd Brasil, an NGO working in defense of marine environment, and regarded the prohibition of whale-watching tourism in the environmental protection area for the Southern White Whale ("Área de Proteção Ambiental da Baleia Franca") in the south of Brazil.[16] The case was the subject of a Public Civil Lawsuit that sought to ensure the free movement of right whales within the limits of the environmental protection area without being harassed, in accordance with the relevant legislation. The practice of whale watching boat tours has been banned. The case had great repercussions and sensitized the population to the importance of nurseries, since it concerns the area where whales usually spend the winter with their young. Today people prefer to do the observation by land, preserving the safety and tranquility of the animals. This case shows a change in the position of the Brazilian judiciary; it also reflects a change in behavior in Brazilian society and a change in public policies regarding animals. Presently, several Brazilian municipalities have specialized departments for animals: in Florianópolis, for example, there is a Board for Animal Welfare, an entity linked to city hall.[17]

Despite this progress, the Brazilian legal system is still dominated by deeply ingrained attitudes and traditions. Therefore, the courts' decisions are often legalistic and lack necessary reflection about social change and the constitutional provisions, taking into account only the wish of an animal's "owner."[18] In June 2017, for example, the National Congress approved Constitutional Amendment 96, which "allows events such as *vaquejada* and rodeos" (*vaquejada* is a variation of rodeo popular in Brazil's northeast). According to the amendment, sports activities that involve the use of animals are not considered cruelty toward animals as long as they are cultural expressions, in accordance with paragraph 1 of article 215 of the Federal Constitution, which guarantees cultural rights. These practices must be regulated by means of specific laws to ensure the well-being of the animals involved.[19] In the same year, as a consequence of this Amendment, an additional paragraph with the same content was added to art. 225 the Federal Constitution. The approval of this constitutional amendment is a setback, especially because only a few months earlier, the Brazilian Supreme Court had ruled the *vaquejada* unconstitutional due to its intrinsic cruelty toward animals.[20] The adoption of Constitutional Amendment 96 shows how the National Congress has adopted legal and even constitutional changes which jeorpardize the protection of both the environment and human rights that were hard-won after the end of the military dictatorship.[21]

SPECIFIC LEGISLATION REGARDING THE BREEDING OF ANIMALS FOR THEIR FUR

As mentioned at the beginning of this text, in Brazil the issue of fur is not as notorious as in Europe or the United States, probably because fur is not a central part of Brazilian fashion culture. There are animals farmed for their fur in Brazil, however, mainly chinchillas. The legal provisions discussed previously (article 225 of the Federal Constitution and article 32 of the Environmental Crimes Law, both of which prohibit cruelty against and mistreatment of animals) cover farmed animals. Currently, federal law does not address the welfare of these animals specifically. However, a federal bill proposed in 2009 and state and municipal legislation promulgated in 2014 and 2015, respectively, deal with the issue of animals farmed and killed for their fur. This last section of this essay is dedicated to Brazilian legislation that specifically addresses the issue of animals farmed for their fur.

The Bill Proposed by Congressman Ricardo Tripoli (Projeto de Lei No. 5.956 de 2009)

In 2009, Congressman Ricardo Tripoli, an advocate of animal welfare in the National Congress, proposed a bill aimed at outlawing the killing of chinchillas for their fur nationwide.[22] The proposal was accepted by the Commission on Environment and Sustainable Development in 2011 and by the Commission on Constitution, Justice and Citizenship in 2016. However, it was rejected by two other commissions, the Commission on Agriculture, Livestock, Supply and Rural Development in 2012 and the Commission on Economic Development, Industry and Trade in 2013. In his proposal of the bill, Congressman Tripoli argued that although chinchilla fur production is very lucrative, interests other than merely commercial ones should be considered; animals should not be killed to make luxury coats merely to satisfy human vanity.[23]

The opinion by the Commission on Environment and Sustainable Development points out that in nature, the long-tailed chinchilla (*Chinchilla lanigera*) is a species threatened by extinction and is listed in the CITES Convention, to which Brazil is a signatory; therefore, the animals' commercialization (import and export) is subject to restrictions. This does not, however, apply to animals reared in captivity. The commission's opinion argues that in the case of chinchillas reared in captivity for their fur, the issue at stake is cruelty against animals, which according to article 225 of the Brazilian Constitution is prohibited. The opinion states that "the constitutional norm preemptively embodied the evergrowing manifestation of Brazilian society in regard to the protection of animal life. It has to do with not only the protection of species, but also with the ethical question of how we treat animals that are part of the chain of production that sustains our economy and share our day to day lives." It concludes, "We do not see why Brazil should abstain from keeping up with the global tendency of ethical concern regarding animals that, in a very logical way, associates the condemnation of superfluous human consumption with the direction of the economy that puts at risk the sustainability of life on the planet."[24] The opinion by the Commission on Constitution, Justice and Citizenship merely examined technical questions (legislative competence and technique).[25] Both the Commission on Agriculture, Livestock, Supply and Rural Development and the Commission on Economic Development, Industry and Trade rejected the bill, highlighting the importance of the chinchilla fur trade for the current Brazilian economy and job market, as well as its potential for future growth. As for the question of animal welfare, these opinions argued that chinchillas on Brazilian territory are reared using humane practices that prioritize the animals' well-being, through adequate management, comfortable facilities, balanced feeding, and specialized veterinary care. The opinions also state that the breeding of chinchillas in captivity guarantees the preservation of their species. They conclude that the prohibition of this economic activity would just shift this industry to competitor countries.[26]

State of São Paulo: State Law No. 15.566/2014

In 2014, the state of São Paulo sanctioned state law no. 15.566/2014, called *Lei AntiPele* ("Anti-Fur Law"), which "aims to preserve the animals used in the coat and accessories industry, such as rabbits, foxes, visons, badgers, seals, coyotes, squirrels and, mainly, chinchillas."[27] The law was proposed in 2011 by Feliciano Filho, deputy to the state's legislative assembly, who already had successfully advocated for four other state laws regarding animal welfare issues.[28]

Law no. 15.566/2014 consists of three articles: Article 1 prohibits "in the State of São Paulo, the creation or maintenance of any domestic, domesticated, native, exotic, wild or ornamental animal for the exclusive purpose of fur extraction." Article 2 states that "the rearing or maintenance of chinchillas of the species *chinchilla lanigera* is allowed to meet the demand for pets." Finally, article 3 establishes penalties (fines) in case of violation.

By virtue of this law, since 2014 it has been illegal in the state of São Paulo to rear animals for the exclusive purpose of extracting their fur. Due to the word "exclusively," this prohibition does not affect articles made of leather, which is considered simply a by-product of the meat industry. Moreover, the breeding of chinchillas to satisfy the demand for "pets" is explicitly allowed. The penalties—fines of 12,500 Brazilian reais per animal—are considerable; in practice, however, enforcement of this law may not always be possible due to the state's lack of sufficient infrastructure.

The comments of the committees that issued opinions during the legislative process are worth noting. In its opinion, the Commission on Constitution, Justice and Writing refers to article 225, paragraph 1, section VII, of the Federal Constitution of 1988, which prohibits cruelty against animals, and argues that the Constitution must be interpreted according to "current social values":

> Thus, the abovementioned article 225 should be interpreted in the light of important concepts adopted by the collectivity: the preservation of animal species, respect for all forms of life, the inadmissibility of cruel acts and the use of nature to the extent of human needs. It is known that animal species are not preserved when slaughtered for fur extraction. There is also no respect for animal life, which represents a value in itself, in the breeding of animals for purely commercial purposes; furthermore the cruelty with which animals are treated during their lives, and especially at the time of their deaths, is proven. Finally, it should be noted that the options that are available today are quite different from those which existed during the prehistoric period. At that time, animal skin was necessary to warm the group. However, given the innumerable possibilities presently available, the use of fur serves solely to satisfy human vanity, thus it cannot be said that it represents a necessary evil.[29]

The opinion concludes with the approval of the anti-fur bill, "since there is constitutional support to prohibit practices that result in animal suffering and are not essential to meet human needs."[30] The opinion of Special Rapporteur Regina Gonçalves reached the same conclusion:

> We observe that this is a measure of significant importance in order to contain the fur industry, which is one of the most hideous practices in the world, causing the cruel death of a huge number of animals. We must point out that all this cruelty is totally immoral and unjustifiable in this day and age, as it is known that there is already a variety of synthetic fur on the market that provides the same thermal comfort as natural ones, and in addition, are more durable.[31]

Municipality of São Paulo: Municipal Law No. 16.222

In 2015, the city of São Paulo sanctioned municipal law no. 16.222, which "prohibits the production and marketing of foie gras and articles of clothing made with animal skin within the City of São Paulo."[32] The bill had been proposed in 2013 by councilman Laércio Benko and had been approved unanimously by the city's House of Representatives.[33] The passage of the law relied on expressive popular pressure from organized civil society: several animal welfare NGOs, the Brazilian Vegetarian Society, and the São Paulo Bar Association (OAB/SP) supported the law. In an effort headed by the Brazilian Vegetarian Society and the National Organization for Animal Protection (Fórum Nacional de Proteção e Defesa Animal, or FNPDA), 95,000 signatures in favor of the law were collected through the online campaign platform Change.org.[34]

Municipal law no. 16.222 prohibits, within the jurisdiction of the municipality of São Paulo, "the commercialization of articles of clothing, even imported ones, made with the fur of animals which were bred exclusively for the purpose of the extraction and use of their skin." The law states that it shall not apply to products constructed from leather originating from farmed animals used in the meat industry.

Municipal law no. 16.2222 also stipulated that the production and marketing of foie gras, *in natura* or canned, shall be prohibited in commercial establishments located within the municipality of São Paulo. Before the law could come into force, however, it was challenged by Brazil's National Restaurant Association, which questioned its constitutionality. The state court (Tribunal de Justiça de São Paulo) first suspended the law. Later it declared the prohibition against producing and marketing foie gras unconstitutional, upholding the plaintiffs' claim that the authority to legislate on this subject matter belonged to the state and not the municipality.[35] On June 26, 2016, São Paulo City Hall and the attorney general of the state of São Paulo appealed this decision to the Brazilian Supreme Court, where the issue is pending at the time of this writing.[36]

The part of the law that prohibits the production and marketing of articles of clothing made with fur was not declared unconstitutional for procedural reasons. Therefore, it is in force today, making the commercialization of articles of clothing, even imported ones, made with the skin of animals who were bred exclusively for the extraction and use of their fur illegal within the jurisdiction of the municipality of São Paulo. As in the case of the aforementioned state law, the penalties are not inconsiderable (5,000 Brazilian reais); however, in practice, enforcement may not always be possible.

CONCLUSION

Although in Brazil animals are reared for the main purpose of extracting their fur, currently there is no specific legislation regulating their welfare, at least not on a national level. The provision of the Constitution of the Federal Republic of Brazil of 1988 that prohibits cruelty toward animals, however, applies to animals used in the fur industry. The federal Environmental Crimes Law also prohibits abuse and mistreatment of animals. As for legislation specifically addressing the breeding of animals for their fur, a bill that aims to outlaw the killing of chinchillas for their fur nationwide is pending in the National Congress. On the state and municipal levels, both the state and the municipality of São Paulo have sanctioned laws regarding the production and marketing of animal skin exclusively for the creation of fashion items. These prohibitions have been justified with the argument that the suffering of animals for the exclusive and mere purpose of satisfying superfluous and vain consumer desires cannot be considered "necessary."

NOTES

1. Ana Carolina Oliveira, "Toda essa confusão é fruto da internet, diz Anderson Birman," *Veja São Paulo*, April 18, 2011, vejasp.abril.com.br/cidades/polemica-arezzo/.
2. Mônica Reolom, "Chinchilas não poderão ser criadas para extração de pele em SP," *O Estado de São Paulo*, October 28, 2014, sao-paulo.estadao.com.br/noticias/geral,chinchilas-nao-poderao-ser-criadas-para-extracao-de-pele-em-sp,1584458.
3. Reolom, "Chinchilas."
4. For an overview, see Fernanda Medeiros, *Direito dos Animais* (Porto Alegre, Brazil: Livraria do Advogado Editora, 2013).
5. Lane Azevedo Clayton, "Overview of Brazil's Legal Structure for Animal Issues," Animal Legal & Historical Center, Michigan State University College of

Law, 2011, accessed October 31, 2017, www.animallaw.info/article/overview-brazils-legal-structure-animal-issues.

6. An official English translation of the Constitution of the Federative Republic of Brazil is available from Brazil's Superior Electoral Court: english.tse.jus.br/arquivos/federal-constitution.

7. Federal Law on Environmental Crimes of February 12, 1998 (law no. 9.605/98), accessed October 31, 2017, www.planalto.gov.br/ccivil_03/LEIS/L9605.htm.

8. Federal Decree no. 24.645 of July 10, 1934, accessed October 31, 2017, www.planalto.gov.br/ccivil_03/decreto/1930-1949/D24645.htm.

9. David N. Cassuto and Sarah Saville, "Hot, Crowded and Legal: A Look at Industrial Agriculture in the United States and Brazil," *Animal Law Review* 8, no. 2 (Spring 2012): 27, papers.ssrn.com/sol3/papers.cfm?abstract_id=2104294.

10. Carlos M. Naconecy, "South American Perspectives on Animals," in *The Global Guide to Animal Protection*, ed. Andrew Linzey (Urbana: University of Illinois Press, 2013), loc. 1560, Kindle.

11. Clayton, "Overview."

12. Supreme Court, Recurso Extraordinário no. 153.531–8/SC.

13. Clayton, "Overview."

14. See Medeiros, *Direito dos Animais*.

15. Federal Supreme Court, ADI 2.514 do Estado de Santa Catarina, 2005; ADI 3.776–5 do Estado do Rio Grande do Norte, 2007; ADI 1.856 dp Estado do Rio de Janeiro, 2011.

16. Cf. Letícia Albuquerque and Kamila Guimarães de Moraes, "Direitos Animais," in *Manual de Direito Ambiental*, ed. José Rubens Morato (São Paulo: Saraiva, 2015), 402–4.

17. "Diretoria do Bem-Estar Animal (DIBEA)," accessed October 31, 2017, www.pmf.sc.gov.br/entidades/bemestaranimal/.

18. Leticia Albuquerque and Fernanda Medeiros, "Constituição e Animais não-humanos: Um impacto no direito contemporâneo," in *Direito Ambiental II—Compedi/Uninove*, ed. Maria Cláudia da Silva Antunes de Souza, Celso Antônio Pacheco Fiorillo, and Consuelo Yatsuda Moralizada (Florianópolis, Brazil: Funjab, 2013), 155.

19. Sergio Vieira, "Promulgada Emenda Constitucional que libera prática da vaquejada," *Senado Notícias*, June 6, 2017, www12.senado.leg.br/noticias/materias/2017/06/06/promulgada-emenda-constitucional-que-libera-pratica-da-vaquejada.

20. Supreme Court, ADI 4983/CE.

21. Cf. Letícia Albuquerque, "Constitutional Environmental Law and Animal Protection: Brazil in Regression," in *Environmental Constitutionalism: What impact on legal systems?*, ed. Jochen Sohnle, (Bruxelles: Peter Lang, 2019), 156.

22. "PL 5.956/2009," accessed October 31, 2017, www.camara.gov.br/proposicoesWeb/fichadetramitacao?idProposicao=448186.

23. "PL 5.959/2009," accessed October 31, 2017, www.camara.gov.br/proposicoesWeb/prop_mostrarintegra?codteor=686596&filename=PL+5956/2009.

24. "Opinion by the Commission on Environment and Sustainable Development," accessed October 31, 2017, www.camara.gov.br/proposicoesWeb/prop_mostrarintegra?codteor=920090&filename=Parecer-CMADS-16-09-2011.

25. "Opinion by the Commission on Constitution, Justice and Citizenship," accessed October 31, 2017, www.camara.gov.br/proposicoesWeb/prop_mostrarintegra?codteor=1478660&filename=Parecer-CCJC-26-07-2016.

26. "Opinion by the Commission on Agriculture, Livestock, Supply and Rural Development," accessed October 31, 2017, www.camara.gov.br/proposicoesWeb/prop_mostrarintegra?codteor=1013711&filename=Parecer-CAPADR-18-07-2012; "Opinion by the Commission on Economic Development, Industry and Trade," accessed October 31, 2017, www.camara.gov.br/proposicoesWeb/prop_mostrarintegra?codteor=1081094&filename=Parecer-CDEIC-25-04-2013.

27. "Lei no. 15.556, de 28 de outubro de 2014," accessed October 31, 2017, www.al.sp.gov.br/norma/?id=173594.

28. "Projeto de Lei no. 616/11," accessed October, 31, 2017, www.al.sp.gov.br/propositura/?id=1019234.

29. "Opinion by the Commission on Constitution, Justice and Redaction," accessed October 31, 2017, www.al.sp.gov.br/propositura/?id=1019234.

30. "Opinion by the Commission on Constitution, Justice and Redaction."

31. "Opinion by the Special Rapporteur Regina Gonçalves, in Substitution of the Commission on Environment and Sustainable Development," accessed October 31, 2017, www.al.sp.gov.br/propositura/?id=1019234.

32. "Lei no. 16.222, de 25 de junho de 2015," accessed October 31, 2017, www3.prefeitura.sp.gov.br/cadlem/secretarias/negocios_juridicos/cadlem/integra.asp?alt=26062015L%20162220000.

33. "Projeto de Lei no. 537/13," accessed October 31, 2017, documentacao.camara.sp.gov.br/iah/fulltext/projeto/PL0537–2013.pdf.

34. Sociedade Vegetariana Brasileira, "Agora é lei: Proibido o comércio de foie gras e peles em São Paulo," accessed October 31, 2017, www.svb.org.br/2296-agora-e-lei-proibido-o-comercio-de-foie-gras-e-peles-em-sao-paulo; see also Pamella Cajano, "Comércio de peles de animais está proibido em São Paulo," *Investimentos e Notícias*, March 2, 2016, www.investimentosenoticias.com.br/noticias/negocios/comercio-de-peles-de-animais-esta-proibido-em-sao-paulo.

35. "Ação direta de inconstitucionalidade n. 2137241.2015.8.26.0000"; Tribunal de Justiça de São Paulo, Relator: Sérgio Rui, Comarca São Paulo; Órgão julgador: Órgão Especial, Data do julgamento: 24/02/2016; Data do registro: 25/02/2016. On this subject, see Rafael Speck de Souza and Letícia Albuquerque, "Direitos animais e o caso *foie gras* no âmbito do município de São Paulo: Análise de julgado do TJSP," in *Annais do 21º congresso brasileiro de Direito Ambiental—Jurisprudência, Ética e Justiça Ambiental no século 21*, ed. Antonio Herman Benjamin and José Rubens Morato Leite (São Paulo: IDPV, 2016), 906–18, www.planetaverde.org/arquivos/biblioteca/arquivo_20161118140350_2664.pdf.

36. "Recurso Extraordinário RE 1030732," Supremo Tribunal Federal, accessed October 31, 2017, www.stf.jus.br/portal/processo/verProcessoAndamento.asp?incidente=5145857.

REFERENCES

Albuquerque, Letícia, and Fernanda Medeiros. "Constituição e Animais não-humanos: Um impacto no direito contemporâneo." In *Direito Ambiental II—Conpedi/Uninove*, edited by Maria Cláudia da Silva Antunes de Souza, Celso Antônio Pacheco Fiorillo, and Consuelo Yatsuda Moralizada, 134–58. Florianópolis, Brazil: Funjab, 2013.

Albuquerque, Letícia, and Kamila Guimarães de Moraes. "Direitos Animais." In *Manual de Direito Ambiental*, edited by José Rubens Morato, 383–411. São Paulo: Saraiva, 2015.

Albuquerque, Letícia. "Constitutional Environmental Law and Animal Protection: Brazil in Regression." In *Environmental Constitutionalism: What impact on legal systems?*, edited by Jochen Sohnle. Bruxelles: Peter Lang, 2019.

Cajano, Pamella. "Comércio de peles de animais está proibido em São Paulo." *Investimentos e Notícias*, March 2, 2016. www.investimentosenoticias.com.br/noticias/negocios/comercio-de-peles-de-animais-esta-proibido-em-sao-paulo.

Cassuto, David N., and Sarah Saville. "Hot, Crowded and Legal: A Look at Industrial Agriculture in the United States and Brazil." *Animal Law Review* 8, no. 2 (Spring 2012): 11–30. papers.ssrn.com/sol3/papers.cfm?abstract_id=2104294.

Clayton, Lane Azevedo. "Overview of Brazil's Legal Structure for Animal Issues." Animal Legal & Historical Center, Michigan State University College of Law, 2011. Accessed October 31, 2017. www.animallaw.info/article/overview-brazils-legal-structure-animal-issues.

Medeiros, Fernanda. *Direito dos Animais*. Porto Alegre, Brazil: Livraria do Advogado Editora, 2013.

Naconecy, Carlos M. "South American Perspectives on Animals." In *The Global Guide to Animal Protection*, edited by Andrew Linzey, loc. 1543–1601. Urbana: University of Illinois Press, 2013. Kindle.

Oliveira, Ana Carolina. "Toda essa confusão é fruto da internet, diz Anderson Birman." *Veja São Paulo*, April 18, 2011. vejasp.abril.com.br/cidades/polemica-arezzo/.

Reolom, Mônica. "Chinchilas não poderão ser criadas para extração de pele em SP." *O Estado de São Paulo*, October 28, 2014. sao-paulo.estadao.com.br/noticias/geral,chinchilas-nao-poderao-ser-criadas-para-extracao-de-pele-em-sp,1584458.

Speck de Souza, Rafael, and Letícia Albuquerque. "Direitos animais e o caso *foie gras* no âmbito do município de São Paulo: Análise de julgado do TJSP." In *Annais do 21º congresso brasileiro de Direito Ambiental—Jurisprudência, Ética e Justiça Ambiental no século 21*, edited by Antonio Herman Benjamin and José Rubens Morato Leite, 906–18. São Paulo: IDPV, 2016. www.planetaverde.org/arquivos/biblioteca/arquivo_20161118140350_2664.pdf.

Sociedade Vegetariana Brasileira. "Agora é lei: Proibido o comércio de foie gras e peles em São Paulo." Accessed October 31, 2017. www.svb.org.br/2296-agora-e-lei-proibido-o-comercio-de-foie-gras-e-peles-em-sao-paulo.

Vieira, Sergio. "Promulgada Emenda Constitucional que libera prática da vaquejada." *Senado Notícias*, June 6, 2017. www12.senado.leg.br/noticias/materias/2017/06/06/promulgada-emenda-constitucional-que-libera-pratica-da-vaquejada.

Chapter 14

Animal Welfare Standards in European Fur Production and the "WelFur" Assessment Program

Heather Pickett

Most fur sold globally is from farmed animals, with Europe and China being the largest producers.[1] The main species farmed exclusively for their fur are mink and foxes. Worldwide, prior to large-scale "culls" or killing in response to the coronavirus pandemic, more than fifty million mink (*Neogale vison*) and more than thirteen million foxes (red/silver foxes, *Vulpes vulpes*, and arctic/blue foxes, *Vulpes lagopus*) were reared and killed for their fur on fur farms in 2019.[2] Smaller numbers of other species are also farmed for fur, and around 10 percent of the global trade in fur comes from hunting and trapping free-living animals.[3]

While fur animals are included in general EU legislation on animal welfare, transport, and slaughter, there is no detailed species-specific EU legislation setting welfare standards for animals farmed for fur. Serious concerns for the welfare of animals farmed for fur were highlighted in the Council of Europe's 1999 *Recommendation Concerning Fur Animals*[4] and a 2001 report of the Scientific Committee on Animal Health and Animal Welfare, titled *The Welfare of Animals Kept for Fur Production*.[5] Recent scientific studies add further weight to the substantial body of evidence demonstrating that the needs of mink and foxes are not being met in current housing systems and cannot be met in any housing system for undomesticated animals used by the fur industry.

MINK AND FOXES USED FOR FUR PRODUCTION ARE NOT DOMESTICATED

Domestication is "an evolutionary process by which a population of animals becomes adapted to man and to the captive environment by genetic changes occurring over generations including those predisposing to environmentally induced developmental events recurring in each generation"[6] (i.e., some of the genetic changes alter the potential for responding to the human contact that precedes taming). The most important aspect of domestication from a welfare perspective is the unique ability of domesticated species to interact with humans in a positive way. The behavioral changes that are associated with domestication are accompanied by an array of alterations in other traits, including coat color, size, and physiology.[7] Domestication does not result in the loss of behaviors from the species' repertoire.[8] Therefore, the needs of domesticated animals remain closely related to the evolutionary history of their ancestors.[9]

Work on the experimental domestication of silver foxes has been carried out at the Russian Academy of Sciences in Novosibirsk, Russia, since the late 1950s, and this study, known as "the farm-fox experiment," is still ongoing.[10] This work demonstrates that if very stringent selection criteria are applied (i.e., if response to humans is the sole selection criterion and less than 10 percent of animals are bred in each generation), it is possible to breed domesticated silver foxes within relatively few generations—that is, foxes who actively seek human attention and are easy to handle. Domestication of mink is also possible,[11] and preliminary research suggests that it may be possible to breed domesticated blue foxes,[12] but no population of domesticated blue foxes currently exists.

Although it has been shown experimentally that silver foxes and mink can be domesticated, this has not occurred—and cannot occur—on fur farms because changes in the coat that are characteristic of domesticated animals are incompatible with the fur industry's demands (e.g., changes observed in the domesticated foxes bred at Novosibirsk included localized depigmentation (piebald patterning), localized yellow-brown mottling, and a lengthened time of molting). On fur farms, the emphasis is on selection for traits associated with pelt color and quality, body size, and litter size, with little attention paid to behavioral traits.[13] Domesticated ferrets, like the silver foxes and mink experimentally bred for domesticated behavior at Novosibirsk, are easy to handle without restraint devices or protective gloves.[14] Mink and foxes on fur farms cannot be handled without protective gloves (for mink) or restraint devices (for foxes) to reduce the risk of injury to the handler. These animals are not adapted to close contact with humans and cannot be considered in any way domesticated. Fear of humans in the undomesticated animals currently used by the fur industry makes them fundamentally unsuitable for farming.

THE WELFARE OF MINK AND FOXES FARMED FOR FUR IN EUROPE IS EXTREMELY POOR

Approaches to assessing animal welfare can be broadly summarized as "biological functioning" (i.e., are the animals physically and mentally healthy?), "affective (emotional) states" (i.e., are the animals happy/feeling good?), and "natural/motivated behaviors" (i.e., do the animals have what they want?).[15] Whichever approach is emphasized, the welfare of mink and foxes farmed for fur is seriously compromised:

- The biological functioning of mink and foxes farmed for fur is impaired, as indicated by levels of stereotypic (abnormal repetitive) behavior; fur-chewing, tail-biting, and other self-injury;[16] physical deformities (bent feet);[17] and high levels of reproductive failure and infant mortality.[18]
- There is evidence of negative affective (emotional) states in farmed fur animals, including fear (as indicated by avoidance of or aggression toward humans),[19] frustration (as indicated by stereotypies),[20] and boredom or under-stimulation (as indicated by fur-chewing and tail-biting,[21] long periods of inactivity when awake, and heightened response to stimuli[22]).
- Animals farmed for fur are unable to perform many natural behaviors that they either have been shown experimentally to be motivated to perform or have been found to be frustrated and stressed by the inability to perform, such as interacting with water (for mink),[23] interacting with a sand or earth floor (for foxes),[24] using multiple nest sites,[25] and foraging/ranging (as indicated by stereotypic behavior).[26]

The "Five Freedoms" were developed by the Farm Animal Welfare Council (FAWC, now the Farm Animal Welfare Committee), the British government's advisory body on farmed animal welfare, and are widely used internationally as a framework for animal welfare assessment, legislation, and assurance standards.[27] Farming systems for mink and foxes fail to satisfy any of the Five Freedoms:

- Freedom from hunger and thirst: Breeding for increased body/pelt size has resulted in animals that tend to become overweight when fed *ad libitum*. Restrictive feeding of overweight animals in preparation for breeding results in hunger[28] and increased stereotypic behavior.[29]

- Freedom from discomfort: Mink and foxes farmed for fur in cages have very little control over their physical and social environment. Foxes are mostly kept without access to a nest box. Handling procedures cause significant stress and discomfort.[30]
- Freedom from pain, injury, and disease: Common problems include fur-chewing, injuries (both self-inflicted and from other animals), high levels of infant mortality, deformities (bent feet), difficulty in moving, diarrhea, and inhumane killing methods.[31]
- Freedom to express normal behavior: The small and largely barren cages used to house mink and foxes on fur farms do not allow the animals to swim, climb, run, dig, hunt or forage, or range or disperse. Maternal deprivation and social stress can result from abrupt early weaning, isolation in individual housing, aggression in group housing, and the close proximity of socially dominant animals.[32]
- Freedom from fear and distress: Fear is a major welfare problem for animals farmed for fur because the mink and foxes used on fur farms are not domesticated.

The FAWC considers that minimum legal requirements should be such that an animal has a "life worth living" and states:

> Achievement of a life worth living requires provision of an animal's needs and certain wants, and care by all involved. Wants are those resources that an animal may not need to survive or to avoid developing abnormal behaviour, but nevertheless improve its quality of life. They may well stem from learned behaviours so that once an animal has become accustomed to their provision then withdrawal may lead to an adverse mental experience. They may also be innate such as space to play, to groom or engage in other normal behaviours.[33]

Levels of fear, stereotypic behavior, fur-chewing and tail-biting, physical deformities, and reproductive failure and infant mortality clearly indicate that the needs of mink and foxes on fur farms are not being met. Mink are semiaquatic and show inelastic demand for access to water.[34] Dawkins states, "Withholding conditions or commodities for which an animal shows 'inelastic demand' (i.e. for which it continues to work despite increasing costs) is very likely to cause suffering."[35] Mink who are accustomed to the provision of water and foxes who are accustomed to access to a clean, dry substrate may show a stress reaction when they can no longer enjoy these resources.[36] Access to these resources would clearly be included within the FAWC's description of a "life worth living."

The welfare of mink and foxes farmed for fur is seriously compromised in current farming systems, which fail to satisfy the Five Freedoms and do not provide a "life worth living." Even if domesticated animals were to be used, current farming systems could not meet the needs of mink or foxes. The 2001 report of the Scientific Committee on Animal Health and Animal Welfare recommends, "Since current husbandry systems cause serious problems for all species of animals reared for fur, efforts should be made for all species to design housing systems which fulfil the needs of the animals."[37] In theory, alternative housing in large, highly enriched outdoor enclosures could potentially provide a more complex and stimulating environment. However, the use of undomesticated animals by the fur industry means that fear of humans and difficulties in handling and management would present insurmountable obstacles to the adoption of more extensive systems. The needs of undomesticated mink and foxes cannot be met in any farming system.

CONSUMER INFORMATION AND VIEWS ON FUR

The majority of citizens recently polled in countries across Europe, including countries with substantial fur production, are opposed to the farming of animals for fur in cages.[38] A number of European countries have already implemented bans, and there is widespread support for a ban at the EU level.

The EU legally requires that textile products containing fur be labeled as containing animal products, but the products do not have to be labeled as specifically containing "fur." A labeling system modeled on the US system, which requires that fur garments be labeled with the species of animal and country of origin, would make it easier for consumers to identify whether trims on garments and furnishings are made of real or imitation fur.

The fur industry's "Furmark®" label (and its predecessor "Origin Assured") is used on fur from animals subjected to standard cage production systems, which have inherently low welfare potential and are opposed by the majority of European citizens. Most consumers would not consider these conditions to be consistent with the scheme's claims of humane treatment of animals.

"WelFur" Will Not Address the Major Welfare Issues for Mink and Foxes Farmed for Fur

The fur industry has tried for many years to argue that conditions on fur farms are satisfactory, and it lobbies hard to maintain the status quo. The industry argues that the public is not well-informed about rearing conditions and welfare standards on fur farms. Partly to address this perceived lack of understanding, the European Fur Breeders' Association launched the

"WelFur" project in 2009 to develop on-farm welfare assessment protocols for mink and foxes. Implementation of the assessments on European fur farms began in 2017 and the first WelFur "certified" pelts were sold at auction in December 2019.[39] The WelFur assessments are now a core part of the fur industry's Furmark labelling scheme. WelFur was modeled on the European Commission's "Welfare Quality" project, which developed welfare assessment protocols for cattle, pigs, and poultry. Examination of the WelFur assessment protocols for mink[40] and foxes[41] reveals the following:

- The protocols have been designed specifically around the very serious limitations of current housing systems and generally reward the status quo, even where this is known to compromise welfare, rather than encourage the development of systems with the potential to provide a higher level of welfare.
- The protocols do not adequately penalize practices that fail to meet existing minimum standards set out in the Council of Europe's recommendations.
- The protocols do not address inhumane handling and killing methods and the lack of training for all personnel carrying out the killing of fur animals.
- The protocols downplay the importance of serious injuries that are associated with extreme suffering.
- The protocols underestimate the true levels of mortality and stereotypies.
- The protocols use inadequate measures of hunger, human–animal relationships, and positive mental states.
- By using complex scoring systems to combine different welfare measures into a single categorization of the overall welfare level, the protocols may allow high scores on some elements to mask serious failings on others.
- The protocols will not achieve WelFur's stated aims of ensuring "a high level of animal welfare" on fur farms and functioning as "the new scientific reference" for fur-farmed species.
- Unlike "Welfare Quality," the protocols do not take account of societal concerns and score welfare only up to a ceiling of "best current practice."
- The use of the protocols as the basis for the fur industry's "WelFur"/"Furmark" labeling system is misleading, giving the false impression of high welfare standards.

WelFur is not able to address the major welfare issues for mink and foxes farmed for fur, the issues associated with inhumane handling and killing methods, or the serious inadequacies in current labeling and regulation. The "best current practice" ceiling makes the WelFur scores of limited use misleading because "best current practice" still represents what the majority of people would consider to be an unacceptable level of welfare. Unlike the other species covered by Welfare Quality, alternative systems with the potential for higher levels of welfare do not exist for mink and foxes.

CONCLUSIONS AND RECOMMENDATION

The welfare of mink and foxes farmed for fur is seriously compromised in current farming systems, which fail to satisfy the Five Freedoms and do not provide a "life worth living." The current regulatory framework for the protection of fur animal welfare in the European Union is inadequate. Enrichment of existing housing systems is not sufficient to address the serious welfare problems inherent in cage systems. The use of undomesticated animals by the fur industry means that fear of humans and difficulties in handling and management would present insurmountable obstacles to the adoption of more extensive systems. It is therefore impossible for the needs of mink and foxes to be met by the fur industry. A ban is the only viable solution to the serious welfare concerns for mink and foxes farmed for fur.

The farming of mink and foxes for fur should be prohibited in accordance with Council Directive 98/58/EC—"No animal shall be kept for farming purposes unless it can reasonably be expected, on the basis of its genotype or phenotype, that it can be kept without detrimental effect on its health or welfare"—and the Council of Europe's *Recommendation concerning Fur Animals*: "No animal shall be kept for its fur if: a. the conditions of this Recommendation cannot be met, or if b. the animal belongs to a species whose members, despite these conditions being met, cannot adapt to captivity without welfare problems."[42] A number of European countries have already implemented bans, and there is widespread support for a ban at the EU level.

NOTES

1. This chapter is based on the report *The Case against Fur Factory Farming: A Scientific Review of Animal Welfare Standards and "WelFur,"* commissioned by Respect for Animals and written by Heather Pickett and Stephen Harris.

2. Finnish Fur Breeders' Association, *FIFUR Statistics 2021*, 15–16.

3. International Fur Federation, *Natural Fur Delivering Sustainability*, 10.

4. Standing Committee of the European Convention for the Protection of Animals Kept for Farming Purposes, *Recommendation concerning Fur Animals* (Council of Europe, 1999), www.coe.int/t/e/legal_affairs/legal_co-operation/biological_safety_and_use_of_animals/farming/Rec%20fur%20animals%20E%201999.asp.

5. Scientific Committee on Animal Health and Animal Welfare (SCAHAW), *The Welfare of Animals Kept for Fur Production* (European Commission, 2001), ec.europa.eu/food/sites/food/files/safety/docs/sci-com_scah_out67_en.pdf.

6. SCAHAW, *The Welfare of Animals Kept for Fur Production*, 37.

7. P. Jensen, "Domestication—From Behaviour to Genes and Back Again," *Applied Animal Behaviour Science* 97 (2006): 3–15.

8. E. O. Price, "Behavioural Development in Animals Undergoing Domestication," *Applied Animal Behaviour Science* 65 (1999): 245–71.

9. P. Jensen et al., "Genetics and Genomics of Animal Behaviour and Welfare—Challenges and Possibilities," *Applied Animal Behaviour Science* 113 (2008): 383–403.

10. M. J. Statham et al., "On the Origin of a Domesticated Species: Identifying the Parent Population of Russian Silver Foxes (*Vulpes vulpes*)," *Biological Journal of the Linnean Society* 103 (2011): 168–75.

11. R. G. Gulevich et al., "The Cortisol and Transcortin Blood Levels in the Mink *Mustela vison* Selected for Behaviour after a Long-Term Maintenance in Pairs," *Zhurnal Evoliutsionnoi Biokhimii I Fiziologii* 36 (2000): 410–13.

12. H. Kenttamies et al., "Selection for More Confident Foxes in Finland and Norway: Heritability and Selection Response for Confident Behaviour in Blue Foxes (*Alopex lagopus*)," *Applied Animal Behaviour Science* 78 (2002): 67–82.

13. SCAHAW, *The Welfare of Animals Kept for Fur Production*; S. W. Hansen and S. H. Moller, "The Application of a Temperament Test to On-Farm Selection of Mink," *Acta Agriculturae Scandinavica Section A, Animal Science* 51, suppl. 30 (2001): 93–98.

14. SCAHAW, *The Welfare of Animals Kept for Fur Production.*

15. D. Fraser, "Assessing Animal Welfare at the Farm and Group Level: The Interplay of Science and Values," *Animal Welfare* 12 (2003): 433–43.

16. SCAHAW, *The Welfare of Animals Kept for Fur Production.*

17. L. K. Ahola et al., "WelFur—Foxes: The Inter-Observer Reliability of the WelFur Health Measures, and the Prevalence of Health Disorders on Fox Farms during the Growth Period," in *Proceedings of the Xth International Scientific Congress in Fur Animal Production,* ed. P. F. Larsen et al. (Wageningen, the Netherlands: Wageningen Academic Publishers, 2012), 441–47.

18. M. Bakken, "Reproduction in Farmed Silver Fox Vixens, *Vulpes vulpes*, in Relation to Own Competition Capacity and That of Neighbouring Vixens," *Journal of Animal Breeding and Genetics* 110 (1993): 305–11.

19. SCAHAW, *The Welfare of Animals Kept for Fur Production.*

20. N. Latham and G. Mason, "Frustration and Perseveration in Stereotypic Captive Animals: Is a Taste of Enrichment Worse than None At All?," *Behavioural Brain Research* 211 (2010): 96–104.

21. SCAHAW, *The Welfare of Animals Kept for Fur Production.*

22. R. K. Meagher and G. J. Mason, "Environmental Enrichment Reduces Signs of Boredom in Caged Mink," *PLoS ONE* 7, no. 11 (2012): e49180.

23. G. J. Mason, J. Cooper, and C. Clarebrough, "Frustrations of Fur-Farmed Mink: Mink May Thrive in Captivity but They Miss Having Water to Romp about In," *Nature* 410 (2001): 35–36.

24. L. Ahola, T. Koistinen, and J. Mononen, "Sand Floor for Farmed Blue Foxes: Effects on Claws, Adrenal Cortex Function, Growth and Fur Properties," *International Journal of Zoology* (2009), doi.org/10.1155/2009/563252.

25. Mason, Cooper, and Clarebrough, "Frustrations of Fur-Farmed Mink"; T. Pyykonen et al., "Nest Provision Influences Reproductive Success in Breeding Blue Fox Vixens: A Preliminary Study," *Animal Welfare* 19 (2010): 101–5.

26. P. M. Svendsen, R. Palme, and J. Malmkvist, "Novelty Exploration, Baseline Cortisol Level and Fur-Chewing in Farm Mink with Different Intensities of Stereotypic Behaviour," *Applied Animal Behaviour Science* 147 (2013)" 182–78; R. Clubb and G. J. Mason, "Natural Behavioural Biology as a Risk Factor in Carnivore Welfare: How Analysing Species Differences Could Help Zoos Improve Enclosures," *Applied Animal Behaviour Science* 102 (2007): 303–28.

27. FAWC, "FAWC Updates the Five Freedoms," *Veterinary Record* 131 (1992): 357.

28. SCAHAW, *The Welfare of Animals Kept for Fur Production.*

29. B. M. Damgaard et al., "Effects of Different Feeding Strategies during the Winter Period on Behaviour and Performance in Mink Females (*Mustela vison*)," *Applied Animal Behaviour Science* 89 (2004): 163–80.

30. H. Korhonen et al., "Effect of Capture, Immobilization and Handling on Rectal Temperatures of Confident and Fearful Male Mink," *Journal of Animal Breeding and Genetics* 117 (2000): 337–45; R. O. Moe and M. Bakken, "Effects of Handling and Physical Restraint on Rectal Temperature, Cortisol, Glucose and Leucocyte Counts in the Silver Fox (*Vulpes vulpes*)," *Acta Veterinaria Scandinavica* 38 (1997): 29–39; L. Osadchuk et al., "Handling during Pregnancy in the Blue Fox (*Alopex lagopus*): The Influence on the Fetal Gonadal Function," *General and Comparative Endocrinology* 132 (2003): 190–97.

31. SCAHAW, *The Welfare of Animals Kept for Fur Production.*

32. SCAHAW, *The Welfare of Animals Kept for Fur Production.*

33. FAWC, *Farm Animal Welfare in Great Britain: Past, Present and Future* (London: Farm Animal Welfare Council, 2009), 15.

34. Mason, Cooper, and Clarebrough, "Frustrations of Fur-Farmed Mink."

35. M. S. Dawkins, "From an Animal's Point of View: Motivation, Fitness, and Animal Welfare," *Behavioural and Brain Sciences* 13 (1990): 1.

36. Mason, Cooper. and Clarebrough, "Frustrations of Fur-Farmed Mink"; Ahola, Koistinen, and Mononen, "Sand Floor for Farmed Blue Foxes."

37. SCAHAW, *The Welfare of Animals Kept for Fur Production*, 186.

38. "Opinion Poll Overview of European Citizens against Fur Farming," Fur Free Alliance, accessed July 17, 2017, www.furfreealliance.com/wp-content/uploads/2016/10/Opinion-poll-overview-of-European-citizens-against-fur-farming.pdf.

39. "World premiere of certified natural fur pelts," Fur Europe, December 19, 2019, www.sustainablefur.com/news_item/world-premiere-of-certified-natural-fur-pelts/.

40. WelFur Consortium, *WelFur Welfare Assessment Protocol for Mink*, version 1, 2nd ed. (Brussels: WelFur Consortium, 2015).

41. WelFur Consortium, *WelFur Welfare Assessment Protocol for Foxes*, version 1, 2nd ed. (Brussels: WelFur Consortium, 2015).

42. Standing Committee of the European Convention, *Recommendation concerning Fur Animals.*

REFERENCES

Ahola, L., T. Koistinen, and J. Mononen. "Sand Floor for Farmed Blue Foxes: Effects on claws, Adrenal Cortex Function, Growth and Fur Properties." *International Journal of Zoology* (2009). doi.org/10.1155/2009/563252.

Ahola, L. K., H. Huuki, A. L. Hovland, T. Koistinen, and J. Mononen. "WelFur—Foxes: The Inter-Observer Reliability of the WelFur Health Measures, and the Prevalence of Health Disorders on Fox Farms during the Growth Period." In *Proceedings of the Xth International Scientific Congress in Fur Animal Production*, edited by P. F. Larsen et al., 441–47. Wageningen, the Netherlands: Wageningen Academic Publishers, 2012.

Bakken, M. "Reproduction in Farmed Silver Fox Vixens, *Vulpes vulpes*, in Relation to Own Competition Capacity and That of Neighbouring Vixens." *Journal of Animal Breeding and Genetics* 110 (1993): 305–11.

Clubb, R., and G. J. Mason. "Natural Behavioural Biology as a Risk Factor in Carnivore Welfare: How Analysing Species Differences Could Help Zoos Improve Enclosures." *Applied Animal Behaviour Science* 102 (2007): 303–28.

Damgaard, B. M., S. W. Hansen, C. F. Borsting, and S. H. Moller. "Effects of Different Feeding Strategies during the Winter Period on Behaviour and Performance in Mink Females (*Mustela vison*)." *Applied Animal Behaviour Science* 89 (2004): 163–80.

Dawkins, M. S. "From an Animal's Point of View: Motivation, Fitness, and Animal Welfare." *Behavioural and Brain Sciences* 13 (1990): 1–61.

Farm Animal Welfare Council. *Farm Animal Welfare in Great Britain: Past, Present and Future.* London: Farm Animal Welfare Council, 2009.

———. "FAWC Updates the Five Freedoms." *Veterinary Record* 131 (1992): 357.

Finnish Fur Breeders' Association. *FIFUR Statistics 2021.* Finnish Fur Breeders' Association and Saga Furs Oyj, 2021. fifur.fi/sites/default/files/fifur_statistics_2021_-_web.pdf.

Fraser, D. "Assessing Animal Welfare at the Farm and Group Level: The Interplay of Science and Values." *Animal Welfare* 12 (2003): 433–43.

Fur Europe. "World Premiere of Certified Natural Fur Pelts." December 19, 2019. www.sustainablefur.com/news_item/world-premiere-of-certified-natural-fur-pelts/.

Fur Free Alliance. "Opinion Poll Overview of European Citizens against Fur Farming." Accessed July 17, 2017. www.furfreealliance.com/wp-content/uploads/2016/10/Opinion-poll-overview-of-European-citizens-against-fur-farming.pdf.

Gulevich, R. G., I. N. Oskina, A. V. Kharlamova, and O. V. Trapezov. "The Cortisol and Transcortin Blood Levels in the Mink *Mustela vison* Selected for Behaviour after a Long-Term Maintenance in Pairs." *Zhurnal Evoliutsionnoi Biokhimii I Fiziologii* 36 (2000): 410–13.

Hansen, S. W., and S. H. Moller. "The Application of a Temperament Test to On-Farm Selection of Mink." *Acta Agriculturae Scandinavica Section A, Animal Science* 51, suppl. 30 (2001): 93–98.

International Fur Federation. *Natural Fur Delivering Sustainability.* International Fur Federation, 2020. www.wearefur.com/wp-content/uploads/2020/02/Natural-Fur-Delivering-Sustainability.pdf.

Jensen, P. "Domestication—From Behaviour to Genes and Back Again." *Applied Animal Behaviour Science* 97 (2006): 3–15.

Jensen, P., B. Buitenhuis, J. Kjaer, A. Zanella, P. Mormede, and T. Pizzari. "Genetics and Genomics of Animal Behaviour and Welfare—Challenges and Possibilities." *Applied Animal Behaviour Science* 113 (2008): 383–403.

Kenttamies, H., N. V. Nordrum, U. T. Brenoe, K. Smeds, K. R. Johannessen, and M. Bakken. "Selection for More Confident Foxes in Finland and Norway: Heritability and Selection Response for Confident Behaviour in Blue Foxes (*Alopex lagopus*)." *Applied Animal Behaviour Science* 78 (2002): 67–82.

Korhonen, H., W. Hansen, J. Malmkvist, and B. Houbak. "Effect of Capture, Immobilization and Handling on Rectal Temperatures of Confident and Fearful Male Mink." *Journal of Animal Breeding and Genetics* 117 (2000): 337–45.

Latham, N., and G. Mason. "Frustration and Perseveration in Stereotypic Captive Animals: Is a Taste of Enrichment Worse than None At All?" *Behavioural Brain Research* 211 (2010): 96–104.

Mason, G. J., J. Cooper, and C. Clarebrough. "Frustrations of Fur-Farmed Mink: Mink May Thrive in Captivity but They Miss Having Water to Romp about In." *Nature* 410 (2001): 35–36.

Meagher, R. K., and G. J. Mason. "Environmental Enrichment Reduces Signs of Boredom in Caged Mink." *PLoS ONE* 7, no. 11 (2012): e49180.

Moe, R. O., and M. Bakken. "Effects of Handling and Physical Restraint on Rectal Temperature, Cortisol, Glucose and Leucocyte Counts in the Silver Fox (*Vulpes vulpes*)." *Acta Veterinaria Scandinavica* 38 (1997): 29–39.

Osadchuk, L., B. O. Braastad, A.-L. Hovland, and M. Bakken. "Handling during Pregnancy in the Blue Fox (*Alopex lagopus*): The Influence on the Fetal Gonadal Function." *General and Comparative Endocrinology* 132 (2003): 190–97.

Pickett, H. and Harris, S. *The Case Against Fur Factory Farming: A Scientific Review of Animal Welfare Standards and "WelFur."* Nottingham: Respect for Animals, 2015. www.furfreealliance.com/wp-content/uploads/2015/11/Case-against-fur-farming.pdf.

Price, E. O. "Behavioural Development in Animals Undergoing Domestication." *Applied Animal Behaviour Science* 65 (1999): 245–71.

Pyykonen, T., L. Ahola, S. Hanninen, and J. Mononen. "Nest Provision Influences Reproductive Success in Breeding Blue Fox Vixens: A Preliminary Study." *Animal Welfare* 19 (2010): 101–5.

Scientific Committee on Animal Health and Animal Welfare. *The Welfare of Animals Kept for Fur Production*. European Commission, 2001. ec.europa.eu/food/sites/food/files/safety/docs/sci-com_scah_out67_en.pdf.

Standing Committee of the European Convention for the Protection of Animals Kept for Farming Purposes. *Recommendation concerning Fur Animals*. Council of Europe, 1999. www.coe.int/t/e/legal_affairs/legal_co-operation/biological_safety_and_use_of_animals/farming/Rec%20fur%20animals%20E%201999.asp.

Statham, M. J., L. N. Trut, B. N. Sacks, A. V. Kharlamova, I. N. Oskina, R. G. Gulevich, J. L. Johnson, S. V. Temnykh, G. M. Ackland, and A. V. Kukekova. "On the Origin of a Domesticated Species: Identifying the Parent Population of Russian Silver Foxes (*Vulpes vulpes*)." *Biological Journal of the Linnean Society* 103 (2011): 168–75.

Svendsen, P. M., R. Palme, and J. Malmkvist. "Novelty Exploration, Baseline Cortisol Level and Fur-Chewing in Farm Mink with Different Intensities of Stereotypic Behaviour." *Applied Animal Behaviour Science* 147 (2013): 172–78.

WelFur Consortium. *WelFur Welfare Assessment Protocol for Foxes*. Version 1, 2nd ed. Brussels: WelFur Consortium, 2015.

———. *WelFur Welfare Assessment Protocol for Mink*. Version 1, 2nd ed. Brussels: WelFur Consortium, 2015.

Chapter 15

The Ethics of Marketing Fur to Children

Kimberly Moore

Children have long been the target of aggressive advertising and marketing strategies, with "cradle to grave" strategies that turn product recognition in childhood into brand loyalty in adulthood.[1] Children today are exposed to all kinds of direct and indirect marketing campaigns in numerous media, including television, print, and the internet. In the United States, companies spent a staggering $100 million on advertising to children in 1983 alone.[2] By 2018, advertising to children in the US had increased to $4.2 billion.[3] According to a report issued by the Federal Trade Commission, in 2004 children in the United States ages two to eleven saw 25,600 advertisements annually on television alone.[4] The American Psychological Association estimates that the number of commercials children view each year is as high as forty thousand.[5] With enormous financial profits at stake, businesses and trade groups invest enormous amounts of time and resources into marketing to children, and the fur industry is no different.

The fur industry targets children through direct and indirect advertising and marketing, knowing that adults will use many of the same products that they used as children.[6] Like other industries, the fur industry is keenly aware of the impact that such advertising can have on children, an impact so profound that some organizations are even calling for restrictions on advertising to children or even bans on advertising to children under a certain age.[7]

MARKETING STRATEGIES FOR CHILDREN

To successfully market fur to children, marketing executives must first familiarize children with fur and desensitize them to its use at a young age. That is, the industry must normalize the use of fur and instill in children the belief that using fur is not cruel. They must connect the use of fur with positive traditions, history, and childhood experiences and instill in children the notions that one can love animals and still use fur and that fur-bearing animals are "different" from companion animals. Finally, biased pro-fur information must be provided to children at a young age, with the ultimate goal of securing their patronage when they are adults. We see many of these marketing efforts used by the fur industry today.

Marketing strategists use basic principles of child psychology[8] as the basis of marketing campaigns. The fur industry knows, for instance, that young children tend to be attracted to bright colors, which are more easily perceived by their developing eyes,[9] so designers are dyeing furs in bright colors. Fur companies are also marketing lighter-weight fur garments designed to appeal to children. Clothing may appeal to some children, but the fur industry knows the value of toys to children, and marketers are working hard to associate fur with prized childhood possessions.

Toys and Trinkets

The addition of fur to children's toys is a common marketing strategy. Glamorizing fur by having favorite childhood possessions, such as Barbie dolls, wear fur products is a subtle but powerful strategy. Combining childhood's most endearing objects, like stuffed animals, with real animal fur aims to normalize the use of fur at a young age. Fur companies even connect fur to the special relationship between grandchildren and grandparents by turning a grandparent's fur coat into a teddy bear for his or her grandchildren. Connecting family "heirlooms" with fur is an example of marketing by association to something positive, and the strategy can be highly effective. It is even alleged by the Coalition against Fur Farms that the Fur Commission USA promotes a program called "Furry Friends," considered to be a "valuable promotional and coalition-building tool" that makes teddy bears from donated, damaged, or older fur garments.[10] It doesn't take a stretch of the imagination to consider how the fur industry might use teddy bears to build coalitions that support the fur trade.

The types of fur products that the fur industry makes available to children are extensive, such as keychains made with genuine mink, pom-poms made with rabbit fur, pencil toppers made with the fur of various animals, and necklaces designed especially for children that include real fur. Connecting fur to popular items, such as iPhone cases, is marketing 101, the marketing message being that fur is "fun" and "stylish" and that popular people use fun and stylish products like fur. Even toys for dogs and cats are available with real fur, perpetuating the subtle yet effective message that fur-bearing animals are somehow less deserving than companion animals and thereby normalizing the use of fur from all animals, including dogs and cats.

We can even surmise that many of the fur industry's marketing efforts involve certain "loss products," products more akin to capital investments that are expected to yield profits when children grow up and buy fur garments, rather than products that generate current profits. The promotion of inexpensive toys and trinkets that contain real fur is intended to normalize the use of animal fur to children and, ultimately, connect positive childhood possessions with adult consumer choices.

Celebrity Endorsements

In addition to direct marketing, the fur industry also uses more subtle, indirect marketing strategies, like celebrity endorsements and celebrity branding.[11] Hiring celebrities to use and promote products is a common marketing tool for all industries, and the fur industry is no exception. We know that the fur industry, like the larger fashion industry, "loans" or "gifts" furs to celebrity role models, though statistics are difficult to locate because such arrangements are generally documented by private contracts. Occasionally, the terms of such arrangements become public, as was the case with a blue- and green-dyed fur jacket given to actress Lily Allen by a London-based fur company to wear to an awards banquet.[12]

The internet is flooded with photographs of child models and celebrity children wearing fur. North West, the young daughter of Kim Kardashian and Kanye West, and Suri Cruise, the daughter of Tom Cruise and Katie Holmes, are often photographed wearing fur.[13] Designers are even using fashion shows to showcase fur garments for children, with children participating in the shows. However, using children to market and promote fashion products like fur can be unsafe and exploitative.[14]

Vogue Paris shocked the world when ten-year-old French model Thylane Blondeau appeared in a series of suggestive images that showed the child posing provocatively on a tiger skin with leopard-print pillows while wearing leopard stilettos and posing with live animals.[15] Associating fur with youth and beauty is a common marketing strategy, but using live animals alongside animal skins is more subtle. Photographs of children wearing animal fur alongside companion animals again perpetuates the notion that one can use the fur of some animals while still loving companion animals.

Advertisements that capture the innocence of children also may be suggesting, albeit with great subtlety, that the product advertised too is innocent. The photos of Thylane Blondeau were widely criticized for sexualizing a child, but they also can be criticized for their attempt to normalize the use of fur.

The Federal Trade Commission, the agency responsible in the United States for ensuring that advertising and marketing claims are neither unfair nor deceptive to consumers, has voiced concern about celebrity endorsement of products that occur without disclosure of payment for the endorsement.[16] The Federal Trade Commission views undisclosed paid endorsements as deceptive to consumers because consumers may consider paid endorsements to be less authentic than actual expressions of consumer preferences. While there are no studies on the impact of paid versus unpaid celebrity endorsements of fur, one may suspect that even children might be less influenced to wear fur if they knew that a celebrity was being paid to wear or promote it.[17]

Fur Design Competitions

The fur industry sponsors a number of design competitions to promote fur and to encourage young fashion designers to use fur. The Hong Kong Fur Federation, for instance, holds an annual Hong Kong Fur Design Competition to identify and nurture local design talent and to encourage younger designers to use fur, with winners earning a fur design course in Copenhagen, Denmark.[18] The International Fur Federation hosts the IFF Remix International Student Fur Design Competition, an event that offers promotional opportunities and showcases young fashion designers who use fur, to introduce young designers to fur fashion.[19] The British Fur Trade Association holds the BFTA Design Competition, which offers a detailed introduction to the fur industry meant to inspire students and encourage young designers to explore the use of fur in fashion.[20] The BFTA Design Competition also offers cash prizes, paid trips to Milan, and an internship in London. The Japanese Fur Association also has hosted design competitions to promote the use of fur in fashion worldwide, offering prizes and exhibits for winning designs. The International Fur Federation is even going into schools and colleges to promote the use of fur, providing opportunities to students to create their own fur design for a garment.[21] Cash prizes, all-expenses-paid trips, and recognition are enormous incentives for young designers, and young designers are an integral part of the fur industry's marketing strategy.

CORPORATIZATION OF EDUCATION

In addition to direct marketing campaigns and more subtle, indirect marketing strategies, children are targeted by advertisers in schools. The US educational system offers enormous profit opportunities from marketing products to children, estimated to be worth around $650 million, including profits derived from donated educational materials that also advertise consumer products.[22] Corporate-sponsored "educational materials" are becoming increasingly popular to schools and classrooms that need additional funding. In exchange for a business receiving advertising rights and/or marketing opportunities, the business donates resources characterized as "educational materials" to the school or classroom.[23] According to Campaign for a Commercial-Free Childhood, when trade groups and businesses donate "educational materials" and supplies to schools and classrooms, the materials are usually biased toward their product or service.[24] Consumers Union, a policy and action division of Consumer Reports, released a report on commercial pressure on children in schools. After reviewing seventy-seven corporate-sponsored "classroom kits," Consumers Union concluded that nearly 80 percent of the kits contained biased or incomplete information, "promoting a viewpoint that favors consumption of the sponsor's product or service or a position that favors the company or its economic agenda," with a few kits even containing "significant inaccuracies."[25] The fur industry is one of many industries that promote products to children by donating "educational materials" to schools and classrooms.

The Fur Council of Canada has developed a fifteen-minute video titled "Furbearing Animals: A Renewable Natural Resource" as an "educational tool" that includes a teachers' guide and quiz. The video purports to "illustrate key environmental concepts in the 5th/6th grade curriculum," while offering an entirely one-sided, positive view of the fur industry. The materials compare animals to water, coal, and plants and argue that trapping is necessary to "balance" species populations in nature. The educational resources for schools are free and are offered on the Fur Council of Canada's website.[26] The Russian Fur Union developed a project to introduce twelve- to fifteen-year-old children to the fur trade.[27] In a lecture titled "Fur Rainbow," students are taught that fur is an "ecological" material that can be used year-round, while teachers demonstrate different kinds of fur and offer information intended to steer children into the fur trade. The British Fur Trade Association launched its own educational initiative in 2008 named "Fur Trails" that targeted children ages twelve to fourteen and included "study" packs, videos, and notes for teachers.[28]

It's not just trade groups and businesses, however, that seek to influence children through in-class marketing. Governmental authorities and politicians, who are often influenced by special interests, also promote materials that are biased toward certain products. The Fur and Alligator Advisory Council of the Louisiana Department of Wildlife and Fisheries funded a package of "educational materials" for classrooms in Louisiana. In the introduction, the packet states that "[h]unting and trapping have been a way of life for many rural people in Louisiana" and that the fur industry "dates back to the 1700s."[29] The materials further state that "hunters and trappers have a true love for the land, for the habitat, and for the animals which live there" and that "from the hunters to the tanners to the manufacturers, they all have a passion for their craft."[30] In the materials for children K–2, a poem is included titled "Fur That Can Purr (You Are What You Wear?)" that arguably promotes the use of animals for various clothing items.[31] Marketing that ties history and tradition to the fur trade not only has a powerful impact on children; it also is marketing at its best, because any challenge to the fur trade can be condemned as an attack on history and tradition, creating a narrative that works in favor of the fur industry. The International Association of Fish and Wildlife Agencies, which represents professionals from the fish and wildlife agencies of the states, provinces, and federal governments of the United States and Canada, developed the "Trapper Education Program" to promote fur trapping. The program highlights the "benefits" that trapping provides to society, including (1) disease control, (2) habitat protection, (3) endangered species protection, (4) property protection, and (5) wildlife restoration and research, and the program provides information on fur trade associations, including the National Trappers Association and the Fur Takers of America.[32]

Allowing businesses and industries like the fur industry to bring "educational materials" into the classroom raises serious ethical concerns, especially when controversial products such as fur are being marketed to children. Not only are such materials biased in favor of the fur trade; children also are naturally inclined to assume that teachers and school officials have endorsed the materials,[33] which further increases the effectiveness of the marketing.

EFFORTS TO REGULATE AND BAN MARKETING TO CHILDREN

The larger issue of marketing and advertising directed toward children is on the radar of a number of organizations, with recommendations ranging from self-regulation by industries to outright bans on advertising to children.

The Responsible Advertising and Children Programme, an industry group that represents advertisers, agencies, and media worldwide, argues against outright bans on marketing to children and instead advocates self-regulation to ensure responsible marketing.[34] The Children's Advertising Review Unit, a division administered by the BBB National Programs in the US, also supports a self-regulatory approach, but one that contains general guidelines for advertising to children under the age of twelve, including certain core principles such as the following: (1) advertisers must recognize that children have limited capacity to evaluate the credibility of information and may not even understand the persuasive intent of advertising; (2) advertising should be neither deceptive nor unfair, as such terms are defined under the Federal Trade Commission Act; (3) products and content that are inappropriate for children should not be advertised directly to them; (4) advertisers should not encourage negative social stereotyping and prejudice; (5) advertisers are encouraged to capitalize on the potential of advertising to serve an informational role and influence positive personal qualities and behaviors in children, such as being honest and respectful of others; and (6) advertisers shall not undermine the parent–child relationship.[35]

Not all organizations, however, support self-regulation when it comes to marketing to children. Research conducted by the American Psychological Association has found that children ages eight and under are not able to critically comprehend advertisements and may accept advertisements as truthful and unbiased.[36] In the *Report of the APA Task Force on Advertising and Children*, Wilcox et al. note that other professional groups, such as the American Academy of Pediatrics, the National Education Association, the National Parent Teacher Association, and the Association for Supervision and Curriculum Development, all have been critical of advertising to children that is done in schools.[37] The American Psychological Association recommends that advertising targeted to children eight and under be restricted and that further investigation be done on the age at which children over the age of eight are able to fully understand the persuasive nature of advertising.[38]

Policy recommendations are helpful, but they are not enforceable. But do laws protect children from marketers? UNICEF, an organization that is mandated by the United Nations General Assembly to advocate for the protection of children around the world, was interested in determining whether sufficient international legal protections were in place with regard to marketing and advertising to children. UNICEF has been working to establish international standards of behavior toward children, and in November 2016, UNICEF commissioned a global report on advertising and marketing to children.[39] The report examined the legal and regulatory framework of thirty-six countries and the European Union, countries considered to be highly diverse in terms of their economic, geographic, and sociocultural environments, to determine the extent to which laws protect children from advertisements and marketing.[40] The authors found that while thirty of the thirty-seven jurisdictions had some form of industry code of practice with respect to marketing and/ or advertising to children, the codes varied widely in terms of scope and coverage.[41] The report found that seventeen countries lacked legislation that explicitly addressed marketing and advertising to children.[42] Nine countries had "some provisions" that addressed marketing and advertising to children,[43] but only ten countries were found to have substantial or complete provisions regulating marketing and/or advertising to children.[44] The report also found that the majority of jurisdictions lacked specific regulations for online spaces, such as websites that target children, with only seven countries having a comprehensive legislative or regulatory obligation to "pre-clear" advertisements.[45] Based on UNICEF's commissioned global report on advertising and marketing to Children, it doesn't appear that, at least on an international basis, sufficient laws are in place to regulate marketing and advertising to children.

HUMANE EDUCATION

Because policy recommendations are helpful but not binding, and because sufficient international laws are not in place to protect children from marketers, a case can be made that humane education should be introduced in schools and classrooms to provide a balanced point of view on the fur industry, including information on the animal welfare concerns and animal cruelty issues inherent in the fur industry. Educators may be reluctant to ban "educational materials" that promote fur, particularly when they are coupled with financial incentives, but humane education materials should also be provided so that children learn viewpoints both for and against the use of fur.

The humane education required to educate children on the arguments against the use of fur would be the opposite of the marketing goals of the fur industry and would include (1) teaching children about animal cruelty at a young age; (2) educating children on the animal welfare and cruelty issues associated with fur farming and trapping; (3) normalizing the use of cruelty-free clothing; (4) connecting fur with living, sentient beings; (5) discussing with children the ethics of taking the skin of an animal and the unnecessary suffering of animals who are killed for their fur; and (6) promoting cruelty-free information and materials to children in schools and classrooms.

While the fur industry may take the position that mandating humane education is morally equivalent to "educational materials" that promote fur, an important distinction is that the materials provided by the fur industry are profit-motivated, whereas humane education is arguably similar to good citizenship education, where principles of respect, kindness, and compassion are taught.

CONCLUSION

The fur industry is actively marketing fur to children. Through direct marketing campaigns that provide toys and trinkets with fur to children and indirect marketing efforts that include more subtle strategies such as celebrity endorsements and pro-fur "educational materials," the fur industry as a whole is investing millions of dollars to market fur to children. By providing pro-fur biased information to children at a young age, the fur industry seeks to normalize the use of fur by children. By tying important institutions like history, tradition, and family to fur, the industry is using principles of child psychology in hopes of securing children as future consumers of fur. When this is packaged together with the fur industry's "fur is green" message that may appeal to older, more environmentally conscientious youth,[46] the impact of the fur industry's marketing efforts is profound. Based on research conducted by the American Psychological Association, a strong case can be made that all advertising of fur to children ages eight and under should be restricted on the basis that children at that age are not able to comprehend the persuasive intent of advertising. Given the extent to which the fur industry is marketing to children, an even stronger case can be made that humane education should be provided to all children, including information on the animal welfare aspects of the fur industry and the ethical issues associated with the use of fur. All children should have access to full, complete, and accurate information on the fur industry and its practices, including educational materials that address the cruelty involved with fur farming and trapping. With humane education we can strike at the core of all animal exploitation—attitudes toward animals that are formed in early childhood, attitudes that the fur industry hopes to influence through advertising and marketing.

NOTES

1. Adriana Barbaro and Jeremy Earp, *Consuming Kids: The Commercialization of Childhood* (Media Education Foundation Study Guide, 2008), 13.

2. Juliet Schor, *Born to Buy: The Commercialized Child and the New Consumer Culture* (New York: Scribner, 2005), 21.

3. A. Guttman, "Spending on Advertising to Children Worldwide from 2012 to 2021, by Format," *Statista*, April 7, 2020, accessed December 10, 2020, www.statista.com/statistics/750865/kids-advertising-spending-worldwide/.

4. Debra J. Holt, Pauline M. Ippolito, Debra M. Desrochers, and Christopher R. Kelley, *Children's Exposure to Television Advertising in 1977 and 2004: Information for the Obesity Debate* (Federal Trade Commission Bureau of Economics Staff Report, June 2007), 63.

5. Brian L. Wilcox et al., *Report of the APA Task Force on Advertising and Children* (American Psychological Association, February 20, 2004), 4.

6. Paul M. Connell, Merrie Brucks, and Jesper H. Nielsen, "How Childhood Advertising Exposure Can Create Biased Product Evaluations That Persist into Adulthood," *Journal of Consumer Research* 41, no. 1 (June 2014): 119–34.

7. Wilcox et al., *Report of the APA Task Force*, 7, 56.

8. Media Smarts, "How Marketers Target Kids," accessed February 8, 2022, mediasmarts.ca/digital-media-literacy/media-issues/marketing-consumerism/how-marketers-target-kids.

9. Rachel Pancare, "How Do Bright Colors Appeal to Kids?," *Sciencing*, April 23, 2018.

10. Coalition against Fur Farms, "Internal Document Reveals the Anatomy of the Fur Commission USA," accessed February 8, 2022, www.coalitionagainstfurfarms.com/internal-document-reveals-the-anatomy-of-the-fur-commission-usa/, citing an internal document of Fur Commission USA titled "Synopsis of FCUSA's Programs" (revised July 2010).

11. Lorraine Fisher, "How the Fur Industry Clawed Its Way Back: Lavishing Gifts on Celebs. Targeting Children in the Classroom. The Cynical Ploys Making Fur 'Respectable' Again," *Daily Mail*, March 16, 2014.

12. Fisher, "How the Fur Industry Clawed."

13. Rachel Maresca, "North West Rocks Estimated $3,500 Fur Coat in New York City," *New York Daily News*, February 12, 2015, accessed February 8, 2022, www.nydailynews.com/entertainment/gossip/north-west-rocks-estimated-3-500-fur-coat-new-york-city-article-1.2112747.

14. Blake Ellis and Melanie Hicken, "How the Modeling Industry Exploits Young and Vulnerable Workers," *CNNMoney*, May 12, 2016.

15. Rheana Murray, "Thylane Loubry Blondeau Photos: 10-Year-Old Model's Sultry *Vogue* Spread Sparks Controversy," *Daily News*, August 4, 2011.

16. Sarah Frier and Matthew Townsend, "FTC to Crack Down on Paid Celebrity Posts That Aren't Clear Ads," *Bloomberg News*, August 5, 2016, accessed February 8, 2022, www.bloomberg.com/news/articles/2016-08-05/ftc-to-crack-down-on-paid-celebrity-posts-that-aren-t-clear-ads.

17. While outside the scope of this paper, a criticism of celebrities wearing faux fur is that it is not always possible to distinguish real from faux fur, so faux fur may be unintentionally promoting the fur trade.

18. Hong Kong Fur Federation, "2019 Fur Design Competition," accessed December 12, 2020, www.hkff.org/furDesign.php?lang=1.

19. International Fur Federation, "2018/2018 IFF ReMix: International Student Fur Design Competition," accessed December 12, 2020, www.fur.org/2018-2019-iff-remix-international-student-fur-design-competition/.

20. British Fur Trade Association, "Reclaim, Recycle, Reimagine: Design Competition 2019/2020," accessed February 8, 2022, britishfur.co.uk/fashion/design-competition/.

21. Fisher, "How the Fur Industry Clawed."

22. Anup Shah, "Children as Consumers," *Global Issues*, November 21, 2010, accessed February 8, 2022, www.globalissues.org/article/237/children-as-consumers.

23. Alex M. Gurn, "Courting Corporate Philanthropy in Public Education: Multi-Disciplinary Literature Review of Public–Private Partnerships (PPPs) in Urban Public Schooling," *SAGE Open*, April 19, 2016, doi.org/10.1177/2158244016635714.

24. Campaign for a Commercial-Free Childhood, "The Facts about Marketing to Kids," accessed December 12, 2020, nepc.colorado.edu/sites/default/files/CERU-0502–115-OWI.pdf.

25. *Captive Kids: A Report on Commercial Pressures on Kids at Schools (Part One),* (Consumer Reports, January 1, 1998), accessed February 8, 2022. advocacy.consumerreports.org/press_release/captive-kids-a-report-on-commercial-pressures-on-kids-at-schools-part-one/.

26. Fur Council of Canada, "Resources for Schools," accessed December 12, 2020, www.furcouncil.com/resources-for-schools/.

27. International Fur Federation, "Russian Fur Union Introduces the Next Generation to Fur," *Fur & Fashion*, December 21, 2016, accessed December 12, 2020, www.wearefur.com/russian-fur-union-introduces-kids-fur-industry/.

28. Fisher, "How the Fur Industry Clawed."

29. Fur and Alligator Advisory Council, Louisiana Department of Wildlife and Fisheries, "Educational Materials," 4, accessed February 8, 2022, www.insta-gatorranch.com/wp-content/uploads/2019/06/FurandAlligatorEd.pdf.

30. Fur and Alligator Advisory Council, "Educational Materials," 4.

31. Fur and Alligator Advisory Council, "Educational Materials," 61.

32. International Association of Fish and Wildlife Agencies, "Introduction to Trapper Education," chap. 1 in *Trapper Education Manual*, 4–5, accessed February 8, 2022, www.fishwildlife.org/application/files/7915/1977/4541/Student_manual_2005.pdf.

33. Wilcox et al., *Report of the APA Task Force*, 7, 56.

34. Responsible Advertising and Children, "What do these codes say in practice?," in FAQs, accessed December 12, 2020, responsibleadvertising.org/faqs/.

35. BBB National Programs, Inc., Children's Advertising Review Unit, *Self-Regulation Guidelines for Children's Advertising* (2021), 2–9, accessed February 8, 2022, bbbprograms.org/media-center/news/CARU-revised-guidelines-for-advertising-to-children.

36. Wilcox et al., *Report of the APA Task Force*, 8.

37. Wilcox et al., *Report of the APA Task Force*, 59.

38. Wilcox et al., *Report of the APA Task Force*, 11–13.

39. DLA Piper, *Advertising & Marketing to Children: Global Report*, report commissioned by UNICEF, November 2016, accessed December 12, 2020, www.lexology.com/library/detail.aspx?g=195d20ef-d179-4556-b572-d9087fd9311b.

40. DLA Piper, *Advertising & Marketing to Children*, 5–11.

41. DLA Piper, *Advertising & Marketing to Children*, 5–11.

42. DLA Piper, *Advertising & Marketing to Children*, 5–12. Countries found to lack explicit legislation addressing marketing and advertising to children included Brazil, Canada, Chile, Ghana, Hong Kong, Indonesia, Italy, Japan, Kenya, Myamar, the Netherlands, Qatar, Saudi Arabia, Spain, Sweden, Switzerland, and Zambia. The

report noted, however, that some countries covered by the report, such as Belgium, Canada, Japan, Pakistan, the United Arab Emirates, and the United States, have an additional level of state or regional legislation that governs advertising and marketing to children.

43. DLA Piper, *Advertising & Marketing to Children*, 5–12. Countries found to have some provisions include Australia, China, Colombia, Jordan, Pakistan, Poland, Russia, Thailand, and the United States.

44. DLA Piper, *Advertising & Marketing to Children*, 5–12. Countries found to have substantial or complete provisions include Argentina, Austria, Belgium, Denmark, Ecuador, France, Germany, India, the United Arab Emirates, and the U.K.

45. DLA Piper, *Advertising & Marketing to Children*, 11.

46. Fur Council of Canada, "Fur Is Green" (website), accessed December 12, 2020, www.furisgreen.com/.

REFERENCES

Barbaro, Adriana, and Jeremy Earp. *Consuming Kids: The Commercialization of Childhood*. Media Education Foundation Study Guide. Media Education Foundation, 2008. Accessed February 8, 2022. downloads.mediaed.org/discussion-guide-consuming-kids.

British Fur Trade Association. "Reclaim, Recycle, Reimagine: Design Competition 2019/2020." Accessed February 8, 2022. britishfur.co.uk/fashion/design-competition/.

Campaign for a Commercial-Free Childhood. "The Facts about Marketing to Kids." Accessed December 12, 2020. nepc.colorado.edu/sites/default/files/CERU-0502–115-OWI.pdf.

Captive Kids: A Report on Commercial Pressures on Kids at Schools (Part One). Consumer Reports. January 1, 1998. Accessed February 8, 2022. advocacy.consumerreports.org/press_release/captive-kids-a-report-on-commercial-pressures-on-kids-at-schools-part-one/.

Coalition against Fur Farms. "Internal Document Reveals the Anatomy of the Fur Commission USA." Accessed February 8, 2022. www.coalitionagainstfurfarms.com/internal-document-reveals-the-anatomy-of-the-fur-commission-usa/.

Connell, Paul M., Merrie Brucks, and Jesper H. Nielsen. "How Childhood Advertising Exposure Can Create Biased Product Evaluations That Persist into Adulthood." *Journal of Consumer Research* 41, no. 1, June 2014. doi.org/10.1086/675218.

DLA Piper. *Advertising & Marketing to Children: Global Report*. Report commissioned by UNICEF. November 2016. Accessed December 12, 2020. www.lexology.com/library/detail.aspx?g=195d20ef-d179-4556-b572-d9087fd9311b.

Ellis, Blake, and Melanie Hicken. "How the Modeling Industry Exploits Young and Vulnerable Workers." *CNNMoney*, May 12, 2016. Accessed February 8, 2022. money.cnn.com/2016/05/04/news/runway-injustice-modeling/index.html.

Fisher, Lorraine. "How the Fur Industry Clawed Its Way Back: Lavishing Gifts on Celebs. Targeting Children in the Classroom. The Cynical Ploys Making

Fur 'Respectable' Again." *Daily Mail*, March 16, 2014. Accessed February 8, 2022. www.dailymail.co.uk/femail/article-2582226/How-fur-industry-clawed-way-Lavishing-gifts-celebs-Targeting-children-classroom-The-cynical-ploys-making-fur-respectable-again.html.

Frier, Sarah, and Matthew Townsend. "FTC to Crack Down on Paid Celebrity Posts That Aren't Clear Ads." *Bloomberg News*. August 5, 2016. Accessed February 8, 2022. www.bloomberg.com/news/articles/2016-08-05/ftc-to-crack-down-on-paid-celebrity-posts-that-aren-t-clear-ads.

Fur and Alligator Advisory Council, Louisiana Department of Wildlife and Fisheries. "Educational Materials." Accessed February 8, 2022. www.insta-gatorranch.com/wp-content/uploads/2019/06/FurandAlligatorEd.pdf.

Fur Council of Canada. "Fur Is Green." Accessed December 12, 2020. www.furisgreen.com/.

———. "Resources for Schools." Accessed December 12, 2020. www.furcouncil.com/resources-for-schools/.

Gurn, Alex M. "Courting Corporate Philanthropy in Public Education: Multi-Disciplinary Literature Review of Public–Private Partnerships (PPPs) in Urban Public Schooling." *SAGE Open*. April 19, 2016. doi.org/10.1177/2158244016635714.

Guttman, A. "Spending on Advertising to Children Worldwide from 2012 to 2021, by Format." *Statista*. April 7, 2020. Accessed December 10, 2020. www.statista.com/statistics/750865/kids-advertising-spending-worldwide/

Holt, Debra J., Pauline M. Ippolito, Debra M. Desrochers, and Christopher R. Kelley. *Children's Exposure to Television Advertising in 1977 and 2004: Information for the Obesity Debate*. Federal Trade Commission Bureau of Economics Staff Report, June 2007. Accessed February 8, 2022. www.ftc.gov/reports/childrens-exposure-television-advertising-1977-2004-information-obesity-debate-bureau.

Hong Kong Fur Federation. "2019 Fur Design Competition." Accessed December 12, 2020. www.hkff.org/furDesign.php?lang=1.

International Fur Federation. "Russian Fur Union Introduces the Next Generation to Fur." *Fur & Fashion*, December 21, 2016. Accessed December 12, 2020. www.wearefur.com/russian-fur-union-introduces-kids-fur-industry/.

———. "2018/2018 IFF ReMix: International Student Fur Design Competition." Accessed December 12, 2020. www.fur.org/2018-2019-iff-remix-international-student-fur-design-competition/.

International Association of Fish and Wildlife Agencies. "Introduction to Trapper Education," chap. 1 in *Trapper Education Manual*. International Association of Fish and Wildlife Agencies, 2005. Accessed February 8, 2022. www.fishwildlife.org/application/files/7915/1977/4541/Student_manual_2005.pdf.

Maresca, Rachel. "North West Rocks Estimated $3,500 Fur Coat in New York City." *New York Daily News*, February 12, 2015. Accessed February 8, 2022. www.nydailynews.com/entertainment/gossip/north-west-rocks-estimated-3-500-fur-coat-new-york-city-article-1.2112747.

Media Smarts. "How Marketers Target Kids." Accessed February 8, 2022. mediasmarts.ca/digital-media-literacy/media-issues/marketing-consumerism/how-marketers-target-kids.

Murray, Rheana. "Thylane Loubry Blondeau Photos: 10-Year-Old Model's Sultry *Vogue* Spread Sparks Controversy." *Daily News*, August 4, 2011. www.nydailynews.com/life-style/fashion/thylane-loubry-blondeau-photos-10-year-old-model-sultry-vogue-spread-sparks-controversy-article-1.944000.

Pancare, Rachel. "How Do Bright Colors Appeal to Kids?" *Sciencing*, April 23, 2018. Accessed February 8, 2022. sciencing.com/do-bright-colors-appeal-kids-5476948.html.

Responsible Advertising and Children. "What do these codes say in practice?" In FAQs. Accessed February 8, 2022. responsibleadvertising.org/faqs/.

Schor, Juliet. *Born to Buy: The Commercialized Child and the New Consumer Culture.* New York: Scribner, 2005.

Self-Regulation Guidelines for Children's Advertising. BBB National Programs, Inc., Children's Advertising Review Unit. 2021. Accessed February 8, 2022. bbbprograms.org/media-center/news/CARU-revised-guidelines-for-advertising-to-children.

Shah, Anup. "Children as Consumers." *Global Issues*, November 21, 2010. Accessed February 8, 2022. www.globalissues.org/article/237/children-as-consumers.

Wilcox, Brian L., Dale Kunkel, Joanne Cantor, Peter Dowrick, Susan Linn, and Edward Palmer. *Report of the APA Task Force on Advertising and Children.* American Psychological Association, February 20, 2004. Accessed February 8, 2022. www.apa.org/pi/families/resources/advertising-children.pdf.

Chapter 16

Fur and Free Speech

Justin Marceau, Jess Beaulieu, Kate Sanford, and Chloe Gleichman

Social movements have a tempestuous relationship with free-speech principles. On the one hand, for politically marginalized groups, education, outreach, and activism are often essential tools of the trade in changing public attitudes and action. A movement or perspective usually cannot gain mainstream acknowledgment and support without finding effective outlets for speech that challenges the dominant viewpoint. On the other hand, unpopular social movements will be tempted to seek speech limits, narrowing constructions of a free-speech principle when the doctrine empowers and gives voice to its politically powerful political opponents. There do not appear to be any robust scholarly projects documenting in detail the willingness of speech-dependent movements to take positions opposing free speech, and this discussion will not do this either. But this chapter starts an overdue discourse about the role of free speech in the debate over the use of animals for personal or commercial benefit, such as fur as a fashion accessory. Civil libertarianism is often good for activists on the ground but may at times be at odds with efforts to regulate commercial animal enterprises, including those within the fur industry.

This chapter is divided into four sections with three main points. First, it will give a basic overview of fur-use trends in the United States. Next, it will discuss the range of federal and state anti-transparency laws that have been enacted in the United States that directly impact activism in the realm of challenging the fur industry. Finally, while avoiding the temptation to fetishize speech, the chapter will argue that anti-fur activists should avoid an overly myopic view of free speech. Speech protections for protests, education, and mobilizing grass roots might be the most important vehicle for eradicating the use of fur, and simultaneously, speech protections may be a critical limit on the scope of legislative victories for anti-fur activists. The chapter concludes that anti-fur activists should grapple with this tension more than they do.

I. HISTORY OF THE FUR INDUSTRY IN THE UNITED STATES

At the beginning of the twentieth century, fur signified status, wealth, and prestige among the European aristocracy, but as the century progressed, fur became a fashion item that was accessible to society at large.[1] This shift in public perception catalyzed the demand for fur across Western societies, and in the years that followed, many species were killed for their skins and fur. Coats made from wolves, leopards, and tigers were coveted, and accessories made from animals such as skunks, beavers, raccoons, and hamsters became popular.[2] Western designers went to great lengths to promote this lucrative industry, and the effectiveness of advertising fur in cultivating consumer interest and shaping public opinion has been a topic of distinct scholarly interest. Over time, as society's taste for fur grew, numerous species neared extinction in Europe and America.[3] Thus, to continue to meet the demand for fur, Western companies turned to farming fur-bearing animals.

Beginning in the 1980s, a coalition of organizations had success in raising awareness about the cruelty inherent in fur production. Utilizing undercover investigations at fur farms, anti-fur advertising, and protests, an impassioned social movement began to foment momentum around abolishing the fur industry. Private investigators were sent into fur farms to document the animals' suffering and slaughter, and the footage obtained was later broadcast on public television, showing thousands of animals kept in tiny, dark cages for their entire lives.[4] The footage also showed the routine slaughter of animals in gruesome ways: anal and oral electrocution, neck breaking, suffocation, and poisonous gas. These methods were often ineffective at killing the animals immediately and left many to suffer for extended periods of time.[5] As awareness of these practices spread, an increasing number of people regarded wearing fur as a social taboo, and the anti-fur movement made considerable strides toward its ultimate goal of abolishing the fur industry.[6]

Throughout the next decade, numerous organizations launched campaigns that drew public attention to the issues surrounding fur.[7] Perhaps most famous is a PETA campaign that began in 1992 featuring celebrities such as Christina Applegate, Eva Mendes, and Pamela Anderson appearing undressed on ads with the message "I'd Rather Go Naked Than Wear Fur."[8] Activists crashed fashion show runways around the world.[9] Expository advertisements were plastered on billboards, and corresponding posters read, "It takes up to 40 dumb animals to make a fur coat. But only one to wear it."[10]

Beyond protests, during this same period, criminal acts of civil disobedience targeting the fur industry also brought attention to the practices of fur farms. The Animal Liberation Front and at least sixteen other groups[11] claimed responsibility for criminal acts of civil disobedience that involved freeing animals held at universities and private research laboratories, fur retailers, and fur farms,[12] and from 1977 to 1993, the US Department of Justice reported approximately 313 incidents of direct action.[13] The fur industry estimates that these incidents caused $100 million in damages, and direct action organizations claim that this economic sabotage resulted in the closure of numerous facilities.[14]

In the face of widespread education, media campaigns, and criminal activism, the interest in fur among Americans appears to have plummeted. In June 2016, the Free Fur Alliance reported that the global number of minks killed for fur had dropped 38 percent in the previous year—from about seventy-two million mink in 2015 to around fifty-two million in 2016.[15] And in 2020, the number of mink killed for their fur in the United States dropped 49 percent to 1.4 million, the lowest number on record according to US Department of Agriculture reports dating back to 1975.[16] Prior lows in annual mink production figures remained around 2.5 million mink in the early 2000s before peaking in 2014 and 2015 at 3.7 million mink.[17]

Public sentiment against wearing fur has also led to some legislative progress restricting fur sales, both in the United States and around the world. San Francisco, Los Angeles, West Hollywood, and Berkeley have complete bans on the sale of fur within their city limits, and other cities are beginning to introduce similar legislation.[18] In 2019, California passed a law banning the production and sale of fur within the state beginning in 2023.[19] And in February 2022, "in voting to approve the America COMPETES Act, the U.S. House of Representatives included a provision to ban mink farming throughout the United States, signaling disapproval of an industry that harms and kills animals for their pelts, exports them to China for a sliver of elite consumers, and presents a threat of SARS-CoV-2 spillover to people in the homeland."[20] Across the world, countries including Austria, the United Kingdom, Japan, and Belgium have banned fur farming, and other countries have either partially or completely banned the sale of fur.[21] In fact, Israel has banned the sale of most fur clothing, becoming the first country to prohibit the controversial material.[22]

With respect to the fashion industry itself, popular clothing companies such as Calvin Klein, Ralph Lauren, and Tommy Hilfiger were among the first to initiate fur-free policies for their collections in 1994, 2006, and 2007, respectively.[23] In 2017, Gucci became one of the first major brands to announce that it was going fur-free,[24] and in 2021, the label's owner announced that its remaining brands—including Alexander McQueen, Balenciaga, and Yves Saint Laurent—would also conform by fall 2022.[25] Most recently, Dolce & Gabbana joined this growing list, announcing in January 2022 that it will begin phasing out fur and will instead use a sustainable "eco-fur" in its future collections.[26] In a press release, the label stated that "Dolce & Gabbana is working towards a more sustainable future that can't contemplate the use of animal fur," and "[t]he entire fashion system has a significant social responsibility role that must be promoted and encouraged."[27] And finally, retailers such as Bloomingdale's and Macy's[28] have also decided to ban fur products, while *Elle* Magazine and London Fashion Week have banned fur items from their editorials and runways, respectively.[29] And despite some designers turning to fur to develop and strengthen their brands, millennials have increasingly shown their support for faux fur as a replacement for real fur.[30] In light of these successes, many Americans appear to believe that fur as a political issue is passé.

However, rumors of the death of fur have been exaggerated as the fur industry is fighting back. Fur industry associations claim fur bans or changes in public opinion have no significant effect on fur sales, but rather point to economic fluctuations.[31] According to the International Fur Trade Federation, global fur sales doubled from $15.6 billion in 2011 to $35.8 billion in 2013, with increased demand from China as the primary driver of this growth.[32] In 2015, fur reappeared on the most esteemed runways around the world, and young fashion-conscious women and men were again choosing fur for its trendiness: 73 percent of 2015's 436 fashion shows in New York, Paris, Milan, and London featured fur.[33] And with mounting global environmental concerns, the fur industry is responding to the rise of faux alternatives by fervently promoting their product as a naturally sustainable choice.[34] The industry continues to gain traction as preserving the fur aesthetic by supporting faux alternatives serves to subsidize fur's endurance in the landscape of fashion.

II. FEDERAL LEGISLATION RELEVANT TO FUR ACTIVISM

The economic damage associated with attacks on animal industries by activists eventually garnered the attention of the government, which conducted several grand-jury investigations targeting major animal rights "extremists" in the years that followed. Driven by the National Association for Biomedical Research,[35] panicked industries[36] pressured Congress to respond, leading to the Animal Enterprise Protection Act ("AEPA") passing in 1992.[37] The

AEPA was a landmark law that made it a federal offense to cause physical disruption to the functioning of an animal enterprise resulting in economic damage exceeding $10,000.[38] If convicted, an offender was subject to fines or imprisonment of up to one year, or up to ten years or life imprisonment for an aggravated offense.[39] Notably, the AEPA was the first piece of legislation to refer to individuals who interfered with animal enterprises as terrorists.

The AEPA's brevity—it was just one page long—was alarming to many activists and legal advocates, who worried the law was overbroad, covering activities protected by the First Amendment. The statute criminalized anyone who "intentionally cause[d] physical disruption to the functioning of an animal enterprise" and broadly defined an "animal enterprise" as "(A) a commercial or academic enterprise that uses animals for food or fiber production, agriculture, research, or testing; (B) a zoo, aquarium, circus, rodeo, or lawful competitive animal event; or (C) any fair or similar event intended to advance agricultural arts and sciences."[40] Most significantly, many worried that the vague language would have a chilling effect, preventing individuals from engaging in protected First Amendment activity because of the threat of criminalization. Notwithstanding this worry, and despite the risk of prosecution under the AEPA, individuals continued to take bold actions to raid fur farms, and representatives of the animal industry lobbied Congress to expand the AEPA's scope.

Using a draft prepared by the American Legislative Exchange Council (ALEC), a corporate-friendly think tank,[41] Congress proposed a new law called the Animal Enterprise Terrorism Act (AETA), which contained a few key provisions enabling further criminalization. The AETA, which President George W. Bush signed into law in 2006, aimed "to provide the Department of Justice the necessary authority to apprehend, prosecute, and convict individuals committing animal enterprise terror."[42] US Senator Dianne Feinstein defended the importance of the bill by stating, "This legislation is crucial to respond to the expanded scope of terrorist activity that has threatened to impede important medical research and scientific innovation."[43] She went on to explain that "all conduct protected by the First Amendment is expressly excluded from the scope of this legislation. This law effectively protects the actions of the law-abiding protestor while carefully distinguishing the criminal activity of extremists."[44] In the US House of Representatives, the AETA was put on a fast track for bills that are "noncontroversial" and was passed by voice vote with only six out of 435 congresspersons present. The law also included a provision saying that nothing in the law should be construed as prohibiting "expressive conduct,"[45] which is a bit like including a statutory provision instructing that the law does not violate core principles of free speech.

In contrast to the AEPA's "physical disruption" requirement, any "interference" with an animal enterprise suffices for prosecution under the AETA.[46] Additionally, the AETA arguably allows a greater variety of harms to count as "economic damage" to an animal enterprise, including "costs resulting from threats, acts or vandalism, property damage, trespass, harassment, or intimidation."[47] The possible penalties under the AETA are also more severe, and the AETA's sentencing guidelines include an "enhancement" that can be imposed whenever the government deems an act to be "terrorism."[48] A person who receives this enhancement can have their term of imprisonment significantly increased. And with the terrorist designation, the individual is assigned to a maximum-security prison meant to confine the most violent criminal offenders. In these facilities, inmates are commonly subjected to twenty-three hours of lockdown and strict limitations on their communication with the outside world.

One notable AETA case involved the prosecution of Kevin Johnson and Tyler Lang, who were indicted for "releasing" and "conspiring to release" about two thousand mink and foxes from Midwest fur farms.[49] Their appeal challenging the AETA's constitutionality failed.[50] More generally, the AETA's enactment and use for prosecutions has been colloquially referred to as the "Green Scare," named after the anticommunist Red Scare in the 1950s.[51] The legislative efforts seem to have had the desired effect. In the years following the enactment of the AETA, the number of activist campaigns targeting fur farms decreased, and mink production in the US increased by 32 percent between 2010 and 2014.[52]

III. STATE "AG-GAG" LAWS: THE NEXT WAVE OF ANTI-TRANSPARENCY LEGISLATION

Beyond the federal laws chilling activism, there are state laws that attempt to criminalize whistleblowing in the agricultural industry, often including fur farms. The laws, colloquially referred to as ag-gag laws, have been introduced in at least twenty-seven states and have been signed into law in seven states since 2012.[53] The basic feature of ag-gag legislation is silencing or gagging undercover investigators and whistleblowers whose efforts enable public scrutiny of animal handling practices.

The purpose of these laws is to curtail and to criminalize negative speech about the agricultural industry. As one of the architects of the Idaho law put it, the laws are an effective way of keeping animal protection advocates "off their soapbox." One legislator explained that the law would not have been necessary if activists had not used their footage to encourage boycotts and bad press. During hearings on that ag-gag bill, the president of the Idaho

Dairymen's Association continually referred to activists as "terrorists" and explained that "these farm terrorists use media and sensationalism to attempt to steal the integrity of the producer and their reputation, and their ability to conduct business in Idaho by declaring him guilty in the court of public opinion."[54] It is beyond dispute that the laws are a legislative response to negative publicity generated by otherwise lawful undercover investigations.

The laws are primarily designed to insulate industrial factory farms from the very sort of publicity that Justice Louis Brandeis once described as a "remedy for social and industrial diseases."[55] Furthermore, the laws have often been written so broadly that they benefit any facility that houses animals for commercial uses or prepares or packages agricultural products, including butchers, restaurants, and facilities involved with the fur trade. Indeed, in the litigation challenging the constitutionality of Utah's ag-gag law, a fur farmer submitted a document styled as an expert report in support of the law. As one judge explained in striking down the Idaho law, these laws were "animated by an improper animus toward animal welfare groups and other undercover investigators."[56]

Ag-gag laws function to prevent transparency regarding the harms that animals on fur farms suffer through two specific prohibitions: barring the use of deception to gain entry and prohibiting acts of audio or visual recording. In practical effect, the laws make whistleblowing and investigative journalism in factory farms, including fur farms, impossible to conduct legally.

Such whistleblowing and reporting can have profound effects. To take one prominent example, the pioneering journalistic efforts of Upton Sinclair in exposing the health problems, environmental concerns, workplace safety issues, and animal suffering of the early twentieth-century slaughterhouse led to public outrage and federal legislative reforms. Sinclair explained, "I was not much better dressed than the workers, and found that by the simple device of carrying a dinner pail I could go anywhere,"[57] but as a biographer clarified, the dress-up routine was not always enough, and frequently Sinclair gained access "with a few simple lies appropriate to the area in which he was investigating."[58] It also has been observed that Sinclair rarely took notes while he was in a slaughterhouse, but rather memorized the details of his observations and then wrote them down later. However, if a journalist employed these same investigative tactics at a slaughterhouse or fur farm in a state with an ag-gag law, even without video and relying exclusively on memory, that journalist would be a criminal.

Moreover, where a state bans recording, even a longtime employee who simply documents with a photograph or video a health risk or cruel condition, to turn it over to authorities or the press, could be treated as a common criminal. Such a prohibition has the practical effect of criminalizing the most reliable, easily distributed, and self-authenticating evidence of animal abuse available. Indeed, if there had been an ag-gag law in California, the Humane Society investigation that resulted in the largest beef recall in US history[59] would not have been possible without the investigators risking severe criminal penalties.

In short, ag-gag laws bar investigators from gaining access, and moreover, they bar traditional whistleblowers from documenting their observations when they are otherwise lawfully present. The laws are a comprehensive barrier to publicity, and as Justice Louis Brandeis noted in 1913, "publicity is justly commended as a remedy for social and industrial diseases. Sunlight is said to be the best of disinfectants; electric light the most efficient policeman."[60]

Although the power of ag-gag laws in blocking the disinfecting force of transparency cannot be gainsaid, the free-speech principles that render such laws intolerable are rather sweeping and were not well-settled when the first round of cases challenging the ag-gag laws were filed. In the absence of a material expansion of the existing free-speech principles, these laws would have to be upheld as constitutional. The aforementioned challenges would go on to serve as test cases for determining whether deception and recording are acts of expression covered by the First Amendment. In 2012, the Animal Legal Defense Fund (ALDF) and PETA, among others, filed the first case against ag-gag legislation, challenging Utah's law. After four years of discovery and motions, the United States District Court for the District of Utah declared the law unconstitutional.[61] Even in the heart of agricultural America, and despite the argument of fur farmers that the law should be upheld, a federal judge provided a blunt assessment of the law: "What the Act appears perfectly tailored toward is preventing undercover investigators from exposing abuses at agricultural facilities."[62] The state of Utah waived its appeal and agreed to pay more than $300,000 in attorney fees.

In 2014, ALDF, PETA, the American Civil Liberties Union of Idaho, and a coalition of other civil rights organizations filed the second challenge to an ag-gag law, against Idaho's law. In 2015, a federal district court in Idaho agreed with the Utah judge, pointing out that the ag-gag law "seeks to limit and punish those who speak out on topics relating to the agricultural industry, striking at the heart of important First Amendment values."[63] The court went on to explain that "the effect of the statute will be to suppress speech by undercover investigators and whistleblowers concerning topics of great public importance" such as safety of the public food supply and the treatment and health of animals.[64]

Additional challenges to ag-gag laws across the country are underway,[65] and as these laws are struck down in agricultural states, transparency on fur farms is better protected. In the absence of these laws, journalists and activists can engage in undercover investigations without risking criminal liability for merely exposing the mistreatment of animals. This allows for powerful investigations revealing the worst abuses of the fur industry, such as PETA's 1998 undercover investigation of a fur farm in Montana, which showed hundreds of animals confined to "fifty concrete pens with stagnant water full of dead and dying beavers."[66]

IV. THE FIRST AMENDMENT AS A TWO-WAY STREET

Defeating ag-gag laws represents a necessary, but by no means sufficient, step in the fight for transparency. Other legal obstacles that impede exposing the truth about industries profiting from the exploitation of animals include defamation lawsuits. In what some commentators have described as one of the most devastating blows to journalistic independence in recent decades,[67] a state court judge in South Dakota allowed a case to go to trial against NBC for the network's news coverage of a meat product that NBC referred to as "pink slime."[68] Facing the potential of a hostile home-court jury, the network's parent company, Disney, settled the lawsuit for approximately $176 million. This is one of the largest defamation recoveries in U.S. history, and it is likely to embolden parties who feel aggrieved by the media to file similar litigation. The payment in the "pink slime" case is somewhat analogous to the liability imposed on the UK anti-fur organization Lynx for its exposé of a fur farm in 1992. Lynx and its founder were bankrupted because of defamation litigation brought by a fur farm after Lynx had conducted an undercover investigation, published its findings, and described the conditions at the fur farm as a "hell hole."[69] Based on these revelations, a UK court imposed liability in excess of the personal and professional assets of the persons and organization involved in the exposé. Lynx went over £400,000 in debt, and a judge subsequently froze its bank account.

Defamation liability, ag-gag laws, anti-terrorism laws targeting civil disobedience, and other measures pursued by the animal industries may leave one with the impression that the animal protection movement is always on the side of civil liberties, at least when it comes to protecting freedom of speech. The reality, however, is a bit more complicated. When speech is critical of animal protection efforts, some would seek to ignore the principles that undergird free-speech protections and instead tolerate or promote censorial activity that would support the animal protection agenda.[70]

More generally, when social movements are fortified by court rulings upholding the constitutionality of their speech-based advocacy, they sometimes become complacent about the fact that speech is a neutral concept available to all sides of a debate. To the extent that the First Amendment must protect the rights of anti-fur advocates to voice their views and shape their message, it must apply with equal force to proponents of the fur industry.

If it is constitutional for animal advocates to craft inflammatory messages to the public about the cruelty occurring within an animal enterprise, those with a stake in animal enterprises are also constitutionally protected in pursuing aggressive efforts to persuade persons about the value of their animal exploitation.[71]

Today, some of the increased popularity of fur can be fairly traced to the fur industry's advertising campaigns presenting fur-bearing animals as humanely raised.[72] For example, a fur marketing website called Fur is Green, run by the Fur Council of Canada, insists that if animals on fur farms were not treated humanely, their fur would not be high-quality: "While providing animals with humane care is an ethical obligation for all livestock farmers, it also makes good business sense since the healthiest animals produce the finest furs" and "farmers who do not care for their animals will not remain in business very long."[73] Moreover, a marketing website called Truth About Fur devotes a significant portion of its website to the ethics of fur farming. The website shows pictures of people affectionately holding animals and states that "mink and foxes are provided with excellent nutrition and care" and that "no unnecessary pain or cruelty is inflicted."[74]

The coalition of fur companies that run Truth About Fur has also deployed a concerted marketing effort portraying fur as a highly sustainable and ethical fashion choice:

> If we really care about the environment (and we all should because nothing else matters if we don't have water and food and clean air), we will want to buy sustainable fashion products that use production processes that are not too harmful to the environment, that are long-lasting, and that are biodegradable. That is exactly what animal skins are.[75]

Likewise, the Fur Commission USA, an organization that represents mink farmers throughout the United States, advertises fur as a natural, earth-friendly, durable, recyclable, and ethical material.[76]

Such comments and other claims of exemplary animal treatment might be belied by undercover investigations. The Fur Commission has publicly endorsed the notion that transparency and investigations are the evil to be avoided, not fur production processes: "Regrettably, it is painfully obvious that often these organizations appear to care less about the animals, than they do about maximizing publicity, self-promotion and fund raising—and that should be the real crime."[77]

Notably, however, it is not just animal exploiters who would like to erect legal barriers to transparency and undercover investigations. Opposition to speech that is contrary to one's desired message has already crept into other social movements, including the pro-choice movement, which has historically benefited from expansive free-speech protections afforded to its advocacy.

In 2015, several undercover journalists from the Center for Medical Progress (CMP)—a pro-life organization—released numerous videos exposing Planned Parenthood's alleged practices of illegally selling the body parts of aborted fetuses. Instead of coming to terms with the fact that the undercover videos would likely be considered constitutionally permissible forms of speech, Planned Parenthood essentially argued that this was a campaign of deception against its practices.[78] In fact, Dawn Laguens, the executive vice president of Planned Parenthood Federation of America, explained, "Previous tapes released by this extremist group were heavily edited to distort what the people on the tapes actually said."[79]

As part of this effort, Planned Parenthood successfully lobbied members of the California legislature to support a bill that criminalizes the publication of confidential interactions with state-licensed medical personnel, including abortion providers and clinic staff, punishable by up to one year in prison and $10,000 fine per violation.[80] Despite considerable concern from liberals and conservatives alike that this would force First Amendment rights to free speech and a free press to become subservient to Planned Parenthood's privacy, the governor of California signed the bill into law September 2016.[81]

Planned Parenthood also filed a lawsuit against CMP, alleging that it violated several federal and state laws.[82] The lawsuit requested restitution for actual losses caused by CMP as well as compensatory and punitive damages and attorneys' fees for the losses Planned Parenthood incurred as a result of the videos. In response, CMP called the lawsuit a "frivolous lawsuit in retaliation for CMP's First Amendment investigative journalism."[83] In 2019, a federal jury in San Francisco ruled in Planned Parenthood's favor on each of its claims[84] and awarded it up to $2.2 million in damages.[85] Claims included engagement in trespass, illegal secret recording, fraud, breach of contract, and violations of the Racketeer Influenced and Corrupt Organizations Act.[86] CMP has an appeal pending in the Ninth Circuit Court of Appeals,[87] and has stated that the verdict sets "a dangerous precedent for citizen journalism and First Amendment civil rights across the country."[88]

If Planned Parenthood's narrow construction of the First Amendment as applied to undercover investigations prevails, the advocacy of animal protection groups and undercover journalists is at risk. And the temptation to impose limits on the marketplace of ideas is something that many animal protection advocates may not be able to resist when speech protection seems to be in tension with short-term animal protection efforts.

Consider the movement's response to the Supreme Court case *United States v. Stevens*.[89] *Stevens* presented the question of whether a federal statute that, among other things, prohibited creating so-called crush videos was unconstitutional. Rather than acknowledging the failings of the statute in question and seeking a more narrowly tailored, targeted statute, the movement (including its lawyers) almost universally argued in public and in briefs for a general shift of First Amendment principles. Specifically, the movement argued that the category of unprotected speech should be expanded substantially by conditioning coverage of the First Amendment on a general balancing test that would weigh the value to society of a category of speech against the harm likely to flow from the speech. Even a decade after *Stevens*, it is nearly blasphemous to suggest among animal protection lawyers that *Stevens* was correctly decided, and nearly all the academic commentary from animal law scholars is deeply critical of the case's outcome. An indeterminate balancing test for speech was treated as an essential good for animal law.

So, what does the First Amendment require when it comes to protecting pro-fur speech? Most obviously, it requires protecting laudatory rhetoric and impassioned (even if mistaken) historical, cultural, or ecological claims about fur. Truthful advertising and propagandizing campaigns are also protected. More controversially, because fur has been a way of communicating one's status, and potentially one's views about the dominion humans enjoy over animals, wearing fur as fashion may also be protected speech. What one chooses to wear may have an expressive element to it—is a fur coat less expressive than a PETA T-shirt? If wearing fur is an expressive act, then perhaps bans on wearing it would implicate free-speech protections.[90]

Likewise, it may be relevant to analogize to ag-gag litigation, which has, perhaps more than any other context, conveyed the importance of protecting non-expressive acts antecedent to speech. Just as acts of recording must be protected as the sort of conduct that is necessary to the editing and distribution of a video, so too must other acts of non-speech that are preparatory to expression be safeguarded. Purchasing paper or paintbrushes may not be an act of speech, but certainly limits on such purchases have the ability to chill the creation of speech. By the same logic, an outright ban on the production or sale of fur—such as that passed in California—might arguably implicate free expression, or it could be viewed as a neutral law of general applicability that only incidentally restricts speech. The stakes for such questions are quite high. If fur production is protected as pre-speech activity, then is there merit to an aquarium's argument that it has a free-speech right to obtain and display cetaceans? Or does a restaurant have a speech-protected right to have items on its menu that have been deemed illegal, such as foie gras? Is hunting or fur trapping expressive activity?

When answering these thorny questions, animal activists would do well to heed Jack Balkin's observation that free-speech doctrine's political valence—that is, whether the doctrine tends to support liberal or conservative causes—has shifted over time.[91] He terms the process by which such shifts occur "ideological drift," and it captures when the political "valence" of "styles of legal argument, theories of jurisprudence, and theories of constitutional interpretation . . . varies over time as they are applied and understood repeatedly in new contexts and situations."[92] Balkin specifically observed the following:

> Since the 1920s left-liberals in the United States have tended to take relatively libertarian views on free speech, while conservatives have been more likely to balance the interest in free speech against the interest in social order, the preservation of important social values, and so on. In the last several years we have seen a gradual and partial reversal of these positions in debates over regulation of sexual and racial harassment, campaign finance, and pornography.[93]

Balkin's framework teaches that activists ought to be mindful that a doctrinal perspective they embrace could be used against them in the future to hamper litigation efforts.[94] Advocates should be careful to avoid a drift in their own advocacy away from protections for the sort of expressive activities that are central to the movement's pro-transparency identity.[95] Moreover, whether a social movement ought to waffle on as potentially foundational an issue as free expression is hardly obvious. As anti-fur activists grapple with whether and how to develop (consistent) positions regarding free-speech principles, their consideration of the potential consequences ought not be too myopic.

The point is neither that everything is speech and that all forms of animal exploitation must be regarded as protected expressive activity, nor that the First Amendment protects none of those acts. The point is, more narrowly, that the lines are not as clear and one-sided as animal advocates often seem to assume. Conservationists and citizen scientists are arguing with some success that collecting soil and water samples is a form of expression.[96] One need not overly fetishize the ideal of free speech to understand how such claims of expression could be weaponized by forces in favor of exploitation, including the fur industry. More research and thinking is necessary on the connection between animals and artistic, or other, expression. How should the law respond to the use of sentient beings as part of one's artistic or expressive endeavor? Whatever the answer, anti-fur activists should at least consider William Kunstler's insight that lawyers are at their best as part of the social-change engine when they keep activists out of jail, and they defend their often inflammatory and unpopular speech. The success of lawyers in doing this sort of work will always be in some tension with the ability of animal advocates to obtain legislatively enacted limits on those who would exploit animals for profit or expression.[97]

NOTES

1. Ann M. Carlos and Frank D. Lewis, "The Economic History of the Fur Trade: 1670 to 1870," *Economic History Association*, accessed September 10, 2017, eh.net/encyclopedia/the-economic-history-of-the-fur-trade-1670-to-1870/.

2. Carlos and Lewis, "The Economic History of the Fur Trade: 1670 to 1870."

3. Bill Adams, *Against Extinction: The Story of Conservation* (New York: Earthscan, 2004), 196–98.

4. For example, in 1988, PETA conducted an undercover investigation at a beaver fur farm in Montana. The investigation showed hundreds of animals confined to "fifty concrete pens with stagnant water full of dead and dying beavers." Rik Scarce, *Eco-Warriors: Understanding the Radical Environmental Movement* (Walnut Creek, CA: Left Coast, 2006), 129–30.

5. See Lise Skov, "The Return of the Fur Coat: A Commodity Chain Perspective," *Current Sociology* 53, no. 1 (2005): 25 (noting that the suffering caused by fur clothing production may be "modest compared to many other ways that humans use animals").

6. Last Chance for Animals, "Fur-Free Friday: A Historical Perspective," accessed September 15, 2017, www.lcanimal.org/index.php/campaigns/fur/fur-trade-facts-2.

7. These organizations included People for the Ethical Treatment of Animals (PETA), Lynx, Greenpeace, and many others.

8. See Kristen Bousquet, "31 Celebrities Who Got Naked for PETA," *StyleCaster*, February 7, 2022, stylecaster.com/celebrities-who-got-naked-for-peta-ads/.

9. See Sara Oliver, "PETA Stormed Runway Shows: How Fur Went out of Style," *PETA*, February 11, 2022, www.peta.org/blog/peta-how-fur-went-out-of-style/.

10. Jeremy Laurance, "Health: Get Warm Fur Winter and Don't Be a Dumb Animal," October 13, 1998, www.independent.co.uk/arts-entertainment/health-get-warm-fur-winter-and-dont-be-a-dumb-animal-1177997.html.

11. These groups include Animal Avengers, Animal Liberation Action Foundation, Animal Liberation Front, Animals Now, Animal Rights Militia, Band of Mercy, Earth First!, Earth Night Action Group, Farm Freedom Fighters, Guardian Apes, Paint Panthers, Socialist Committee for the Protection of Animals, True Friends, Undersea Railroad, Urban Gorillas, and the Western Wildlife Unit/Cell (of the Animal Liberation Front). U.S. Department of Justice and U.S. Department of Agriculture, *Report to Congress on the Extent and Effects of Domestic and International Terrorism on Animal Enterprises* (October 1993), 4–5.

12. For example, in 1991 the Animal Liberation Front went into the Oregon State University Experimental Fur Farm and removed files and videotapes, destroyed equipment, and painted slogans on the walls. See Peter Young, "How They Got In (Blast from the Past, Still Pertinent Today!)," *Animal Liberation Front*, December 9, 2021, animalliberationpressoffice.org/NAALPO/2019/12/09/how-they-got-in-blast-from-the-past-still-pertinent-today/.

13. U.S. Departments of Justice and Agriculture, *Report to Congress*, 4–5.

14. See John E. Lewis, Deputy Assistant Director of Federal Bureau of Investigation, "Before the Senate Judiciary Committee Washington DC," May 18, 2004, archives.fbi.gov/archives/news/testimony/animal-rights-extremism-and-ecoterrorism.

15. Fur Free Alliance, "Drastic Drop of Mink Fur Production Worldwide," June 30, 2016, www.furfreealliance.com/drastic-price-drop-mink-fur/.

16. Kitty Block and Sara Amundson, "Mink Fur Production Drops to Historic All-Time Low in the US," *The Humane Society of the United States*, July 28, 2021, blog.humanesociety.org/2021/07/us-mink-fur-production-drops-to-historic-low.html. Additionally, the United States mink trade's value dropped to $47 million, which is a 19 percent decline from 2019, the recorded lowest.

17. Block and Amundson, "Mink Fur Production Drops to Historic All-Time Low in the US."

18. See Humane Society International, "The Fur Trade," accessed February 14, 2022, www.hsi.org/news-media/fur-trade/. The towns of Wellesley and Weston in Massachusetts and Ann Arbor, Michigan banned the sale of fur in 2020 and 2021, and more cities and states in the United States look to follow suit.

19. See Cal. Stat. Ch. 764 § 2023.

20. Animal Wellness Action, "U.S. House Passes Sweeping Ban on Mink Farming Citing Cruelty and Contagion Risks," *GlobeNewswire*, February 04, 2022, www.globenewswire.com/news-release/2022/02/04/2379463/0/en/U-S-House-Passes-Sweeping-Ban-on-Mink-Farming-Citing-Cruelty-and-Contagion-Risks.html.

21. PETA, "PETA Is Taking Down Fur, and These Fur Bans Are Helping Us Secure Victory," February 3, 2022, www.peta.org/features/fur-bans-fur-free-future/.

22. NPR, "Israel Has Become the 1st Country to Ban the Sale of Most Fur Clothing," June 14, 2021, www.npr.org/2021/06/14/1006279660/israel-has-become-the-first-country-to-ban-the-sale-of-fur-clothing.

23. Ana Colón, "All the Fashion Brands that have Banned Fur," *Glamour*, October 22, 2019, www.glamour.com/gallery/fashion-brands-that-have-banned-fur. The rise of fake fur also has been accompanied by some efforts to sell real (but inexpensive) fur as fake fur. Wayne Pacelle, "Breaking News: Fur Flies with New HSUS Exposé of Retailers Selling Real Fur as Fake," *A Humane World*, August 9, 2016, blog.humanesociety.org/2016/08/breaking-news-fur-flies-new-hsus-expose-retailers-selling-real-fur-fake.html.

24. Allyssia Alleyne, "Gucci Will Go Fur-Free in 2018," *CNN*, October 12, 2017, www.cnn.com/style/article/gucci-fur-free/index.html.

25. Leah Dolan, "Luxury Fashion Giant Kering Bans Fur Across All Its Businesses," *CNN*, September 24, 2021, www.cnn.com/style/article/kering-bans-fur/index.html.

26. Oscar Holland, "Dolce & Gabbana to Drop Animal Fur in Favor of 'Eco' Alternative," *CNN*, February 1, 2022, www.cnn.com/style/article/dolce-gabbana-fur-ban/index.html. Dolce and Gabbana has faced increased demand to ban fur from its collections as brands such as Prada, Chanel, and Burberry have pledged to ban fur in recent years. Jacopo Prisco, "Prada to Go fur-free in 2020," *CNN*, May 22, 2019, edition.cnn.com/style/article/prada-goes-fur-free-2020/index.html; Lianne Kolirin, "Chanel Bans Fur and Exotic Animal Skins," *CNN*, December 4, 2018, www.cnn.com

/style/article/chanel-fur-ban-scli-intl/index.html; Bard Wilkinson, "Burberry Bans Destroying Unsold Goods and Using Fur," *CNN*, September 6, 2018, www.cnn.com/style/article/fashion-burberry-environment-intl/index.html.

27. Holland, "Dolce & Gabbana to Drop Animal Fur in Favor of 'Eco' Alternative."

28. David Williams, "Macy's and Bloomingdale's Will Stop Selling Fur in 2021," *CNN*, October 22, 2019, www.cnn.com/2019/10/22/business/macys-fur-free-trnd/index.html.

29. Reuters, "Elle Magazine Bans Fur in All its Titles," *CNN*, December 2, 2021, www.cnn.com/style/article/elle-magazine-bans-fur-scli-intl/index.html; Rob Picheta, "London Fashion Week Drops Fur from Runway," *CNN*, September 7, 2018, www.cnn.com/style/article/london-fashion-week-drops-fur-intl/index.html.

30. See, e.g., Georgia Alexia Benjou, "8 Ways to Wear This Season's Sassiest Trend: Faux Fur," *5280*, October 23, 2017, www.5280.com/2017/10/winter-2017-trend-faux-fur/.

31. Annachiara Biondi, "The Fur Industry is Fighting Back," *Vogue Business*, December 18, 2019, www.voguebusiness.com/sustainability/materials-fur-industry-faux-vegan-prada-chanel-yoox-net-a-porter-burberry.

32. Kate Abnett, "Inside the Growing Global Fur Industry," *Business of Fashion*, June 7, 2015, www.businessoffashion.com/articles/news-analysis/inside-the-growing-global-fur-industry/.

33. Alex Williams, "Fur Is Back in Fashion and Debate," *New York Times*, July 3, 2015, www.nytimes.com/2015/07/05/fashion/fur-is-back-in-fashion-and-debate.html.

34. Biondi, "The Fur Industry is Fighting Back." The industry argues that real fur's long lifecycle, biodegradable nature, and the absence of harsh chemicals in its processing is proof of its inherent sustainability compared to faux fur, which is commonly made of synthetic materials such as modacrylic or polyester. However, studies finding high levels of alkylphenols, alkylphenol ethoxylates, and formaldehyde in selected fur samples dispute the industry's sustainability claims. See Bremer Umweltinstitut, "Report," accessed February 14, 2022, www.furfreealliance.com/wp-content/uploads/2016/01/ToxicFur_Bremer-Umweltinstitut.pdf.

35. The National Association for Biomedical Research is a nonprofit organization that advocates for the use of animals in medical research.

36. Notably, in the years leading up to the passage of this bill, the American Medical Association—a powerful lobbying group on behalf of the animal enterprises—ranked second in contributions to federal candidates. Federal Election Commission, "PAC Activity Rebounds in 1991–1992 Election Cycle: Unusual Nature of Contests Seen as Reason," April 29, 1993.

37. Animal Enterprise Protection Act, Pub. L. No. 102–346, 106 Stat. 928 (1992) (codified as amended by 2006 Animal Enterprise Terrorism Act at 18 U.S.C. § 43 [2020]). The Animal Enterprise Terrorism Act has been officially renamed under § 43 as "Force, violence, and threats involving animal enterprises." For practical purposes, it is referred to as "AETA" in this chapter.

38. Animal Enterprise Protection Act, § 1(a), 106 Stat. at 928.

39. Animal Enterprise Protection Act, § 1(a), 106 Stat. at 928.

40. Animal Enterprise Protection Act, § 1(a), 106 Stat. at 928–29. Fiber production here refers to "animal fibers," including silk, hair, fur, wool, and feathers. See also H.R. Rep. No. 102–498(II), at 4 (1992), reprinted in 1992 U.S.C.C.A.N. 816: "The ambiguous term 'physical disruption' is not defined, and could be construed to make criminal whistleblowing activity that results in a facility being shut down by regulators or protests. At best, this would have chilled whistleblowing; at worst, it could have resulted in actual prosecutions of whistleblowers."

41. See, generally, "ALEC Exposed," *Center for Media and Democracy*, accessed February 14, 2022, www.alecexposed.org.

42. Animal Enterprise Terrorism Act, Pub. L. No. 109–374, 120 Stat. 2652, 2652 (2006) (codified at 18 U.S.C. § 43).

43. 152 Cong. Rec. 9254, 9254 (2006).

44. 152 Cong. Rec. 9254, 9255 (2006).

45. Force, Violence, and Threats Involving Animal Enterprises, 18 U.S.C. § 43(e)(1) (2020).

46. Force, Violence, and Threats Involving Animal Enterprises, 18 U.S.C. § 43(a)(1).

47. Force, Violence, and Threats Involving Animal Enterprises, 18 U.S.C. § 43(d)(3)(A).

48. "Animal Enterprise Terrorism Act (AETA): Introduction," *Civil Liberties Defense Center*, April 24, 2014, cldc.org/animal-enterprise-terrorism-act-aeta/.

49. United States v. Johnson, No. 14-CR-390, 2015 WL 1058087 (N.D. Ill. Mar. 5, 2015).

50. See Johnson v. United States, 875 F.3d 360, 364 (7th Cir. 2017).

51. See Dean Kuipers, *Operation Bite Back* (New York: Bloomsbury USA, 2009).

52. In 2010, around 2.84 million mink pelts were produced. In 2014, that number grew to 3.76 million. See National Agricultural Statistics Service, "Pelt Production Down 49 Percent," July 22, 2021, downloads.usda.library.cornell.edu/usda-esmis/files/2227mp65f/8c97mm649/hd76sx594/mink0721.pdf.

53. See "Anti-Whistleblower ('Ag-Gag') Legislation," *Animal Welfare Institute*, accessed February 14, 2022, awionline.org/content/anti-whistleblower-legislation.

54. Hearing before the House Agricultural Affairs Committee, 2014 Leg., 2d Reg. Sess. 6, 21 (Idaho 2014).

55. Louis D. Brandeis, "What Publicity Can Do," *Harper's Weekly* (1913): 10.

56. Animal Legal Defense Fund v. Otter, 118 F. Supp. 3d. 1195, 1211 (D. Idaho 2015).

57. Upton Sinclair, *The Autobiography of Upton Sinclair* (1962), 109.

58. Alan K. Chen and Justin Marceau, "High Value Lies, Ugly Truths, and the First Amendment," *Vanderbilt Law Review* 68 (2015): 1457 (compiling sources regarding Sinclair's work).

59. See Stephen J. Hedges, "Beef Recall is Largest in History," *Chicago Tribune*, February 17, 2008, www.chicagotribune.com/news/ct-xpm-2008-02-18-0802170492-story.html.

60. Leading scholar Timothy Pachirat challenges this quote as empirically unfounded. Pachirat's research shows that at least in certain contexts, transparency

does not lead to public disgust or serve as an impetus for changing dietary practices. For these purposes, it suffices to note that industry experts made ag-gag laws a legislative priority, suggesting they see financial value in the enactment of such secrecy provisions.

61. Specifically, the court found that the law's prohibition on lying to gain entry to an agricultural facility and filming once inside was a violation of the First Amendment.

62. Animal Legal Defense Fund v. Herbert, 263 F. Supp. 3d 1193, 1213 (D. Utah 2017).

63. Animal Legal Defense Fund v. Otter, 118 F. Supp. 3d. 1195, 1201 (D. Idaho 2015).

64. Animal Legal Defense Fund v. Otter, 118 F. Supp. 3d. 1195, 1201 (D. Idaho 2015).

65. See "Anti-Whistleblower ('Ag-Gag') Legislation."

66. Scarce, *Eco-Warriors: Understanding the Radical Environmental Movement*, 129–30.

67. Steven D. Zansberg, "Recent High-Profile Cases Highlight the Need for Greater Procedural Protections for Freedom of the Press," *Communications Lawyer* 33, no. 2 (Fall 2017): 7–14, dx.doi.org/10.2139/ssrn.3067163.

68. See Beef Products Inc. v. American Broadcasting Companies, Inc., 949 F. Supp. 2d 936 (D.S.D. 2013).

69. David Connett, "Lynx Anti-Fur Group Faces Extinction Over Libel Loss," *Independent*, December 24, 1992, www.independent.co.uk/news/uk/lynx-antifur-group-faces-extinction-over-libel-loss-1565298.html.

70. Justin Marceau, *Beyond Cages: Animal Law and Criminal Punishment* (Cambridge: Cambridge University Press, 2019).

71. There are those who would prefer a view of speech protections that empowers the courts to select low-value speech and deem it unworthy of protection. The Court has, for example, allowed legislatures to prohibit "fighting words," so why not, some would argue, just let courts expand that category of low-value speech to include advocating harm to animals? It is this sort of balancing, or ad hoc decisions, about what speech warrants protection that this chapter rejects as a matter of principle. But moreover, it is unlikely in the extreme that animals would consistently fare well under such an ad hoc balancing approach to determining when speech or expression ought to be protected.

72. See, e.g., Truth About Fur, "How Fur Is Produced in 5 Easy Steps," accessed September 27, 2017, www.truthaboutfur.com/en.

73. Fur is Green, "Animal Welfare: Fur Farming," accessed February 15, 2022, www.furisgreen.com/animal-welfare/fur-farming/.

74. Truth About Fur, "The Ethics of Fur," accessed October 30, 2017, www.truthaboutfur.com/en/ethics-of-fur.

75. Truth About Fur, "5 Reasons Why We Must Wear Leather and Fur," October 12, 2016, www.truthaboutfur.com/blog/5-reasons-must-wear-leather-fur/.

76. Fur Commission USA, "Natural Fur—The Responsible Choice," accessed February 15, 2022, furcommissionx.wpengine.com/fur-fashion-posts/natural-fur-the-responsible-choice/.

77. Fur Commission USA, "Undercover Videos: Concerned Citizens or Shameless Self Promoters?," accessed October 5, 2017, furcommission.com/undercover-videos-concerned-citizens-or-shameless-self-promoters/.

78. To the extent that editing made the message conveyed by the video inaccurate or grossly misleading, then the edited video might be unprotected as defamatory.

79. Carolyn Y. Johnson, "Antiabortion Group Posts Another Video Attacking Planned Parenthood," *Washington Post*, August 4, 2015, www.washingtonpost.com/news/wonk/wp/2015/08/04/antiabortion-group-posts-another-video-attacking-planned-parenthood/.

80. Aubree Poole, "California: New Bill Would Limit Free Speech to Protect Planned Parenthood, *Washington Examiner*," June 7, 2016, www.washingtonexaminer.com/red-alert-politics/california-new-bill-limit-free-speech-protect-planned-parenthood.

81. Alexandra Desanctis, "California Governor Signs Bill to Criminalize Whistleblowing," *National Review*, September 30, 2016, www.nationalreview.com/corner/california-whistleblower-law-governor-brown-signs-bill-criminalizing-whistleblowing/.

82. Associated Press, "Planned Parenthood Sues Anti-Abortion Activists Over Undercover Videos," *Los Angeles Times*, January 14, 2016, www.latimes.com/local/california/la-me-planned-parenthood-lawsuit-20160114-story.html.

83. Michelle Goldberg, "Planned Parenthood Is Going on the Offensive with Massive Lawsuit," *Slate*, January 14, 2016, slate.com/human-interest/2016/01/planned-parenthood-is-going-on-the-offensive-with-massive-lawsuit.html. Notably, a federal judge in California actually imposed a prior restraint on the distribution of undercover video footage pursuant to Planned Parenthood's request. This tactic could be adopted by animal exploiters seeking to avoid the release of undercover videos filmed in slaughterhouses. Strikingly, the litigation involving investigations of Planned Parenthood has already yielded federal decisions limiting the reach of the First Amendment in ways that are relevant to ag-gag type restrictions. See, e.g., *Planned Parenthood Federation of America, Inc. v. Center for Medical Progress*, 402 F. Supp. 3d 615, 684 (N.D. Cal. 2019) (describing investigations designed to create "public outrage" or to assist with "fundraising" as outside of the scope of speech protections).

84. Planned Parenthood Federation of America, Inc. v. Center for Medical Progress, 402 F. Supp. 3d 615, 726–727 (N.D. Cal. 2019).

85. Sabrina Tavernise, "Planned Parenthood Awarded $2 Million in Lawsuit Over Secret Videos," *New York Times*, November 15, 2019, www.nytimes.com/2019/11/15/us/planned-parenthood-lawsuit-secret-videos.html.

86. Planned Parenthood Federation of America, Inc. v. Center for Medical Progress, 402 F. Supp. 3d 615, 726–727 (N.D. Cal. 2019).

87. For this appeal, Justin Marceau, on behalf of free-speech scholars and animal-advocacy organizations, filed an amicus brief in support of neither party, with "an interest in preserving robust constitutional protections for speech (and the

precursors of speech) and for those who gather news and report on matters of public concern." Brief of Amici Curiae Free Speech Scholars and Animal-Advocacy Organizations in Support of Neither Party at 1, *Planned Parenthood Federation of America, Inc. v. Center for Medical Progress* (9th Cir. March 5, 2021) (Nos. 20–16068, 20–16070, 20–16773, & 20–16820). Amici argued that to continue the American tradition of essential journalism conducted using undercover techniques, individuals must remain capable of using undercover methods to investigate and report on matters that might otherwise remain inaccessible or unavailable to the public. Brief of Amici Curiae Free Speech Scholars and Animal-Advocacy Organizations in Support of Neither Party at 1–2, *Planned Parenthood Federation of America, Inc. v. Center for Medical Progress* (9th Cir. March 5, 2021) (Nos. 20–16068, 20–16070, 20–16773, & 20–16820). They additionally asserted that as the "First Amendment protects rights essential to permit the individual citizen to effectively participate in and contribute to our republican system of self-government, and to render public debate well informed—capable of advancing knowledge, discovering truth, and informing rational decisions," the district court's decision raises many grave First Amendment issues. Brief of Amici Curiae Free Speech Scholars and Animal-Advocacy Organizations in Support of Neither Party at 2, *Planned Parenthood Federation of America, Inc. v. Center for Medical Progress* (9th Cir. March 5, 2021) (Nos. 20–16068, 20–16070, 20–16773, & 20–16820).

88. Sabrina Tavernise, "Planned Parenthood Awarded $2 Million in Lawsuit Over Secret Videos."

89. 559 U.S. 460 (2010).

90. The point here is not that a ban on wearing fur would necessarily be unconstitutional. Assuming the prohibition implicated expressive conduct, the ban could still be upheld under U.S. law if some form of heightened scrutiny were satisfied. And in many ways, this is a key point. If one is confident that the protection of animals should be more robustly recognized in speech and expression law, then legal research should direct more effort towards the science and social psychology that could demonstrate a compelling government interest in prohibiting certain expressive practices that involve injury to animals.

91. See J. M. Balkin, "Ideological Drift and the Struggle over Meaning," *Connecticut Law Review* 25 (1993): 869, 871.

92. Balkin, "Ideological Drift," 870; see also David E. Pozen, "Transparency's Ideological Drift," *Yale Law Journal* 128 (2018): 106 (explaining that "ideological drift occurs" if "1. at Time One, an idea tends to be associated with policy outcomes or reform agendas that have political orientation *X*; and 2. at Time Two, the idea becomes substantially (though not necessarily exclusively) associated with policy outcomes or reform agendas that have political orientation not-*X*").

93. Balkin, "Ideological Drift," 871.

94. Balkin, "Ideological Drift," 874.

95. See, e.g., Balkin, "Ideological Drift," 887: "It is the job of the lawyer to argue in one way for client *A* on Monday, and in the opposite way for client *B* on Tuesday."

96. See Media, Freedom, and Information Access Clinic, "Data Gathering and the Right to Petition," *Yale Law School*, January 2, 2019, law.yale.edu/mfia/case-disclosed/data-gathering-and-right-petition.

97. To briefly recap the central point: We take as a starting point, though we concede it is contestable, that free-speech principles can be applied relatively evenly. Thus, a narrow view of speech rights for those who seek to promote the harm of animals will mean a narrow set of speech rights for animal activists as well. There are, then, two crudely simplified options: (a) recognize a broad set of speech rights for both animal activists and animal exploiters, or (b) recognize a very limited set of protections for those who seek to promote animal harm and understand that pro-animal speech will also be diminished such that legislative restraints on it might be tolerated. There will be hard questions to answer about where the appropriate lines should be drawn, but this brief chapter simply suggests that given the range of speech restrictions that animal activists have faced, the animal rights movement should think more carefully about the trade-offs involved in arguing for narrow or broad conceptions of expression rights.

REFERENCES

Abnett, Kate. "Inside the Growing Global Fur Industry." *Business of Fashion*, June 7, 2015. www.businessoffashion.com/articles/news-analysis/inside-the-growing-global-fur-industry/.

Adams, Bill. *Against Extinction: The Story of Conservation*. New York: Earthscan, 2004.

"ALEC Exposed." *Center for Media and Democracy*. Accessed February 14, 2022. www.alecexposed.org.

Alleyne, Allyssia. "Gucci Will Go Fur-Free in 2018." *CNN*, October 12, 2017. www.cnn.com/style/article/gucci-fur-free/index.html.

"Animal Enterprise Terrorism Act (AETA): Introduction." *Civil Liberties Defense Center*, April 24, 2014. cldc.org/animal-enterprise-terrorism-act-aeta/.

Animal Wellness Action. "U.S. House Passes Sweeping Ban on Mink Farming Citing Cruelty and Contagion Risks." *GlobeNewswire*, February 04, 2022. www.globenewswire.com/news-release/2022/02/04/2379463/0/en/U-S-House-Passes-Sweeping-Ban-on-Mink-Farming-Citing-Cruelty-and-Contagion-Risks.html.

"Anti-Whistleblower ('Ag-Gag') Legislation." *Animal Welfare Institute*. Accessed February 14, 2022, awionline.org/content/anti-whistleblower-legislation.

Associated Press. "Planned Parenthood Sues Anti-Abortion Activists Over Undercover Videos." *Los Angeles Times*, January 14, 2016. www.latimes.com/local/california/la-me-planned-parenthood-lawsuit-20160114-story.html.

Balkin, J. M. "Ideological Drift and the Struggle over Meaning." *Connecticut Law Review* 25 (1993): 869–891.

Benjou, Georgia Alexia. "8 Ways to Wear This Season's Sassiest Trend: Faux Fur." *5280*, October 23, 2017. www.5280.com/2017/10/winter-2017-trend-faux-fur/.

Biondi, Annachiara. "The Fur Industry is Fighting Back." *Vogue Business*, December 18, 2019. www.voguebusiness.com/sustainability/materials-fur-industry-faux-vegan-prada-chanel-yoox-net-a-porter-burberry.

Block, Kitty, and Amundson, Sara. "Mink Fur Production Drops to Historic All-Time Low in the US." *The Humane Society of the United States*, July 28, 2021. blog.humanesociety.org/2021/07/us-mink-fur-production-drops-to-historic-low.html.

Bousquet, Kristen. "31 Celebrities Who Got Naked for PETA." *StyleCaster*, February 27, 2017. stylecaster.com/celebrities-who-got-naked-for-peta-ads/.

Brandeis, Louis D. "What Publicity Can Do." *Harper's Weekly* (1913).

Carlos, Ann M., and Frank D. Lewis. "The Economic History of the Fur Trade: 1670 to 1870." Economic History Association. Accessed September 10, 2017. eh.net/encyclopedia/the-economic-history-of-the-fur-trade-1670-to-1870/.

Chen, Alan K., and Justin Marceau. "High Value Lies, Ugly Truths, and the First Amendment." *Vanderbilt Law Review* 68 (2015): 1435–1507.

Colón, Ana. "All the Fashion Brands that have Banned Fur." *Glamour*, October 22, 2019. www.glamour.com/gallery/fashion-brands-that-have-banned-fur.

Connett, David. "Lynx Anti-Fur Group Faces Extinction Over Libel Loss." *Independent*, December 24, 1992. www.independent.co.uk/news/uk/lynx-antifur-group-faces-extinction-over-libel-loss-1565298.html.

Desanctis, Alexandra. "California Governor Signs Bill to Criminalize Whistleblowing." *National Review*, September 30, 2016. www.nationalreview.com/corner/440611/california-whistleblower-law-governor-brown-signs-bill-criminalizing-whistleblowing.

Dolan, Leah. "Luxury Fashion Giant Kering Bans Fur Across All Its Businesses." *CNN*, September 24, 2021. www.cnn.com/style/article/kering-bans-fur/index.html.

Federal Election Commission. "PAC Activity Rebounds in 1991–1992 Election Cycle: Unusual Nature of Contests Seen as Reason." April 29, 1993.

Fur Commission USA. "Natural Fur—The Responsible Choice." Accessed February 15, 2022. furcommissionx.wpengine.com/fur-fashion-posts/natural-fur-the-responsible-choice/.

———. "Undercover Videos: Concerned Citizens or Shameless Self Promoters?" Accessed October 5, 2017. furcommission.com/undercover-videos-concerned-citizens-or-shameless-self-promoters/.

Fur Free Alliance. "Drastic Drop of Mink Fur Production Worldwide." June 30, 2016. www.furfreealliance.com/drastic-price-drop-mink-fur/

Fur is Green. "Animal Welfare: Fur Farming." Accessed February 15, 2022. www.furisgreen.com/animal-welfare/fur-farming/.

Goldberg, Michelle. "Planned Parenthood Is Going on the Offensive with Massive Lawsuit." *Slate*, January 14, 2016. www.slate.com/blogs/xx_factor/2016/01/14/planned_parenthood_is_going_on_the_offensive_with_massive_lawsuit.html.

Hearing before the House Agricultural Affairs Committee. 2014 Leg., 2d Reg. Sess. 6 (Idaho 2014).

Hedges, Stephen J. "Beef Recall is Largest in History." *Chicago Tribune*, February 17, 2008. www.chicagotribune.com/news/ct-xpm-2008-02-18-0802170492-story.html.

Holland, Oscar. "Dolce & Gabbana to Drop Animal Fur in Favor of 'Eco' Alternative." *CNN*, February 1, 2022. www.cnn.com/style/article/dolce-gabbana-fur-ban/index.html.

Humane Society International. "The Fur Trade." Accessed February 14, 2022. www.hsi.org/news-media/fur-trade/.

Johnson, Carolyn Y. "Antiabortion Group Posts Another Video Attacking Planned Parenthood." *Washington Post*, August 4, 2015. www.washingtonpost.com/news/wonk/wp/2015/08/04/antiabortion-group-posts-another-video-attacking-planned-parenthood/.

Kolirin, Lianne. "Chanel Bans Fur and Exotic Animal Skins." *CNN*, December 4, 2018. www.cnn.com/style/article/chanel-fur-ban-scli-intl/index.html.

Kuipers, Dean. *Operation Bite Back*. New York: Bloomsbury USA, 2009.

Last Chance for Animals. "Fur-Free Friday: A Historical Perspective." Accessed September 15, 2017. www.lcanimal.org/index.php/campaigns/fur/fur-trade-facts-2.

Laurance, Jeremy. "Health: Get Warm Fur Winter and Don't Be a Dumb Animal." *Independent*, October 13, 1998. www.independent.co.uk/arts-entertainment/health-get-warm-fur-winter-and-dont-be-a-dumb-animal-1177997.html.

Lewis, John E. Deputy Assistant Director of Federal Bureau of Investigation. "Before the Senate Judiciary Committee Washington DC." May 18, 2004. archives.fbi.gov/archives/news/testimony/animal-rights-extremism-and-ecoterrorism.

Marceau, Justin. *Beyond Cages: Animal Law and Criminal Punishment*. Cambridge: Cambridge University Press, 2019.

Media, Freedom, and Information Access Clinic. "Data Gathering and the Right to Petition." *Yale Law School*, January 2, 2019. law.yale.edu/mfia/case-disclosed/data-gathering-and-right-petition.

National Agricultural Statistics Service, "Pelt Production Down 49 Percent," July 22, 2021, downloads.usda.library.cornell.edu/usda-esmis/files/2227mp65f/8c97mm649/hd76sx594/mink0721.pdf.

NPR. "Israel Has Become the 1st Country to Ban the Sale of Most Fur Clothing." June 14, 2021. www.npr.org/2021/06/14/1006279660/israel-has-become-the-first-country-to-ban-the-sale-of-fur-clothing.

Oliver, Sara. "PETA Stormed Runway Shows: How Fur Went out of Style." *PETA*, February 11, 2022. www.peta.org/blog/peta-how-fur-went-out-of-style/.

Pacelle, Wayne. "Breaking News: Fur Flies with New HSUS Exposé of Retailers Selling Real Fur as Fake." *A Humane World*, August 9, 2016. blog.humanesociety.org/2016/08/breaking-news-fur-flies-new-hsus-expose-retailers-selling-real-fur-fake.html.

PETA. "PETA Is Taking Down Fur, and These Fur Bans Are Helping Us Secure Victory." December 22, 2021. www.peta.org/features/fur-bans-fur-free-future/.

Picheta, Rob. "London Fashion Week Drops Fur from Runway." *CNN*, September 7, 2018. www.cnn.com/style/article/london-fashion-week-drops-fur-intl/index.html.

Poole, Aubree. "California: New Bill Would Limit Free Speech to Protect Planned Parenthood. *Washington Examiner*," June 7, 2016. www.washingtonexaminer.com/red-alert-politics/california-new-bill-limit-free-speech-protect-planned-parenthood.

Pozen, David E. "Transparency's Ideological Drift." *Yale Law Journal* 128 (2018): 100–165.

Prisco, Jacopo. "Prada to Go fur-free in 2020." *CNN*, May 22, 2019. edition.cnn.com/style/article/prada-goes-fur-free-2020/index.html.

Reuters, "Elle Magazine Bans Fur in All its Titles." *CNN*, December 2, 2021. www.cnn.com/style/article/elle-magazine-bans-fur-scli-intl/index.html.

Scarce, Rik. *Eco-Warriors: Understanding the Radical Environmental Movement*. Walnut Creek, CA: Left Coast, 2006.

Sinclair, Upton. *The Autobiography of Upton Sinclair* (1962).

Skov, Lise. "The Return of the Fur Coat: A Commodity Chain Perspective." *Current Sociology* 53, no. 1 (2005): 9–32. doi:10.1177/0011392105048286.

Tavernise, Sabrina. "Planned Parenthood Awarded $2 Million in Lawsuit Over Secret Videos." *New York Times*, November 15, 2019. www.nytimes.com/2019/11/15/us/planned-parenthood-lawsuit-secret-videos.html.

Truth About Fur. "The Ethics of Fur." Accessed October 30, 2017. www.truthaboutfur.com/en/ethics-of-fur.

———. "5 Reasons Why We Must Wear Leather and Fur." October 12, 2016. www.truthaboutfur.com/blog/5-reasons-must-wear-leather-fur/.

———. "How Fur Is Produced in 5 Easy Steps." Accessed September 27, 2017. www.truthaboutfur.com/en.

Umweltinstitut, Bremer. "Report." Accessed February 14, 2022. www.furfreealliance.com/wp-content/uploads/2016/01/ToxicFur_Bremer-Umweltinstitut.pdf.

U.S. Department of Justice and U.S. Department of Agriculture. *Report to Congress on the Extent and Effects of Domestic and International Terrorism on Animal Enterprises*. October 1993.

Wilkinson, Bard. "Burberry Bans Destroying Unsold Goods and Using Fur." *CNN*, September 6, 2018. www.cnn.com/style/article/fashion-burberry-environment-intl/index.html.

Williams, Alex. "Fur Is Back in Fashion and Debate." *New York Times*, July 3, 2015. www.nytimes.com/2015/07/05/fashion/fur-is-back-in-fashion-and-debate.html.

Williams, David. "Macy's and Bloomingdale's Will Stop Selling Fur in 2021." *CNN*, October 22, 2019. www.cnn.com/2019/10/22/business/macys-fur-free-trnd/index.html.

Young, Peter. "How They Got In (Blast from the Past, Still Pertinent Today!)." *Animal Liberation Front*, December 9, 2021. animalliberationpressoffice.org-/NAALPO/2019/12/09/how-they-got-in-blast-from-the-past-still-pertinent-today/.

Zansberg, Steven D. "Recent High-Profile Cases Highlight the Need for Greater Procedural Protections for Freedom of the Press." *Communications Lawyer* 33, no. 2 (Fall 2017): 7–14. dx.doi.org/10.2139/ssrn.3067163.

LEGAL AUTHORITIES

152 Cong. Rec. 9254 (2006).

Animal Enterprise Protection Act, Pub. L. No. 109–374, 18 U.S.C.A. § 43 (1992).

Animal Enterprise Terrorism Act, Pub. L. No. 109–374, 18 U.S.C. § 43 (2006).
Animal Legal Defense Fund v. Otter, 118 F. Supp. 3d. 1195 (D. Idaho 2015).
Animal Legal Defense Fund v. Herbert, 263 F. Supp. 3d 1193 (D. Utah 2017).
Beef Products Inc. v. American Broadcasting Companies, Inc., 949 F. Supp. 2d 936 (D.S.D. 2013).
Brief of Amici Curiae Free Speech Scholars and Animal-Advocacy Organizations in Support of Neither Party, *Planned Parenthood Federation of America, Inc. v. Center for Medical Progress* (9th Cir. March 5, 2021) (Nos. 20–16068, 20–16070, 20–16773, & 20–16820).
Cal. Stat. Ch. 764 § 2023.
H.R. Rep. No. 102–498(II) (1992).
Johnson v. United States, 875 F.3d 360 (7th Cir. 2017).
Planned Parenthood Federation of America, Inc. v. Center for Medical Progress, 402 F. Supp. 3d 615 (N.D. Cal. 2019).
United States v. Johnson, No. 14-CR-390, 2015 WL 1058087 (N.D. Ill. Mar. 5, 2015).
United States v. Stevens, 559 U.S. 460 (2010).

Chapter 17

The Myth That "Fur Is Green" and the Real Impact of the Fur Industry on the Environment

Kimberly Moore

Research shows that "green" labels yield greater profits. A global study conducted by Nielsen in 2014 found that consumers across sixty countries are willing to pay more for products from companies that are committed to positive social and environmental impact, with millennials being the most willing to pay extra for sustainable products.[1] A national survey conducted by Tiller, LLC in 2014 revealed a growing concern for the environment across all generations in the United States, with more than eight in ten Americans willing to look for more opportunities to "go green" in 2015 and 60 percent of Americans committed to making "green" resolutions for 2015.[2] The rise in demand for environmentally friendly products has been met with an explosion of advertising claims that products are "green," "eco-friendly," "sustainable," and "natural," including many marketing claims that are deceptive and aimed solely at capturing profits from green marketing, and the fur industry is one of many industries that seek to profit from the public's growing concern for the environment. After the industry suffered declining profits in the 1990s, the emerging green economy arguably provided a lifeline to the fur industry, with manufacturers and trade groups promoting fur as a "green" and "eco-friendly" product. The marketing of fur as a green product enables consumers to both legitimize and justify their use of fur when they would not otherwise be inclined to do so.

DEFINING "ECO-FRIENDLY" PRODUCTS AND IDENTIFYING GREENWASHING

Background

In the most general terms, "eco-friendly" means not harmful to the environment,[3] but there are currently no standard, universal definitions for the terms "green," "sustainable," "natural," and "environmentally friendly" for clothing. The lack of uniformity creates enormous financial incentives for manufacturers and industries to promote products using vague terms and to engage in "greenwashing," a term that refers to deceptive or false environmental claims in advertising, where marketing is used to promote the perception that products are environmentally friendly,[4] or where marketing is used to promote green-based environmental initiatives or images when an entity actually operates in a way that is damaging to the environment.[5] Based on the enormous number of "green" advertisements that we see today, it is clear that tremendous resources are being spent claiming that products are green and environmentally friendly, but how do we know if an industry, like the fur industry, is engaging in greenwashing?

The Greenwashing Report

TerraChoice Environmental Marketing, Inc., now part of the Underwriters Laboratories global network, evaluated thousands of products for their environmental claims and concluded in a 2010 report that greenwashing is still "rampant," with over 95 percent of "green" products committing at least one of the seven "Sins of Greenwashing": (1) the "sin of the hidden trade-off" (suggesting that a product is "green" based on "an unreasonably narrow set of attributes without attention to other important environmental issues," such as water and air pollution and greenhouse gas emissions); (2) the "sin of no proof" (claims that "cannot be substantiated by easily accessible supporting information or by a reliable third party certification"); (3) the "sin of vagueness" (claims that are "so poorly defined or broad" that they are likely to be misunderstood by consumers); (4) the "sin of irrelevance" ("an environmental claim that may be truthful but is unimportant or unhelpful"); (5) the "sin of lesser of two evils" (claims that may be true but that distract consumers from the larger environmental impact); (6) the "sin of fibbing" (false environmental claims); and (7) the "sin of worshiping false labels" (giving the impression that a third party has endorsed a product where no endorsement exists).[6]

Updated Green Guidelines

TerraChoice's greenwashing report was highly influential. Two years after the report was issued, the US Federal Trade Commission (FTC) issued updated guidelines for the use of environmental marketing claims (the "Green Guides") in an effort to halt unfair or deceptive marketing claims.[7] The FTC's green guidelines do not preempt US federal, state, or local laws but rather reflect the FTC's current views about environmental claims, although the FTC can undertake an enforcement action under Section 5 of the Federal Trade Commission Act "if a marketer makes an environmental claim inconsistent with the guides."[8]

The Green Guides provide general principles that apply to all environmental marketing claims and state that marketing claims "should not overstate, directly or by implication, an environmental attribute or benefit" and should not "state or imply environmental benefits if the benefits are negligible."[9] These guidelines also state that "it is deceptive to misrepresent, either directly or by implication, that a product . . . offers a general environmental benefit"—for instance, by using such terms as "greener" or "eco-friendly"—since "unqualified environmental benefit claims are difficult to interpret" and are likely to convey the message that the product has "specific and far-reaching environmental benefits" with no adverse environmental impact.[10] Similar to the TerraChoice greenwashing report's position on the "sin of vagueness," the FTC agreed that claims that are so poorly defined or broad are likely to be misunderstood by consumers and are therefore considered deceptive under US federal law.

The Green Guides caution against making confusing "comparative environmental marketing claims," a concern similar to the "sin of lesser of two evils" described in the TerraChoice greenwashing report. The FTC's green guidelines state that any qualifications or disclosures should be "clear and prominent" to prevent deception and that any environmental claims should specifically identify to what they refer (e.g., a product, a product's packaging, a component of the product).[11] The Green Guides further state that "it is deceptive to mispresent, directly or by implication, that a product . . . is degradable, [or] biodegradable" and that unqualified degradable claims "should have competent and reliable scientific evidence that the entire item will completely break down and return to nature (i.e., decompose into elements found in nature) within a reasonably short period of time after customary disposal."[12] The FTC's guidelines also provide that it is deceptive to indicate "that a product . . . is made with renewable materials" unless marketers "have substantiation for all their express and reasonably implied claims" and "clearly and prominently qualify their renewable materials claims."[13]

The Green Guides state that whether a claim is deceptive depends on "the net impression" of the advertisement or label.[14]

ENVIRONMENTAL MARKETING CLAIMS INVOLVING FUR

The fur industry makes broad and far-reaching environmental claims regarding fur and in doing so arguably commits the "sins of greenwashing" identified in the TerraChoice greenwashing report, with many of the environmental claims even being contrary to the general principles established by the FTC's Green Guides. The environmental claims at issue are analyzed in the following paragraphs.

Promotion of Fur as "Natural"

Fur trade associations, including the Fur Council of Canada and the International Fur Federation, an organization that represents the international fur industry, promote fur on their websites as a "green" and "natural" product.[15] Kopenhagen Fur, the Danish fur trade association, claims that fur is an excellent example of a "natural" resource,[16] the British Fur Trade Association too describes fur as a "natural" resource,[17] and the Hong Kong Fur Federation describes fur as the "natural" and "responsible" choice.[18] Although the FTC's Green Guides do not define "natural," consumers may interpret a marketing claim that fur is "natural" as meaning that the product is not chemically treated. In fact, a number of toxic chemicals must be used in order to preserve animal skins and prevent decay. According to a report published by the Humane Society of the United States, chemical and organic compounds are required to "dress" and "dye" fur and include formaldehyde, chromium, naphthalene, sulfuric acid, toluene, ammonia, chlorine, lead, copper, zinc, and chlorobenzene,[19] chemicals that are listed as causing cancer or other chronic human health effects, significant adverse acute human health effects, and/or significant adverse environmental effects under the US Environmental Protection Agency's Toxics Release Inventory Program.[20] The National Cancer Institute even warns that the EPA has designated formaldehyde as a probable human carcinogen.[21]

The tanning process used to preserve animal pelts and hides poses significant health risks to workers, particularly in places that lack environmental protection and worker safety standards. The World Health Organization has previously warned that tannery pollution threatens the health of a half-million Bangladesh residents, with a large number of tannery workers suffering from gastrointestinal, dermatological, and other diseases thought to be related to pollution, with 90 percent of workers dying before the age of fifty.[22] The World Health Organization has recently reported that 90 percent of individuals who live and work in the urban areas of Hazaribagh and Kamrangirchar, where toxic chemicals from tanneries are discharged into the air, streets, and river, also die before they reach the age of fifty, a report that received widespread media attention.[23] In 2012, Human Rights Watch produced a report titled *Toxic Tanneries*, which revealed unregulated industrial pollution of air, water, and soil, a de facto policy of non-implementation of environmental laws, dangerous working conditions, child labor, health issues and illnesses among local residents, and anecdotal evidence suggesting elevated cancer rates among workers working with chemicals.[24] In addition to the health risks for workers engaged in the production of fur, toxic chemicals including chrome VI (Hexavalent), chrome III (Trivalent), formaldehyde, and nonylphenol ethoxylate also have been discovered in fur trim on garments intended for children under the age of thirty-six months.[25] Based on the growing body of reports and scientific studies regarding the toxic chemicals used in the production of fur, as well as chemicals found to exist on furs after production, the promotion of fur as "natural" arguably commits a number of sins of greenwashing, including the sins of vagueness, no proof, and even fibbing. The claim that fur is "natural" is arguably deceptive under US federal law as well, based on principles set forth in the Green Guides, because it implies an unqualified general environmental benefit claim that is likely to be misunderstood by consumers.

Promotion of Fur as "Green" and "Environmentally Friendly"

Fur trade associations also promote fur on their websites as a "green" and "environmentally friendly" product. The International Fur Federation claims that fur is "environmentally-friendly" and "sustainable" and that using fur makes environmental sense because "to waste these beautiful furs would be disrespectful to the animals and environment that created them."[26] A claim that leaves consumers with the impression that furs are "wasted" if not worn is misleading because more than 85 percent of the global fur trade comes from fur-farmed animals who are not raised for food, such as minks and foxes.[27] The Fur Council of Canada claims that "fur is green" and promotes the use of fur as a "renewable and sustainable resource" that does not deplete populations of free animals or "damage the natural habitats that sustain them."[28] Fur Europe, the European fur trade association, promotes fur farming as "sustainable" because the industry contributes to "waste reduction" for the environment.[29] Kopenhagen Fur claims that fur farming is "respectful of the environment" and a renewable and sustainable resource.[30] The British

Fur Trade Association describes trapping as "an important conservation tool" and a "renewable and sustainable resource,"[31] while Fur Commission USA includes articles that promote fur under the heading of "Sustainability" on its website.

Fur farming, like agricultural factory farming, has been identified as an industry that is detrimental to the environment, in part due to animal waste that ends up in waterways. The David Suzuki Foundation studied the impact that the mink industry has on the freshwater lakes of Nova Scotia and found that lakes and rivers in parts of southwest Nova Scotia are under "serious threat," with several lakes "artificially eutrophied as a result of nutrient inputs from human activities, with some developing blue-green algae (cyanobacteria) blooms."[32] A 2013 water quality survey commissioned by Nova Scotia Environment to study lakes located within the Carleton River watershed areas of Digby and Yarmouth Counties, Nova Scotia, also revealed that a number of lakes were "seriously degraded, primarily with respect to high nutrient over-enrichment resulting in the development of high algal concentrations"—the result of "high phosphorus inputs resulting from releases emanating from mink farming operations."[33] Prior studies by Nova Scotia Environment showed "high algal concentrations" containing "species of cyanobacteria (blue-green algae), known to produce microcystins, a toxin that, under certain conditions, may be harmful to humans, livestock and wildlife."[34] The 2013 study found that the highest levels of phosphorus and nitrogen occur in regions where the highest concentration of mink farms is located.[35] Although mink farmers are required under new laws to take steps to reduce nutrient releases that can adversely impact waterways, there are concerns that such measures do not go far enough,[36] and in any case it is expected to require a considerable amount of time before improvements in water quality become apparent.[37]

Eutrophication is a serious environmental concern and, according to the EPA, a major cause of degradation of US waters. As the EPA describes, nutrient pollution from excess nitrogen and phosphorus is a "leading cause of degradation of U.S. water quality," causing depletion of dissolved oxygen that fish and other aquatic life need to survive and increasing "harmful algal blooms, which may endanger human health through the production of toxins that can contaminate recreational and drinking water resources."[38] According to the EPA, field and laboratory studies have "found the production of microcystin, a common cyanotoxin that is linked to human illness, to be strongly associated with nitrogen concentration."[39] The EPA describes nutrient pollution caused by excess nitrogen and phosphorus in the air and water as "one of America's most widespread, costly and challenging environmental problems"; it "has impacted many streams, rivers, lakes, bays and coastal waters . . . resulting in serious environmental and human health issues," and the EPA warns that some algal blooms "are harmful to humans because they produce elevated toxins and bacterial growth that can make people sick" if they consume contaminated food or water or come in contact with polluted water.[40] The EPA further warns that nutrient pollution in groundwater, which is used by millions of people in the United States for drinking water, can be harmful even at low levels and that "excess nitrogen in the atmosphere can produce pollutants such as ammonia . . . which can impair our ability to breathe, limit visibility and alter plant growth," as well as harm the health of forests, soils, and waterways when it comes back to earth from the atmosphere.[41] The EPA notes that the animal manure is one of the primary sources of nutrient pollution.[42]

In addition to animal waste, animal carcasses and chemical waste also pollute waterways. News of pollution from fur and leather industries has been reported in countries around the world where such industries exist. Rivers near Daying, known as "the home of furs in China," are reported to be so severely contaminated from fur and leather processing chemicals that the river water is brown and black.[43] In 2015, disturbing photographs emerged from Leningrad, Russia, of thousands of mink carcasses dumped near a fur farm, alongside a waterway.[44] Tanneries in India also have been severely criticized for polluting water in India, including the Ganges river, with heavy metals such as chromium, a chemical agent used in leather production.[45]

Independent research also concludes that using pelts and hides comes with a high environmental cost. In 2011, CE Delft released a groundbreaking independent research report on the environmental impact of mink fur production.[46] The CE Delft report analyzed the environmental impact of mink fur as compared to other common textiles, including cotton, polyester fabric, and polyacryl fabric, with regard to eighteen different environmental concerns: climate change, water depletion, minerals depletion, fossil depletion, ozone layer depletion, ionizing radiation, agricultural land occupation, urban land occupation, freshwater ecotoxicity, marine ecotoxicity, particulate matter formation, terrestrial ecotoxicity, freshwater eutrophication, marine eutrophication, terrestrial acidification, human toxicity, photochemical oxidant formation, and natural land transformation.[47] The 2011 CE Delft report concluded that in seventeen of the eighteen environmental impacts studied for the various textiles, mink fur scored worst in terms of its environmental impact, and that the environmental impact of mink fur was two to twenty-eight times higher than common textiles.[48]

The environmental costs of fur are so great that even the fashion industry itself is advocating for the use of more sustainable textiles, including innovative human-made fibers. The 2017 *Pulse of the Fashion Industry*, a report from Global Fashion Agenda and the Boston Consulting Group, focused in large part on environmental and sustainability issues as they relate to the fashion industry.[49] The report acknowledged that "the planet is already beyond its safe operating space in terms of climate change, waste pollution, changes in land use, and biochemical output" and recognized that the fashion industry's "present linear business model is an obvious contributor to stress on natural resources."[50] The authors concluded that of fourteen common fashion materials, animal products are among the most environmentally detrimental materials in terms of global warming, water scarcity, eutrophication, and abiotic resource depletion[51] and that synthetic leather has only a third of the environmental impact of cow leather.[52] The report also recommended establishing common standards for animal treatment "to guarantee the ethical treatment of animals, enabling them to live healthy lives without suffering from pain, fear or distress," and using more sustainable materials than animal skins.[53] The promotion of fur to consumers as "green" and "environmentally friendly" in the face of such overwhelming evidence to the contrary is nothing less than greenwashing by the fur industry.

Promotion of Fur as Not Using Endangered Species

The Fur Council of Canada claims that "wearing fur also helps to protect nature" and that "absolutely no endangered species are used,"[54] but trapping is known to catch nontarget species, including companion animals,[55] endangered species,[56] and even children.[57] According to a 2008 report published by the American Veterinary Medical Association, nontarget animals account for up to 67 percent of total trapped animals.[58] In testimony to Congress, a former federal trapper stated, "My trapping records show that for each target animal I trapped, about two unwanted individuals were caught."[59] A claim that "no endangered species are used" that fails to take into account the endangered animals who are inadvertently caught by trapping arguably commits the "sin of the hidden trade-off" and is arguably inconsistent with the general principle in the FTC's Green Guides that an environmental marketing claim "should not overstate . . . an environmental attribute or benefit."[60]

Promotion of Fur as "Biodegradable" and Promotion of Real Fur over Faux Fur

To promote fur, trade groups claim that fur is "biodegradable" and that faux fur is detrimental to the environment.[61] Mark Oaten, CEO of the International Fur Federation, claims that "while the fake furs sit on landfills alongside plastic rubbish bags poisoning the world, natural fur either stays in the coat closet . . . or quietly biodegrades."[62] The CEO further claims that "fake fur, comprising polyacrylates, requires the extraction and fractionating of petroleum" and is "not only incredibly energy-intensive but also produce[s] a lot of extremely unpleasant chemical compounds."[63] While it may be true that the untreated pelt of an animal is biodegradable, pelts are chemically treated to prevent rot and decomposition, and in that regard, even the fur federation CEO acknowledges that fur garments have their own environmental issues with respect to the chemicals required to dress and dye pelts.[64]

Although it is true that faux fur comes with its own set of environmental concerns, the promotion of fur as biodegradable without scientific evidence is arguably inconsistent with the FTC's green guidelines. As discussed previously, the Green Guides require that any unqualified degradable claims be backed by "competent and reliable scientific evidence that the entire item will completely break down and return to nature (i.e., decompose into elements found in nature) within a reasonably short period of time"[65] and specifically states that "it is deceptive to make an unqualified degradable claim for items entering the solid waste stream if the items do not completely decompose within one year after customary disposal."[66] Moreover, the promotion of fur as more environmentally friendly than faux fur, even if true, commits the "sin of lesser of two evils" because it fails to take into account other more environmentally friendly textiles, thereby distracting consumers from the larger environmental impact of both products. Further, it is not clear based on scientific studies that real fur is in fact more environmentally friendly than faux fur. In June 2013, CE Delft released a second report, *Natural Mink Fur and Faux Fur Products: An Environmental Comparison*, which compared the environmental impact of a natural fur coat versus a faux fur coat.[67] The 2013 CE Delft report concluded that "the environmental impact of natural mink fur coats and trims is higher than the impact of faux fur coats and trims," even when it is assumed that the natural fur trim is reused once or twice on a new product, and the faux fur trim is not.[68]

CONCLUSION

The deceptive marketing and advertising of fur as a "green" or "eco-friendly" product misleads consumers, who may rely on such claims to justify their purchase and use of fur. Without the environmental claims that seek to legitimize and justify the use of fur, claims that arguably commit each of the "sins of greenwashing" and that arguably are inconsistent with the general principles set forth in the FTC's Green Guides, the fur industry might not be the industry that it is today. The impact that "green" marketing has for the fur industry is significant, in part because of the public's growing concern for the environment and in part because green advertising dominates the marketing campaigns of the fur industry. The "green" marketing of fur presents ethical considerations beyond deceptive advertising to consumers, however.

The deceptive advertising and marketing of fur as green and environmentally friendly has profound consequences not only for the environment but also for millions of fur-bearing animals who, like their agricultural counterparts, are held in extreme confinement in small cages during their short lives, devoid of anything natural. Public awareness of the indisputable cruelty involved with fur farming and trapping was increasing in the 1990s, and declining sales in the fur industry during that period suggest that some consumers were reluctant to purchase a product that involved such extreme cruelty to animals. The fur industry knew that it needed to rebrand itself—and rebrand itself it did. The industry has worked hard to promote fur as the "environmentally friendly" option, and as a consequence, the industry has seemed to stabilize in the last two decades.

The green economy in many respects is still in its infancy, and so too are laws governing marketing claims by businesses and industries, so deceptive green marketing claims must be challenged not only with governmental authorities and in courts, but also in the court of public opinion. Green consumers are, after all, the ultimate arbiters of green marketing claims, but they must have full, complete, and accurate information to make informed purchasing decisions. Until deceptive "eco-friendly" labels are removed from all fur garments and "green" marketing claims are prohibited, consumers will continue to be misled by "fur is green" marketing claims. Only when these deceptive marketing claims are gone will consumers see the fur industry for what it is, an industry motivated solely by profit, and only when the distracting greenwashing advertisements are gone will consumers see the real impact that the fur industry has on the environment.

NOTES

1. The Nielsen Global Survey of Corporate Social Responsibility, conducted between February 17, 2014, and March 7, 2014, polled more than 30,000 consumers in sixty countries throughout North America, the Asia-Pacific, Europe, Latin America, the Middle East, and Africa. Nielsen, *Doing Well by Doing Good: Increasingly, Consumers Care about Corporate Social Responsibility*, June 17, 2014.

2. Tiller, LLC, "National Survey Finds . . . " (press release), December 29, 2014, accessed December 15, 2020, www.tillerllc.com/wp-content/uploads/2014/12/Tiller-Green-Survey-Press-Release-Final.pdf.

3. *Merriam-Webster*, s.v. "eco-friendly," accessed December 15, 2020, www.merriam-webster.com/dictionary/eco-friendly.

4. *Wikipedia*, s.v. "Greenwashing," accessed December 15, 2020, en.m.wikipedia.org/wiki/Greenwashing.

5. Will Kenton, "What Is Greenwashing?," *Investopedia*, January 30, 2020, accessed December 15, 2020, www.investopedia.com/terms/g/greenwashing.asp.

6. TerraChoice, "The Sins of Greenwashing Home and Family Edition 2010," at 6, 10 and 21, accessed February 7, 2022, faculty.wwu.edu/dunnc3/rprnts.TheSinsof-Greenwashing2010.pdf.

7. 16 C.F.R. § 260 (2012).

8. 16 C.F.R. § 260.1(b) (2012).

9. 16 C.F.R. § 260.3(c) (2012).

10. 16 C.F.R. § 260.4(a)–(b) (2012).

11. 16 C.F.R. § 260.3(a)–(b) (2012).

12. 16 C.F.R. § 260.8(a)–(b) (2012).

13. 16 C.F.R. § 260.16(a)–(b) (2012).

14. 16 C.F.R. § 260.1(d) (2012).

15. The Fur Council of Canada claims that "fur is green" on its website of the same name, while the International Fur Trade Federation includes a video under the heading "Environmentalism: Fur Is Sustainable" on its website.

16. Kopenhagen Fur, "Sustainable Fur—A Natural Resources," accessed February 7, 2022, www.kopenhagenfur.com/en/responsibility/fur-and-the-enviroment/sustainable-fur-a-natural-resource/.

17. British Fur Trade Association, "Sustainability," accessed on February 7, 2022, britishfur.co.uk/sustainability/.

18. Hong Kong Fur Federation, "Fur & Ecology," accessed December 15, 2020, www.hkff.org/furFacts3.php?lang=1.

19. Humane Society of the United States, "Toxic Fur: The Impacts of Fur Production on the Environment and Risks to Human Health," January 29, 2009, accessed December 15, 2020, www.humanesociety.org/assets/pdfs/fur/toxic-fur-january-22-2009.pdf.

20. United States Environmental Protection Agency, "Toxics Release Inventory (TRI) Program: TRI-Listed Chemicals," accessed February 7, 2022, www.epa.gov/toxics-release-inventory-tri-program/tri-listed-chemicals.

21. National Cancer Institute, "Formaldehyde and Cancer Risk," June 10, 2011, accessed December 15, 2020, www.cancer.gov/cancertopics/factsheet/Risk/formaldehyde.

22. John Maurice, "Tannery Pollution Threatens Health of Half-Million Bangladesh Residents," *Bulletin of the World Health Organization*, January 2001, accessed December 15, 2020, www.scielosp.org/scielo.php?script=sci_arttext&pid=S0042-96862001000100018.

23. Sarah Boseley, "Child Labourers Exposed to Toxic Chemicals Dying before 50, WHO Says," *Guardian*, March 17, 2017, accessed December 15, 2020, www.theguardian.com/world/2017/mar/21/plight-of-child-workers-facing-cocktail-of-toxic-chemicals-exposed-by-report-bangladesh-tanneries.

24. Richard Pearshouse, *Toxic Tanneries: The Health Repercussions of Bangladesh's Hazaribagh Leather* (Human Rights Watch, October 2012).

25. LAV, "Toxic Fur 2," December 15, 2014, accessed December 15, 2020, www.bontvoordieren.nl/wp-content/uploads/2016/09/2014-LAV-Toxic-Fur-2-EN-1.pdf.

26. International Fur Federation, "Wild Fur: Population Management," accessed December 15, 2020, www.wearefur.com/responsible-fur/environment/wild-fur/.

27. Fur Commission USA, "Mink Farming Fuels Rural Economies, Multi-Generation Family Owned Businesses," accessed December 15, 2020, furcommission.com/mink-farming-2/.

28. Fur Council of Canada, "Fur, A Renewable Resource," Fur Is Green, accessed December 15, 2020, www.furisgreen.com/fur-is-eco-logical/fur-a-renewable-resource/.

29. Fur Europe, "Sustainable Fur, Environment," accessed February 7, 2022, www.sustainablefur.com/environment/.

30. Kopenhagen Fur, "Sustainable Fur—A Natural Resource," accessed February 7, 2022, www.kopenhagenfur.com/en/responsibility/fur-and-the-enviroment/sustainable-fur-a-natural-resource/.

31. British Fur Trade Association, "Sustainability" and "Production," accessed February 7, 2022, britishfur.co.uk/sustainability/, britishfur.co.uk/sustainability/production/.

32. David Suzuki Foundation, *The Impacts of the Mink Industry on Freshwater Lakes in Nova Scotia: An Overview of Concerns* (technical brief), April 25, 2011, 1.

33. M. Brylinsky and J. Sollows, *Results of the 2013 Water Quality Survey of Eleven Lakes Located in the Carleton River Watershed Area of Digby and Yarmouth Counties, Nova Scotia*, prepared for Nova Scotia Environment, June 2014, Summary, accessed December 15, 2020, novascotia.ca/nse/surface.water/docs/carleton-river-watershed-survey-2013.pdf.

34. Brylinsky and Sollows, *Results of the 2013 Water Quality Survey*, 1.

35. Brylinsky and Sollows, *Results of the 2013 Water Quality Survey*, 6.

36. Judith Lavoie, "Mink Farm Pollution Key Culprit in Rendering Nova Scotia Lakes Unswimmable," *DeSmog Canada*, August 15, 2014, accessed December 15, 2020, thenarwhal.ca/mink-farm-pollution-key-culprit-rendering-nova-scotia-lakes-unswimmable-report/.

37. Brylinsky and Sollows, *Results of the 2013 Water Quality Survey*, 17.

38. United States Environmental Protection Agency, *Preventing Eutrophication: Scientific Support for Dual Nutrient Criteria*, February 2015, accessed February 7, 2022, www.epa.gov/sites/production/files/documents/nandpfactsheet.pdf.

39. United States Environmental Protection Agency, *Preventing Eutrophication: Scientific Support for Dual Nutrient Criteria.*

40. United States Environmental Protection Agency, "Nutrient Pollution: The Issue," accessed December 15, 2020, www.epa.gov/nutrientpollution/problem.

41. United States Environmental Protection Agency, "Nutrient Pollution: The Issue."

42. United States Environmental Protection Agency, "Nutrient Pollution: Sources and Solutions," accessed December 15, 2020, www.epa.gov/nutrientpollution/sources-and-solutions.

43. Xu Wei, "Fur and Leather Industry Leads to Hair-Raising Pollution Problems," *Shanghai Daily*, May 16, 2015, accessed December 15, 2020, www.shanghaidaily.com/feature/news-feature/Fur-and-leather-industry-leads-to-hairraising-pollution-problems/shdaily.shtml.

44. Will Stewart, "'I Have No Sympathy for the Animals . . . I Feel a Deep Satisfaction': Barbarity of Russian Fur Farms Where Thousands Are Slaughtered . . . ," *Daily Mail*, May 4, 2016, accessed December 15, 2020, www.dailymail.co.uk/news/article-3572756/Barbarity-Russian-mink-farms-thousands-slaughtered-make-1m-sable-coats-blankets-left-rot-stinking-corpse-mountain.html.

45. Pete McBride, "Industry on the Banks: Deep Inside Kanpur's Tanneries," *National Geographic*, August 6, 2014, accessed December 15, 2020, www.nationalgeographic.com/photography/proof/2014/08/06/industry-on-the-banks-deep-inside-kanpurs-tanneries/.

46. Marijn Bijleveld, Marisa Korteland, and Maartje Sevenster, *The Environmental Impact of Mink Fur Production* (CE Delft, January 2011), accessed December 15, 2020, www.cedelft.eu/publicatie/the_environmental_impact_of_mink_fur_production/1131. CE Delft is an independent research and consultancy organization that specializes in developing structural and innovative solutions to environmental problems.

47. Bijleveld, Korteland, and Sevenster, *Environmental Impact*, 47.

48. Bijleveld, Korteland, and Sevenster, *Environmental Impact*, 53, 61. Only in the case of water depletion did fur score worse than cotton; however, water used to produce chicken feed was not included in the mink life cycle, nor was water used for barn cleaning or water used for fur treatment.

49. Sebastian Boger et al., *Pulse of the Fashion Industry* (Global Fashion Agenda and the Boston Consulting Group, 2017).

50. Boger et al., *Pulse of the Fashion Industry*, 10.

51. Boger et al., *Pulse of the Fashion Industry*, 77.

52. Boger et al., *Pulse of the Fashion Industry*, 80.

53. Boger et al., *Pulse of the Fashion Industry*, 80.

54. Fur Council of Canada, "Fur, A Renewable Resource."

55. PETA, "The Jaws of Death: How Steel-Jaw Traps Torture and Kill Animals," accessed December 15, 2020, www.peta.org/features/steel-jaw-trap-fur-cruelty/.

56. Joshua Gardner, "Trapped Bald Eagle Rescued by Police," *ABC News*, November 26, 2012, accessed December 15, 2020, abcnews.go.com/blogs/headlines/2012/11/trapped-bald-eagle-rescued-by-police/.

57. Benjamin F. Powell, "Animal Trap Catches, Injures 12-Year-Old Triad Boy," *USA Today*, May 3, 2015.

58. American Veterinary Medical Association, *Literature Review on the Welfare Implications of Leghold Trap Use in Conservation and Research*, April 30, 2008, accessed December 15, 2020, www.avma.org/KB/Resources/LiteratureReviews/Documents/leghold_traps_bgnd.pdf

59. Dick Randall, statement in *Hearings before the 94th Congress to Discourage the Use of Painful Devices in the Trapping of Animals and Birds* (Washington, DC: US Government Printing Office, 1975).

60. 16 C.F.R. § 260.3(c) (2012).

61. The Fur Commission USA includes a featured article titled "Should You Be Faking It?" on its website, which discusses the environmental issues associated with faux fur (accessed December 15, 2020, furcommission.com/should-you-be-faking-it/).

62. Mark Oaten, "Faux Fur Is More Than a Faux Pas, It's Poison," International Fur Federation, August 2, 2016, accessed December 15, 2020, www.wearefur.com/FAUX-FUR-MORE-FAUX-PAS-ITS-POISON/.

63. Oaten, "Faux Fur."

64. Oaten, "Faux Fur."

65. 16 C.F.R. § 260.8(b) (2012).

66. 16 C.F.R. § 260.8(c) (2012).

67. Marijn Bijleveld, *Natural Mink Fur and Faux Fur Products: An Environmental Comparison* (CE Delft, June 2013), accessed December 15, 2020, www.furfreealliance.com/wp-content/uploads/2016/01/CE_Delft_22203_Natural_mink_fur_and_faux_fur_products_DEF-1.pdf.

68. Bijleveld, *Natural Mink Fur and Faux Fur*, 5–6.

REFERENCES

American Veterinary Medical Association. *Literature Review on the Welfare Implications of Leghold Trap Use in Conservation and Research.* April 30, 2008. Accessed December 15, 2020. www.avma.org/KB/Resources/LiteratureReviews/Documents/leghold_traps_bgnd.pdf.

Bijleveld, Marijn. *Natural Mink Fur and Faux Fur Products: An Environmental Comparison.* CE Delft, June 2013. Accessed December 15, 2020. www.furfreealliance.com/wp-content/uploads/2016/01/CE_Delft_22203_Natural_mink_fur_and_faux_fur_products_DEF-1.pdf.

Bijleveld, Marijn, Marisa Korteland, and Maartje Sevenster. *The Environmental Impact of Mink Fur Production.* CE Delft, January 2011. Accessed December 15, 2020. www.cedelft.eu/publicatie/the_environmental_impact_of_mink_fur_production/1131.

Boger, Sebastian, Caroline Chalmer, Sofia Tarneberg, Jonas Eder-Hansen, Kristina Jager, Lise Kristensen, Javier Seara, Sebastian Schwarz, Gabriele Theelen, and Thomas Tochtermann. *Pulse of the Fashion Industry.* Global Fashion Agenda and the Boston Consulting Group, 2017.

Boseley, Sarah. "Child Labourers Exposed to Toxic Chemicals Dying before 50, WHO Says." *Guardian*, March 17, 2017. Accessed December 15, 2020. www.theguardian.com/world/2017/mar/21/plight-of-child-workers-facing-cocktail-of-toxic-chemicals-exposed-by-report-bangladesh-tanneries.

British Fur Trade Association. "Dressing and Dyeing." Accessed December 15, 2020. britishfur.co.uk/creativity/dyeing-tanning/.

British Fur Trade Association. "Sustainability" and "Production." Accessed February 7, 2022. britishfur.co.uk/sustainability/. britishfur.co.uk/sustainability/production/.

Brylinsky, M., and J. Sollows. *Results of the 2013 Water Quality Survey of Eleven Lakes Located in the Carleton River Watershed Area of Digby and Yarmouth Counties, Nova Scotia.* Prepared for Nova Scotia Environment, June 2014. Accessed December 15, 2020. novascotia.ca/nse/surface.water/docs/carleton-river-watershed-survey-2013.pdf.

David Suzuki Foundation. *The Impacts of the Mink Industry on Freshwater Lakes in Nova Scotia: An Overview of Concerns*. Technical brief, April 25, 2011.

Federal Trade Commission. "Guides for the Use of Environmental Marketing Claims." 16 C.F.R. § 260 (October 11, 2012).

Fur Commission USA. "Mink Farming Fuels Rural Economies: Multi-Generation Family Owned Businesses." Accessed December 15, 2020. furcommission.com/mink-farming-2/.

———. "Should You Be Faking It?" Accessed December 15, 2020. furcommission.com/should-you-be-faking-it/.

———. "Sustainable Fashion: Why Fur Is the Best Material in Your Closet." Accessed December 15, 2020. furcommission.com/fur-fashion-3–1/sustainable-fashion-why-fur-is-the-best-material-in-your-closet/.

Fur Council of Canada. "Fur, a Renewable Resource." Fur Is Green. Accessed December 15, 2020. www.furisgreen.com/fur-is-eco-logical/fur-a-renewable-resource/.

———. Fur Is Green. Accessed December 15, 2020. www.furisgreen.com/.

Fur Europe. "Sustainable Fur, Environment." Accessed February 7, 2022. www.sustainablefur.com/environment/.

Gardner, Joshua. "Trapped Bald Eagle Rescued by Police." *ABC News*, November 26, 2012. Accessed December 15, 2020. abcnews.go.com/blogs/headlines/2012/11/trapped-bald-eagle-rescued-by-police/.

Hong Kong Fur Federation. "Fur & Ecology." Accessed December 15, 2020. www.hkff.org/furFacts3.php?lang=1.

Humane Research Council. *Public Attitudes towards Fur: An HRC Research Primer*. Accessed December 15, 2020. faunalytics.org/wp-content/uploads/2015/05/Fundamentals_Fur.pdf.

Humane Society of the United States. "Toxic Fur: The Impacts of Fur Production on the Environment and Risks to Human Health." January 29, 2009. Accessed December 15, 2020. www.humanesociety.org/assets/pdfs/fur/toxic-fur-january-22-2009.pdf.

International Fur Trade Federation. "About Fur." Accessed December 15, 2020. www.wearefur.com/about-fur/.

———. "Environmentalism: Fur Is Sustainable." Video. Accessed December 15, 2020. www.wearefur.com/responsible-fur/responsible-fur-in-video/.

———. "Wild Fur: Population Management." Accessed December 15, 2020. www.wearefur.com/responsible-fur/environment/wild-fur/.

———. "Wild Fur and Trapping." April 17, 2019. Accessed December 15, 2020. www.wearefur.com/wild-fur-and-trapping/.

Kenton, Will. "What Is Greenwashing?" *Investopedia*, January 30, 2020. Accessed December 15, 2020. www.investopedia.com/terms/g/greenwashing.asp.

Kopenhagen Fur. "Sustainable Fur—A Natural Resources." Accessed February 7, 2022. www.kopenhagenfur.com/en/responsibility/fur-and-the-enviroment/sustainable-fur-a-natural-resource/.

LAV. "Toxic Fur 2." December 15, 2014. Accessed on December 15, 2020. www.bontvoordieren.nl/wp-content/uploads/2016/09/2014-LAV-Toxic-Fur-2-EN-1.pdf.

Lavoie, Judith. "Mink Farm Pollution Key Culprit in Rendering Nova Scotia Lakes Unswimmable." *DeSmog Canada*, August 15, 2014. Accessed December 15, 2020. thenarwhal.ca/mink-farm-pollution-key-culprit-rendering-nova-scotia-lakes-unswimmable-report/.

Maurice, John. "Tannery Pollution Threatens Health of Half-Million Bangladesh Residents." *Bulletin of the World Health Organization*, January 2001. Accessed December 15, 2020. www.scielosp.org/scielo.php?script=sci_arttext&pid=S0042-96862001000100018.

McBride, Pete. "Industry on the Banks: Deep Inside Kanpur's Tanneries." *National Geographic*, August 6, 2014. Accessed December 15, 2020. www.nationalgeographic.com/photography/proof/2014/08/06/industry-on-the-banks-deep-inside-kanpurs-tanneries/.

National Cancer Institute. "Formaldehyde and Cancer Risk." June 10, 2011. Accessed December 15, 2020. www.cancer.gov/cancertopics/factsheet/Risk/formaldehyde.

Nielsen. *Doing Well by Doing Good: Increasingly, Consumers Care about Corporate Social Responsibility*. Nielsen Global Survey of Corporate Social Responsibility, June 17, 2014.

Oaten, Mark. "Faux Fur Is More Than a Faux Pas, It's Poison." International Fur Federation, August 2, 2016. Accessed December 15, 2020. www.wearefur.com/FAUX-FUR-MORE-FAUX-PAS-ITS-POISON/.

Pearshouse, Richard. *Toxic Tanneries: The Health Repercussions of Bangladesh's Hazaribagh Leather*. Human Rights Watch, October 2012.

PETA. "The Jaws of Death: How Steel-Jaw Traps Torture and Kill Animals." Accessed December 15, 2020. www.peta.org/features/steel-jaw-trap-fur-cruelty/.

Powell, Benjamin F. "Animal Trap Catches, Injures 12-Year-Old Triad Boy." *USA Today*, May 3, 2015.

Randall, Dick. Statement in *Hearings before the 94th Congress to Discourage the Use of Painful Devices in the Trapping of Animals and Birds*. Washington, DC: US Government Printing Office, 1975.

Steel Jaw Leghold Traps: Hearings on H.R. 1797, before Committee on Energy and Commerce House of Representatives, 98th Congress (1984) (statement of D. Randall).

Stewart, Will. "'I Have No Sympathy for the Animals . . . I Feel a Deep Satisfaction': Barbarity of Russian Fur Farms Where Thousands Are Slaughtered to Make $1m Coats and Blankets then Left to Rot in Stinking Corpse Mountain." *Daily Mail*, May 4, 2016. Accessed December 15, 2020. www.dailymail.co.uk/news/article-3572756/Barbarity-Russian-mink-farms-thousands-slaughtered-make-1m-sable-coats-blankets-left-rot-stinking-corpse-mountain.html.

TerraChoice. *The Sins of Greenwashing: Home and Family Edition*. TerraChoice, Part of the UL Global Network, 2010. Accessed February 7, 2022. faculty.wwu.edu/dunnc3/rprnts.TheSinsofGreenwashing2010.pdf

Tiller, LLC. "National Survey Finds . . . " Press release. December 29, 2014. Accessed December 15, 2020. www.tillerllc.com/wp-content/uploads/2014/12/Tiller-Green-Survey-Press-Release-Final.pdf.

Underwriters Laboratories. "Sins of Greenwashing." Accessed December 15, 2020. www.ul.com/insights/sins-greenwashing.

United States Environmental Protection Agency. "Nutrient Pollution: The Issue." Accessed December 15, 2020. www.epa.gov/nutrientpollution/problem.

———. "Nutrient Pollution: Sources and Solutions." Accessed December 15, 2020. www.epa.gov/nutrientpollution/sources-and-solutions.

———. *Preventing Eutrophication: Scientific Support for Dual Nutrient Criteria*. February 2015. Accessed December 15, 2020. www.epa.gov/sites/production/files/documents/nandpfactsheet.pdf.

———. "Toxics Release Inventory (TRI) Program: TRI-Listed Chemicals." Accessed December 15, 2020. www.epa.gov/toxics-release-inventory-tri-program/tri-listed-chemicals.

Wei, Xu. "Fur and Leather Industry Leads to Hair-Raising Pollution Problems." *Shanghai Daily*, May 16, 2015. Accessed December 15, 2020. www.shanghaidaily.com/feature/news-feature/Fur-and-leather-industry-leads-to-hairraising-pollution-problems/shdaily.shtml.

Index

About the Editors and Contributors

Andrew Linzey (editor) is director of the Oxford Centre for Animal Ethics and has been a member of the Faculty of Theology in the University of Oxford for twenty-eight years. He is a visiting professor of animal theology at the University of Winchester and a professor of animal ethics at the Graduate Theological Foundation. He is the author or editor of more than thirty books, including *Animal Theology* (SCM Press/University of Illinois Press, 1994); *Why Animal Suffering Matters* (Oxford University Press, 2009); *The Global Guide to Animal Protection* (University of Illinois Press, 2013); and *The Palgrave Handbook of Practical Animal Ethics* (Palgrave Macmillan, 2018).

Clair Linzey (editor) is the deputy director of the Oxford Centre for Animal Ethics. She is a professor of animal theology at the Graduate Theological Foundation. She gained her doctorate in theology from the University of St Andrews and is coeditor of the *Journal of Animal Ethics*, and coeditor of the Palgrave Macmillan Animal Ethics Series. She is coeditor with Andrew Linzey of *Animal Ethics for Veterinarians* (University of Illinois Press, 2017); *The Ethical Case against Animal Experiments* (University of Illinois Press, 2018); *The Routledge Handbook of Religion and Animal Ethics* (Routledge, 2018); *The Palgrave Handbook of Practical Animal Ethics* (Palgrave Macmillan, 2018); and *Ethical Vegetarianism and Veganism* (Routledge, 2018).

Letícia Albuquerque is a professor in the Law Faculty of the Federal University of Santa Catarina, Brazil, where she teaches both undergraduate and postgraduate students. She is the cofounder and codirector of the Environmental Justice Observatory, a research and action group in the areas of environment, human rights, and animal rights linked to the graduate program in law of the Federal University of Santa Catarina.

Jess Beaulieu manages the Animal Law Program at the University of Denver Sturm College of Law. Prior to this role, she practiced as a public interest attorney in the field of dependency and neglect at Muhaisen & Muhaisen, LLC. Previously, she was a fellow at the Center for Biological Diversity in Denver, Colorado, advocating for the protection of western wildlife. Jess received her J.D. from Stetson University College of Law, where she focused on environmental and animal law. She additionally holds a Bachelor of Science degree in Wildlife Ecology and Conservation from the University of Florida. In 2020, Jess was able to contribute a chapter to Randall Abate's Second Edition of *What Can Animal Law Learn From Environmental Law?* (Environmental Law Institute, 2020).

Sidney Blankenship is an associate fellow of the Oxford Centre for Animal Ethics. He holds a BA in Bible and Greek from Abilene Christian University in Texas. After studying divinity at the University of Edinburgh, he gained a further BA in theology from the University of Oxford, where he was president of the Junior Common Room of Mansfield College. He received his MA in theology from Oxford in 1974. He is a charter member of the National Museum of the American Indian in Washington, DC, where he participated with the Cherokee tribe in the inaugural procession on the National Mall at the museum's grand opening in 2004. He has also supported the Archaeology Conservancy, based in Albuquerque, New Mexico, for Native American sites' preservation. He is the author of "Native American Religion: Restoring Species to the Circle of Life" in the *Routledge Handbook of Religion and Animal Ethics* (Routledge, 2018); also "Ecological Hermeneutics and Native American Ethics" in Christina Nellist, ed. *Climate Crisis and Creation Care* (Cambridge Scholars, 2021). A forthcoming book on the animals of Deuteronomy 14 and Leviticus 11 explores the animal implications of identity in translation, literary analysis, and history as well ethical perspectives from the Hebrew Bible and the New Testament. This work has been undertaken concurrently with research for a concordance of biblical animals. He is a member of the Society of Biblical Literature and the Biblical Archaeology Society, as well as the American Academy of Religion with interests in Native American, environmental, and animal issues.

Adam Bridgen is a research fellow in Eighteenth-Century Literature and Culture in the School of English at the University of St. Andrews, and an associate fellow of the Oxford Centre for Animal Ethics. He gained a DPhil in English from the University of Oxford in 2020 and has previously held fellowships from the Huntington Library and the Royal Historical Society. His research concerns the influence of social class and religion on writing about transatlantic slavery, empire, and the natural world during the long eighteenth century, as well as the theological and transatlantic contexts of animal rights thinking in Britain. He has published numerous articles on labouring-class poetry, on abolitionist verse, and on lesser-known literary forms, and has recently contributed chapters on Thomas Tryon and Humphry Primatt to *Animal Theologians*, forthcoming with Oxford University Press.

Simon Brooman is a senior lecturer in animal law at Liverpool John Moores University. He is coauthor of *Law Relating to Animals* (Cavendish Publishing, 1997) and is widely published in the area of animal law. He is a fellow of the Oxford Centre for Animal Ethics and senior fellow of the Higher Education Academy. His research interests include all aspects of animal law, including developing methodologies for introducing animal law into the higher-education curriculum.

Jen Clements is a PhD candidate at the University of Exeter. She gained her undergraduate degree in archaeology and anthropology from St John's College, Oxford. While at Oxford, she was president of the Oxford University Animal Ethics Society and is now an honorary life member. Her research interests include agricultural policy and practice, human–nonhuman relationships, and sustainability.

Chloe Gleichman received her juris doctor from the University of Denver in 2018. Chloe began practicing criminal defense at the Colorado State Public Defender's office. She continues to practice criminal defense full-time at a firm in Denver. Professionally and personally, Chloe maintains an active interest in animal rights and prison abolition.

Robyn Hederman, JD, is an associate court attorney in New York State Supreme Court and a fellow of the Oxford Centre for Animal Ethics. As co-chair of the Animal Law Committee of the New York City Bar Association, she writes and reviews legal reports analyzing pending legislation and organizes public programs examining issues affecting nonhuman animals. She has a Master of Arts in history and is a member of the Phi Alpha Theta History Honor Society. Her publications include "Gender and the Animal Experiments Controversy in Nineteenth-Century America," published in *The Ethical Case against Animal Experiments*, edited by Andrew Linzey and Clair Linzey (University of Illinois Press, 2018), and "The Cost of Cruelty: Henry Bergh and the Abattoirs," in *Ethical Vegetarianism and Veganism*, edited by Andrew Linzey and Clair Linzey (Routledge, 2019).

Linda M. Johnson is curator at Hancock Shaker Village. She was previously a lecturer in the Department of Art History at the University of Michigan–Flint and an adjunct professor at the Massachusetts College of Liberal Arts. She received her PhD from Michigan State University in 2011. She has received fellowships from Historic Deerfield in art history and is a fellow at the Oxford Centre for Animal Ethics. She has taught courses on Renaissance to modern art, science and art, and art and animal ethics, and was an affiliate faculty member and graduate advisor in the Arts Administration program at the University of Michigan–Flint. Johnson is author of the book, *Art, Ethics and the Human-Animal Relationship* (Palgrave Macmillan, 2021), and "A Pre-Millennial Portrait during the Revocation of the Massachusetts Charter" in *American Literature and the New Puritan Studies*, edited by Bryce Traister (Cambridge University Press, 2017).

Justin Marceau is a professor of law, the Brooks Institute Faculty Research Scholar of Animal Law and Policy, and the Faculty Director of the Animal Law Program at the University of Denver Sturm College of Law. Justin joined the College of Law in 2008. The focus of his teaching and scholarship includes criminal law, criminal procedure, constitutional law, and animal law. He graduated first in his class from Boston College and cum laude from Harvard Law School. He is a coauthor of textbooks on the death penalty (West, 2016) and habeas corpus (Carolina, 2012), the coauthor of more than two dozen scholarly articles, and the author of *Beyond Cages: Animal Law and Criminal Punishment* (Cambridge University Press, 2019). In addition, he is currently working on two forthcoming books, one titled *Undercover Investigations and Democracy*, that demonstrates the way investigations have emerged as an essential tool for advocates in a variety of movements (co-authored with Alan Chen), and the other an edited volume on animal law and social justice issues titled *Carceral Logics: Human Incarceration and Animal Captivity* (with Lori Gruen), both of which are with Cambridge University Press.

Kimberly Moore is a senior attorney at Pillsbury Winthrop Shaw Pittman LLLP in Washington, DC, where she specializes in federal income tax law, private equity investments, and public–private partnerships and where she is a national expert on tax-advantaged affordable housing programs. She is a graduate of the University of Virginia School of Law, where she served as managing editor of the Virginia Tax Return and received an elite LLM degree from New York University in taxation. She is an active member of the D.C. Bar, an associate member of the Virginia State Bar, and a member of the Animal Law Committee of the American Bar Association. She is the director of public relations for Fur Free Society and has worked on state legislation to ban the sale and manufacture of fur. Her research interests include improving the legal status of animals and exploring the use of established public–private partnership paradigms to improve the lives of animals on factory farms.

Kimberly is currently working on a book that will examine why our legal treatment of animals matters for humanity.

Heather Pickett is a freelance researcher with twenty years' experience in research, analysis, and writing in the fields of, inter alia, animal behavior and welfare, animal agriculture, and environment and sustainability. Her clients include a number of high-profile organizations, primarily within the nonprofit sector. Her work has been instrumental in achieving policy change at UK and European Union levels and at major companies. For more on her work, see www.animalwelfareresearch.com.

Frances M. C. Robinson is an associate fellow of the Oxford Centre for Animal Ethics. She was a practicing veterinary surgeon from 1971 to 1989, having earned a bachelor's degree in veterinary medicine and surgery from the University of Glasgow in 1971. In 2000 she graduated with a BA in philosophy and environmental management from Keele University, and in 2001 she received an MA in values and the environment from the University of Lancaster. In 2011 she graduated with an MPhil in philosophy from the University of Lancaster with a thesis titled "Animal Experimentation, Complexity and Animal Ethics." She was a member of the working group of the Oxford Centre for Animal Ethics that led to the report titled *Normalising the Unthinkable: The Ethics of Using Animals in Research* (2015). Her main research interests include environmental ethics, animal ethics, and the ethics of the use of animals in scientific experiments.

Kurt Remele is an associate professor emeritus and former director of the Institute for Ethics and Social Teaching at the Department of Catholic Theology at Graz University in Austria. He was a visiting professor at several US and British universities and is a fellow of the Oxford Centre for Animal Ethics. In 2019, a revised edition of his book on the inviolable dignity of animals and what it entails was published: *Die Würde der Tiere ist unantastbar: Eine zeitgemäße christliche Tierethik* (Topos premium, 2019). His latest book (2021) deals with an extended concept of the common good that includes animals. Its title *Es geht uns allen besser, wenn es allen besser geht* (Gruenewald, 2022) is the German translation of a dictum by the late Minnesota Senator Paul Wellstone: "We all do better when we all do better."

Kate Sanford is at attorney at Davis Graham & Stubbs in Denver. She is passionate about finding ways to strengthen legal frameworks to better protect animals. She received her juris doctor from the University of Denver in 2018.

Gabriela Franziska Schoch Santos Carvalho holds a master's degree (MLaw) from the University of Fribourg, Switzerland, and a master's degree in law (MSc) from the Federal University of Santa Catarina, Brazil. Born in Switzerland, Gabriela is currently an independent researcher based in Brazil. She is also a member of the Environmental Justice Observatory. Her 2018 master's thesis, "The Constitutional Protection of Animals in Brazil and in Switzerland: Cruelty, Well-Being and Dignity," examines the scope and underlying ethical assumptions of the constitutional protection granted to animals in Brazil and in Switzerland.

Rebecca Rose Stanton completed a PhD in animal studies at Northumbria University in 2019. She is an associate fellow of the Oxford Center for Animal Ethics, and she leads the "Animals and Animation" group for the Society of Animation Studies. She is the author of *The Disneyfication of Animals* (Palgrave Macmillan, 2020). She is also a member of the Vegan Society's researcher network.

Ambrose Tinarwo is a senior lecturer in animal behavior and welfare at the University of Lincoln. He has a PhD in animal welfare physiology from the University of Bristol, an MSc in applied animal behavior and welfare from the University of Edinburgh, and a BSc (Hons) in animal science from the University of Zimbabwe. His interests are in animal behavior, animal welfare, and anthrozoology. After completing his PhD, he worked for animal welfare charities, for colleges, and in research. He currently is the program lead for the MSc in clinical animal behavior at the University of Lincoln, where he lectures on animal welfare, animal behavior, and animal ethics. His research interests are in applied farmed animal welfare, companion animal behavior, and animal ethics.

K. York is a PhD student in philosophy at the University of Colorado at Boulder. They got their BA at the University of Colorado at Denver, their MA in philosophy at the University of Tartu in Estonia, and spent time researching at Lingnan University in Hong Kong. Kyle's writing has appeared (sometimes under "Kaya") in *The Journal of Value Inquiry*, *Essays in Philosophy*, and *Philosophy Now*.

Milton Keynes UK
Ingram Content Group UK Ltd.
UKHW040127070224
437369UK00004B/16

9 781666 937947